Legal Studies:
TERMINOLOGY
and
Transcription

Fourth Edition

Wanda Roderick-Bolton
R&W Associates
Naples, Florida

JOIN US ON THE INTERNET
WWW: http://www.thomson.com
EMAIL: findit@kiosk.thomson.com   A service of I(T)P®

South-Western Educational Publishing
an International Thomson Publishing company I(T)P®

Cincinnati • Albany, NY • Belmont, CA • Bonn • Boston • Detroit • Johannesburg • London • Madrid
Melbourne • Mexico City • New York • Paris • Singapore • Tokyo • Toronto • Washington

Managing Editor: Karen Schmohe
Editor: Inell Bolls
Production Coordinator: Jane Congdon
Art Coordinator: Ann Small
Marketing Manager: Al S. Roane

Understanding legal terminology is an essential requirement for the nonlawyer employee in the legal office. In order to be able to transcribe and key legal documents and follow legal procedures, you must understand the tools with which you are working. In the legal field, these tools are the legal words that are used. Many misunderstandings and frustrations on the job can be eliminated with a basic understanding of legal terms. The study of legal terminology is only a part of the skills and knowledge necessary for the nonlawyer employee, but it is a very vital and necessary element for success in the legal field. With a basic understanding of legal vocabulary, the job will be much easier, and you, the legal employee, will be a more effective participant and contributor in the legal profession.

During my many years of teaching in the area of court reporting, the frequency of errors in student transcripts resulting from lack of knowledge of legal terms pointed out the need for a systematic approach for the learning of basic legal vocabulary. Errors, such as the land was measured by "leaps and bounds" instead of "metes and bounds," "quickclaim deed" instead of "quitclaim deed," and a "causal relationship" transcribed as a "casual relationship," may appear humorous on the surface but are not so funny when the fortunes or the lives of people are at stake.

OBJECTIVES

This text-workbook is intended to give you knowledge and understanding of over 900 terms commonly used in the legal profession. You will learn to define the terms and to use them in legal context. Pronunciation guides are provided for each word, and the correct pronunciation is reinforced by taped dictation. Keyboarding practice from printed copy will assist you in learning the correct spelling of each term, and all objectives are reinforced as you learn to transcribe the terms from taped dictation. Therefore, upon successful completion of this course, you should be able to

1. correctly spell, pronounce, and define the legal terms presented;
2. transcribe the legal terms on a typewriter or computer either directly from the tape or from shorthand notes.

INSTRUCTIONAL LEVEL

This course can be used in a regular classroom, but it is also very adaptable to an individualized instructional system. It will provide a good background if you want to work in a legal office as a receptionist/typist, secretary, stenographer, paralegal, or research assistant. Should you plan to become a court reporter, captionist, realtime reporter, note-reader/transcriber, or transcriptionist, you can also benefit from this course since the transcription is either from a phonetically written word or from taped dictation. Should you choose work in a legal office or in the court reporting field, you must, of course, have a much broader knowledge of legal vocabulary than this course provides. However, this course will give you an excellent background for legal keyboarding, legal shorthand, legal office procedures, and business law courses.

In order to succeed in legal/terminology transcription, you should be able to key—a prerequisite for any of the named jobs in the legal field. Shorthand is not required, but the course is designed so that if you do use a shorthand system (either pen or machine), you can integrate that skill into the study of this course.

Because of the tear-out feature of the text-workbook, the author suggests that pages to be copied on a typewriter or computer be torn out first and put to the side of the machine. If the shorthand procedure is used, tear out the appropriate page and put it on the desk when writing the outlines. In both instances, you will find it easier to work with individual pages than with an open book.

LENGTH OF COURSE

The course consists of 32 lessons, each containing 25–30 terms. If you plan to follow the keyboarding/transcription procedure, the course will take approximately 40 clock hours to complete. It will take approximately 50 clock hours to follow the shorthand/transcription procedure.

SELF-EVALUATIONS

At the end of each section, there is a short quiz that you will use as a self-evaluation. This enables you to check your understanding and comprehension of the subject matter presented in each lesson. These self-evaluations should not be used for grading purposes. Answers to the self-evaluations begin on page 494 in the Appendix.

TESTS

The Instructor's Manual contains evaluations to be given after every two text-workbook lessons. These evaluations will be used as a measurement of your comprehension of the material and should be graded by your instructor. The evaluations consist of taped dictation material to be transcribed on a typewriter or computer and objective questions that you will complete.

DICTATION TAPES

Practice Dictation. The practice dictation for each of the 32 lessons is on one side of a cassette. This means there are two lessons on a single cassette (16 practice dictation cassettes all totaled). The dictation rate is approximately 80 words a minute. Each term presented in a given lesson is included in the dictation material for that lesson.

Evaluation Tapes. In addition to the lesson practice dictation material, there are eight evaluation cassettes. After every two lessons, there is dictated material on a cassette similar to what you will hear on the practice cassettes. Each cassette has one evaluation per side to be given at the completion of every two text-workbook lessons. These will be administered by your instructor or a specially designated person. Each evaluation consists of three sections—A, B, and C. Be sure that you complete all three sections before going to the next lesson. This edition contains an additional audiocassette for lessons 31 and 32 which can be purchased separately upon request.

AREAS OF LAW COVERED

The various areas of law are listed and arranged in a logical sequence to provide some continuity as you progress through the course. The general areas are introduced first, followed by the most common specific areas, such as criminal and civil. Progression is then made into other specific areas that will give you an understanding of the terminology used in most law firms, whether the lawyer happens to be in general law practice or in a specialized area. Most of the areas require two lessons to cover the terminology. However, for areas such as bankruptcy and partnerships where the number of specific terms are limited, there is only one lesson. After Lesson 10, Lessons 11–30 may be rearranged or a specific selection may be made to meet your individual needs. Lessons 31–32 should be completed after all the other lessons have been studied.

SELECTION OF TERMINOLOGY

The terminology was selected from books on legal secretarial training, law books, legal dictionaries, legal documents, and court transcripts. Also, attorneys and other legal personnel were consulted regarding specific terms.

The most commonly used terms, as well as those with special legal meanings in each area, were selected. Terms that are used very infrequently were avoided, as one of the main objectives was to develop a general basic background in legal terms. The use of certain terms will vary from state to state, and those are identified throughout the course. Some of the most commonly used Latin terms are also included. Even though you will learn some legal procedures from the study of the terminology, this is not intended to be a course in law.

PRONUNCIATIONS

The pronunciations for most of the terms in this course are based on the pronunciation guide of *Webster's Tenth New Collegiate Dictionary,* 1993, Merriam-Webster, Inc., Springfield, Massachusetts.

TRANSCRIPTION SOFTWARE

A transcription software training package is available for this text-workbook. This package features a word processor with a built-in spell checker that is able to check each word as it is keyed and highlight any word that is not in the specialized 13,000-word dictionary. The Spell Help function suggests a list of possible replacements to highlighted words. The program updates the list of misspelled words and replacements while a file is being keyed in. This list, along with the file, can later be shown on the screen or printed on paper. The program can also monitor the total time spent on a file and calculate the average transcription rate. The two new lessons (31 and 32) are not included in this software.

The program runs on IBM compatible computers with at least 256K of memory, running under PC-DOS or MS-DOS, Version 2.0 or higher. The program operates with either one or two floppy disk drives, but it cannot be installed on a hard drive. A User's Guide is provided with the software package.

ILLUSTRATIONS

Legal forms and documents illustrating many of the terms have been added to this edition. These forms and documents are provided only for the purpose of assisting you in learning the definitions of the terms and how they are used in the legal field. You should be aware that the forms and documents shown in the illustrations will vary from state to state except for those used in federal courts, such as the bankruptcy forms.

SPECIFIC COMMENTS ON LESSONS AND EVALUATIONS

At the beginning of each lesson there is a general introduction that explains the content of the lesson and gives the objectives that you are to complete for the lesson.

Part A—Terminology and Definitions

The first list of legal terms presented in each lesson consists of 12 to 16 terms. The pronunciation and definition for each term is given.

Illustrations are also provided for many of the legal terms. The illustrations will assist you in further understanding the definition and usage of the terms.

You should study the words carefully and be sure that you understand the definition of each term and can spell and pronounce the term correctly.

Self-Evaluation A—Terminology and Definition Recall

This self-evaluation will require you to recall the terms that were presented in Part A. The format will be blanks, multiple choice, or matching. The answers are provided in the Appendix so that you can check the answers as soon as you have completed the self-evaluation. This provides reinforcement for learning, and you should restudy any incorrect answers. These evaluations were designed as a self-help tool for you.

Part A—Keying Legal Terms

Further reinforcement of the terms and definitions is provided in this part. In the first part, you will key the legal terms presented in the lesson. This will assist you in learning the correct spelling for each of the terms. The sentences in the second part reemphasize the terms and the definitions. The terms are presented in legal context or usage whenever possible. If you are following the shorthand procedure, write the shorthand outlines for the material in your shorthand notebook or on your shorthand machine. Then transcribe from your shorthand notes on your typewriter or computer.

Part A—Transcribing from Dictation

Since the material dictated on the cassette is the same as you just practiced keying from printed copy, your main adaptation in this part will be to transcribe from sound or from your shorthand notes. By practicing the material beforehand, you will minimize your frustrations as you move into this section. Also, the tapes will help you learn the correct pronunciation of the legal terms.

This part of the lesson provides you with the opportunity to transcribe from dictation, make mistakes, and relearn before an evaluation. After you have transcribed the dictation, check your transcript with the printed copy and restudy any part that gave you difficulty.

Part B is a repeat of the above learning situations using 12 to 16 more new legal terms.

Evaluations

Section A. This part of the evaluation is taped for you to transcribe either directly on your typewriter or computer or from your shorthand notes. It consists of the same legal terms, but the dictation varies in content from that given in the lessons. A form with directions is provided at proper intervals in your text-workbook. You will turn in this evaluation to your instructor for checking and grading. Each dictated evaluation is dictated at approximately 80 words per minute.

Sections B and C. These parts provide a written evaluation of your knowledge of the legal terms and definitions. They are to be turned in to your instructor for checking, along with Section A. Both parts recap the lesson and are an indication, along with the dictation section, of whether or not you have fully comprehended the lesson and are ready to continue. Sections B and C of the evaluation consist of multiple choice and matching questions.

REFERENCE SECTION

The Reference Section consists of four parts:

Latin Words and Phrases: Approximately 30 additional Latin words and phrases with pronunciations and definitions are in this section. This will provide you with a further understanding of Latin terms that are used in the legal field.

Proofreading Guidelines: Information to help improve your proofreading skills is presented in this section along with a list of proofreader's marks and a list of words that are often confused are also included.

Words Often Confused: A list of words that are often confused.

Legal Transcription Basics: This section covers some general and basic rules for preparing legal instruments.

INDEX OF TERMS

An index of terms is included at the end of the text-workbook. It is an alphabetized listing of the terms, including the page number where the term is presented.

INSTRUCTOR'S MANUAL

An *Instructor's Manual* is available for instructors using this text-workbook. The manual contains additional information on teaching methods, grading procedures, and grading scales. It also includes the 16 evaluations for testing purposes.

ACKNOWLEDGMENTS

Many students, instructors, secretaries, court reporters, business people, legal personnel, and lawyers assisted with the content and organization of this text-workbook.

The author expresses thanks to all who contributed time and suggestions and especially to those who used the first three editions and made suggestions for this fourth edition.

Wanda Roderick-Bolton

Contents

Lesson 1

Courts and Legal Systems

> "The state without law would be like the human body without mind."
> —Cicero

A knowledge of the federal and state court systems, of the sources of our laws, and of the classifications of law is an essential basis for the understanding of legal terminology. The names and types of courts may vary from state to state, but the ones most commonly used are defined. Our law is an outgrowth of the legal systems of other countries. Therefore, the most common types of law upon which our system is based are also included. When you complete this lesson, you will have an understanding of the general terms used in reference to our courts and legal systems, which will help you learn the terminology taught in the following lessons.

Part A   TERMINOLOGY AND DEFINITIONS

Directions: Study the terms, pronunciations, and definitions until you are thoroughly familiar with them. In order to complete this lesson successfully, you must understand the meaning and usage of all the legal terms presented. If you are using shorthand, write your shorthand outline for each legal term in your shorthand notebook or on your shorthand machine.

Legal Term	Pronunciation	Definition
		Federal Court System: (See Figure 1-1, page 3.)
1. U.S. Supreme Court	ū s sə-ˈprēm kōrt	The highest court in the federal judicial system. Composed of a chief justice and eight associate justices. This court has final jurisdiction in matters tried in the lower federal courts and can also hear certain cases on appeal from the highest courts in the state systems if a constitutional question of federal law is involved.
2. U.S. Court of Appeals	ū s kōrt əv ə-ˈpēls	An appellate court. Reviews cases from lower federal courts. There are currently 13 judicial circuits, each of which has a U.S. Court of Appeals.
3. U.S. District Court	ū s ˈdis-trikt kōrt	A federal trial court or a federal court of original jurisdiction. The court in which a case is first tried in the federal court system.
4. special courts	ˈspesh-əl kōrts	There are several special U.S. courts that have limited jurisdiction, including the Court of Claims, the Court of Customs and Patent Appeals, and the Tax Court.
		State Court System: (See Figure 1-2, page 3.)
5. supreme court	sə-ˈprēm kōrt	The highest court in most state court systems. Certain cases decided in a state supreme court may be appealed to the U.S. Supreme Court if a constitutional question of federal law is involved.

6. court of appeal	kōrt əv ə-'pēl	A court that reviews cases from the trial courts or lower courts. The highest court in states not having a supreme court.
7. appellate court	ə-'pel-ət kōrt	Same as court of appeal. A court that reviews cases that are appealed from a lower court.
8. trial court	trīl kōrt	A court of original jurisdiction. Hears a case the first time it is tried in court.
9. court of original jurisdiction	kōrt əv ə-'rij-ən-l jür-əs-'dik-shən	A court that hears a case the first time it is tried in court. A trial court is a court of original jurisdiction.
10. court of record	kōrt əv 'rek-ərd	A court in which all proceedings are recorded for future reference. Trial courts, appellate courts, and supreme courts are usually courts of record.
11. probate court	'prō-bāt kōrt	A court that deals with the probate of wills and the settlement of estates. May also be called orphan's court or surrogate court. In some states the probate court has jurisdiction over the estates of minors and the appointment of guardians.
12. lower or inferior court	lōr ər in-'fir-ē-ər kōrt	A court that has a very limited jurisdiction and whose cases may be appealed to a higher court. In some states a written record is not required for the proceedings.
13. court not of record	kōrt nät əv 'rek-ərd	A court in which the proceedings are not required to be recorded. Usually the lower or inferior courts are courts not of record. However, many states now require all courts to be courts of record. A court not of record, such as a small claims court, cannot impose fines or imprisonment.
14. small claims court	smȯl klāms kōrt	A court established in some states to settle minor disputes between individuals in which the parties represent themselves without the assistance of attorneys. Usually the judge's decision is final, and the case cannot be appealed to a higher court.

FIGURE 1-1 Federal Court System

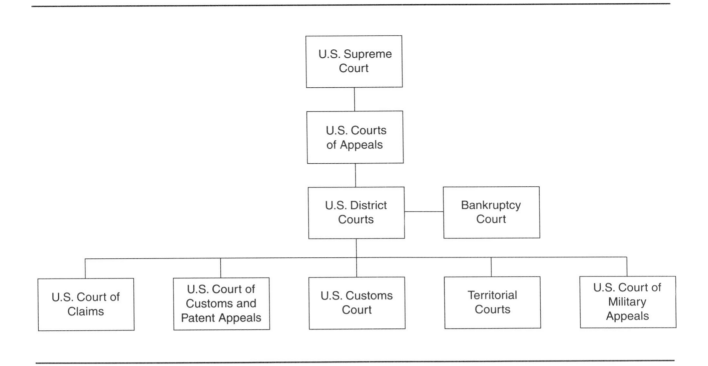

FIGURE 1-2 State Court Systems (The courts in each state vary, so this chart is intended to give only a general overview of the structure of the state court systems.)

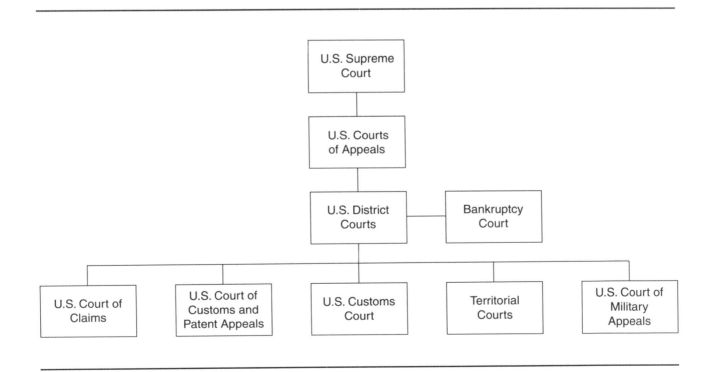

Self-Evaluation A   TERMINOLOGY AND DEFINITION RECALL   X

Directions: In the Answers column at the right of each statement, write the letter that represents the word or group of words that correctly completes the statement. After you have completed this self-evaluation, check your answers with the key on page 494. If you have any incorrect answers, restudy the definitions for those terms before going on with this lesson. Then unless otherwise directed, submit this self-evaluation to your instructor.

Answers

1. If you lost the decision in a case in a court of original jurisdiction or a trial court, you could appeal the decision in a/an (a) supreme court, (b) probate court, (c) appellate court.

   1. C

2. If someone damages your personal property and a small amount of money is involved, you would probably file the case in a/an (a) small claims court, (b) appellate court, (c) special court.

   2. A

3. If there is a dispute between states or residents of two different states, the case would be filed in the (a) U.S. Court of Appeals, (b) U.S. District Court, (c) supreme court.

   3. B

4. In the federal court system, the Court of Claims, the Court of Customs and Patents, and the Tax Court are (a) U.S. District Courts, (b) special courts, (c) U.S. Courts of Appeals.

   4. B

5. A federal trial court or a federal court of original jurisdiction is a (a) U.S. Supreme Court, (b) U.S. Court of Appeals, (c) U.S. District Court.

   5. C

6. The federal appellate court is called the (a) U.S. Court of Appeals, (b) U.S. District Court, (c) U.S. Special Court.

   6. A

7. A state court that reviews cases from the trial courts is referred to as a (a) court of original jurisdiction, (b) court of appeal, (c) supreme court.

   7. B

8. A court that has very limited jurisdiction and whose cases may be appealed to a higher court is a (a) court of original jurisdiction, (b) probate court, (c) lower or inferior court.

   8. C

9. A court in which all proceedings are recorded for future reference is a (a) court of record, (b) court not of record, (c) small claims court.

   9. A

10. A court having jurisdiction over wills, the settlement of estates, the estates of minors, and the appointment of guardians is known as a/an (a) appellate court, (b) special court, (c) probate court.

    10. C

11. A court in which the proceedings are not required to be recorded is referred to as a (a) court not of record, (b) court of record, (c) trial court.

    11. A

12. A court that hears a case the first time it is tried in court is called a (a) lower or inferior court, (b) court of original jurisdiction, (c) court of appeal.

    12. B

13. The highest court in the federal judicial system is composed of a chief justice and (a) seven associate justices, (b) eight associate justices, (c) nine associate justices.

    13. B

14. The highest court in the federal judicial system is called the (a) U.S. Supreme Court, (b) special court, (c) supreme court.

    14. A

15. The highest court in most states is called the (a) U.S. Supreme Court, (b) special court, (c) supreme court.

    15. C

KEYING LEGAL TERMS

Directions: Unless otherwise instructed, use a 70-space line (typewriter) or 1-inch margins (computer) and double spacing. Correct all errors. Follow one of the procedures below.

WORDS

Keyboarding Procedure
On your typewriter or computer, key the following words at least two times, concentrating on the correct spelling and pronunciation.

Shorthand Procedure
On your typewriter or computer, key the following words once, concentrating on the correct spelling and pronunciation. Then write the shorthand outline for each word in your shorthand notebook or on your shorthand machine. Transcribe from the shorthand outlines one time on your typewriter or computer.

special courts	**U.S. Supreme Court**	**U.S. District Court**
court of original jurisdiction	**U.S. Court of Appeals**	**supreme court**
trial court	**court of record**	**appellate court**
court of appeal	**lower or inferior court**	**court not of record**
probate court	**small claims court**	

SENTENCES

Keyboarding Procedure
Key each of the following sentences one time on your typewriter or computer. Concentrate on the correct spelling and pronunciation of each underlined legal term.

Shorthand Procedure
Write the correct shorthand outlines for the following sentences in your shorthand notebook or on your shorthand machine. Transcribe from your shorthand outlines one time on your typewriter or computer.

These sentences will be used for practice dictation on the cassettes.

The American judicial system has a dual court system, consisting of one federal court system and fifty state court systems. The federal court system deals with cases involving the federal government, suits between states, suits between citizens of two different states, and specific matters in the various special courts established for that purpose.

The U.S. Supreme Court is the highest court in the federal judicial system and is composed of a chief justice and eight associate justices. The U.S. District Court is a federal trial court or court of original jurisdiction. If the state of Illinois were suing the state of Missouri, the case would be filed in a U.S. District Court. A case tried in the U.S. District Court may be appealed to the U.S. Court of Appeals. The U.S. Supreme Court may then be petitioned to hear the case. There are several special courts in the federal court system, such as the Court of Claims, the Court of Customs and Patent Appeals, and the Tax Court.

The highest court in most states is called the supreme court. A trial court or court of original jurisdiction hears a case the first time it is tried in court. If you were going to sue another resident or business located in your state, you would file the case in a trial court. A trial court is usually a court of record, meaning that all the proceedings are recorded verbatim, or word for word. A case tried in a trial court may be appealed to an appellate court or a court of appeal and then to the supreme court. Certain cases heard by the state supreme court, or the highest court in a state system, may be appealed to the U.S. Supreme Court.

A court of small or restricted jurisdiction, such as a municipal court, is known generally as a lower or inferior court and, in most cases, is a court not of record. However, the trend in many states is to require all courts to be courts of record. A case tried in a lower or inferior court may be reviewed in a trial court and could then follow the appellate procedure, the same as a case originally tried in a trial court.

A probate court has jurisdiction over the probate of wills, the settlement of estates, and, in some states, the estates of minors and the appointment of guardians.

Small claims courts have been established in some states to handle minor disputes between individuals. For example, if the dry cleaners ruin your slacks, you could file the case to be settled in a small claims court without the assistance of an attorney.

TRANSCRIBING FROM DICTATION

Directions: This dictation emphasizes and reinforces the legal terms and definitions you have studied. Listen carefully to the pronunciation of each of the legal terms. Unless otherwise directed, use a 70-space line (typewriter) or 1-inch margins (computer) and double spacing. Correct all errors. Follow one of the procedures below.

Keyboarding Procedure
Using the cassette from Lesson 1, Part A, transcribe the dictation directly at your typewriter or computer.

Shorthand Procedure
Using the cassette from Lesson 1, Part A, take the dictation using your shorthand system and then transcribe from your shorthand notes on your typewriter or computer.

When you have finished transcribing Part A of the practice dictation, check your transcript with the printed copy. If you made any mistakes in the transcription, you should practice those words several times before going on.

Part B TERMINOLOGY AND DEFINITIONS

Directions: Study the terms, pronunciations, and definitions until you are thoroughly familiar with them. In order to complete this lesson successfully, you must understand the meaning and usage of all the legal terms presented. If you are using shorthand, write your shorthand outline for each legal term in your shorthand notebook or on your shorthand machine.

Legal Term	Pronunciation	Definition
		Sources of Law:
1. constitutional law	kän-stə-tü-shən-l lö	A branch of public law that deals with the interpretation and validity of federal and state constitutions. Constitutional law may be amended by the U.S. Supreme Court or by the highest state courts.
2. statutory law	'stach-ə-tōr-ē lö	Law that has been created by statute or legislation passed by the U.S. Congress or the state legislatures. Sometimes called written law.

3. common law	'käm-ən lȯ	A body of law that originated in England and has been adopted as the major source of law in the United States. Common law operates through the rule of precedent (like cases in the future to be decided in a like manner). Under common law, the rights of the individual are emphasized over the rights of the government.
4. case law	kās lȯ	Same as common law or unwritten law. Based on cases used as precedents rather than on statutes or other sources of law.
5. Napoleonic Code	nə-'pō-lē-ən-ik kōd	Law that originated in France and was adopted by the state of Louisiana as the basis for its state law. It is also referred to as Code Civil, Civil law, or Code Napoleon. Emphasis is on the rights of the state over the rights of the individual.

Classifications of Law:

6. public law	'pəb-lik lȯ	A body of law to which the general public is subject, including constitutional, administrative, and criminal law.
7. private law	'prī-vət lȯ	A body of law that deals with relationships between private individuals, such as contracts, civil injuries, domestic relations, and partnerships.
8. substantive law	'səb-stən-tiv lȯ	The body of law that creates and defines our rights and duties.
9. procedural law	prə-'sēj-rəl lȯ	The body of law that establishes the procedures to be followed for remedial action in court when one's rights have been violated. Also called adjective law.
10. administrative law	əd-'min-ə-strāt-iv lȯ	A branch of public law that deals with the various administrative agencies created by the government and defines the scope of power of those administrative agencies.
11. federal law	'fed-rəl lȯ	Law that is created by the federal government and is unaffected by state laws.
12. state law	stāt lȯ	Laws that are created by a state and are effective only in that state.
13. local and municipal ordinances	'lō-kəl ən myù-'nis-pəl 'ȯrd-nəns-əs	Laws or rules that are created by a local or municipal government and are effective only in that particular governmental unit.

Date <u>Sara Stone</u> — Name

Self-Evaluation B   TERMINOLOGY AND DEFINITION RECALL

Directions: In the Answers column, write the letter from Column 1 that represents the word or phrase that best matches each item in Column 2. After you have completed this self-evaluation, check your answers with the key on page 494. If you have any incorrect answers, restudy the definitions for those terms before going on with this lesson. Then unless otherwise directed, submit this self-evaluation to your instructor.

Column 1	Column 2	Answers
a. administrative law	1. Law that establishes the steps to be followed when one's rights have been violated.	1. _j_
b. case law	2. The part of law that deals with relationships between private individuals.	2. _i_
c. civil law	3. A law, a rule, or an ordinance enacted or adopted by a county, city, or township; it is effective only in the governmental unit that created it.	3. _g_
d. common law	4. A branch of public law that deals with the interpretation and validity of federal and state constitutions.	4. _e_
e. constitutional law	5. The body of law that includes constitutional, administrative, and criminal law to which the general public is subject.	5. _k_
f. federal law	6. The form of law that originated in France and was adopted by the state of Louisiana.	6. _h_
g. local and municipal ordinances	7. Law that is created by a state and is effective only in that state.	7. _l_
h. Napoleonic Code	8. Law that is based on cases used as precedents rather than on statutes or other sources of law.	8. _b_
i. private law	9. Law that is created by the federal government and is unaffected by state laws.	9. _f_
j. procedural law	10. Law that creates and defines our rights and duties.	10. _n_
k. public law	11. Law that is created by statute in the legislatures and is sometimes called written law.	11. _m_
l. state law	12. Law that originated in England and is the basis for the laws in most of our states.	12. _d_
m. statutory law	13. The branch of public law that deals with the various administrative agencies created by the government and defines the scope of their power.	13. _a_
n. substantive law		

KEYING LEGAL TERMS

Directions: Unless otherwise instructed, use a 70-space line (typewriter) or 1-inch margins (computer) and double spacing. Correct all errors. Follow one of the procedures below.

WORDS

Keyboarding Procedure
On your typewriter or computer, key the following words at least two times, concentrating on the correct spelling and pronunciation.

Shorthand Procedure
On your typewriter or computer, key the following words once, concentrating on the correct spelling and pronunciation. Then write the shorthand outline for each word in your shorthand notebook or on your shorthand machine. Transcribe from the shorthand outlines one time on your typewriter or computer.

public law	private law	constitutional law
administrative law	statutory law	case law
Napoleonic Code	common law	substantive law
procedural law	federal law	state law
local and municipal ordinances		

SENTENCES

Keyboarding Procedure
Key each of the following sentences one time on your typewriter or computer. Concentrate on the correct spelling and pronunciation of each underlined legal term.

Shorthand Procedure
Write the correct shorthand outlines for the following sentences in your shorthand notebook or on your shorthand machine. Transcribe from your shorthand outlines one time on your typewriter or computer.

These sentences will be used for practice dictation on the cassettes.

The sources of law in the United States are the federal and state constitutions, statutes enacted by the U.S. Congress and the state legislatures, common or case law principles, and the Napoleonic or Civil Code. Law that is classified on the basis of the parties involved is known as public law or private law. Public law is that body of law to which the general public is subject. It includes constitutional law, administrative law, and criminal law. Constitutional law is based on the federal and state constitutions and may be amended by the U.S. Supreme Court or the highest state courts. For example, the right to vote is a constitutional law. Administrative law governs the various agencies created by the government and defines the scope of their authority. The licensing of builders or pharmacists is an example of administrative law. Private law deals with relationships between private individuals, such as contracts, civil injuries, domestic relations, and partnerships.

The form of law is another basis for classifying law. Statutory law, common or case law, and the Napoleonic Code are based on the form of law. Statutory law, sometimes called written law, is created by statute or legislation passed by the U.S. Congress or the state legislatures. The laws giving individuals the right to work are statutory laws. Common law, or case law, originated in England and is the basis for the law in most of our states. Under common law, the rights of the individual are emphasized over the rights of the government. It is based on cases used as precedents rather than on statutes, and the rights of the individual are emphasized over the rights of the government. The Napoleonic Code originated in France and is used in the state of Louisiana. It is also referred to as Code Civil, Civil law, or Code Napoleon. The Napoleonic Code emphasizes the rights of the state over the rights of the individual. Under this system of law, you are presumed to be guilty until you prove you are innocent.

Substantive law and procedural law are two classifications based on the nature of law. Substantive law creates and defines our rights and duties; whereas procedural law, which is also known as adjective law, establishes the procedures to be followed for remedial action in court when one's rights have been violated. Other types of law are federal law, state law, and local and municipal ordinances. Federal law is created by the federal government and applies to all states. State law and local and municipal ordinances are created by states, counties, cities, or townships and are effective only in the state or governmental unit that created them.

TRANSCRIBING FROM DICTATION

Directions: This dictation emphasizes and reinforces the legal terms and definitions you have studied. Listen carefully to the pronunciation of each of the legal terms. Unless otherwise directed, use a 70-space line (typewriter) or 1-inch margins (computer) and double spacing. Correct all errors. Follow one of the procedures below.

Keyboarding Procedure
Using the cassette from Lesson 1, Part B, transcribe the dictation directly at your typewriter or computer.

Shorthand Procedure
Using the cassette from Lesson 1, Part B, take the dictation using your shorthand system and then transcribe from your shorthand notes on your typewriter or computer.

When you have finished transcribing Part B of the practice dictation, check your transcript with the printed copy. If you made any mistakes in the transcription, you should practice those words several times before going on to Lesson 2.

CHECKLIST
I have completed the following for Lesson 1:

	Part A, Date	Part B, Date	Submitted to Instructor Yes	No
Terminology and Definitions	_____	_____	_____	_____
Self-Evaluation	_____	_____	_____	_____
* Keying Legal Terms	_____	_____	_____	_____
Words	_____	_____	_____	_____
Sentences	_____	_____	_____	_____
* Transcribing from Dictation	_____	_____	_____	_____

When you have successfully completed all the exercises in this lesson and submitted to your instructor those requested, you are ready to proceed with Lesson 2.

* If you are using a shorthand system, submit to your instructor your shorthand notes along with your transcript.

Lesson 2

General Legal Terminology

"There's no disputing about rules of law."
—Legal Maxim

There are many legal terms that apply to the entire field of law. Several of these are presented in this lesson so that you will be familiar with them as you get into the study of the more specific areas of law. Legal terms are mostly everyday English words, but often they have a totally different meaning when used in the legal field. For example, you will find that the words suit, party, bench, and bar have different legal meanings than they have in common usage. When you complete this lesson, you will have a knowledge of some of the general terminology used in its legal context.

Part A TERMINOLOGY AND DEFINITIONS

Directions: Study the terms, pronunciations, and definitions until you are thoroughly familiar with them. In order to complete this lesson successfully, you must understand the meaning and usage of all the legal terms presented. If you are using shorthand, write your shorthand outline for each legal term in your shorthand notebook or on your shorthand machine.

Legal Term	Pronunciation	Definition
1. lex	leks	Latin term for law. A system of written or unwritten law for a given jurisdiction.
2. lexicon	′lek-sə-kän	Latin. A dictionary of legal terms.
3. code books	kōd bùks	Books containing the laws that have been created by state and federal legislatures.
4. Corpus Juris Secundum	′kȯr-pəs ′jür-əs si-′kənd-əm	An encyclopedia of laws commonly used as a reference by lawyers.
5. jurisprudence	jür-ə-′sprüd-ns	The philosophy or science of law.
6. statute	′stach-üt	A law created by a state or federal legislature.
7. bar	bär	The legal profession. Lawyers are members of the bar. An attorney guilty of misconduct may be censored by the bar association.
8. judge	jəj	The presiding officer of a court of law.
9. bench	bench	A court of law. Also, the judge's seat in a court of law.
10. jurist	′jür-əst	One who has a thorough knowledge of law and has written extensively on legal subjects. Do not confuse with a juror.

11. prosecuting attorney	′präs-i-kyüt-iŋ ə-′tər-nē	An appointed or elected official who represents the people or the state in criminal cases. For example, whenever a public law has been violated, such as the commission of murder, the prosecuting attorney, who may also be called a district attorney in some jurisdictions, represents the "People," or the public, and attempts to prosecute the defendant.
12. defense attorney	di-′fens ə-′tər-nē	One who represents the defendant in court cases or legal matters.
13. in propria persona	in prō-′prē-ə pər-′sō-nə	Latin. In one's own proper person. One who acts without the assistance of an attorney. Sometimes shortened to in pro per. For example, if a defendant chooses not to be represented by an attorney, he or she is said to appear in propria persona, or in pro per.
14. esquire	′es-kwīr	A title written after the surname of an attorney. Usually abbreviated to Esq., and no personal or professional title is prefixed to the name.

Self-Evaluation A   TERMINOLOGY AND DEFINITION RECALL

Directions: In the Answers column, write the legal term that is most representative of the corresponding statement. After you have completed this self-evaluation, check your answers with the key on page 494. If you have any incorrect answers, restudy the definitions for those terms before going on with this lesson. Then unless otherwise directed, submit this self-evaluation to your instructor.

Answers

1. An encyclopedia of laws commonly used as a reference by lawyers is known as a/an _____.

   1. _Corpis Juris Secundum_

2. A title that is written after the surname of an attorney is ___(a)___ and it is sometimes abbreviated as ___(b)___.

   2a. _esquire_
   2b. _defense attorney_

3. One who represents the defendant in court cases or other legal matters is the _____.

   3. _Esq._

4. An appointed or elected official who represents the people, or the public, in a criminal case is the _____.

   4. _prosecuting attorney_

5. If you did not know the meaning of a legal term, you would probably look it up in a dictionary of legal terms called a/an _____.

   5. _lexicon_

6. The philosophy or science of law is referred to as _____.

   6. _jurisprudence_

7. The Latin term for law is _____.

   7. _lex_

8. All members of the legal profession are collectively referred to as the _____.

   8. _Bar_

9. The presiding officer in a court of law is known as the _____.

   9. _judge_

10. Books containing laws that have been created by state and federal legislatures are _____.

    10. _code books_

11. A court of law and, also, the judge's seat in a court of law are called the _____.

    11. _bench_

12. A law created by a state or federal legislature is a/an _____.

    12. _Statute_

13. If you chose to represent yourself in a lawsuit without the assistance of an attorney, you would be referred to as appearing ___(a)___, or ___(b)___.

    13a. _In propria persona_
    13b. _proper_

14. One who has a thorough knowledge of law and has written extensively on legal subjects is a/an _____.

    14. _jurist_

KEYING LEGAL TERMS

Directions: Unless otherwise instructed, use a 70-space line (typewriter) or 1-inch margins (computer) and double spacing. Correct all errors. Follow one of the procedures below.

WORDS

Keyboarding Procedure
On your typewriter or computer, key the following words at least two times, concentrating on the correct spelling and pronunciation.

Shorthand Procedure
On your typewriter or computer, key the following words once, concentrating on the correct spelling and pronunciation. Then write the shorthand outline for each word in your shorthand notebook or on your shorthand machine. Transcribe from the shorthand outlines one time on your typewriter or computer.

lex	lexicon	code books
Corpus Juris Secundum	jurisprudence	statute
bar	judge	bench
jurist	prosecuting attorney	defense attorney
in propria persona	esquire	

SENTENCES

Keyboarding Procedure
Key each of the following sentences one time on your typewriter or computer. Concentrate on the correct spelling and pronunciation of each underlined legal term.

Shorthand Procedure
Write the correct shorthand outlines for the following sentences in your shorthand notebook or on your shorthand machine. Transcribe from your shorthand outlines one time on your typewriter or computer.

These sentences will be used for practice dictation on the cassettes.

The Latin term for law is lex. Lex is a system of written or unwritten law for a given jurisdiction. A lexicon is a dictionary of legal terms. If you do not know the meaning of a legal term, you can look up the term in a lexicon. The code books contain the laws that have been created by state and federal legislatures. The Corpus Juris Secundum is an encyclopedia of laws. The Corpus Juris Secundum is commonly used as a legal reference by lawyers.

The philosophy or science of law is known as jurisprudence. Jurisprudence deals with the principles of law and legal relations. A statute is a law created by a state or federal legislature. The violation of a statute will usually result in a legal proceeding in a court of law.

All members of the legal profession are collectively referred to as the bar. Attorneys follow a code of ethics established by the American Bar Association and may be censored by the bar association if they are found guilty of misconduct in their profession. A judge presides over and administers the law in a court of justice. A court of law may also be referred to as the bench. Also, the bench can mean the seat occupied by the judge in court. A jurist is a person who has a thorough knowledge of the law and who has written extensively on legal subjects. Do not confuse a jurist with a juror.

When a statute has been violated, the judge will hear the case as presented by the prosecuting and defense attorneys. The prosecuting attorney conducts criminal prosecutions on behalf of the state or the people, whereas the defense attorney tries a case in court on behalf of the one who is charged with the crime in the case. If you were charged with a criminal act and you did not want the assistance of a defense attorney, you could appear in court in propria persona, or in pro per. Someone who is in propria persona, or in pro per, is acting in his or her own behalf and does not have the assistance of an attorney.

The title "Esquire" is sometimes written after an attorney's surname. The word esquire is usually abbreviated to Esq., and a personal or professional title is not prefixed to the name. An example is William D. Flannagan, Esq.

TRANSCRIBING FROM DICTATION

Directions: This dictation emphasizes and reinforces the legal terms and definitions you have studied. Listen carefully to the pronunciation of each of the legal terms. Unless otherwise directed, use a 70-space line (typewriter) or 1-inch margins (computer) and double spacing. Correct all errors. Follow one of the procedures below.

Keyboarding Procedure
Using the cassette from Lesson 2, Part A, transcribe the dictation directly at your typewriter or computer.

Shorthand Procedure
Using the cassette from Lesson 2, Part A, take the dictation using your shorthand system and then transcribe from your shorthand notes on your typewriter or computer.

When you have finished transcribing Part A of the practice dictation, check your transcript with the printed copy. If you made any mistakes in the transcription, you should practice those words several times before going on.

Part B TERMINOLOGY AND DEFINITIONS

Directions: Study the terms, pronunciations and definitions until you are thoroughly familiar with them. In order to complete this lesson successfully, you must understand the meaning and usage of all the legal terms presented. If you are using shorthand, write your shorthand outline for each legal term in your shorthand notebook or on your shorthand machine.

Legal Term	Pronunciation	Definition
1. legal procedure	′lē-gəl prə-′sē-jər	The method or steps to be followed in any action in a court of law.
2. proceeding	prō-′sēd-iŋ	Any action in a court of law.
3. suit	süt	Any action or proceeding in a court of law whereby one seeks relief or recovery from another who has caused injury to or violated the rights of that person.
4. litigation	lit-ə-′gā-shən	A legal action or suit in a court of law whereby one seeks relief or recovery from another.
5. action	′ak-shən	A legal proceeding or suit in a court of law whereby one seeks relief from another for an injury or a violated right.
6. due process	dü ′präs-es	The legal procedures established which provide that every person has the benefit and protection of the law.

7. justice	′jəs-təs	A just and fair application of the law for every person. Also, a judge is referred to as a justice.
8. client	′klī-ənt	One who employs an attorney to represent or advise him or her in court cases or legal matters.
9. party	′pärt-ē	Any person involved in or affected by a legal proceeding. The plaintiff and the defendant are both parties to a suit.
10. litigant	′lit-i-gənt	A party to an action, a suit, a litigation, or a legal proceeding.
11. plaintiff	′plānt-əf	One who starts an action, a suit, or a proceeding in a court of law. If you file the suit, you are the plaintiff.
12. defendant	di-′fen-dənt	The one against whom an action, a suit, a litigation, or a proceeding is started in a court of law. If you file a suit, the one against whom you file is the defendant.
13. et alius	et ′āl-ē-us	Latin. And others. Abbreviated et al. When et al. is used in a legal document with more than one plaintiff or defendant named, it means all persons previously named are included. For example, if the case title includes the names of Kozak, Wayland, Morris, and Jones as plaintiffs, they may be referred to in the legal document as Kozak, et al.
14. versus	′vər-səs	Latin. Against. When used in a case title, the plaintiff's name is first, followed by "versus," then the defendant's name; for example, Durand versus Selmar. May be abbreviated as vs. or v. (i.e., Durand vs. Selmar or Durand v. Selmar).

Self-Evaluation B   TERMINOLOGY AND DEFINITION RECALL

Directions: In the Answers column, write the letter from Column 1 that represents the word or phrase that best matches each item in Column 2. After you have completed this self-evaluation, check your answers with the key on page 494. If you have any incorrect answers, restudy the definitions for those terms before going on with this lesson. Then unless otherwise directed, submit this self-evaluation to your instructor.

Column 1	Column 2	Answers
a. action	1. Another name for a legal proceeding, suit, or litigation in a court of law by which one person seeks recovery from another for an injury or a violated right.	1.
b. client	2. The one against whom an action, a suit, or a proceeding is started in a court of law.	2. c
c. defendant	3. The legal procedure established that provides that every person has the benefit and protection of the law.	3. d
d. due process	4. One who starts an action, a suit, or a proceeding in a court of law.	4. L
e. et alius	5. The legal term meaning and others.	5. e
f. jurisprudence	6. Another name for a proceeding, an action, or a suit in a court of law whereby one seeks recovery from another who has caused injury to or violated the rights of that person.	6.
g. justice	7. Another name for a litigant involved in or affected by a legal proceeding.	7. K
h. legal procedure	8. The method to be followed in any action in a court of law.	8. h
i. litigant	9. A party to an action, a suit, or a legal proceeding.	9. i
j. litigation	10. Another name for a litigation, a suit, or an action whereby one seeks recovery from another who has caused injury to or violated the rights of that person.	10. m
k. party	11. The word in the title of a case that means against.	11. O
l. plaintiff	12. One who employs an attorney to represent or advise him or her in court cases or legal matters.	12. b
m. proceeding	13. A just and fair application of law for every person.	13. g
n. suit	14. Another name for a proceeding, a litigation, or an action whereby one seeks recovery from another who has caused injury to or violated the rights of that person.	14. a
o. versus		

KEYING LEGAL TERMS

Directions: Unless otherwise instructed, use a 70-space line (typewriter) or 1-inch margins (computer) and double spacing. Correct all errors. Follow one of the procedures below.

WORDS

Keyboarding Procedure
On your typewriter or computer, key the following words at least two times, concentrating on the correct spelling and pronunciation.

Shorthand Procedure
On your typewriter or computer, key the following words once, concentrating on the correct spelling and pronunciation. Then write the shorthand outline for each word in your shorthand notebook or on your shorthand machine. Transcribe from the shorthand outlines one time on your typewriter or computer.

legal procedure	proceeding	suit
litigation	action	justice
due process	client	party
litigant	plaintiff	defendant
et alius	versus	

SENTENCES

Keyboarding Procedure
Key each of the following sentences one time on your typewriter or computer. Concentrate on the correct spelling and pronunciation of each underlined legal term.

Shorthand Procedure
Write the correct shorthand outlines for the following sentences in your shorthand notebook or on your shorthand machine. Transcribe from your shorthand outlines one time on your typewriter or computer.

These sentences will be used for practice dictation on the cassettes.

When a person starts a legal case, there is a certain legal procedure that must be followed throughout the legal proceeding. A suit, a litigation, a proceeding, and an action all refer to a dispute in a court of law whereby one seeks relief or recovery from another who has caused injury to or violated the rights of that person. If someone owes you money and will not pay, you can start a legal action against that person to recover the money that is owed to you.

Our system of justice strives to apply the law fairly and justly to every person involved in a litigation. The parties to a proceeding are seeking justice by following a course of legal procedures usually referred to as due process. Every person is entitled to due process in our system of justice.

A client is one who employs an attorney to represent or advise him or her in legal proceedings or other legal matters. Any person involved in or affected by a lawsuit is known as a party or litigant. A client who hires an attorney to start a legal proceeding becomes known as the plaintiff in the suit. When a plaintiff starts an action, the person charged with a wrongdoing is called the defendant. Thus, the two most common parties in a lawsuit are the plaintiff and the defendant.

Sometimes there may be more than one plaintiff or defendant in a suit. A group of plaintiffs or defendants may be referred to by using the name of the first one listed followed by et alius, which may be abbreviated to et al. If the case title includes the names of Kozak, Wayland, Morris, and Jones as plaintiffs, they may be referred to in the legal document as Kozak, et al. This means that all the others are also included.

The word <u>versus</u> means against. In the title of a suit, an action, a litigation, or a proceeding, the plaintiff's name is first, followed by versus, then the defendant's name. Versus may be abbreviated vs. or v. If Mr. Cook were suing Mr. Walters, the title of the suit would be Cook versus Walters.

TRANSCRIBING FROM DICTATION

Directions: This dictation emphasizes and reinforces the legal terms and definitions you have studied. Listen carefully to the pronunciation of each of the legal terms. Unless otherwise directed, use a 70-space line (typewriter) or 1-inch margins (computer) and double spacing. Correct all errors. Follow one of the procedures below.

Keyboarding Procedure
Using the cassette from Lesson 2, Part B, transcribe the dictation directly at your typewriter or computer.

Shorthand Procedure
Using the cassette from Lesson 2, Part B, take the dictation using your shorthand system and then transcribe from your shorthand notes on your typewriter or computer.

When you have finished transcribing Part B of the practice dictation, check your transcript with the printed copy. If you made any mistakes in the transcription, you should practice those words several times before going on to Evaluation 1.

CHECKLIST
I have completed the following for Lesson 2:

	Part A, Date	Part B, Date	Submitted to Instructor Yes	No
Terminology and Definitions				
Self-Evaluation				
* **Keying Legal Terms**				
Words				
Sentences				
* **Transcribing from Dictation**				

When you have successfully completed all the exercises in this lesson and submitted to your instructor those requested, you are ready to proceed with Evaluation 1.

* If you are using a shorthand system, submit to your instructor your shorthand notes along with your transcript.

Evaluation No. 1   SECTION A

Directions: This dictation/transcription evaluation will test your spelling and transcription abilities on the legal terms that you studied in the two preceding lessons. Use a 5-space paragraph indention, a 70-space line (typewriter) or 1-inch margins (computer), and double spacing unless otherwise instructed. Correct all errors. Follow one of the procedures below.

Keyboarding Procedure

Using the cassette from Evaluation 1, transcribe the dictation directly at your typewriter or computer.

Shorthand Procedure

Using the cassette from Evaluation 1, take the dictation using your shorthand system and then transcribe from your shorthand notes on your typewriter or computer.

Sections B and C are available from your instructor.

Lesson 3

General Legal Terms

"The act of God does injury to no one."
—Legal Maxim

Terms that describe the various types of claims and defenses of the parties to a lawsuit are presented in the following exercises. Also included are some related and general legal terms. When you complete this lesson, you should have a knowledge and understanding of terminology involving pleadings and other general legal activities.

Part A   TERMINOLOGY AND DEFINITIONS

Directions: Study the terms, pronunciations, and definitions until you are thoroughly familiar with them. In order to complete this lesson successfully, you must understand the meaning and usage of all the legal terms presented. If you are using shorthand, write your shorthand outline for each legal term in your shorthand notebook or on your shorthand machine.

Legal Term	Pronunciation	Definition
1. retainer	ri-′tā-ner	The fee a client pays to an attorney for representation or assistance in a legal matter.
2. tribunal	trī-′byün-l	A court of justice. Also, all the judges in a particular jurisdiction.
3. adjudicate	ə-′jüd-i-kāt	To decide a case by law.
4. complaint	kəm-′plānt	The first pleading filed in a civil action whereby the plaintiff states the facts on which the suit is based. (See Figure 3-1, page 31.)
5. declaration	dek-lə-′rā-shən	Another name for a first pleading filed in a civil action whereby the plaintiff states the facts on which the suit is based.
6. narratio	na-′rā-shē-ō	The Latin word for the first pleading filed in a civil action by the plaintiff in which the facts for the basis of the suit are stated.
7. plea	plē	The first pleading filed by a defendant in an action that states the defendant's answer, based on fact, to the plaintiff's claims.
8. pleadings	′plēd-iŋs	The written allegations of what the plaintiff claims and what the defendant denies in a lawsuit. (See Figure 3-1, page 31.)
9. gravamen	grə-′vā-mən	The grievance or injury specifically complained of in a pleading. The substantial cause of the action.
10. count	kaůnt	The various charges in a complaint or declaration made by the plaintiff against a defendant. (See Figure 3-2, page 32.)

11. contest	kən-'test	To dispute the plaintiff's claim in a court of law. If you contest a lawsuit, you are denying the charge.
12. petition	pə-'tish-ən	A written application to the court for action upon a legal matter. There are many different kinds of petitions that may be filed with the court. For example, a party to an action may petition the court to set a trial date, to issue a bench warrant, or to probate a will. (See Figure 3-3, page 32.)
13. writ	rit	A written command issued by a court that requires some specified action. The person receiving the writ may be required to do or not to do a specific act. Some of the various types of writs are a writ of habeas corpus, a writ of garnishment, or a writ of restitution. (See Figure 3-4, page 33.)
14. champerty	'cham-pərt-ē	An illegal procedure whereby one not involved in the lawsuit makes a deal with a party to the suit to pay the costs of the litigation in exchange for a share of the proceeds from the suit.

FIGURE 3-1 A Complaint

STATE OF MICHIGAN

IN THE CIRCUIT COURT FOR THE COUNTY OF INGHAM

SARAH ANN STONE,

      Plaintiff,

v.   File No. 83-52179

IMAGE GRAPHICS, INC.,

      Defendant.

_____

JASON C. O'MALLEY (P 23345)
PATRICK B. STILWELL (P 36588)
Attorneys for Plaintiff

COMPLAINT

NOW COMES Sarah Ann Stone, by and through her attorneys, O'Malley & Stilwell, P.C., and for her complaint against defendant states the following:

COMMON ALLEGATIONS

1. Plaintiff, Sarah Ann Stone ("Stone"), is a resident and citizen of the State of Michigan and resides at 6447 Whitmore Avenue, Lansing, Michigan 48810.

2. Defendant, Image Graphics, Inc. ("Image"), is a corporation chartered under the laws of the State of Michigan, whose principal administrative offices and place of business is located at 7850 South Washington Avenue, Lansing, Michigan 48933.

3. Stone was employed by Image as a commercial artist from 1985 until September 1996.

4. In 1992, Stone, working in conjunction with other staff members at Image, undertook development of certain audiovisual materials ("AV materials") designed to be used by various businesses for in-service training programs.

Pleadings

FIGURE 3-2 A Count

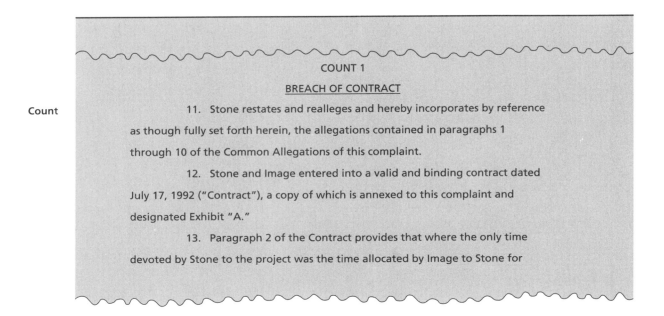

Count

COUNT 1

BREACH OF CONTRACT

    11. Stone restates and realleges and hereby incorporates by reference as though fully set forth herein, the allegations contained in paragraphs 1 through 10 of the Common Allegations of this complaint.

    12. Stone and Image entered into a valid and binding contract dated July 17, 1992 ("Contract"), a copy of which is annexed to this complaint and designated Exhibit "A."

    13. Paragraph 2 of the Contract provides that where the only time devoted by Stone to the project was the time allocated by Image to Stone for

FIGURE 3-3 A Petition

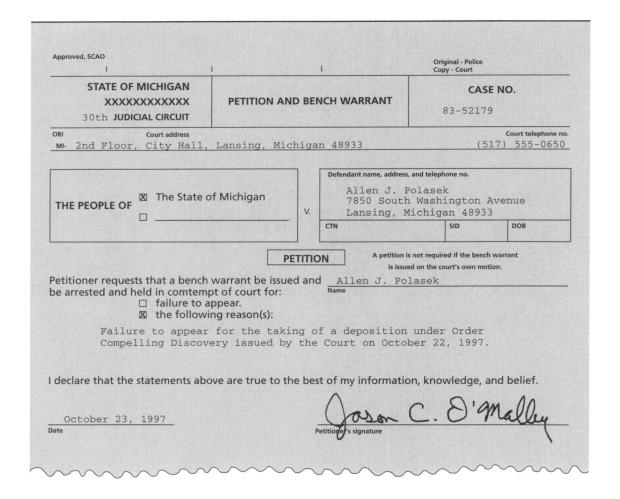

FIGURE 3-4 A Writ

| | | | |

ORIGINAL - OFFICER RETURN
1st COPY - COURT
2nd COPY - DEFENDANT

| STATE OF MICHIGAN
54A **DISTRICT COURT** | **WRIT OF RESTITUTION**
LANDLORD/TENANT - LAND CONTRACT | CASE NO.
885599-LT |

6th Floor, City Hall, Lansing, Michigan   (517) 555-3445
Court address   Court telephone no.

Plaintiff name and address	Defendant name(s) and address(es)
Capitol Management, Inc. 7720 Wildwood Drive Lansing, Michigan 48912	Justin H. Story 6453 Fairlane Drive, Apt. 201 Lansing, Michigan 48906

Plaintiff's attorney, bar no., and telephone no.
Margo B. Griffin (P 55220)
7885 South Cedar Street
Lansing, Michigan 48910   555-7781

APPLICATION

The undersigned makes application for a writ of restitution and states:

1. On <u>November 24, 1997</u> judgment was entered against Defendant(s), and Plaintiff was awarded
   Date
   possessionof the following described property. <u>Apartment 201, 6453 Fairlane Drive, Lansing,</u>

   <u>Michigan 48906</u>
   _____

2. No payment has been made on the judgment and/or no rent has been received since the date of

   judgment,except the sum of $ _____ received under the following conditions: _____
   _____
   _____

3. The party awarded judgment has complied with its terms.
4. The time stated in the judgment to precede the issuance of a writ of restitution has elapsed.

I declare, under penalty of contempt of court, that to the best of my knowledge, information and belief,
there is good ground to support the contents of this pleading.

December 4, 1997   *Margo B. Griffin* (P 55220)
Date   Signature of Attorney/ Bar no.
                                                                    7885 South Cedar Street
                                                                    Address
                                                                    Lansing, Michigan 48912   555-7781
                                                                    City, state, zip   Telephone no.

WRIT

IN THE NAME OF THE PEOPLE OF THE STATE OF MICHIGAN:
To the Court Officer: Based upon the facts set forth in the above application, you are commanded to remove the above
named Defendant(s) and other occupants from the premises described, and to restore Plaintiff to peaceful possession.

SEAL   _12/4/97_   *Hunter G. Mitchell*
             Date issued   District Judge

NOTE: This writ must be served within 60 days of the issuance date.

OFFICER RETURN
WRIT OF RESTITUTION, LANDLORD TENANT, LAND CONTRACT, Form no. DCH107, (3 part, pink) Revised 4/80

Self-Evaluation A   TERMINOLOGY AND DEFINITION RECALL

Directions: In the Answers column, write the legal term that is most representative of the corresponding statement. After you have completed this self-evaluation, check your answers with the key on page 494. If you have any incorrect answers, restudy the definitions for those terms before going on with this lesson. Then unless otherwise directed, submit this self-evaluation to your instructor.

Answers

1. A written application to the court for action upon a legal matter, such as the setting of a court date, is a/an _____.
   1. petition

2. A Latin term for the first pleading filed by the plaintiff in an action is _____.
   2. narratio

3. The first pleading filed in an action whereby the plaintiff states the facts on which the suit is based is a/an _____.
   3. declaration

4. A written command issued by a court that requires a person to do or not to do a specific act is a/an _____.
   4. writ

5. The first pleading filed by a defendant in a lawsuit that states the defendant's answer, based on fact, to the plaintiff's claims is a/an _____.
   5. plea

6. A court of justice is also referred to as a/an _____.
   6. tribunal

7. To dispute the plaintiff's claim in a court of law is to _____ the claim.
   7. contest

8. The first pleading filed in an action by the plaintiff is a/an _____.
   8. complaint

9. A charge in a complaint or declaration made by the plaintiff against a defendant is called a/an _____.
   9. count

10. To decide a case by law is to _____ the case.
    10. adjudicate

11. An illegal procedure whereby one not involved in the lawsuit makes a deal with a party to the suit to pay the costs of the litigation in exchange for a share of the proceeds is called _____.
    11. Champerty

12. The written allegations of what the plaintiff claims and what the defendant denies in a lawsuit are referred to as _____.
    12. pleadings

13. The grievance or injury specifically complained of in a pleading is _____.
    13. gravamen

14. The fee that a client pays to an attorney for representation or assistance in a legal matter is a/an _____.
    14. retainer

KEYING LEGAL TERMS

Directions: Unless otherwise instructed, use a 70-space line (typewriter) or 1-inch margins (computer) and double spacing. Correct all errors. Follow one of the procedures below.

WORDS

Keyboarding Procedure
On your typewriter or computer, key the following words at least two times, concentrating on the correct spelling and pronunciation.

Shorthand Procedure
On your typewriter or computer, key the following words once, concentrating on the correct spelling and pronunciation. Then write the shorthand outline for each word in your shorthand notebook or on your shorthand machine. Transcribe from the shorthand outlines one time on your typewriter or computer.

retainer	tribunal	adjudicate
complaint	declaration	narratio
plea	pleadings	gravamen
count	contest	petition
writ	champerty	

SENTENCES

Keyboarding Procedure
Key each of the following sentences one time on your typewriter or computer. Concentrate on the correct spelling and pronunciation of each underlined legal term.

Shorthand Procedure
Write the correct shorthand outlines for the following sentences in your shorthand notebook or on your shorthand machine. Transcribe from your shorthand outlines one time on your typewriter or computer.

These sentences will be used for practice dictation on the cassettes.

If you hire an attorney to represent or assist you in a legal matter, the fee you pay the attorney is called a retainer. To decide or settle a case in a court of law, or a tribunal, is to adjudicate the case. A tribunal may also be used when referring to all the judges in a particular jurisdiction.

Depending upon the state, court, and type of proceeding, an initial pleading whereby the plaintiff states the facts on which the suit is based may be referred to as a complaint or a declaration or by the Latin term narratio. Once a client has retained an attorney for representation in a legal matter, the attorney will prepare a complaint, declaration, or narratio, which will state the facts on which the suit is based. When the defendant in a suit receives the plaintiff's complaint, the defendant will file a plea, which states the defendant's answer, based on fact, to the plaintiff's claim. The plaintiff's written claims and the defendant's written denials make up the pleadings in a lawsuit. The grievance or injury specifically complained of in a pleading is referred to as gravamen.

A count is one of the various charges in a complaint or declaration made by the plaintiff against a defendant. The defendant's plea will answer each count or charge listed in the plaintiff's declaration or complaint. When the defendant disputes the plaintiff's claim, the defendant is said to contest the claim made by the plaintiff. Of course, a complaint that is contested will be adjudicated in a tribunal, or a court of law.

The attorney for either party may <u>petition</u> the court for various matters, such as the setting of a trial date.

The judge may issue a <u>writ</u>, which requires one of the parties to a lawsuit to do or not to do a specific thing.

If someone who is not involved in the lawsuit makes a deal with a party in the lawsuit whereby the uninvolved

party will pay all the legal fees in exchange for a share of any money awarded in the suit, this procedure is

referred to as <u>champerty</u>. Champerty constitutes an illegal act and is not permitted under law.

TRANSCRIBING FROM DICTATION

Directions: This dictation emphasizes and reinforces the legal terms and definitions you have studied. Listen carefully to the pronunciation of each of the legal terms. Unless otherwise directed, use a 70-space line (typewriter) or 1-inch margins (computer) and double spacing. Correct all errors. Follow one of the procedures below.

Keyboarding Procedure
Using the cassette from Lesson 3, Part A, transcribe the dictation directly at your typewriter or computer.

Shorthand Procedure
Using the cassette from Lesson 3, Part A, take the dictation using your shorthand system and then transcribe from your shorthand notes on your typewriter or computer.

When you have finished transcribing Part A of the practice dictation, check your transcript with the printed copy. If you made any mistakes in the transcription, you should practice those words several times before going on.

Part B TERMINOLOGY AND DEFINITIONS

Directions: Study the terms, pronunciations, and definitions until you are thoroughly familiar with them. In order to complete this lesson successfully, you must understand the meaning and usage of all the legal terms presented. If you are using shorthand, write your shorthand outline for each legal term in your shorthand notebook or on your shorthand machine.

Legal Term	Pronunciation	Definition
1. allege	ə-'lej	To make an allegation or a charge.
2. malicious prosecution	mə-'lish-əs präs-i-'kyü-shən	An action started by a plaintiff without justification and with the intention of damaging the defendant.
3. double jeopardy	'dəb-əl 'jep-ərd-e	A second prosecution for the same offense. Our laws prohibit double jeopardy. If one is found innocent of a crime, he or she cannot be tried again for the same crime.
4. act of God	akt əv gäd	A disaster that occurs as a result of natural causes unaided by any human action. One cannot sue for damages caused by an act of God.
5. jointly and severally	'jȯint-lē ən 'sev-rəl-ē	When a liability involves more than one party, they may all be sued together or they may be sued separately. If you and a friend rent an apartment together and your friend refuses to pay the rent, you may be held liable for all the rent if the lease contains a jointly and severally clause.
6. feasance	'fēz-ns	The proper performance of a legal act.

7. malfeasance	mal-'fēz-ns	The performance of an illegal act. Misconduct.
8. statute of limitations	'stach-üt əv lim-ə-'tā-shəns	A law that requires an action to be started within a certain length of time after the alleged cause occurred. If a case is not filed within the statute of limitations, then it cannot be filed.
9. statute of frauds	'stach-üt əv frȯdz	An act that requires that certain kinds of contracts must be in writing and signed before an action based on the contracts can be instituted.
10. per se	pər 'sā	Latin. In itself or by itself.
11. alias	'ā-lē-əs	Latin. Otherwise. An assumed name by which one is also known. If Jane Rosewell also uses the name Jean Rosswell, she is said to have an alias. The abbreviation AKA or a/k/a which stands for "also known as" is sometimes used to denote an alias. The abbreviation may also be written as A/K/A or aka.
12. minor	'mī-nər	One who is too young to be considered as legally competent. That person is also referred to as an infant.
13. sui juris	'sü-ī 'jür-əs	Latin. One that is legally capable of managing his or her own actions or affairs.

Date _Sara Stone_ Name _____

Self-Evaluation B TERMINOLOGY AND DEFINITION RECALL

Directions: In the Answers column at the right of each statement, write the letter that represents the word or group of words that correctly completes the statement. After you have completed this self-evaluation, check your answers with the key on page 494. If you have any incorrect answers, restudy the definitions for those terms before going on with this lesson. Then unless otherwise directed, submit this self-evaluation to your instructor.

Answers

1. To make a charge or an allegation that someone committed a wrongful act is to (a) allege, (b) feasance, (c) malfeasance.

   1. A

2. One who is too young to be considered as legally competent is a/an (a) sui juris, (b) alias, (c) minor.

   2. C

3. If a plaintiff starts an action without justification and with the intention of damaging the defendant, it is called a (a) double jeopardy, (b) malicious prosecution, (c) feasance.

   3. B

4. If a legal act is properly performed, it is called (a) feasance, (b) malfeasance, (c) jointly and severally.

   4. A

5. A disaster that occurs as a result of natural causes unaided by any human action is a/an (a) act of God, (b) statute of limitations, (c) double jeopardy.

   5. A

6. An act that requires that certain kinds of contracts must be in writing and signed before an action based on the contracts can be commenced is the (a) act of God, (b) statute of limitations, (c) statute of frauds.

   6. C

7. If a person performs an illegal act or is guilty of misconduct, that person is guilty of (a) double jeopardy, (b) feasance, (c) malfeasance.

   7. C

8. If someone is prosecuted twice for the same offense, it is called (a) double jeopardy, (b) per se, (c) jointly and severally.

   8. A

9. A law that requires an action to be started within a certain length of time after the alleged cause occurred is the (a) statute of limitations, (b) statute of frauds, (c) act of God.

   9. A

10. The Latin term for an assumed name or a second name by which one is also known is a/an (a) sui juris, (b) per se, (c) alias.

    10. C

11. A liability involving more than one party who may be sued together or sued separately is expressed as (a) double jeopardy, (b) jointly and severally, (c) malicious prosecution.

    11. B

12. A Latin term meaning in itself or by itself is (a) alias, (b) sui juris, (c) per se.

    12. C

13. A Latin term meaning that one is legally capable of managing his or her own affairs or actions is (a) alias, (b) sui juris, (c) per se.

    13. B

KEYING LEGAL TERMS

Directions: Unless otherwise instructed, use a 70-space line (typewriter) or 1-inch margins (computer) and double spacing. Correct all errors. Follow one of the procedures below.

WORDS

Keyboarding Procedure
On your typewriter or computer, key the following words at least two times, concentrating on the correct spelling and pronunciation.

Shorthand Procedure
On your typewriter or computer, key the following words once, concentrating on the correct spelling and pronunciation. Then write the shorthand outline for each word in your shorthand notebook or on your shorthand machine. Transcribe from the shorthand outlines one time on your typewriter or computer.

allege	malicious prosecution	double jeopardy
act of God	jointly and severally	feasance
malfeasance	statute of limitations	statute of frauds
per se	alias	minor
sui juris		

SENTENCES

Keyboarding Procedure
Key each of the following sentences one time on your typewriter or computer. Concentrate on the correct spelling and pronunciation of each underlined legal term.

Shorthand Procedure
Write the correct shorthand outlines for the following sentences in your shorthand notebook or on your shorthand machine. Transcribe from your shorthand outlines one time on your typewriter or computer.

These sentences will be used for practice dictation on the cassettes.

Allege means to make a charge or an allegation. If the plaintiff starts a legal action without justification and with the intention of damaging the defendant, it is called malicious prosecution. Malicious prosecution cases terminate in favor of the defendant, and the plaintiff cannot recover in such cases. A second prosecution for the same offense is referred to as double jeopardy. Under our laws, a person cannot be tried for the same crime twice. So, if a person has been found innocent of a crime in a court of law, that person can never be tried for the same crime again.

When a disaster occurs as a result of natural causes unaided by any human action, it is called an act of God. No person can be held responsible for an act of God, and, therefore, no legal action can be taken for any loss from such an occurrence.

Jointly and severally refers to a situation where there is more than one party responsible for a liability, and they may all be sued together or they may be sued separately. If, for example, you and a friend rent an apartment together and the lease contains a jointly and severally clause, then either one of you may be held totally responsible for the full amount of the rent.

The proper performance of a legal act is feasance, but the performance of an illegal act or misconduct is called malfeasance. The statute of limitations is a law that requires an action to be started within a certain length of time after the alleged cause occurred. The <u>statute of frauds</u> is an act that requires that certain kinds of contracts must be in writing before an action based on the contracts can be instituted.

<u>Per se</u> is a Latin term meaning by itself or in itself. If a person is called by an assumed name, he or she is said to have an <u>alias</u>. A <u>minor</u> is one who is too young to be considered legally competent, but <u>sui juris</u> refers to one that is legally capable of managing his or her own actions.

TRANSCRIBING FROM DICTATION

Directions: This dictation emphasizes and reinforces the legal terms and definitions you have studied. Listen carefully to the pronunciation of each of the legal terms. Unless otherwise directed, use a 70-space line (typewriter) or 1-inch margins (computer) and double spacing. Correct all errors. Follow one of the procedures below.

Keyboarding Procedure
Using the cassette from Lesson 3, Part B, transcribe the dictation directly at your typewriter or computer.

Shorthand Procedure
Using the cassette from Lesson 3, Part B, take the dictation using your shorthand system and then transcribe from your shorthand notes on your typewriter or computer.

When you have finished transcribing Part B of the practice dictation, check your transcript with the printed copy. If you made any mistakes in the transcription, you should practice those words several times before going on to Lesson 4.

CHECKLIST
I have completed the following for Lesson 3:

	Part A, Date	Part B, Date	Submitted to Instructor Yes	No
Terminology and Definitions				
Self-Evaluation				
* Keying Legal Terms				
Words				
Sentences				
* Transcribing from Dictation				

When you have successfully completed all the exercises in this lesson and submitted to your instructor those requested, you are ready to proceed with Lesson 4.

* If you are using a shorthand system, submit to your instructor your shorthand notes along with your transcript.

Lesson 4

General Legal Terms

"Ignorance of the law is no excuse."
—Legal Maxim

This lesson continues the study of some of the general legal terms that are applicable to all areas of law. When you have completed these exercises, you will have a knowledge and an understanding of the most common general legal terminology. This information will give you a good background for studying the terms dealing with specific legal procedures and the various areas of law.

Part A TERMINOLOGY AND DEFINITIONS

Directions: Study the terms, pronunciations, and definitions until you are thoroughly familiar with them. In order to complete this lesson successfully, you must understand the meaning and usage of all the legal terms presented. If you are using shorthand, write your shorthand outline for each legal term in your shorthand notebook or on your shorthand machine.

Legal Term	Pronunciation	Definition
1. ancillary	′an-sə-ler-ē	A secondary proceeding that is based upon another proceeding. An example of an ancillary proceeding would be a situation where a person who dies owned property in a state other than the one where he or she lived. The will would be probated in the state in which that person had lived, and an ancillary proceeding would be filed in the other state in which property was owned.
2. cause of action	′kȯz əv ′ak-shən	The facts that are the basis for a lawsuit. This is a general term that varies from state to state and from one case to another.
3. interpolate	in-′tər-pə-lāt	To alter a document by adding an additional word or words.
4. ipso facto	′ip-sō ′fak-tō	Latin. By the fact itself.
5. sui generis	′sü-ī ′jen-ə-rəs	Latin. Of its own kind. Unique.
6. to wit	tü wit	Namely or scilicet. When used in legal documents, it is preceded by a general term and followed by a term that specifically identifies the general term (for example, assault with a deadly weapon, to wit: a gun).
7. scilicet	′si-lə-set	Latin. To wit. Namely. May be abbreviated as ss. or SS.
8. testimonium clause	tes-tə-′mō-nē-əm klȯz	A clause at the end of a document stating that the parties have signed under oath as to the document's contents. Usually begins with "In Witness Whereof" or "In Testimony Whereof" and includes the signatures of the parties. (See Figure 4-1, page 47.)

9. acknowledgment	ik-'näl-ij-mənt	A formal statement made before an authorized person, usually a notary public, whereby one states that the instrument was signed willfully and freely. (See Figure 4-2, page 47.)
10. notary public	'nōt-ə-rē 'pəb-lik	A public officer who is authorized to administer oaths and to certify that documents or instruments are genuine and that the documents were signed in the notary public's presence.
11. seal	sēl	A sign or an impression used to certify that a document or an instrument is genuine.
12. locus sigilli	'lō-kəs si-'jil-ī	Latin. The place of the seal. Abbreviation L.S. is often used.
13. legal back	'lē-gəl bak	A cover prepared for legal documents on which the endorsement is usually printed. It usually includes the names of the parties, the document title, the date executed, and the attorney's name or law firm that prepared it. (See Figure 4-3, page 48.)
14. endorsement	in-'dȯr-smənt	Information written on the back of a legal document. (See Figure 4-3, page 48.)

FIGURE 4-1   A Testimonium Clause

On this 16th day of _June_, A.D., 1997,
JAMES NELSON COLE, the above-named Testator, signed the foregoing
instrument in our presence and at the same time declared it to be
his Last Will and Testament, and we do now at his request and in
his presence and in the presence of each other, subscribe our names
as witnesses hereof.

Brenda S. Reynolds   residing at _411 Saunders Road_
BRENDA S. REYNOLDS   _Lansing_, Michigan

Scott W. Morrison   residing at _809 Vanderbilt Drive_
SCOTT W. MORRISON   _Okemos_, Michigan

Candace N. Ivy   residing at _8943 University Drive_
CANDACE N. IVY   _East Lansing_, Michigan

-Page Eight and Last-

FIGURE 4-2   An Acknowledgment

IN WITNESS WHEREOF, The said party of the first part
has hereunto set her hand the day and year first above written.

Andrea M. Sanson   **Seal**
ANDREA M. SANSON

STATE OF MICHIGAN)
) ss.
COUNTY OF INGHAM)

On _____ June 11 _____, 1997, before me, a Notary
Public, in and for said County, personally appeared ANDREA M.
SANSON to me known to be the same person described in and who
executed the within instrument, who acknowledged the same to be
her free act and deed.

Robert T. Gates   **Notary Public**
                Notary Public

Ingham County, Michigan,

My commission expires: _July 2_, 2001.

FIGURE 4-3   A Legal Back

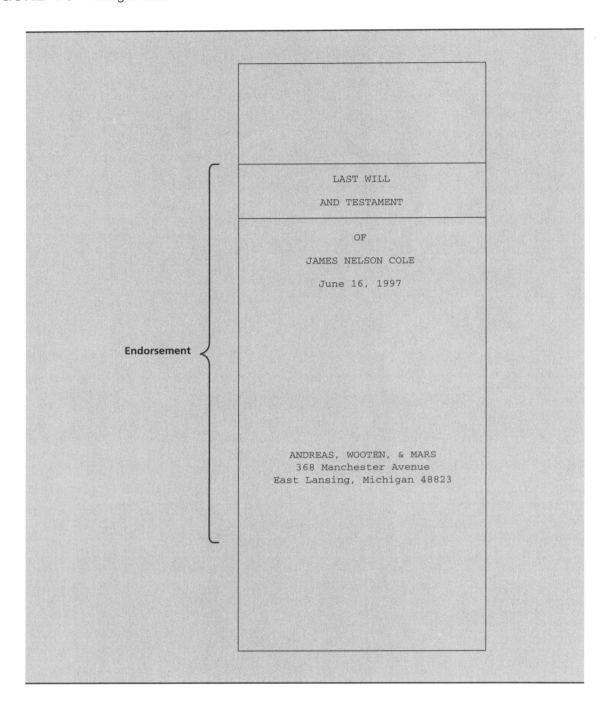

Self-Evaluation A   TERMINOLOGY AND DEFINITION RECALL

Directions: In the Answers column, write the legal term that is most representative of the corresponding statement. After you have completed this self-evaluation, check your answers with the key on page 494. If you have any incorrect answers, restudy the definitions for those terms before going on with this lesson. Then unless otherwise directed, submit this self-evaluation to your instructor.

Answers

1. A public officer who is authorized to administer oaths and to certify that documents or instruments are genuine is a/an _____.

   1. *notary public*

2. Information written on the back of a legal document is called a/an _____.

   2. *endorsement*

3. A Latin term meaning by the fact itself is _____.

   3. *ipso facto*

4. A formal statement made before an authorized person, usually a notary public, whereby one states that the instrument was signed willfully and freely, is referred to as a/an _____.

   4. *acknowledgment*

5. A clause at the end of a document stating that the parties have signed under oath as to the document's contents is a/an _____.

   5. *testimonium clause*

6. A sign or an impression used to certify that a document or an instrument is genuine is a/an _____.

   6. *seal*

7. A term meaning namely or scilicet, which when used in legal documents, is preceded by a general term and followed by a term that specifically identifies the general term, is _____.

   7. *to wit*

8. A Latin term for to wit is _____.

   8. *scilicet*

9. A Latin term meaning of its own kind or unique is _____.

   9. *sui generis*

10. The facts that are the basis for a lawsuit are referred to as the _____.

    10. *cause of action*

11. To alter a document by adding an additional word or words is to _____.

    11. *interpolate*

12. A secondary proceeding that is based upon another proceeding is a/an _____ proceeding.

    12. *ancillary*

13. The Latin term for the place of the seal is _____.

    13. *locus sigilli*

14. A cover prepared for legal documents on which the endorsement is printed is called a/an _____.

    14. *legal back*

KEYING LEGAL TERMS

Directions: Unless otherwise instructed, use a 70-space line (typewriter) or 1-inch margins (computer) and double spacing. Correct all errors. Follow one of the procedures below.

WORDS

Keyboarding Procedure
On your typewriter or computer, key the following words at least two times, concentrating on the correct spelling and pronunciation.

Shorthand Procedure
On your typewriter or computer, key the following words once, concentrating on the correct spelling and pronunciation. Then write the shorthand outline for each word in your shorthand notebook or on your shorthand machine. Transcribe from the shorthand outlines one time on your typewriter or computer.

ancillary	cause of action	interpolate
ipso facto	sui generis	to wit
scilicet	testimonium clause	acknowledgment
notary public	seal	locus sigilli
legal back	endorsement	

SENTENCES

Keyboarding Procedure
Key each of the following sentences one time on your typewriter or computer. Concentrate on the correct spelling and pronunciation of each underlined legal term.

Shorthand Procedure
Write the correct shorthand outlines for the following sentences in your shorthand notebook or on your shorthand machine. Transcribe from your shorthand outlines one time on your typewriter or computer.

These sentences will be used for practice dictation on the cassettes.

An ancillary proceeding is a secondary proceeding that is based upon another proceeding. For example, if you were living in the state of Kansas and owned property in the state of New Mexico, your will would be probated in Kansas, and an ancillary proceeding would be filed in New Mexico.

A cause of action refers to the facts that are the basis for a lawsuit. To interpolate is to alter a document by adding an additional word or words. Ipso facto is a Latin term meaning by the fact itself. The Latin term sui generis means of its own kind or unique. To wit and scilicet are synonymous terms. Scilicet is the Latin word for to wit. Scilicet and to wit mean that is to say or namely. When used in legal documents, they are preceded by a general term and followed by a term that specifically identifies the general term.

The testimonium clause is a clause at the end of a document stating that the parties have signed under oath as to the document's contents. An acknowledgment, made before an authorized person, usually states that the party willfully and freely signed the instrument.

Documents or instruments are certified as genuine by a notary public. A notary public may also administer oaths. The notary public seal is a sign or an impression used to certify that a document or an instrument is genuine. Locus sigilli is a Latin term meaning the place of the seal. The place where the seal is on a legal document is usually indicated by L.S., the abbreviation for locus sigilli.

A **legal back** is a cover prepared for a legal document that provides a place for the **endorsement**. An endorsement is information written on the back of a legal document. The endorsement on the back of a legal document usually includes the names of the parties, the title of the document, the date executed, and the attorney's name.

TRANSCRIBING FROM DICTATION

Directions: This dictation emphasizes and reinforces the legal terms and definitions you have studied. Listen carefully to the pronunciation of each of the legal terms. Unless otherwise directed, use a 70-space line (typewriter) or 1-inch margins (computer) and double spacing. Correct all errors. Follow one of the procedures below.

Keyboarding Procedure
Using the cassette from Lesson 4, Part A, transcribe the dictation directly at your typewriter or computer.

Shorthand Procedure
Using the cassette from Lesson 4, Part A, take the dictation using your shorthand system and then transcribe from your shorthand notes on your typewriter or computer.

When you have finished transcribing Part A of the practice dictation, check your transcript with the printed copy. If you made any mistakes in the transcription, you should practice those words several times before going on.

Part B TERMINOLOGY AND DEFINITIONS

Directions: Study the terms, pronunciations, and definitions until you are thoroughly familiar with them. In order to complete this lesson successfully, you must understand the meaning and usage of all the legal terms presented. If you are using shorthand, write your shorthand outline for each legal term in your shorthand notebook or on your shorthand machine.

Legal Term	Pronunciation	Definition
1. incriminate	in-'krim-ə-nāt	To accuse one of a crime. Also, to put oneself or another in danger of being charged with a crime.
2. quasi	'kwā-zī	Latin. Almost, but not actually, the same as. This term is usually used with another term (for example, quasi ex contractu, which means as if from a contract).
3. chose in action	'shōz in 'ak-shən	Personal property that one has a right to but is in the possession of another. Such property may be recovered through a lawsuit.
4. irrevocable	ir-'ev-ə-kə-bəl	Something that is final and cannot be undone or taken back.
5. recidivist	ri-'sid-ə-vəst	One who repeatedly commits criminal acts and cannot be reformed.
6. penal	'pēn-l	Having to do with punishment or a penalty.
7. ensue	in-'sü	To follow or to come after.
8. collusion	kə-'lü-zhən	When two or more persons secretly agree to participate in a fraudulent act.

9. fraud	frȯd	A misrepresentation of the facts done intentionally to deceive or mislead another. If you buy a ring that you are told is a diamond and it is really cut glass, the person who sold it to you is guilty of fraud.
10. duress	du̇-ʹres	The use of force to get someone to do something unwillingly. If you do something because another person threatens you, then you did the act under duress.
11. malice	ʹmal-əs	Purposely doing something that will harm another. An evil intent.
12. turpitude	ʹtər-pə-tüd	Something that is corrupt, shameful, wicked, or immoral.
13. mens rea	menz ʹrē-ə	Latin. A guilty mind or a criminal intent.

Self-Evaluation B   TERMINOLOGY AND DEFINITION RECALL

Directions: In the Answers column, write the letter from Column 1 that represents the word or phrase that best matches each item in Column 2. After you have completed this self-evaluation, check your answers with the key on page 494. If you have any incorrect answers, restudy the definitions for those terms before going on with this lesson. Then unless otherwise directed, submit this self-evaluation to your instructor.

Column 1	Column 2	Answers
a. chose in action	1. Intangible personal property that one has a right to but is in the possession of another and may be recovered through a lawsuit.	1. A
b. collusion		
c. duress	2. Intentionally deceiving or misleading another by misrepresenting the facts.	2. e
d. ensue	3. To accuse one of a crime or to put oneself or another in danger of being charged with a crime.	3. f
e. fraud		
f. incriminate	4. Purposely doing something that will harm another or an evil intent.	4. h
g. irrevocable	5. To follow or to come after.	5. D
h. malice	6. A Latin term meaning almost, but not actually, the same as.	6. L
i. malfeasance	7. A Latin term meaning a guilty mind or a criminal intent.	7. j
j. mens rea	8. The use of force or threats to get someone to do something against his or her will.	8. C
k. penal	9. Something that is corrupt, shameful, wicked, or immoral.	9. n
l. quasi	10. Two or more persons secretly agreeing to participate in a fraudulent act.	10. b
m. recidivist	11. A legal term that refers to punishment or a penalty.	11. k
n. turpitude	12. One who repeats criminal acts and cannot be reformed.	12. m
	13. Something that is final and cannot be undone or taken back.	13. g

KEYING LEGAL TERMS

Directions: Unless otherwise instructed, use a 70-space line (typewriter) or 1-inch margins (computer) and double spacing. Correct all errors. Follow one of the procedures below.

WORDS

Keyboarding Procedure
On your typewriter or computer, key the following words at least two times, concentrating on the correct spelling and pronunciation.

Shorthand Procedure
On your typewriter or computer, key the following words once, concentrating on the correct spelling and pronunciation. Then write the shorthand outline for each word in your shorthand notebook or on your shorthand machine. Transcribe from the shorthand outlines one time on your typewriter or computer.

incriminate	quasi	chose in action
irrevocable	recidivist	penal
ensue	collusion	fraud
duress	malice	turpitude
mens rea		

SENTENCES

Keyboarding Procedure
Key each of the following sentences one time on your typewriter or computer. Concentrate on the correct spelling and pronunciation of each underlined legal term.

Shorthand Procedure
Write the correct shorthand outlines for the following sentences in your shorthand notebook or on your shorthand machine. Transcribe from your shorthand outlines one time on your typewriter or computer.

These sentences will be used for practice dictation on the cassettes.

Incriminate is a term that means to accuse one of a crime or to put oneself or another in danger of being charged with a crime. One cannot be forced to testify in a case to anything that a person feels might incriminate himself or herself in a crime. Quasi is used to indicate that something is almost, but not actually, the same as. A quasi-legal matter would refer to one that is almost, but not entirely, a legal matter.

A chose in action is a right to personal property that is in the possession of another. A chose in action may be recovered through a lawsuit. If an act or deed is final and cannot be undone or changed, it is said to be irrevocable.

A recidivist, one who repeats criminal acts and cannot be reformed, would probably spend many years in a penal institution. Penal refers to something having to do with punishment or a penalty. To ensue is a term meaning to follow or to come after.

Collusion, fraud, duress, malice, turpitude, and mens rea are all terms that refer to some kind of illegal act. If you make an agreement with another person to defraud someone of their rights or to obtain an object forbidden by law, it is collusion. If a person intentionally lies for the purpose of deceiving or misleading another, that person is guilty of fraud. Therefore, if only one person is involved in committing the illegal act, it is fraud. If two or more persons are involved, it is collusion. Duress is the use of force to get someone to do something unwillingly. Duress, fraud, and collusion all involve malice and mens rea because the intent is evil and wrongful. Turpitude also applies to something that is corrupt, shameful, wicked, or immoral.

TRANSCRIBING FROM DICTATION

Directions: This dictation emphasizes and reinforces the legal terms and definitions you have studied. Listen carefully to the pronunciation of each of the legal terms. Unless otherwise directed, use a 70-space line (typewriter) or 1-inch margins (computer) and double spacing. Correct all errors. Follow one of the procedures below.

Keyboarding Procedure
Using the cassette from Lesson 4, Part B, transcribe the dictation directly at your typewriter or computer.

Shorthand Procedure
Using the cassette from Lesson 4, Part B, take the dictation using your shorthand system and then transcribe from your shorthand notes on your typewriter or computer.

When you have finished transcribing Part B of the practice dictation, check your transcript with the printed copy. If you made any mistakes in the transcription, you should practice those words several times before going on to Evaluation 2.

CHECKLIST
I have completed the following for Lesson 4:

	Part A, Date	Part B, Date	Submitted to Instructor Yes	No
Terminology and Definitions				
Self-Evaluation				
* Keying Legal Terms				
Words				
Sentences				
* Transcribing from Dictation				

When you have successfully completed all the exercises in this lesson and submitted to your instructor those requested, you are ready to proceed with Evaluation 2.

* If you are using a shorthand system, submit to your instructor your shorthand notes along with your transcript.

Evaluation No. 2   SECTION A

Directions: This dictation/transcription evaluation will test your spelling and transcription abilities on the legal terms that you studied in the two preceding lessons. Use a 5-space paragraph indention, a 70-space line (typewriter) or 1-inch margins (computer), and double spacing unless otherwise instructed. Correct all errors. Follow one of the procedures below.

Keyboarding Procedure

Using the cassette from Evaluation 2, transcribe the dictation directly at your typewriter or computer.

Shorthand Procedure

Using the cassette from Evaluation 2, take the dictation using your shorthand system and then transcribe from your shorthand notes on your typewriter or computer.

Sections B and C are available from your instructor.

Lesson 5

Litigation—Pretrial

"No one is responsible
for that which no one
can control."

—Legal Maxim

Before a case goes to trial, many pretrial activities must take place. Many of these activities involve nonlawyer personnel; therefore, you should have knowledge and a good understanding of these terms. The terms to be studied in the following exercises will acquaint you with the terminology involved with several of the pretrial activities. To complete this lesson successfully, you should be able to spell, define, pronounce, and transcribe correctly from dictation each of the terms presented.

Part A   TERMINOLOGY AND DEFINITIONS

Directions: Study the terms, pronunciations, and definitions until you are thoroughly familiar with them. In order to complete this lesson successfully, you must understand the meaning and usage of all the legal terms presented. If you are using shorthand, write your shorthand outline for each legal term in your shorthand notebook or on your shorthand machine.

Legal Term	*Pronunciation*	*Definition*
1. caption	′kap-shən	The title page of a court document, which includes the case title, the jurisdiction, the venue, the court or docket number, and the document title. Also called style of case. (See Figure 5-1, page 63.)
2. venue	′ven-yü	The geographical location where a case is tried. A change of venue for a case means that the case is tried at a location different from where the case originated. (See Figure 5-1, page 63.)
3. jurisdiction	jür-əs-′dik-shən	The right or authority of a court to hear and adjudge cases. (See Figure 5-1, page 63.)
4. case title	kās ′tīt-l	The part of a legal document that contains the names of the parties to the suit. (See Figure 5-1, page 63.)
5. Doe clause	dō klōz	Fictitious names in a case title. When the name or names of all defendants involved are not known, the unknown defendants are usually referred to as John and Mary Doe. (See Figure 5-1, page 63.)
6. ad damnum clause	ad ′dam-nəm klòz	Latin. A clause in a complaint that states the plaintiff's damage. (See Figure 5-2, page 63.)
7. prayer for relief	prar fər ri-′lēf	The summary at the end of a complaint that requests the court to grant the plaintiff's demands. (See Figure 5-2, page 63.)

8. filed	fīld	When papers are placed with the clerk of a court, the papers have been filed.
9. summons	'səm-ənz	A writ that notifies a defendant that a lawsuit has been filed and an appearance must be made before the court at a specified time to answer the charges. (See Figure 5-3, page 64.)
10. service	'sər-vəs	The delivery of a summons to the person named therein. When a person receives a summons, that person has been served. Depending on the state and the type of case, service may be made by a process server (in person or by attachment—posting on the door of the address listed in the summons), by mail, or by publication.
11. appearance	ə-'pir-əns	To be present in court as a party to a lawsuit.
12. answer	'an-sər	A pleading that states the defendant's defense against the plaintiff's claims. Also referred to as a response and is sometimes called a responsive pleading.
13. demurrer to complaint	di-'mər-ər tü kəm-'plānt	Disputes the sufficiency in law of the pleading of the other side. The defendant states in a demurrer to complaint that even if the facts in the case are true, there is no legal basis for the complaint; therefore, the defendant should not have to answer the charges.
14. bill of particulars	bil əv pə-'tik-ə-lərs	The detailed facts upon which a complaint is based. Usually supplied by the plaintiff upon the request of the defendant.

FIGURE 5-1 A Caption

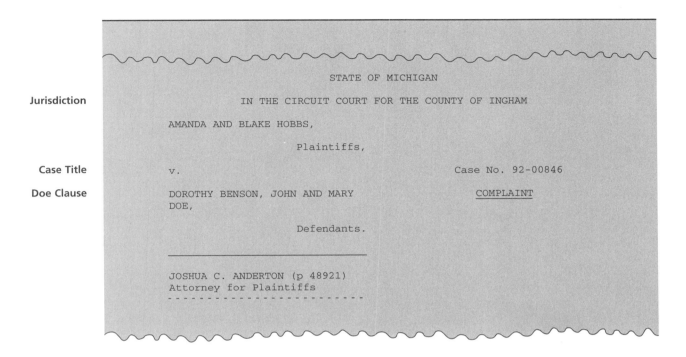

Jurisdiction

Case Title

Doe Clause

FIGURE 5-2 An Ad Damnum Clause and A Prayer for Relief

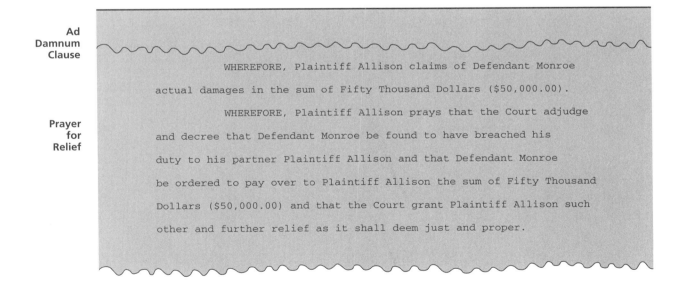

Ad Damnum Clause

Prayer for Relief

FIGURE 5-3 A Summons

Approved, SCAO

ORIGINAL - Court   2nd copy - Plaintiff
1st copy - Defendant   3rd copy - Return

STATE OF MICHIGAN XXXXXXXXXXXX 30th **JUDICIAL CIRCUIT**	**SUMMONS AND COMPLAINT**	**CASE NO.** 92-00846

Court address
2nd Floor, City Hall, Lansing, Michigan 48933

Court telephone no.
(517) 555-0650

Plaintiff name(s) and address(es) and telephone no(s).
Amanda and Blake Hobbs
2421 Seaview River Road
Lansing, Michigan 48906
(517) 555-9788

Plaintiff attorney, bar no., address and telephone no.
Joshua C. Anderton (P 48921)
688 S. Capitol Avenue, Suite 11
Lansing, Michigan 48933
(517) 555-1664

V.

Defendant name(s), address(es) and telephone no(s).
Dorothy Benson, John and Mary Doe
55 Sandalwood Avenue
Okemos, Michigan 48864

NOTICE TO THE DEFENDANT: In the name of the people of the State of Michigan you are notified:

1. You are being sued.

2. YOU HAVE 21 DAYS after receiving this summons to file an answer or to take other lawful action (28 days if you were served by mail or you were served outside this state).

3. If you do not answer or take other action within the time allowed, judgment may be entered against you for the relief demanded in the complaint.

Issued 6/11/97	This summons expires 12/10/97	Court clerk *Lois McMahon*

*This summons is invalid unless served on or before its expiration date.

☒ There is no other civil action between these parties arising out of the same transaction or occurrence as alleged in this complaint pending in this court, nor has any such action been previously filed and dismissed or transferred after having been assigned to a judge.

☐ There is now on file in this court a civil action between these parties arising out of the same transaction or occurrence as alleged in the complaint. The action ☐ is pending ☐ was dismissed ☐ was transferred. The case number and assigned judge are:

Case no.	Judge	Bar no.

VENUE		
Plaintiff(s) residence Lansing, Ingham Co., Michigan	**Defendant(s) residence** Okemos, Ingham Co., Michigan	
Place where action arose or business conducted Lansing, Ingham Co., Michigan		

I declare that the complaint information above and attached is true to the best of my information, knowledge, and belief.

June 11, 1997
Date

Joshua C. Anderton
Signature of attorney XXXX

COMPLAINT IS STATED ON ATTACHED PAGES. EXHIBITS ARE ATTACHED IF REQUIRED BY COURT RULE.

MC 01 (10/85) **SUMMONS AND COMPLAINT**   MCR 2.102(B)(11), MCR 2.104, MCR 2.107, MCR 2.113(C)(2)(a) and (b)

COURT

Self-Evaluation A   TERMINOLOGY AND DEFINITION RECALL

Directions: In the Answers column at the right of each statement, write the letter that represents the word or group of words that correctly completes the statement. After you have completed this self-evaluation, check your answers with the key on page 494, 495. If you have any incorrect answers, restudy the definitions for those terms before going on with this lesson. Then unless otherwise directed, submit this self-evaluation to your instructor.

Answers

1. A writ notifying a defendant that a lawsuit has been filed and an appearance must be made before the court at a specified time to answer the charges is a/an (a) demurrer to complaint, (b) summons, (c) appearance.   **1.** _B_

2. If a defendant answers the claims of the plaintiff by stating that even if the facts as presented are true, the claims are not sufficient for a legal action, the answer is called a/an (a) ad damnum clause, (b) Doe clause, (c) demurrer to complaint.   **2.** _C_

3. A clause in a complaint that states the plaintiff's damages is the (a) Doe clause, (b) prayer for relief, (c) ad damnum clause.   **3.** _C_

4. When the names of one or more defendants in a suit are not known, they are identified in the case title by a (a) Doe clause, (b) venue, (c) service.   **4.** _A_

5. The title page of a court document is the (a) caption, (b) bill of particulars, (c) case title.   **5.** _A_

6. The detailed facts upon which a complaint is based that are usually supplied by the plaintiff upon request of the defendant are contained in a document called a/an (a) summons, (b) answer, (c) bill of particulars.   **6.** _C_

7. Papers that are placed with the clerk of a court are said to be (a) served, (b) filed, (c) answered.   **7.** _B_

8. To be present in a court as a party to a lawsuit is to make a/an (a) caption, (b) service, (c) appearance.   **8.** _C_

9. The summary at the end of a complaint that requests the court to grant the plaintiff's demands is the (a) prayer for relief, (b) demurrer to complaint, (c) ad damnum clause.   **9.** _A_

10. The right or authority of a court to hear and adjudge cases is referred to as (a) service, (b) venue, (c) jurisdiction.   **10.** _C_

11. The pleading that states the defendant's defense against the plaintiff's claims is the (a) prayer for relief, (b) answer, (c) bill of particulars.   **11.** _B_

12. The part of a legal document that contains the names of the parties to the suit is called the (a) case title, (b) caption, (c) jurisdiction.   **12.** _A_

13. The delivery of a summons to the person named therein is called (a) service, (b) filed, (c) venue.   **13.** _A_

14. The geographical location where a case is tried is the (a) jurisdiction, (b) appearance, (c) venue.   **14.** _C_

KEYING LEGAL TERMS

Directions: Unless otherwise instructed, use a 70-space line (typewriter) or 1-inch margins (computer) and double spacing. Correct all errors. Follow one of the procedures below.

WORDS

Keyboarding Procedure
On your typewriter or computer, key the following words at least two times, concentrating on the correct spelling and pronunciation.

Shorthand Procedure
On your typewriter or computer, key the following words once, concentrating on the correct spelling and pronunciation. Then write the shorthand outline for each word in your shorthand notebook or on your shorthand machine. Transcribe from the shorthand outlines one time on your typewriter or computer.

caption	venue	jurisdiction
case title	Doe clause	ad damnum clause
prayer for relief	filed	summons
appearance	service	answer
demurrer to complaint	bill of particulars	

SENTENCES

Keyboarding Procedure
Key each of the following sentences one time on your typewriter or computer. Concentrate on the correct spelling and pronunciation of each underlined legal term.

Shorthand Procedure
Write the correct shorthand outlines for the following sentences in your shorthand notebook or on your shorthand machine. Transcribe from your shorthand outlines one time on your typewriter or computer.

These sentences will be used for practice dictation on the cassettes.

The caption is the title page of a court document and includes the venue, the jurisdiction, the case title, the court case number, and the document title. The venue is the geographical location where a case is tried. A request for change of venue would be a request to have the case tried in another court in a different geographical area. This might occur when the court feels that a defendant could not get a fair trial in the area where the case originated because of too much publicity before the trial. The jurisdiction is the right or authority of a court to hear and adjudge cases. Courts can only hear and decide cases that fall within their jurisdiction. The case title, which is also located in the caption, names the parties to the lawsuit. If the names of one or more of the defendants to a suit are not known, a Doe clause is used in the case title. The unknown defendants are then referred to as John and Mary Doe.

The statement of the plaintiff's damages in the complaint is called the ad damnum clause. The summary at the end of a complaint that requests the court to grant the plaintiff's demands is the prayer for relief. Court documents are filed with the clerk of a court. All documents involving a court must be filed with the clerk.

If a person is served with a summons, that person is a defendant in a lawsuit and must make an appearance before the court at a specified time to answer the charges. The delivery of a summons to the person named therein is known as the service. When the defendant has received the summons, the defendant is said to have been served.

An appearance is to be present in court as a party to a lawsuit. If one makes an appearance, the person comes into court as a party to a suit. The pleading by which the defendant states the defense against the plaintiff's claims is an answer. A demurrer to complaint is a formal method of saying that the claims of the other side are not sufficient in law for a legal action. In a demurrer to complaint, the defendant states that even though the facts in the plaintiff's charges may be true, there is no legal basis for the suit. Therefore the defendant should not have to answer the charges. The bill of particulars supplies the defendant with the detailed facts upon which a complaint is based.

TRANSCRIBING FROM DICTATION

Directions: This dictation emphasizes and reinforces the legal terms and definitions you have studied. Listen carefully to the pronunciation of each of the legal terms. Unless otherwise directed, use a 70-space line (typewriter) or 1-inch margins (computer) and double spacing. Correct all errors. Follow one of the procedures below.

Keyboarding Procedure
Using the cassette from Lesson 5, Part A, transcribe the dictation directly at your typewriter or computer.

Shorthand Procedure
Using the cassette from Lesson 5, Part A, take the dictation using your shorthand system and then transcribe from your shorthand notes on your typewriter or computer.

When you have finished transcribing Part A of the practice dictation, check your transcript with the printed copy. If you made any mistakes in the transcription, you should practice those words several times before going on.

Part B TERMINOLOGY AND DEFINITIONS

Directions: Study the terms, pronunciations, and definitions until you are thoroughly familiar with them. In order to complete this lesson successfully, you must understand the meaning and usage of all the legal terms presented. If you are using shorthand, write your shorthand outline for each legal term in your shorthand notebook or on your shorthand machine.

Legal Term	Pronunciation	Definition
1. omnibus clause	′äm-ni-bəs klȯz	A clause at the end of the prayer for relief in a complaint that makes it possible for the court to award relief other than that specifically requested by the plaintiff. (See Figure 5-4, page 70.)
2. motion	′mō-shən	A written or an oral application made to a court or judge for a rule or an order. (See Figure 5-5, page 71.)
3. court docket	kōrt ′däk-ət	A record of the dates and times that cases are to be tried in court.

4. counterclaim	'kaủnt-ər-klām	A claim made by the defendant as a result of the plaintiff's charges in the lawsuit.
5. cross plaintiff	krȯs 'plānt-əf	A defendant who brings a crossclaim against a plaintiff in the same action. Also referred to as cross complainant.
6. cross defendant	'krȯs di-'fen-dənt	The plaintiff who is named as defendant in a crossclaim.
7. crossclaim	'krȯs-klām	A claim brought by a defendant against a plaintiff and/or a codefendant to seek relief against either in the event that there is recovery.
8. reply	ri-'plī	The plaintiff's answer to the defendant's answer or counterclaim.
9. recrimination	ri-krim-ə-'nā-shən	A countercharge or a counterclaim.
10. intervenor	int-ər-'vē-nər	A person not originally a party to a suit who voluntarily enters into the action to protect some interest that he or she claims to have in the case.
11. affidavit	af-ə-'dā-vət	A voluntary written statement made under oath before a notary public or other qualified official. (See Figure 5-6, page 72.)
12. affiant	ə-'fī-ənt	A person who makes an affidavit. (See Figure 5-6, page 72.)
13. jurat	'jủr-at	A clause at the end of an affidavit that verifies the time, place, and person before whom the affidavit was made. A jurat begins with the words "SWORN TO AND SUBSCRIBED." (See Figure 5-6, page 72.)
14. verification	ver-ə-fə-'kā-shən	Confirmation of the truth of a document made under oath before a notary public.

FIGURE 5-4 An Omnibus Clause

Omnibus Clause

> WHEREFORE, Plaintiff Allison prays that the Court adjudge and decree that Defendant Monroe be found to have breached his duty to his partner Plaintiff Allison and that Defendant Monroe be ordered to pay over to Plaintiff Allison a sum in excess of Ten Thousand Dollars ($10,000.00) and that the Court grant Plaintiff Allison such other and further relief as it shall deem just and proper.

FIGURE 5-5 A Motion

STATE OF MICHIGAN

IN THE CIRCUIT COURT FOR THE COUNTY OF INGHAM

AMANDA AND BLAKE HOBBS,

                Plaintiffs,   Case No. 92-00846

v.   MOTION TO QUASH

DOROTHY BENSON, JOHN AND MARY   SUBPOENA DUCES TECUM
DOE,

                Defendants.

JOSHUA C. ANDERTON (P 48921)
Attorney for Plaintiffs
688 S. Capitol Avenue, Suite 11
Lansing, MI 48933
(517) 555-1664

MARIE S. STANLEY (P 55901)
Attorney for Defendants
- -

        NOW COMES Plaintiffs Amanda and Blake Hobbs, by and through their attorney, Joshua C. Anderton, and moves this Court under MCR 2.302(c) for an order to quash the subpoena served upon plaintiffs, and in support thereof states as follows:

        1. The attached subpoena (Exhibit A) was served upon Plaintiffs Amanda and Blake Hobbs, seeking production of plaintiffs' income tax returns for the years 1994 through 1995.

        2. The subpoena requests documentation which is totally irrelevant to the instant case in which plaintiffs seek recovery under a contract between the parties. MCR 2.302(B)(1) limits discovery of nonprivileged materials to those which are relevant.

        3. The subpoena served upon plaintiffs is incapable of being complied with without undue burden, annoyance, embarrassment, expense, and oppression.

        4. The time in the subpoena in which plaintiff is given to produce the required documents is unreasonably short.

        WHEREFORE, plaintiffs respectfully request this Court to quash the subpoena. Further, plaintiffs respectfully request this Court to award them their attorney fees and costs necessitated and incurred in obtaining this order.

                      Respectfully submitted,

Dated: *July 28, 1997*   *Joshua C. Anderton*
                         Joshua C. Anderton (P.48921)
                         Attorney for Plaintiffs

FIGURE 5-6 An Affidavit

AFFIDAVIT

STATE OF MICHIGAN)
) ss.
COUNTY OF INGHAM)

Affiant

       DARREL L. KELLY being first duly sworn, says and deposes as follows:

       1. That he resides at 4330 Spartan Boulevard, Mason, Michigan 48854.

       2. On or about January 17, 1997, he was the purchaser in the closing of a transaction for real property commonly known as 516 Linden Street, East Lansing, Michigan, legally described as Lots 20 and 21, Assessor's Plat of Lot 51, of Angell's Subdivision, being Lot 80 and parts of Lots 78 and 79 of College Grove, City of East Lansing, Ingham County, Michigan.

       3. The Warranty Deed delivered at said closing inadvertently listed Daryl L. Kelly as the purchaser.

       4. The undersigned is one and the same as Daryl L. Kelly. Further, Deponent saith not.

Darrel C. Kelly
DARREL L. KELLY

Jurat

SWORN TO AND SUBSCRIBED before me this _23rd_ day of _October_ 1997, by DARREL L. KELLY.

Robert T. Gates
Notary Public,
Ingham County, Michigan

My commission expires: *July 2, 2001*

Self-Evaluation B   TERMINOLOGY AND DEFINITION RECALL

Directions: In the Answers column, write the letter from Column 1 that represents the word or phrase that best matches each item in Column 2. After you have completed this self-evaluation, check your answers with the key on page 495. If you have any incorrect answers, restudy the definitions for those terms before going on with this lesson. Then unless otherwise directed, submit this self-evaluation to your instructor.

Column 1

a. affiant
b. affidavit
c. counterclaim
d. court calendar
e. court docket
f. cross defendant
g. cross plaintiff
h. crossclaim
i. intervenor
j. jurat
k. motion
l. omnibus clause
m. recrimination
n. reply
o. verification

Column 2

1. A person not originally a party to a suit who voluntarily enters into the action to protect some interest that he or she claims to have in the case.

2. A written or an oral application made to a court or judge for a rule or an order.

3. A claim brought by a defendant against a plaintiff and/or a codefendant to seek relief against either in the event there is recovery in the suit.

4. An attachment to a document that confirms the truthfulness of the contents of the document.

5. A clause at the end of the prayer for relief in a complaint that makes it possible for the court to award relief other than that specifically requested by the plaintiff.

6. A clause at the end of an affidavit that verifies the time, place, and person before whom the affidavit was made.

7. The person who makes an affidavit.

8. A claim made by the defendant as a result of the plaintiff's charges in a lawsuit.

9. A countercharge or a counterclaim.

10. The defendant's title when the defendant brings a crossclaim against the plaintiff in the same proceeding.

11. A voluntary written statement made under oath before a notary public.

12. A record of the dates and times that cases are to be tried in court.

13. The plaintiff's title when the plaintiff is named as defendant in a crossclaim.

14. The plaintiff's response to the defendant's answer or counterclaim.

Answers

1. B
2. K
3. g
4. _____
5. _____
6. _____
7. _____
8. _____
9. _____
10. _____
11. _____
12. _____
13. _____
14. _____

KEYING LEGAL TERMS

Directions: Unless otherwise instructed, use a 70-space line (typewriter) or 1-inch margins (computer) and double spacing. Correct all errors. Follow one of the procedures below.

WORDS

Keyboarding Procedure
On your typewriter or computer, key the following words at least two times, concentrating on the correct spelling and pronunciation.

Shorthand Procedure
On your typewriter or computer, key the following words once, concentrating on the correct spelling and pronunciation. Then write the shorthand outline for each word in your shorthand notebook or on your shorthand machine. Transcribe from the shorthand outlines one time on your typewriter or computer.

omnibus clause	motion	court docket
counterclaim	cross plaintiff	cross defendant
crossclaim	reply	recrimination
intervenor	affidavit	jurat
affiant	verification	

SENTENCES

Keyboarding Procedure
Key each of the following sentences one time on your typewriter or computer. Concentrate on the correct spelling and pronunciation of each underlined legal term.

Shorthand Procedure
Write the correct shorthand outlines for the following sentences in your shorthand notebook or on your shorthand machine. Transcribe from your shorthand outlines one time on your typewriter or computer.

These sentences will be used for practice dictation on the cassettes.

An omnibus clause makes it possible for the court to award relief other than that specifically requested by the plaintiff. For example, a plaintiff may request damages in excess of $10,000, whereby the court can then award more than $10,000 if the court so decides.

A written or an oral motion may be made to the court to have the trial date set. If the motion is honored, the trial date will be set and will be entered on the court docket. The defendant may file a counterclaim against the plaintiff in the same proceeding, the defendant becomes the cross plaintiff, or cross complainant, and the plaintiff then becomes the cross defendant. A defendant may bring a crossclaim against a codefendant or the plaintiff or both seeking relief from either in the event there is a recovery in the suit. The plaintiff files a reply, which is to answer to the defendant's counterclaim. A countercharge, or a counterclaim, is also called recrimination. Recrimination would be a countercharge against the person who made the original charge.

An intervenor is a person not originally a party to a suit who voluntarily enters into the action to protect some interest that he or she claims to have in the case.

An affidavit, which is a voluntary written statement made under oath before a notary public or other qualified official, has a jurat clause at the end that verifies the time, place and person before whom the affidavit was made. The person who makes an affidavit is an affiant. A verification may be attached to a document to confirm the truthfulness of the contents of the document.

TRANSCRIBING FROM DICTATION

Directions: This dictation emphasizes and reinforces the legal terms and definitions you have studied. Listen carefully to the pronunciation of each of the legal terms. Unless otherwise directed, use a 70-space line (typewriter) or 1-inch margins (computer) and double spacing. Correct all errors. Follow one of the procedures below.

Keyboarding Procedure
Using the cassette from Lesson 5, Part B, transcribe the dictation directly at your typewriter or computer.

Shorthand Procedure
Using the cassette from Lesson 5, Part B, take the dictation using your shorthand system and then transcribe from your shorthand notes on your typewriter or computer.

When you have finished transcribing Part B of the practice dictation, check your transcript with the printed copy. If you made any mistakes in the transcription, you should practice those words several times before going on to Lesson 6.

CHECKLIST
I have completed the following for Lesson 5:

	Part A, Date	Part B, Date	Submitted to Instructor Yes	No
Terminology and Definitions	_____	_____	_____	_____
Self-Evaluation	_____	_____	_____	_____
* Keying Legal Terms	_____	_____	_____	_____
Words	_____	_____	_____	_____
Sentences	_____	_____	_____	_____
* Transcribing from Dictation	_____	_____	_____	_____

When you have successfully completed all the exercises in this lesson and submitted to your instructor those requested, you are ready to proceed with Lesson 6.

* If you are using a shorthand system, submit to your instructor your shorthand notes along with your transcript.

Lesson 6

Litigation—Pretrial

"The law helps the vigilant, before those who sleep on their rights."

—Legal Maxim

This lesson continues the study of the terminology involved in pretrial litigation activities. Several of the terms in this lesson deal with the discovery process; i.e., before a case goes to trial, all parties have an opportunity to learn what evidence and facts anyone connected with the case might have. Upon successful completion of these exercises, you should be able to spell, define, pronounce, and transcribe correctly from dictation each of the terms presented.

Part A TERMINOLOGY AND DEFINITIONS

Directions: Study the terms, pronunciations, and definitions until you are thoroughly familiar with them. In order to complete this lesson successfully, you must understand the meaning and usage of all the legal terms presented. If you are using shorthand, write your shorthand outline for each legal term in your shorthand notebook or on your shorthand machine.

Legal Term	Pronunciation	Definition
1. contempt of court	kən-'temt əv kōrt	Intentionally doing something that is against the court rules or that interferes with the administration of justice.
2. bench warrant	bench 'wȯr-ənt	A warrant issued by a judge or the court for the arrest of a person charged with contempt of court or of a person who has been indicted for a crime. (See Figure 6-1, page 79.)
3. subpoena	sə-'pē-nə	A document compelling a witness to appear in court and give testimony at a specified time for the party named therein. A bench warrant may be issued for the arrest of a person who does not obey a subpoena. (See Figure 6-2, page 80.)
4. subpoena duces tecum	sə-'pē-nə 'dü-səs 'tē-kəm	Latin. A writ commanding the person named to produce in court certain designated documents relating to the case.
5. interrogatories	int-ə-'räg-ə-tōr-ēs	Written questions that a witness or a party to the action must answer under oath as a part of the discovery process.
6. disclosure	dis-'klō-zhər	Making known all the facts that one has about a case.
7. concealment	kən-'sēl-mənt	Failure to disclose or reveal the facts a person has about a case that the law requires him or her to make known.
8. court reporter	kort ri-'port-ər	One who records verbatim the deposition of a witness or the proceedings in court and produces a written transcript thereof.

9. verbatim	vər-'bāt-əm	Something that is stated in exactly the same words. Word for word.
10. deposition	dep-ə-'zish-ən	Part of the discovery process whereby the witness answers questions under oath outside of court, and a verbatim transcript is prepared of the questions asked and the answers given. The witness testifying in a deposition is called a deponent.
11. transcript	'trans-kript	A printed verbatim copy of a deposition or a court proceeding usually prepared by a court reporter.
12. pretrial stipulations	prē-'trīl stip-yə-'lā-shəns	Agreements made between the attorneys as to the conditions or procedures that will be followed in the taking of a deposition.
13. fishing expedition	'fish-iŋ ek-spə-'dish-ən	A tactic used by some attorneys in the discovery process to try to obtain information from a witness that is not based upon or supported by the allegations.

FIGURE 6-1 A Bench Warrant

Approved, SCAO

Original - Police
Copy - Court

STATE OF MICHIGAN XXXXXXXXXXXX 30th JUDICIAL CIRCUIT	PETITION AND BENCH WARRANT	CASE NO. 83-52179

ORI MI-	Court address 2nd Floor, City Hall, Lansing, Michigan 48933	Court telephone no. (517) 555-0650

THE PEOPLE OF	☒ The State of Michigan ☐ _____	V.	Defendant name, address, and telephone no. Allen J. Polasek 7850 South Washington Avenue Lansing, Michigan 48933

CTN	SID	DOB

PETITION

A petition is not required if the bench warrant
is issued on the court's own motion.

BENCH WARRANT

Respondent failed to comply with an order of this court.

IN THE NAME OF THE PEOPLE OF THE STATE OF MICHIGAN:

TO ANY PEACE OFFICER OR COURT OFFICER AUTHORIZED TO MAKE ARREST:

I order you to arrest:

Name and address of respondent Allen J. Polasek 7850 South Washington Avenue Lansing, Michigan 48933	Race Caucasian	Sex M
	DLN M-563-788-955	

Bring the respondent before the court immediately, or respondent may be released when a cash or surety bond in the

amount of $5,000.00 is posted for personal appearance before the court at its next session.

October 23, 1997   (SEAL)   *Tomas Rodriguez* (P 33991)
Date   Judge   Bar no.

RETURN

I have, on October 24, 1997 , taken respondent into custody as ordered by this warrant.
          Date
October 24, 1997   *Carol M. Rossi*
Date   Peace Officer

MC 229 (3/87) **PETITION AND BENCH WARRANT**   MCR 3 606

FIGURE 6-2 A Subpoena

Approved, SCAO			Original - Return 1st copy - Witness 2nd copy - File

STATE OF MICHIGAN XXXXXXXXXX 30th JUDICIAL CIRCUIT XXXXXXXXXXXXXXX	SUBPOENA ORDER TO APPEAR	CASE NO. 92-00846

Court address   2nd Floor, City Hall, Lansing, Michigan 48933   **Court telephone no.**   (517) 555-0650

Plaintiff(s) ☐ People of the State of Michigan ☒ Amanda and Blake Hobbs	V.	**Defendant(s)** Dorothy Benson, John and Mary Doe
☒ CIVIL ☐ CRIMINAL		**Charge**
☐ PROBATE In the matter of		

In the Name of the People of the State of Michigan. TO: Dorothy Benson
55 Sandalwood Avenue
Okemos, Michigan 48864

YOU ARE ORDERED to appear personally at the time and place stated: You may be required to appear from time to time and day to day until you are excused.

Appear at:
1. ☒ The court address above   ☐ Other:

Day 2. Friday	**Date** August 15, 1997	**Time** 9:30 a.m.

YOU ARE ALSO ORDERED to:

3. ☒ Testify at trial/examination/hearing.

4. ☐ Produce the following items: _____

_____

_____ ☐ Injunction attached

5. ☐ *Testify as to your assets, and bring with you the items listed in line 4 above.
    *Affidavit on reverse side must be completed for judgment debtor examination.

6. ☐ Testify at deposition.

7. ☐ Other: _____

Person requesting subpoena 8. Joshua C. Anderton (P 48921)	**Telephone** (517) 555-1664
Address **City** **State** 688 S. Capitol Avenue, Suite 11, Lansing, Michigan	**Zip** 48933

FAILURE TO APPEAR AT STATED TIME AND PLACE MAY SUBJECT YOU TO PENALTY FOR CONTEMPT OF COURT.

July 25, 1997
Date

X _Joshua C. Anderton_ (P 48921)
XXXXXXXXXX/Attorney   Bar no.

JUDGMENT DEBTOR JUDICIAL ENDORSEMENT	Court use only
_____ _____ Date Judge	☐ Served ☐ Not served

MC 11 (10/85) **SUBPOENA, Order To Appear** MCLA 600.1455, 600.1701, 600.6110; MSA 27A.1455, 27A.1701, 27A .6110, MCR 2.506

RETURN

Self-Evaluation A   TERMINOLOGY AND DEFINITION RECALL

Directions: In the Answers column, write the legal term that is most representative of the corresponding statement. After you have completed this self-evaluation, check your answers with the key on page 495. If you have any incorrect answers, restudy the definitions for those terms before going on with this lesson. Then unless otherwise directed, submit this self-evaluation to your instructor.

Answers

1. Agreements made between the attorneys as to the conditions or procedures that will be followed in the taking of a deposition are _____.

   1. _____

2. Intentionally doing something that is against the court rules or that interferes with the administration of justice is _____.

   2. _____

3. A tactic used by some attorneys in the discovery process to try to obtain information from a witness that is not based upon or supported by the allegations is called a/an _____.

   3. _____

4. A warrant issued by a judge or the court for the arrest of a person charged with contempt of court or of a person who has been indicted for a crime is a/an _____.

   4. _____

5. The part of the discovery process whereby the witness answers questions under oath outside of court and a verbatim transcript is prepared of the questions asked and the answers given is a/an _____.

   5. _____

6. Written questions that a witness must answer under oath as a part of the discovery process are _____.

   6. _____

7. The making known of all the facts that one has about a case is _____.

   7. _____

8. A document compelling a witness to appear in court and give testimony at a specified time for the party named therein is a/an _____.

   8. _____

9. A printed verbatim copy of a deposition or a court proceeding usually prepared by a court reporter is a/an _____.

   9. _____

10. A writ commanding the person named therein to produce in court certain designated documents is a/an _____.

    10. _____

11. Failure to disclose or reveal the facts a person has about a case that the law requires him or her to make known is referred to as _____.

    11. _____

12. Something that is stated in exactly the same words, or word for word, is _____.

    12. _____

13. One who records verbatim the deposition of a witness or the proceedings in court and produces a written transcript thereof is a/an _____.

    13. _____

KEYING LEGAL TERMS

Directions: Unless otherwise instructed, use a 70-space line (typewriter) or 1-inch margins (computer) and double spacing. Correct all errors. Follow one of the procedures below.

WORDS

Keyboarding Procedure
On your typewriter or computer, key the following words at least two times, concentrating on the correct spelling and pronunciation.

Shorthand Procedure
On your typewriter or computer, key the following words once, concentrating on the correct spelling and pronunciation. Then write the shorthand outline for each word in your shorthand notebook or on your shorthand machine. Transcribe from the shorthand outlines one time on your typewriter or computer.

contempt of court	subpoena	bench warrant
subpoena duces tecum	interrogatories	disclosure
concealment	court reporter	transcript
verbatim	deposition	pretrial stipulations
fishing expedition		

SENTENCES

Keyboarding Procedure
Key each of the following sentences one time on your typewriter or computer. Concentrate on the correct spelling and pronunciation of each underlined legal term.

Shorthand Procedure
Write the correct shorthand outlines for the following sentences in your shorthand notebook or on your shorthand machine. Transcribe from your shorthand outlines one time on your typewriter or computer.

These sentences will be used for practice dictation on the cassettes.

If a party intentionally does something that interferes with the administration of justice, a contempt of court charge could be made against the party. In cases of contempt of court or if a witness does not obey a subpoena, the judge may issue a bench warrant. A subpoena is a document that compels a witness to appear in court and give testimony at a specified time for the party named therein. If a party has certain designated documents that are required in court, a subpoena duces tecum is issued commanding the person to bring those documents into court. If the party fails to do so, he or she may be charged with contempt of court, and a bench warrant may be issued for the party's arrest.

A witness may be required to answer interrogatories prior to a trial. Interrogatories are written questions about a case, and they must be answered under oath. A party is required under law to make a disclosure of all facts known about a case. If a party does not disclose the known facts about a case and withholds information that the law requires one to make known, the party is guilty of concealment.

A court reporter is a person who records the proceedings in the discovery process or in court and produces a written transcript of what transpired. The transcript must be verbatim, or word for word. A deposition is the part of the discovery process whereby the attorneys ask a witness questions that the witness must answer orally and under oath prior to the trial. The court reporter prepares a verbatim transcript of the deposition. Prior to the taking of a deposition, the attorneys for each party may agree to certain pretrial stipulations that affect certain procedures in the taking of the deposition. In a deposition, attorneys may ask a wide range of questions regarding the case, but they may not go on a fishing expedition. A fishing expedition refers to a tactic used by some attorneys in the discovery process to try to obtain information from a witness that is not based upon or supported by the allegations.

TRANSCRIBING FROM DICTATION

Directions: This dictation emphasizes and reinforces the legal terms and definitions you have studied. Listen carefully to the pronunciation of each of the legal terms. Unless otherwise directed, use a 70-space line (typewriter) or 1-inch margins (computer) and double spacing. Correct all errors. Follow one of the procedures below.

Keyboarding Procedure
Using the cassette from Lesson 6, Part A, transcribe the dictation directly at your typewriter or computer.

Shorthand Procedure
Using the cassette from Lesson 6, Part A, take the dictation using your shorthand system and then transcribe from your shorthand notes on your typewriter or computer.

When you have finished transcribing Part A of the practice dictation, check your transcript with the printed copy. If you made any mistakes in the transcription, you should practice those words several times before going on.

Part B TERMINOLOGY AND DEFINITIONS

Directions: Study the terms, pronunciations, and definitions until you are thoroughly familiar with them. In order to complete this lesson successfully, you must understand the meaning and usage of all the legal terms presented. If you are using shorthand, write your shorthand outline for each legal term in your shorthand notebook or on your shorthand machine.

Legal Term	Pronunciation	Definition
1. precedent	′pres-əd-ənt	A judicial decision serving as a guide for future cases that are similar in nature.
2. notice of lis pendens	′nōt-əs əv lis ′pen-dəns	Latin. A notice issued to inform persons that there is a litigation pending in regard to certain property. (See Figure 6-3, page 86.)
3. chambers	′cham-bərs	The private office of the judge where business outside of the courtroom is conducted.
4. pretrial conference	prē-′trīl ′kän-frəns	An informal conference between judge and counsel to discuss a case before it is tried in court in an effort to clarify and expedite its disposition. It is also used to determine if there is adequate evidence to justify proceeding to trial.
5. examination before trial	ig-zam-ə-′nā-shən bi-′fōr trīl	Inquiry into the facts prior to the trial of a case in order to obtain the information needed to prosecute or defend the action. Sometimes abbreviated as EBT.
6. moot	müt	Something that can be debated, argued, or discussed. A moot point is one that can be argued and is not settled by a court decision.

7. recusation	rē-kyü-'zā-shən	An exception or a plea that a particular judge should be disqualified or removed from hearing a case because he or she is prejudiced or has a personal interest in the case. The judge may also recuse or remove himself or herself if he or she deems there is a personal conflict of interest.
8. bond	bänd	A document certifying that one will pay a certain amount of money if certain acts are not performed. A bond may be posted to assure the appearance of a defendant in court. (See Figure 6-4, page 87.)
9. recognizance	ri-'käg-nə-zəns	A commitment made and recorded before a court that a certain act will be done. Serves as a bond in some states and is referred to as released on personal recognizance. A person released on personal recognizance does not have to post a bond.
10. surety bond	'shủr-ət-ē bänd	A bond insuring that a debt or an obligation will be paid.
11. attachment	ə-'tach-mənt	A document issued so that persons or property may be legally taken and held in the custody of the law.
12. garnishment	'gär-nish-mənt	A legal notice to a person holding property belonging to a defendant that states the property is the subject of a garnishment, or the act of withholding a defendant's property by the order of the court. Under a garnishment, your employer may be required to withhold a portion of your wages to pay a debt that you owe to another party. (See Figure 6-5, page 88.)
13. garnishee	gär-nə-'shē	The one who is in possession of the defendant's property that is the subject of a garnishment or to serve with a garnishment.

FIGURE 6-3 A Notice of Lis Pendens

State of Michigan,

Circuit Court for the County of _____Ingham_____

DARREL L. KELLY _____

                              PLAINTIFF

NOTICE LIS PENDENS

VS.

SACHICO P. LIN _____   **File No.** _45-3175_____

                        DEFENDANT.

    Notice is Hereby Given, That an action has been commenced and is pending in said Court, upon a Complaint filed by the above named Plaintiff _____ against the above named Defendant _____ for

a defect in title _____

_____

_____

_____

_____

and that the premises affected by the said action were, at the time of commencement of said action, and at the time of filing this notice, situated in the __City_____ of _East Lansing_____

County of __Ingham_____ State of Michigan, and are described in said _Warranty_____

Deed_____ as follows, to-wit: _Lots 20 and 21, Assessor's Plat of_

Lot 51, Angell's Subdivision, being Lot 80 and parts of Lots 78

and 79 of College Grove, City of East Lansing, Ingham County,

_Michigan._____

_____

_____

_____

_____

_____

_____

Dated ___November 14,_____ 19_97___

BUSINESS ADDRESS:

4598 Westcott Drive_____

East Lansing, MI 48823_____

Janet Atwell

Attorney,   JANET ATWELL   (P 45502)

FIGURE 6-4 A Bond

	Original - Court	2nd copy - Defendant
	1st copy - Sheriff or court officer	3rd copy - Plaintiff

STATE OF MICHIGAN XXXXXXXXXXXX 30th **JUDICIAL CIRCUIT**	**BOND** Claim and Delivery	**CASE NO.** 83-52179

Court address

2nd Floor, City Hall, Lansing, Michigan 48933

Court telephone no.
(517) 555-0650

Plaintiff name(s) and address(es)

SARAH ANN STONE
6447 Whitmore Avenue
Lansing, MI 48810

V.

Defendant name(s) and address(es)

IMAGE GRAPHICS, INC.
7850 South Washington Avenue
Lansing, MI 48933

Plaintiff's attorney, bar no., address, and telephone no.

Jason C. O'Malley (P 23345)
Patrick B. Stilwell (P 36588)
5219 West Parkway
Holt, MI 48842

Amount of bond	Type of bond	Principal	
$ 5,000.00	☒ Cash ☐ Surety	Allan J. Polasek	☐ Plaintiff ☒ Defendant

Type or print name(s), address(es), and telephone number(s) of sureties

The principal, and surety if applicable, is/are bound jointly and severally to the ☒ sheriff or court officer ☐ plaintiff or their ☐ defendant successors, assigns or legal representatives in the sum stated if the principal fails to perform any of the following obligations:

1. Surrender the property to the person judged entitled to possession;
2. Pay any money that may be recovered against him/her in the action;
3. Diligently prosecute/defend this suit to final judgment; and
4. Perform all other acts required by the court.

October 27, 1997
Date

Allan J. Polasek
Principal signature

Surety signature

Surety signature

The surety(ies) in this bond acknowledge(s) personal worth in the amount of twice the penalties in the bond, over and above all debts and legal exemptions.

Date

Surety

Surety

Subscribed and sworn to before me on _____ County, Michigan.
Date

My commission expires: _____ Signature: _____
Date   Court Clerk/Notary Public

This bond is approved and filed.

October 27, 1997
Date

Tomas Rodriguez (P 33991)
Judge   Bar no.

MC 38 (6/86) **BOND, CLAIM AND DELIVERY**

MCLA 600.2920; MSA 27A.2920, MCR 3.105, MCR 3.604

COURT

FIGURE 6-5 A Garnishment

Self-Evaluation B   TERMINOLOGY AND DEFINITION RECALL

Directions: In the Answers column at the right of each statement, write the letter that represents the word or group of words that correctly completes the statement. After you have completed this self-evaluation, check your answers with the key on page 495. If you have any incorrect answers, restudy the definitions for those terms before going on with this lesson. Then unless otherwise directed, submit this self-evaluation to your instructor.

Answers

1. Something that can be debated, argued, or discussed and has not been settled by court decisions is (a) moot, (b) precedent, (c) chambers.

    1. _____

2. A legal notice to a person holding property belonging to a defendant that said property is to be held for the payment of a debt to the plaintiff is a/an (a) attachment, (b) garnishment, (c) garnishee.

    2. _____

3. A bond that insures that a debt or obligation will be paid is a (a) surety bond, (b) garnishment, (c) subpoena.

    3. _____

4. A notice to inform persons that there is a litigation pending in regard to a certain property is a/an (a) attachment, (b) surety bond, (c) notice of lis pendens.

    4. _____

5. An informal meeting between judge and counsel to discuss a case before it is tried in court in an effort to clarify and expedite its disposition or to determine if there is adequate evidence to justify proceeding to trial is a/an (a) examination before trial, (b) pretrial conference, (c) chambers.

    5. _____

6. A commitment made and recorded before a court that a certain act will be done and that serves in some states as a bond is a (a) recognizance, (b) surety bond, (c) garnishment.

    6. _____

7. The one who is in possession of the defendant's property that is the subject of a garnishment, or the act of withholding a defendant's property by the order of the court, is called a (a) precedent, (b) garnishment, (c) garnishee.

    7. _____

8. The private office of the judge where business outside of the courtroom is conducted is the (a) pretrial conference, (b) chambers, (c) moot.

    8. _____

9. Inquiry into the facts prior to the trial of a case in order to obtain the information needed to prosecute or defend the action is a/an (a) recusation, (b) chambers, (c) examination before trial.

    9. _____

10. A document that certifies that one will pay a certain amount of money if certain acts are not performed, such as the appearance of a defendant in court, is a/an (a) attachment, (b) bond, (c) notice of lis pendens.

    10. _____

11. A document issued so that persons or property may be legally taken and held in the custody of the law is a/an (a) attachment, (b) garnishee, (c) surety bond.

    11. _____

12. A judicial decision that serves as a guide for future cases that are similar in nature is a/an (a) attachment, (b) recusation, (c) precedent.

    12. _____

13. An exception or a plea that a judge should be disqualified from hearing a case because of prejudice or a personal interest in the case is (a) recognizance, (b) subpoena, (c) recusation.

    13. _____

KEYING LEGAL TERMS

Directons: Unless otherwise instructed, use a 70-space line (typewriter) or 1-inch margins (computer) and double spacing. Correct all errors. Follow one of the procedures below.

WORDS

Keyboarding Procedure
On your typewriter or computer, key the following words at least two times, concentrating on the correct spelling and pronunciation.

Shorthand Procedure
On your typewriter or computer, key the following words once, concentrating on the correct spelling and pronunciation. Then write the shorthand outline for each word in your shorthand notebook or on your shorthand machine. Transcribe from the shorthand outlines one time on your typewriter or computer.

precedent	notice of lis pendens	chambers
pretrial conference	examination before trial	moot
recusation	bond	recognizance
surety bond	attachment	garnishment
garnishee		

SENTENCES

Keyboarding Procedure
Key each of the following sentences one time on your typewriter or computer. Concentrate on the correct spelling and pronunciation of each underlined legal term.

Shorthand Procedure
Write the correct shorthand outlines for the following sentences in your shorthand notebook or on your shorthand machine. Transcribe from your shorthand outlines one time on your typewriter or computer.

These sentences will be used for practice dictation on the cassettes.

A precedent is a judicial decision that serves as a guide for future cases that are similar in nature. If a title to property is involved in litigation, a notice of lis pendens is filed to inform persons that there is a litigation pending in regard to certain property. The private office of the judge is called chambers. The judge may hold the pretrial conference in chambers rather than in the courtroom. A pretrial conference may be held before a case is tried in court in an effort to determine if there is adequate evidence to justify proceeding to trial.

An examination before trial, commonly referred to as an EBT, is an inquiry into the facts prior to the trial of a case so as to obtain the information needed to prosecute or defend the action. A moot point is one that can be debated, argued, or discussed. A moot point or issue is one that has not been settled by court decisions.

Recusation is an exception or a plea that a particular judge should be disqualified from hearing a case because he or she is prejudiced or has a personal interest in the matter. For example, the judge's ability to hear a case fairly may be challenged if the judge has a personal or business involvement with a party in the case.

A bond is a document that certifies that one will pay a certain amount of money if certain acts are not performed. A bond may be posted to assure the appearance of the defendant in court, or the court may release a person on personal recognizance. A person released on personal recognizance does not have to post a bond. In some cases, a plaintiff must post a <u>surety bond</u> before attaching property owned by a defendant. A surety bond insures that a debt or an obligation will be paid. An <u>attachment</u> is issued so that persons or property may be legally taken and held in the custody of the law.

If the defendant's property is being held by another party, the plaintiff may acquire the property by filing a <u>garnishment</u>. To <u>garnishee</u> a defendant's property, a legal notice is issued to the person holding said property stating that the property is to be held for the payment of a debt to the plaintiff.

TRANSCRIBING FROM DICTATION

Directions: This dictation emphasizes and reinforces the legal terms and definitions you have studied. Listen carefully to the pronunciation of each of the legal terms. Unless otherwise directed, use a 70-space line (typewriter) or 1-inch margins (computer) and double spacing. Correct all errors. Follow one of the procedures below.

Keyboarding Procedure
Using the cassette from Lesson 6, Part B, transcribe the dictation directly at your typewriter or computer.

Shorthand Procedure
Using the cassette from Lesson 6, Part B, take the dictation using your shorthand system and then transcribe from your shorthand notes on your typewriter or computer.

When you have finished transcribing Part B of the practice dictation, check your transcript with the printed copy. If you made any mistakes in the transcription, you should practice those words several times before going on to Evaluation 3.

CHECKLIST
I have completed the following for Lesson 6:

	Part A, Date	Part B, Date	Submitted to Instructor Yes	No
Terminology and Definitions	_____	_____	_____	_____
Self-Evaluation	_____	_____	_____	_____
* Keying Legal Terms	_____	_____	_____	_____
Words	_____	_____	_____	_____
Sentences	_____	_____	_____	_____
* Transcribing from Dictation	_____	_____	_____	_____

When you have successfully completed all the exercises in this lesson and submitted to your instructor those requested, you are ready to proceed with Evaluation 3.

* If you are using a shorthand system, submit to your instructor your shorthand notes along with your transcript.

Evaluation No. 3   SECTION A

Directions: This dictation/transcription evaluation will test your spelling and transcription abilities on the legal terms that you studied in the two preceding lessons. Use a 5-space paragraph indention, a 70-space line (typewriter) or 1-inch margins (computer), and double spacing unless otherwise instructed. Correct all errors. Follow one of the procedures below.

Keyboarding Procedure

Using the cassette from Evaluation 3, transcribe the dictation directly at your typewriter or computer.

Shorthand Procedure

Using the cassette from Evaluation 3, take the dictation using your shorthand system and then transcribe from your shorthand notes on your typewriter or computer.

Sections B and C are available from your instructor.

Lesson 7

Litigation—Trial and Proceedings

"The law is not concerned with trifles."

—Legal Maxim

Many nonlawyer personnel do not have an opportunity to observe the proceedings that take place in a courtroom. However, regardless of your legal position, having a knowledge of what transpires once a case goes to trial will help you to understand the importance of the various aspects of your particular involvement in a case. This lesson introduces legal terms that are used in the courtroom during a trial or legal proceeding. Upon successful completion of this lesson, you should have a better understanding of the terms used in litigation.

Part A TERMINOLOGY AND DEFINITIONS

Directions: Study the terms, pronunciations, and definitions until you are thoroughly familiar with them. In order to complete this lesson successfully, you must understand the meaning and usage of all the legal terms presented. If you are using shorthand, write your shorthand outline for each legal term in your shorthand notebook or on your shorthand machine.

Legal Term	Pronunciation	Definition
1. trial	trīl	The examination of a civil or criminal case in a court of law with the purpose of deciding an issue.
2. counsel	ˈkaủn-səl	An attorney who represents or assists a client in a court case.
3. jury	ˈjủr-ē	A group of persons selected to hear a case in a court of law and sworn to render a verdict based upon the evidence presented in the case. Sometimes referred to as petit jury.
4. juror	ˈjủr-ər	One who is a member of a jury.
5. veniremen	və-ˈnī-rē-mən	Jurors.
6. impanel	im-ˈpan-l	The process of selecting a jury.
7. voir dire	vwä-ˈdir	French. A preliminary examination by the court of a prospective juror to determine if the person is competent to serve as a juror.
8. challenge	ˈchal-ənj	To object to a certain person serving as a juror. The challenge may be made by the attorney representing either party in the case.
9. challenge to the array	ˈchal-ənj tü thē ə-ˈrā	An objection made to the entire panel of jurors.

10. challenge for cause	'chal-ənj fər kȯz	An objection made to a juror based on a specified reason, such as a previous criminal record.
11. peremptory challenge	pə-'rem-trē 'chal-ənj	An objection made to a juror for which no cause is given. There is a limited number of peremptory challenges allowed to each party in a case.
12. oath	ōth	A swearing or an affirming that one will act faithfully and truthfully.
13. foreman or forewoman	'fōr-mən ȯr fōr-wům-ən	A juror selected by the other members of the jury to preside over the deliberations and to speak for the jury. Also referred to as the foreperson.

Self-Evaluation A   TERMINOLOGY AND DEFINITION RECALL

Directions: In the Answers column, write the letter from Column 1 that represents the word or phrase that best matches each item in Column 2. After you have completed this self-evaluation, check your answers with the key on page 495. If you have any incorrect answers, restudy the definitions for those terms before going on with this lesson. Then unless otherwise directed, submit this self-evaluation to your instructor.

Column 1

a. challenge

b. challenge for cause

c. challenge to the array

d. counsel

e. foreman or forewoman

f. impanel

g. jurist

h. juror

i. jury

j. oath

k. peremptory challenge

l. trial

m. veniremen

n. voir dire

Column 2

1. A swearing or an affirming that one will act faithfully and truthfully.

2. A group of persons selected to hear a case in a court of law and sworn to render a verdict based upon the evidence presented in the case.

3. A juror selected by the other members of the jury to preside over the deliberations and to speak for the jury.

4. The examination of a civil or criminal case in a court of law with the purpose of deciding an issue.

5. One who is a member of a jury.

6. To object to a certain person serving as a juror.

7. Another name for jurors.

8. A preliminary examination by the court of a prospective juror to determine if the person is competent to serve as a juror.

9. An objection made to a juror based on a specified reason, such as a previous criminal record.

10. To go through the process or steps of selecting a jury.

11. An objection made to the entire panel of jurors.

12. An attorney who represents or assists a client in a court case.

13. An objection made to a juror for which no cause is given.

Answers

1. _____

2. _____

3. _____

4. _____

5. _____

6. _____

7. _____

8. _____

9. _____

10. _____

11. _____

12. _____

13. _____

KEYING LEGAL TERMS

Directions: Unless otherwise instructed, use a 70-space line (typewriter) or 1-inch margins (computer) and double spacing. Correct all errors. Follow one of the procedures below.

WORDS

Keyboarding Procedure
On your typewriter or computer, key the following words at least two times, concentrating on the correct spelling and pronunciation.

Shorthand Procedure
On your typewriter or computer, key the following words once, concentrating on the correct spelling and pronunciation. Then write the shorthand outline for each word in your shorthand notebook or on your shorthand machine. Transcribe from the shorthand outlines one time on your typewriter or computer.

trial	counsel	jury
juror	impanel	voir dire
challenge	challenge to the array	challenge for cause
peremptory challenge	oath	veniremen
foreman or forewoman		

SENTENCES

Keyboarding Procedure
Key each of the following sentences one time on your typewriter or computer. Concentrate on the correct spelling and pronunciation of each underlined legal term.

Shorthand Procedure
Write the correct shorthand outlines for the following sentences in your shorthand notebook or on your shorthand machine. Transcribe from your shorthand outlines one time on your typewriter or computer.

These sentences will be used for practice dictation on the cassettes.

A trial is the examination of a civil or criminal case in a court of law with the purpose of deciding an issue. Counsel is an attorney who represents or assists a client in a court case. Cases tried in courts of original jurisdiction or trial courts may be decided by a jury, which is sometimes referred to as petit jury. A jury is a group of persons who are selected to hear a case in a court of law and who have sworn to render a verdict based upon the evidence presented in the case. A juror is one who is a member of a jury.

To impanel a jury is to select the jurors who will decide the issue. Part of the impaneling process is the voir dire, which is the preliminary examination by the court of a prospective juror to determine if the person is competent to serve as a juror.

During the voir dire, counsel for either party may challenge the capability of a juror or jurors. There are three common types of challenges that counsel may exercise. They are challenge to the array, challenge for cause, and peremptory challenge. A challenge to the array is a challenge to the entire panel of jurors. A challenge to a juror based on a specific reason is a challenge for cause. The specific reason for the challenge must be stated to the judge, who will then decide whether or not the prospective juror may sit as a member of the jury. A peremptory challenge is one for which no cause is given. Each party has a certain number of peremptory challenges that they may exercise without giving the judge a reason for the challenge.

Each juror must take an <u>oath</u> to act truthfully and faithfully. Once the jury has been impaneled, the jurors, or the <u>veniremen</u>, will select a <u>foreman or forewoman</u> to preside over the deliberations and to speak for the jury. Veniremen is another name for jurors.

TRANSCRIBING FROM DICTATION

Directions: This dictation emphasizes and reinforces the legal terms and definitions you have studied. Listen carefully to the pronunciation of each of the legal terms. Unless otherwise directed, use a 70-space line (typewriter) or 1-inch margins (computer) and double spacing. Correct all errors. Follow one of the procedures below.

Keyboarding Procedure
Using the cassette from Lesson 7, Part A, transcribe the dictation directly at your typewriter or computer.

Shorthand Procedure
Using the cassette from Lesson 7, Part A, take the dictation using your shorthand system and then transcribe from your shorthand notes on your typewriter or computer.

When you have finished transcribing Part A of the practice dictation, check your transcript with the printed copy. If you made any mistakes in the transcription, you should practice those words several times before going on.

Part B TERMINOLOGY AND DEFINITIONS

Directions: Study the terms, pronunciations, and definitions until you are thoroughly familiar with them. In order to complete this lesson successfully, you must understand the meaning and usage of all the legal terms presented. If you are using shorthand, write your shorthand outline for each legal term in your shorthand notebook or on your shorthand machine.

Legal Term	Pronunciation	Definition
1. opening statement	ˉop-niŋ ˈstāt-mənt	The first step in a jury trial after the jury has been selected in which the attorneys state to the jury what they plan to prove in the trial.
2. testimony	ˈtes-tə-mō-nē	Evidence presented by a witness under oath in a court of law. (See Figure 7-1, page 102.)
3. witness	ˈwit-nəs	One who is called to give testimony under oath in court as to any facts that pertain to the case.
4. direct examination	də-ˈrekt ig-zam-ə-ˈnā-shən	The first questioning of a witness in court by the attorney for the party who called the witness to testify. (See Figure 7-1, page 102.)
5. cross-examination	kròs ig-zam-ə-ˈnā-shən	The questioning of a witness by counsel for the party who is in opposition to the party who called the witness to testify.
6. admissible	əd-ˈmis-ə-bəl	Evidence that is relevant to a case and may, therefore, be presented in court.
7. colloquy	ˈkäl-ə-kwē	A talking together, conference, or conversation between the judge and counsel or the judge and witness. Could be in the form of an objection. Deviates from the normal question and answer that takes place between counsel and witness. (See Figure 7-2, page 103.)

8. objection	əb-'jek-shən	A protest made by counsel to the judge pertaining to certain evidence or a procedure in the trial. (See Figure 7-1, page 102.)
9. irrelevant	ir-'el-ə-vənt	Evidence presented that is not applicable or related to the issues in the case. An attorney may make an objection to irrelevant evidence.
10. motion to strike	'mō-shən tü strīk	A request made by counsel to eliminate improper evidence from consideration in deciding an issue. Evidence that is ordered stricken cannot be considered but remains as a part of the record in the event the case is appealed.
11. physically expunge	'fiz-i-klē 'ik-spənj	To actually remove certain evidence from the record. Only the judge can order evidence to be physically expunged from the record.
12. sustained	sə-'stānd	The answer of the court when supporting an objection made by counsel.
13. overruled	ō-və-'rüld	The answer of the court when refusing to support an objection made by counsel.
14. mistrial	mis-'trīl	A trial that is declared invalid because of an error in the proceedings or the failure of a jury to reach a verdict. When a mistrial occurs, a new jury must be impaneled, and the trial must start over from the beginning.

FIGURE 7-1 Testimony

<u>DIRECT EXAMINATION</u>

BY MRS. SHAPIRO

Q. Mr. Baker, I believe your name was mentioned in yesterday's testimony from the witness stand relative to this particular incident that occurred on December 28, 1997. Do you remember that day, sir?

A. I remember the incident.

Q. Where were you employed at that time?

A. I was employed part time for Midtown Mall as a security guard.

Q. Do you recall being in the security office on that particular day?

A. On that day, yes, ma'am.

~~~~~~

Q. The type of staple that can be removed by a thumbnail or penknife? You can lift them off if you wish to?

A. I would assume so. Yes, ma'am.

          MR. DANIELS: I object, your Honor. It's obvious the staples are removable.

          THE COURT: I sustain the objection. Ask the direct question, not what is possible.

Q. Was the staple of a nature that with a simple ordinary penknife you could easily open the bag and remove the staples from it?

A. In this particular case I never tried, but I assume you could. Yes, ma'am.

~~~~~~

FIGURE 7-2 Colloquy

Q. The only people that have access to it then are the five
   security guards?

A. The people in the security department have a key. Yes.

           MRS. SHAPIRO: I have no further
questions of this witness, your Honor.

           THE COURT: Anything further, MR.
Daniels?

           MR. DANIELS: No questions of this
witness, your Honor.

           THE COURT: You may step down, please.

           MRS. SHAPIRO: Your Honor, I ask the
Court's permission to have Mr. Baker excused.

           THE COURT: Any objections, Mr. Daniels?

           MR. DANIELS: No objections, your Honor.

           THE COURT: The witness is excused.

Self-Evaluation B   TERMINOLOGY AND DEFINITION RECALL

Directions: In the Answers column, write the legal term that is most representative of the corresponding statement. After you have completed this self-evaluation, check your answers with the key on page 495. If you have any incorrect answers, restudy the definitions for those terms before going on with this lesson. Then unless otherwise directed, submit this self-evaluation to your instructor.

Answers

1. The first questioning of a witness in court by the attorney for the party who called the witness to testify is _____.

   1. _____

2. The answer of the court in refusing to support an objection made by counsel is _____.

   2. _____

3. A request made by counsel to eliminate improper evidence from consideration in deciding an issue is a/an _____.

   3. _____

4. Evidence presented that is not applicable or related to the issues in the case is _____.

   4. _____

5. A trial that is declared invalid because of an error in the proceedings or the failure of a jury to reach a verdict is a/an _____.

   5. _____

6. The questioning of a witness by counsel for the party who is in opposition to the party who called the witness to testify is _____.

   6. _____

7. To actually remove certain evidence from the record is to _____ it.

   7. _____

8. The first step in a jury trial after the jury has been selected in which the attorneys state to the jury what they plan to prove in the trial is the _____.

   8. _____

9. A talking together, conference, or conversation between the judge and counsel or the judge and witness is _____.

   9. _____

10. Evidence presented by a witness under oath in a court of law is _____.

    10. _____

11. Evidence that is relevant to a case and therefore may be presented in court is _____ evidence.

    11. _____

12. A protest made by counsel to the judge pertaining to certain evidence or a procedure in the trial is a/an _____.

    12. _____

13. One who is called to give testimony under oath in court as to any facts that pertain to the case is a/an _____.

    13. _____

14. The answer of the court when supporting an objection made by counsel is _____.

    14. _____

KEYING LEGAL TERMS

Directions: Unless otherwise instructed, use a 70-space line (typewriter) or 1-inch margins (computer) and double spacing. Correct all errors. Follow one of the procedures below.

WORDS

Keyboarding Procedure
On your typewriter or computer, key the following words at least two times, concentrating on the correct spelling and pronunciation.

Shorthand Procedure
On your typewriter or computer, key the following words once, concentrating on the correct spelling and pronunciation. Then write the shorthand outline for each word in your shorthand notebook or on your shorthand machine. Transcribe from the shorthand outlines one time on your typewriter or computer.

opening statement	**testimony**	**witness**
direct examination	**cross-examination**	**admissible**
colloquy	**objection**	**irrelevant**
motion to strike	**physically expunge**	**sustained**
overruled	**mistrial**	

SENTENCES

Keyboarding Procedure
Key each of the following sentences one time on your typewriter or computer. Concentrate on the correct spelling and pronunciation of each underlined legal term.

Shorthand Procedure
Write the correct shorthand outlines for the following sentences in your shorthand notebook or on your shorthand machine. Transcribe from your shorthand outlines one time on your typewriter or computer.

These sentences will be used for practice dictation on the cassettes.

At the beginning of a trial, counsel for both sides usually presents an opening statement to the jury. In the opening statements, the attorneys tell the jury what they plan to prove during the trial. Each attorney will then call persons to the witness stand to give testimony under oath as to any facts that pertain to the case. A person who gives testimony is called a witness.

The first questioning of a witness in court by the attorney for the party who called the witness to testify is the direct examination. After the direct examination, the witness may be subjected to a cross-examination by the counsel for the opposing party. Evidence that is admissible in court is evidence that is relevant to a case. During the direct examination or the cross-examination, counsel and judge may engage in colloquy, or conversation relevant to the case. An objection to the testimony or evidence by counsel is a form of colloquy.

Counsel may object to certain evidence on the grounds that it is irrelevant, meaning that it is not applicable or related to the issues in the case. Counsel may make a motion to strike certain irrelevant testimony or evidence. The judge may rule in favor of the motion to strike and order the court reporter to physically expunge the testimony or evidence from the record. To physically expunge testimony from the record means to strike it totally from the record. An objection must be either sustained or overruled by the judge. If an objection is sustained, the judge agrees with the counsel who made the objection; if the objection is overruled, the judge does not agree with the counsel who made the objection. A <u>mistrial</u>, or dismissal of a case, may result if a fundamental legal procedure is violated during a trial.

TRANSCRIBING FROM DICTATION

Directions: This dictation emphasizes and reinforces the legal terms and definitions you have studied. Listen carefully to the pronunciation of each of the legal terms. Unless otherwise directed, use a 70-space line (typewriter) or 1-inch margins (computer) and double spacing. Correct all errors. Follow one of the procedures below.

Keyboarding Procedure
Using the cassette from Lesson 7, Part B, transcribe the dictation directly at your typewriter or computer.

Shorthand Procedure
Using the cassette from Lesson 7, Part B, take the dictation using your shorthand system and then transcribe from your shorthand notes on your typewriter or computer.

When you have finished transcribing Part B of the practice dictation, check your transcript with the printed copy. If you made any mistakes in the transcription, you should practice those words several times before going on to Lesson 8.

CHECKLIST
I have completed the following for Lesson 7:

	Part A, Date	Part B, Date	Submitted to Instructor Yes	No
Terminology and Definitions				
Self-Evaluation				
***** **Keying Legal Terms**				
Words				
Sentences				
***** **Transcribing from Dictation**				

When you have successfully completed all the exercises in this lesson and submitted to your instructor those requested, you are ready to proceed with Lesson 8.

* If you are using a shorthand system, submit to your instructor your shorthand notes along with your transcript.

Lesson 8

Litigation—Trial and Proceedings

"For every wrong there is a remedy."
—Legal Maxim

Additional legal terms relating to courtroom proceedings are introduced in these exercises. When you have successfully completed this lesson, you should have knowledge and a better understanding of the terminology used during the trial of a case.

Part A   TERMINOLOGY AND DEFINITIONS

Directions: Study the terms, pronunciations, and definitions until you are thoroughly familiar with them. In order to complete this lesson successfully, you must understand the meaning and usage of all the legal terms presented. If you are using shorthand, write your shorthand outline for each legal term in your shorthand notebook or on your shorthand machine.

Legal Term	Pronunciation	Definition
1. adduce	ə-'düs	To present or introduce evidence in a case.
2. evidence	'ev-əd-əns	Testimony, exhibits, or other matter presented in the trial of a case to prove the alleged facts.
3. opinion evidence	ə-'pin-yən 'ev-əd-əns	Testimony given by a witness (usually an expert) as to what that witness thinks or believes about the facts in the case.
4. expert evidence	'ek-spərt 'ev-əd-əns	Testimony given by a person who has special qualifications to testify in regard to specific facts in the case.
5. circumstantial evidence	sər-kəm-'stan-chəl 'ev-əd-əns	Indirect evidence. An inference or assumption that may be made from other facts proven in the case. For example, if you have stolen property in your possession, it could be assumed that you stole it even though no one saw you do it.
6. incompetent	in-'käm-pət-ənt	Not qualified legally. Pertains to evidence that is not admissible in a court case.
7. exhibit	ig-'zib-ət	Any document or object presented to the court as evidence in a case. Exhibits must be accepted by the court before they become a part of the evidence. An exhibit is marked for identification (usually by the court reporter) when it is introduced. (See Figure 8-1, page 111.)
8. hearsay	hir-'sā	The repeating of what one heard another say. Hearsay evidence is generally not admissible in court.
9. res gestae	rēz 'jes-tē	Latin. Things done. Things that are a part of a case. Hearsay evidence may be admitted if it can be shown that it is res gestae.

10. impeach	im-'pēch	To prove in a trial that a witness cannot or should not be believed.
11. perjury	'pərj-rē	Intentionally or knowingly giving false testimony under oath. A person who commits perjury may have criminal charges brought against him or her.
12. rebuttal	ri-'bət-l	An attempt to disprove the evidence presented by the other side.
13. hostile witness	'häs-tl 'wit-nəs	A witness who is openly prejudiced against the party who called the witness to testify in the case. A hostile witness may be cross-examined by the party who called the witness to testify.
14. averment	ə-'vər-mənt	A declaration positively stating that the facts are true.

FIGURE 8-1 An Exhibit

RECEIPT Date December 29 19 97 No. **5614**

Received From Sandra Nichols

Address 38 Meadowlark, Lansing, MI

Three Hundred fifty and 00/100 Dollars $ 350.00

For Security Deposit on Apt. 501, Arbor Village Apartments

ACCOUNT			HOW PAID		
AMT. OF ACCOUNT	350	00	CASH	350	00
AMT. PAID	350	00	CHECK		
BALANCE DUE	-0-		MONEY ORDER		

By Mark W. Adams

DEPOSITION EXHIBIT

12

PENGAD-Bayonne, N.J.

Self-Evaluation A TERMINOLOGY AND DEFINITION RECALL

Directions: In the Answers column, write the legal term that is most representative of the corresponding statement. After you have completed this self-evaluation, check your answers with the key on page 495. If you have any incorrect answers, restudy the definitions for those terms before going on with this lesson. Then unless otherwise directed, submit this self-evaluation to your instructor.

Answers

1. To prove in a trial that a witness cannot or should not be believed is to _____ the witness.

    1. _____

2. Testimony, exhibits, or other matter presented in the trial of a case to prove the alleged facts are _____.

    2. _____

3. A witness who intentionally or knowingly gives false testimony under oath is guilty of _____.

    3. _____

4. A witness who is openly prejudiced against the party who called the witness to testify in the case and who may be cross-examined by that party is a/an _____.

    4. _____

5. An exception to the hearsay rule and a term meaning things done is _____.

    5. _____

6. A positive declaration or assertion as to the facts in a case is a/an _____.

    6. _____

7. Testimony given by a person who has special qualifications to testify in regard to specific facts in the case is _____.

    7. _____

8. An attempt to disprove the evidence presented by the other side is a/an _____.

    8. _____

9. A term meaning to introduce or present evidence in a case is _____.

    9. _____

10. A word that means not qualified legally and pertains to evidence that is not admissible in court is _____.

    10. _____

11. Any document or object presented to the court as evidence in a case is a/an _____.

    11. _____

12. Testimony given by a witness, usually an expert, as to what the witness thinks or believes about the facts in the case is _____.

    12. _____

13. The repeating of what one heard another say is _____.

    13. _____

14. Indirect evidence or an inference that may be made from other facts proven in the case is _____.

    14. _____

KEYING LEGAL TERMS

Directions: Unless otherwise instructed, use a 70-space line (typewriter) or 1-inch margins (computer) and double spacing. Correct all errors. Follow one of the procedures below.

WORDS

Keyboarding Procedure
On your typewriter or computer, key the following words at least two times, concentrating on the correct spelling and pronunciation.

Shorthand Procedure
On your typewriter or computer, key the following words once, concentrating on the correct spelling and pronunciation. Then write the shorthand outline for each word in your shorthand notebook or on your shorthand machine. Transcribe from the shorthand outlines one time on your typewriter or computer.

adduce	**evidence**	**opinion evidence**
expert evidence	**circumstantial evidence**	**incompetent**
exhibit	**hearsay**	**res gestae**
impeach	**perjury**	**rebuttal**
hostile witness	**averment**	

SENTENCES

Keyboarding Procedure
Key each of the following sentences one time on your typewriter or computer. Concentrate on the correct spelling and pronunciation of each underlined legal term.

Shorthand Procedure
Write the correct shorthand outlines for the following sentences in your shorthand notebook or on your shorthand machine. Transcribe from your shorthand outlines one time on your typewriter or computer.

These sentences will be used for practice dictation on the cassettes.

Adduce is to present or introduce evidence in a case. Evidence consists of testimony, exhibits, or other matter presented in the trial of a case to prove the alleged facts. Opinion evidence, expert evidence, and circumstantial evidence are some of the various types of evidence that may be presented in a trial. Opinion evidence is testimony given by a witness, usually an expert, as to what the witness thinks or believes about the facts in a case. Testimony given by a person who has special qualifications to testify in regard to specific facts in a case is called expert evidence.

An expert witness may be deemed incompetent to testify if his or her knowledge is lacking in the specified field. Indirect evidence, or an inference that may be made based on other facts proven in a case, is referred to as circumstantial evidence. The evidence is circumstantial if the facts infer that you did something even though no one saw you do it.

An exhibit is any document or object presented to the court as evidence in a case. An exhibit that has been accepted by the court as evidence is marked for identification and made part of the case. Hearsay evidence is what the witness heard another person say. Hearsay evidence may be admitted if it can be shown that it is part of the res gestae. Res gestae means things that are a part of the case or things done.

To impeach a witness is to prove in a trial that the witness cannot or should not be believed. A witness who intentionally or knowingly gives false testimony under oath is guilty of perjury and may have criminal charges brought against him or her. A rebuttal is an attempt to disprove the evidence presented by the other side. A hostile witness is one who is openly prejudiced against the party who called the witness to testify in the case and may be cross-examined by that party. An averment is a positive declaration or assertion as to the facts in a case.

TRANSCRIBING FROM DICTATION

Directions: This dictation emphasizes and reinforces the legal terms and definitions you have studied. Listen carefully to the pronunciation of each of the legal terms. Unless otherwise directed, use a 70-space line (typewriter) or 1-inch margins (computer) and double spacing. Correct all errors. Follow one of the procedures below.

Keyboarding Procedure
Using the cassette from Lesson 8, Part A, transcribe the dictation directly at your typewriter or computer.

Shorthand Procedure
Using the cassette from Lesson 8, Part A, take the dictation using your shorthand system and then transcribe from your shorthand notes on your typewriter or computer.

When you have finished transcribing Part A of the practice dictation, check your transcript with the printed copy. If you made any mistakes in the transcription, you should practice those words several times before going on.

Part B TERMINOLOGY AND DEFINITIONS

Directions: Study the terms, pronunciations, and definitions until you are thoroughly familiar with them. In order to complete this lesson successfully, you must understand the meaning and usage of all the legal terms presented. If you are using shorthand, write your shorthand outline for each legal term in your shorthand notebook or on your shorthand machine.

Legal Term	Pronunciation	Definition
1. bailiff	′bā-lef	An officer of the court who is in charge of the jury. May also guard prisoners when they appear in court.
2. causal	′kȯ-zel	Implying a cause. Having to do with cause and effect.
3. prima facie	′prī-mə ′fā-shə	Latin. At first view. Evidence that is sufficient to prove or establish a fact unless contrary evidence is presented.
4. credible evidence	′kred-ə-bəl ′ev-əd-əns	Evidence presented in a case that is believable.
5. alibi	′al-ə-bī	Latin. Elsewhere. An excuse. In a criminal case, if the defendant presents proof of being in another place at the time the crime was committed, the defendant has an alibi.
6. pendente lite	′pen-dən-tē ′lī-tē	Latin. Pending litigation. The time during which the case is in court.
7. amicus curiae	ə-′mē-kəs ′kur-ē-ī	Latin. Friend of the court. A person who has no interest in a case but is called in by the judge to give advice regarding some matter of law.

8. closing arguments	ˈklō-ziŋ ˈär-gyə-mənts	The presentations given by counsel at the end of a case summarizing the evidence presented in the trial in an effort to persuade the jury to decide the case in favor of their client.
9. burden of proof	ˈbərd-n əv prüf	The plaintiff in a case has the duty of proving that the defendant is guilty; therefore, the burden of proof is on the plaintiff.
10. charge to the jury	ˈchärj tü thə ˈjùr-ē	The instructions given by the judge to the jury before deliberations as to the rules of law that apply to the case.
11. deliberations	di-lib-ə-ˈrā-shəns	The process of the jury discussing the case in an effort to reach a verdict.
12. sequestered	si-ˈkwes-tərd	Latin. Secluded. The seclusion of witnesses or evidence during a case, or the seclusion of the jury until a verdict is reached.
13. preponderance of evidence	pri-ˈpän-drəns əv ˈev-əd-əns	Greater weight of evidence. Evidence that has greater value. Does not mean the greater number of witnesses but rather the greater weight of the evidence. The jury will return a verdict in a civil case for the party that has the preponderance of evidence.

Self-Evaluation B   TERMINOLOGY AND DEFINITION RECALL

Directions: In the Answers column at the right of each statement, write the letter that represents the word or group of words that correctly completes the statement. After you have completed this self-evaluation, check your answers with the key on page 495. If you have any incorrect answers, restudy the definitions for those terms before going on with this lesson. Then unless otherwise directed, submit this self-evaluation to your instructor.

Answers

1. Implying a cause or having to do with cause and effect is (a) bailiff, (b) causal, (c) alibi.

    1. _____

2. An officer of the court who is in charge of the jury or who may also guard prisoners when they appear in court is a/an (a) bailiff, (b) causal, (c) amicus curiae.

    2. _____

3. A person who has no interest in a case but is called in by the judge to give advice regarding some matter of law is a/an (a) bailiff, (b) amicus curiae, (c) pendente lite.

    3. _____

4. Evidence presented in a case that is believable is (a) preponderance of evidence, (b) prima facie, (c) credible evidence.

    4. _____

5. A Latin term meaning pending litigation or the time during which the case is in court is (a) alibi, (b) deliberations, (c) pendente lite.

    5. _____

6. In a criminal case, if the defendant presents proof of being in another place at the time the crime was committed, the defendant is said to have a/an (a) alibi, (b) credible evidence, (c) causal.

    6. _____

7. Evidence that has greater weight or greater value is referred to as the (a) preponderance of evidence, (b) credible evidence, (c) pendente lite.

    7. _____

8. If a jury is secluded from the public until a verdict is reached, the jury is said to be (a) closing arguments, (b) sequestered, (c) amicus curiae.

    8. _____

9. The instructions given by the judge to the jury before deliberations as to the rules of law that apply to the case are known as the (a) burden of proof, (b) preponderance of evidence, (c) charge to the jury.

    9. _____

10. A Latin term meaning at first view or evidence that is sufficient to prove or establish a fact unless contrary evidence is presented is (a) prima facie, (b) amicus curiae, (c) alibi.

    10. _____

11. The duty that the plaintiff has in a case to prove the defendant guilty is the (a) preponderance of evidence, (b) burden of proof, (c) causal.

    11. _____

12. The process of the jury discussing the case in an effort to reach a verdict is called (a) sequestered, (b) charge to the jury, (c) deliberations.

    12. _____

13. The presentations given by counsel at the end of a case in an effort to persuade the jury to decide the case in favor of their client are the (a) deliberations, (b) closing arguments, (c) prima facie.

    13. _____

KEYING LEGAL TERMS

Directions: Unless otherwise instructed, use a 70-space line (typewriter) or 1-inch margins (computer) and double spacing. Correct all errors. Follow one of the procedures below.

WORDS

Keyboarding Procedure
On your typewriter or computer, key the following words at least two times, concentrating on the correct spelling and pronunciation.

Shorthand Procedure
On your typewriter or computer, key the following words once, concentrating on the correct spelling and pronunciation. Then write the shorthand outline for each word in your shorthand notebook or on your shorthand machine. Transcribe from the shorthand outlines one time on your typewriter or computer.

bailiff	causal	prima facie
credible evidence	alibi	pendente lite
amicus curiae	closing arguments	burden of proof
charge to the jury	deliberations	sequestered
preponderance of evidence		

SENTENCES

Keyboarding Procedure
Key each of the following sentences one time on your typewriter or computer. Concentrate on the correct spelling and pronunciation of each underlined legal term.

Shorthand Procedure
Write the correct shorthand outlines for the following sentences in your shorthand notebook or on your shorthand machine. Transcribe from your shorthand outlines one time on your typewriter or computer.

These sentences will be used for practice dictation on the cassettes.

The <u>bailiff</u> is an officer of the court who is in charge of the jury. A bailiff may also guard prisoners when they appear in court. <u>Causal</u> implies a cause or having to do with cause and effect. <u>Prima facie</u> is evidence that is sufficient to prove or establish a fact unless contrary evidence is presented. Evidence that is believable is referred to as <u>credible evidence</u>. If a defendant was somewhere else at the time a crime was committed, the defendant is said to have an <u>alibi</u>. <u>Pendente lite</u> is a Latin term meaning pending litigation or during the time the case is in court.

A person who has no interest in a case but is called in by the judge to give advice regarding some matter of law is an <u>amicus curiae</u>. An amicus curiae is also referred to as a friend of the court. After all evidence in a case is presented, counsel for each party gives speeches called <u>closing arguments</u>. In the closing arguments, counsel states his or her side of a case in an effort to persuade the jury to decide the case in favor of his or her client. The <u>burden of proof</u>, or the proving of the facts that are disputed, is usually the duty of the plaintiff. In other words, the plaintiff must prove that the defendant is in the wrong or guilty before the jury will return a verdict for the plaintiff.

The <u>charge to the jury</u> is given by the judge. When giving the charge to the jury, the judge instructs the jury as to the rules of law they must follow in their <u>deliberations</u>. The deliberations consist of the jury weighing and examining all the evidence in the case. During the course of the trial or deliberations, the jury may be <u>sequestered</u> from the public. Among the things that must be considered by the jury is which party has the greater weight of evidence, or the <u>preponderance of evidence</u>. This does not mean the greater number of witnesses but rather the evidence that carries the most weight. In a civil case, the verdict of the jury will be in favor of the party having the preponderance of evidence.

TRANSCRIBING FROM DICTATION

Directions: This dictation emphasizes and reinforces the legal terms and definitions you have studied. Listen carefully to the pronunciation of each of the legal terms. Unless otherwise directed, use a 70-space line (typewriter) or 1-inch margins (computer) and double spacing. Correct all errors. Follow one of the procedures below.

Keyboarding Procedure
Using the cassette from Lesson 8, Part B, transcribe the dictation directly at your typewriter or computer.

Shorthand Procedure
Using the cassette from Lesson 8, Part B, take the dictation using your shorthand system and then transcribe from your shorthand notes on your typewriter or computer.

When you have finished transcribing Part B of the practice dictation, check your transcript with the printed copy. If you made any mistakes in the transcription, you should practice those words several times before going on to Evaluation 4.

CHECKLIST
I have completed the following for Lesson 8:

	Part A, Date	Part B, Date	Submitted to Instructor Yes	No
Terminology and Definitions				
Self-Evaluation				
* **Keying Legal Terms**				
Words				
Sentences				
* **Transcribing from Dictation**				

When you have successfully completed all the exercises in this lesson and submitted to your instructor those requested, you are ready to proceed with Evaluation 4.

* If you are using a shorthand system, submit to your instructor your shorthand notes along with your transcript.

Evaluation No. 4   SECTION A

Directions: This dictation/transcription evaluation will test your spelling and transcription abilities on the legal terms that you studied in the two preceding lessons. Use a 5-space paragraph indention, a 70-space line (typewriter) or 1-inch margins (computer), and double spacing unless otherwise instructed. Correct all errors. Follow one of the procedures below.

Keyboarding Procedure

Using the cassette from Evaluation 4, transcribe the dictation directly at your typewriter or computer.

Shorthand Procedure

Using the cassette from Evaluation 4, take the dictation using your shorthand system and then transcribe from your shorthand notes on your typewriter or computer.

Sections B and C are available from your instructor.

Lesson 9

Litigation—Verdicts and Judgments

"A matter which has been decided is considered true."
—Legal Maxim

Verdicts by a jury and judgments by the presiding judge involve certain basic legal terminology with which all nonlawyer personnel should be familiar. The terminology in this lesson covers the most common types of verdicts and judgments. Upon successful completion of the exercises, you should be able to spell, pronounce, define, and transcribe correctly the litigation terms that are presented.

Part A TERMINOLOGY AND DEFINITIONS

Directions: Study the terms, pronunciations, and definitions until you are thoroughly familiar with them. In order to complete this lesson successfully, you must understand the meaning and usage of all the legal terms presented. If you are using shorthand, write your shorthand outline for each legal term in your shorthand notebook or on your shorthand machine.

Legal Term	Pronunciation	Definition
1. opinion	ə-ˈpin-yən	A statement by a judge that gives the reasons for the decision made in a case.
2. advisement	əd-ˈvīz-mənt	The consideration and thought that a judge gives a case before a decision is made. The case is said to be under advisement.
3. dictum	ˈdik-təm	Latin. An authoritative opinion by a judge on points other than the actual issue in the case.
4. per curiam	pər ˈkur-ē-äm	Latin. By the court. Indicates an opinion by the entire court, such as the court of appeals or the supreme court.
5. res judicata	ˈrēz jüd-i-ˈkät-ə	Latin. A thing decided. Something that has been decided in a court of law.
6. judgment	ˈjəj-mənt	The decision of the court. (See Figure 9-1, page 127.)
7. judgment by default	ˈjəj-mənt bī di-ˈfȯlt	A judgment given against a party in a suit who fails to make an appearance in court. If you do not appear in court, the case will not be decided in your favor. Sometimes referred to as a default judgment.
8. verdict	ˈvər-dikt	The decision of a jury on a case submitted to it for determination.
9. polling the jury	ˈpōl-iŋ thə ˈjür-ē	After the foreman or forewoman presents the verdict of the jury to the court, each juror may be asked to state what his or her individual verdict is in the case and if he or she agrees with the verdict as presented to the court.

10. hung jury	hən 'jür-ē	A jury that cannot reach a verdict.
11. exonerate	ig-'zän-ə-rāt	To prove or declare a person innocent of the charges made against him or her.
12. acquittal	ə-'kwit-l	The verdict that declares one innocent of a crime.
13. guilty	'gil-tē	Convicted of committing a crime. Not innocent.

FIGURE 9-1 A Judgment

Original - Court
1st copy - Plaintiff
2nd copy - Defendant

STATE OF MICHIGAN 30th JUDICIAL CIRCUIT	JUDGMENT Civil	CASE NO. 92-00846

Court address   Court telephone no.
2nd Floor, City Hall, Lansing, Michigan 48933   (517) 555-0650

Plaintiff(s)
Amanda and Blake Hobbs

v.

Defendant(s)
Dorothy Benson, John and Mary Doe

Joshua C. Anderton (P 48921)
688 S. Capitol Avenue, Suite 11
Lansing, Michigan 48933
(517) 555-1664

Plaintiff/Attorney

In pro per

Defendant/Attorney

☒ **JUDGMENT**

For: Amanda and Blake Hobbs

Against: Dorothy Benson, John and

Mary Doe

☒ After trial   ☐ Consent
☐ Non appearance default

☐ **DISMISSAL**

☐ Without prejudice   ☒ With prejudice

ORDER OF JUDGMENT

Damages $ 1,087.00   Other conditions, if any:
Interest $ 32.00
Costs $ 61.00
Other (specify) $ _____
          $ _____
Judgment $ 1,180.00
This judgment will earn interest at current statutory rates.

☐ A note or other written evidence of indebtedness has been filed with the clerk for cancellation.

☒ Approved as to form, notice of entry waived.

IT IS ORDERED that this judgment is granted.

August 15, 1997
Judgment date

Joshua C. Anderton (P 48921)
XXXXXX/Attorney

Tomas Rodriguez
XXXXXXXJudge/XXXXXXX
Dorothy Benson
Defendant/XXXXXXX

ENTRY, NOTICE OF JUDGMENT AND CERTIFICATE OF MAILING

This judgment has been entered and will be final unless within 21 days of the judgment date a motion for a new trial or an appeal is filed. Satisfaction of the judgment may be made by payment to the clerk of the entire amount of the judgment, or by filing a satisfaction signed by either the party for whom judgment was rendered or their attorney.

I certify that copies of this judgment and notice were served upon the parties and/or their attorneys by ordinary mail.

August 18, 1997
Date of mailing

Lois McMahon
Deputy Court Clerk

DC 10 (6/86) **JUDGMENT, CIVIL**   MCR 2.601, 2.602, 2.603

COURT

Self-Evaluation A   TERMINOLOGY AND DEFINITION RECALL

Directions: In the Answers column, write the letter from Column 1 that represents the word or phrase that best matches each item in Column 2. After you have completed this self-evaluation, check your answers with the key on page 495. If you have any incorrect answers, restudy the definitions for those terms before going on with this lesson. Then unless otherwise directed, submit this self-evaluation to your instructor.

Column 1

a. acquittal

b. advisement

c. dictum

d. exonerate

e. guilty

f. hung jury

g. judgment

h. judgment by default

i. opinion

j. per curiam

k. polling the jury

l. res gestae

m. res judicata

n. verdict

Column 2

1. To prove or declare a person innocent of the charges made against him or her.

2. The consideration and thought that a judge gives a case before a decision is made.

3. An authoritative opinion by a judge on points other than the actual issue involved in the case.

4. A Latin term that means a thing decided or something that has been decided in a court of law.

5. The asking of each individual juror what that juror's verdict is in the case.

6. The decision of the court.

7. The decision of the jury on a case submitted to it for determination.

8. The verdict in a case when a person is convicted of a crime.

9. The verdict that declares one innocent of a crime.

10. A judgment given against a person who fails to make an appearance in court.

11. A Latin term that means by the court and indicates an opinion by the entire court.

12. A jury that cannot reach a verdict.

13. A statement by a judge that gives the reasons for the decision made in a case.

Answers

1. _____

2. _____

3. _____

4. _____

5. _____

6. _____

7. _____

8. _____

9. _____

10. _____

11. _____

12. _____

13. _____

KEYING LEGAL TERMS

Directions: Unless otherwise instructed, use a 70-space line (typewriter) or 1-inch margins (computer) and double spacing. Correct all errors. Follow one of the procedures below.

WORDS

Keyboarding Procedure
On your typewriter or computer, key the following words at least two times, concentrating on the correct spelling and pronunciation.

Shorthand Procedure
On your typewriter or computer, key the following words once, concentrating on the correct spelling and pronunciation. Then write the shorthand outline for each word in your shorthand notebook or on your shorthand machine. Transcribe from the shorthand outlines one time on your typewriter or computer.

opinion	advisement	dictum
per curiam	res judicata	judgment
judgment by default	verdict	polling the jury
hung jury	exonerate	acquittal
guilty		

SENTENCES

Keyboarding Procedure
Key each of the following sentences one time on your typewriter or computer. Concentrate on the correct spelling and pronunciation of each underlined legal term.

Shorthand Procedure
Write the correct shorthand outlines for the following sentences in your shorthand notebook or on your shorthand machine. Transcribe from your shorthand outlines one time on your typewriter or computer.

These sentences will be used for practice dictation on the cassettes.

If a judge hears a case instead of a jury, the judge may give an opinion that gives the reasons for the decision made in a case. Before rendering an opinion, the court takes the case under consideration and thought, which is referred to as taking the case under advisement. Sometimes a judge will give an opinion on points other than the actual issue involved in the case. This authoritative opinion is called a dictum. When the court of appeals or the Supreme Court gives an opinion and the opinion represents the opinion of the entire court rather than just one judge, it is referred to as per curiam. Per curiam can also refer to an opinion written by the chief justice or presiding judge of the court.

Res judicata is a Latin term meaning a thing decided or something that has been decided in a court of law. The decision of the court is a judgment. A judgment that is rendered because one of the parties failed to appear at the time specified by the court is a judgment by default. If you fail to appear in court, the case will not be decided in your favor.

The verdict is the decision of a jury on a case submitted to them for their determination. Polling the jury is asking each juror if the verdict announced by the foreman or forewoman is his or her individual verdict. The attorney for the losing party will usually request that a jury be polled, anticipating that there may be one juror who will waiver on the verdict when each has to stand and announce that the verdict is his or her own verdict. A jury that cannot reach a verdict is referred to as a hung jury.

To exonerate means to prove or declare a person innocent of the charges. A verdict of acquittal proves or declares a person innocent of the charges. If the verdict of the jury is guilty, then the jury is convinced that the person so charged did commit the crime.

TRANSCRIBING FROM DICTATION

Directions: This dictation emphasizes and reinforces the legal terms and definitions you have studied. Listen carefully to the pronunciation of each of the legal terms. Unless otherwise directed, use a 70-space line (typewriter) or 1-inch margins (computer) and double spacing. Correct all errors. Follow one of the procedures below.

Keyboarding Procedure
Using the cassette from Lesson 9, Part A, transcribe the dictation directly at your typewriter or computer.

Shorthand Procedure
Using the cassette from Lesson 9, Part A, take the dictation using your shorthand system and then transcribe from your shorthand notes on your typewriter or computer.

When you have finished transcribing Part A of the practice dictation, check your transcript with the printed copy. If you made any mistakes in the transcription, you should practice those words several times before going on.

Part B   TERMINOLOGY AND DEFINITIONS

Directions: Study the terms, pronunciations, and definitions until you are thoroughly familiar with them. In order to complete this lesson successfully, you must understand the meaning and usage of all the legal terms presented. If you are using shorthand, write your shorthand outline for each legal term in your shorthand notebook or on your shorthand machine.

Legal Term	Pronunciation	Definition
1. nonsuit	'nän-'süt	A judgment that terminates a lawsuit because the plaintiff is unable or refuses to prove the case.
2. adjudge	ə-'jəj	To decide, settle, or sentence by law.
3. decision	di-'sizh-ən	The judgment of the court rendered in a case brought before it.
4. decree	di-'krē	An official decision or order made by a court or a judge.
5. interlocutory decree	int-ər-'läk-yə-tor-e di-'krē	A temporary decree. Not final.
6. final decree	'fīn-l di-'krē	A final decision of the court that resolves all issues in a case.
7. decree nisi	di-'krē 'nī-sī	Latin. A decree that will take effect unless it is successfully contested.
8. order	'órd-ər	A rule of law. A command issued in writing by a court. Not a judgment. (See Figure 9-2, page 134.)
9. restraining order	ri-'strā-niŋ 'órd-ər	An order issued by the court to prevent someone from doing something until the court decides whether or not to issue an injunction.

10. dismiss	dis-ʹmis	To refuse to consider a case in court. Also, during the court proceedings, either counsel may make a motion to dismiss a case.
11. dismissal without prejudice	dis-ʹmis-əl with-ʹaůt ʹprej-əd-əs	The case is dismissed, but the plaintiff is not prevented from suing again on the same cause of action.
12. dismissal with prejudice	dis-ʹmis-əl with ʹprej-əd-əs	The case is dismissed, and the plaintiff cannot sue again on the same cause of action.
13. stare decisis	ʹster-ē di-ʹsī-səs	Latin. Let the decision stand. Pertains to the policy of a court to follow precedent when deciding cases.
14. sine die	ʹsī-ni dī	Latin. Without day. The final adjournment or dismissal of a case against a defendant.

FIGURE 9-2 An Order

Approved, SCAO

Original - Return
1st copy - Witness
2nd copy - File

| STATE OF MICHIGAN XXXXXXXXXX 30th JUDICIAL CIRCUIT XXXXXXXXXXXXXX | SUBPOENA ORDER TO APPEAR | CASE NO. 92-00846 |

Court address
2nd Floor, City Hall, Lansing, Michigan 48933

Court telephone no.
(517) 555-0650

Plaintiff(s)
☐ People of the State of Michigan
☒ Amanda and Blake Hobbs

V.

Defendant(s)
Dorothy Benson, John and Mary Doe

☒ CIVIL   ☐ CRIMINAL

Charge

☐ PROBATE   In the matter of

In the Name of the People of the State of Michigan. TO: Dorothy Benson
55 Sandalwood Avenue
Okemos, Michigan 48864

YOU ARE ORDERED to appear personally at the time and place stated: You may be required to appear from time to time and day to day until you are excused.

Appear at:
1. ☒ The court address above   ☐ Other:

| Day 2. Friday | Date August 15, 1997 | Time 9:30 a.m. |

YOU ARE ALSO ORDERED to:

3. ☒ Testify at trial/examination/hearing.

4. ☐ Produce the following items: _____

_____

_____   ☐ Injunction attached

5. ☐ *Testify as to your assets, and bring with you the items listed in line 4 above.
*Affidavit on reverse side must be completed for judgment debtor examination.

6. ☐ Testify at deposition.

7. ☐ Other: _____

Person requesting subpoena
8. Joshua C. Anderton (P48921)

Telephone
(517) 555-1664

Address
688 S. Capitol Avenue, Suite 11, Lansing, Michigan

City   State

Zip
48933

FAILURE TO APPEAR AT STATED TIME AND PLACE MAY SUBJECT YOU TO PENALTY FOR CONTEMPT OF COURT.

July 25, 1997
Date

Tomas Rodriguez   (P 48921)
Issuing Judge/XXXXXXXXXX   Bar no,

JUDGMENT DEBTOR JUDICIAL ENDORSEMENT

Date   Judge

Court use only

☐ Served   ☐ Not served

MC 11 (10/85) **SUBPOENA, Order To Appear** MCLA 600.1455, 600.1701, 600.6110; MSA 27A.1455, 27A.1701, 27A .6110, MCR 2.506

RETURN

Self-Evaluation B   TERMINOLOGY AND DEFINITION RECALL

Directions: In the Answers column at the right of each statement, write the letter that represents the word or group of words that correctly completes the statement. After you have completed this self-evaluation, check your answers with the key on page 495. If you have any incorrect answers, restudy the definitions for those terms before going on with this lesson. Then unless otherwise directed, submit this self-evaluation to your instructor.

Answers

1. A Latin term that means let the decision stand and pertains to the policy of a court to follow precedent when deciding cases is (a) stare decisis, (b) sine die, (c) decree nisi.

   1. _____

2. The judgment of the court that is rendered in a case brought before it is a/an (a) order, (b) decision, (c) stare decisis.

   2. _____

3. A rule of law or a command issued in writing by a court is a/an (a) order, (b) decision, (c) decree nisi.

   3. _____

4. An official decision or order made by a court or a judge is a/an (a) interlocutory decree, (b) injunction, (c) decree.

   4. _____

5. A judgment that terminates a lawsuit because the plaintiff is unable or refuses to prove the case is a (a) nonsuit, (b) judgment by default, (c) dismissal with prejudice.

   5. _____

6. To refuse to consider a case in court is to (a) order the case, (b) dismiss the case, (c) adjudge the case.

   6. _____

7. A dismissal that does not prevent the plaintiff from suing again on the same cause of action is a (a) restraining order, (b) dismissal with prejudice, (c) dismissal without prejudice.

   7. _____

8. A dismissal stating that a plaintiff cannot sue again on the same cause of action is a (a) restraining order, (b) dismissal without prejudice, (c) dismissal with prejudice.

   8. _____

9. The adjournment or dismissal of a case in which no future date is set to hear it is a/an (a) interlocutory decree, (b) sine die, (c) nonsuit.

   9. _____

10. An order issued by the court to prevent someone from doing something until the court decides whether or not to issue an injunction is a/an (a) restraining order, (b) order, (c) final decree.

    10. _____

11. A final decision of the court that resolves all issues in a case is a/an (a) interlocutory decree, (b) final decree, (c) decree nisi.

    11. _____

12. A decree that will take effect unless it is successfully contested is a/an (a) final decree, (b) interlocutory decree, (c) decree nisi.

    12. _____

13. A temporary decree is a/an (a) adjudge, (b) decree nisi, (c) interlocutory decree.

    13. _____

14. To decide, settle, or sentence by law is to (a) decree, (b) adjudge, (c) dismiss.

    14. _____

KEYING LEGAL TERMS

Directions: Unless otherwise instructed, use a 70-space line (typewriter) or 1-inch margins (computer) and double spacing. Correct all errors. Follow one of the procedures below.

WORDS

Keyboarding Procedure
On your typewriter or computer, key the following words at least two times, concentrating on the correct spelling and pronunciation.

Shorthand Procedure
On your typewriter or computer, key the following words once, concentrating on the correct spelling and pronunciation. Then write the shorthand outline for each word in your shorthand notebook or on your shorthand machine. Transcribe from the shorthand outlines one time on your typewriter or computer.

nonsuit	adjudge	decision
decree	interlocutory decree	final decree
decree nisi	order	restraining order
dismiss	dismissal without prejudice	dismissal with prejudice
stare decisis	sine die	

SENTENCES

Keyboarding Procedure
Key each of the following sentences one time on your typewriter or computer. Concentrate on the correct spelling and pronunciation of each underlined legal term.

Shorthand Procedure
Write the correct shorthand outlines for the following sentences in your shorthand notebook or on your shorthand machine. Transcribe from your shorthand outlines one time on your typewriter or computer.

These sentences will be used for practice dictation on the cassettes.

Nonsuit is a judgment that terminates a lawsuit in the defendant's favor because the plaintiff is unable or refuses to prove the case. To adjudge a case is to decide or settle it by law. A decision is a judgment of the court rendered in a case brought before it.

A decree is an official decision or order made by a court or judge. A decree is final and is made when the case is heard in court. The words judgment and decree are sometimes used synonymously. An interlocutory decree is a temporary decree that is issued prior to a final decree. The final decree is a final decision of the court that resolves all the issues in a case. A decree nisi is a temporary decree that will be made final on motion unless it is successfully contested.

An order is a rule of law or a command issued in writing by the court. A restraining order is an order issued by the court to prevent a person from doing something until the court decides whether or not to issue an injunction. If someone is harassing you, you can get a restraining order to prevent further harassment until the case is decided in court.

To dismiss an action or a suit is to refuse to consider a case in court. A case that has no basis in law will be dismissed. A dismissal without prejudice permits the plaintiff to sue again on the same cause of action, whereas a dismissal with prejudice prevents the plaintiff from suing again on the same cause of action.

Stare decisis is a Latin term meaning let the decision stand. Stare decisis pertains to the policy of a court to follow precedent when deciding cases. **Sine die** is a Latin term meaning without day. When a case is adjourned sine die, the case is dismissed and no future date is set to hear it.

TRANSCRIBING FROM DICTATION

Directions: This dictation emphasizes and reinforces the legal terms and definitions you have studied. Listen carefully to the pronunciation of each of the legal terms. Unless otherwise directed, use a 70-space line (typewriter) or 1-inch margins (computer) and double spacing. Correct all errors. Follow one of the procedures below.

Keyboarding Procedure
Using the cassette from Lesson 9, Part B, transcribe the dictation directly at your typewriter or computer.

Shorthand Procedure
Using the cassette from Lesson 9, Part B, take the dictation using your shorthand system and then transcribe from your shorthand notes on your typewriter or computer.

When you have finished transcribing Part B of the practice dictation, check your transcript with the printed copy. If you made any mistakes in the transcription, you should practice those words several times before going on to Lesson 10.

CHECKLIST
I have completed the following for Lesson 9:

	Part A, Date	Part B, Date	Submitted to Instructor Yes	No
Terminology and Definitions				
Self-Evaluation				
* Keying Legal Terms				
Words				
Sentences				
* Transcribing from Dictation				

When you have successfully completed all the exercises in this lesson and submitted to your instructor those requested, you are ready to proceed with Lesson 10.

* If you are using a shorthand system, submit to your instructor your shorthand notes along with your transcript.

Lesson 10

Litigation—Judgments and Appeals

"Extreme justice is extreme injustice."
—Legal Maxim

Litigation activities in the courtroom usually terminate in a judgment in favor of one of the parties to the action. If the party against whom judgment is rendered is not satisfied with the outcome of the case, that party may file an appeal to a higher court to have the case reviewed. The appellate court may reverse the decision of the lower court, uphold the decision, modify the decision, or order a new trial. Additional terminology dealing with judgments and terms involved in the appellate process are introduced in this lesson. Upon successful completion of the following exercises, you should be able to spell, pronounce, define, and transcribe correctly the litigation terms that are presented.

Part A TERMINOLOGY AND DEFINITIONS

Directions: Study the terms, pronunciations, and definitions until you are thoroughly familiar with them. In order to complete this lesson successfully, you must understand the meaning and usage of all the legal terms presented. If you are using shorthand, write your shorthand outline for each legal term in your shorthand notebook or on your shorthand machine.

Legal Term	Pronunciation	Definition
1. nunc pro tunc	nənk prō tənk	Latin. Now for then. A decision or an order of the court that is retroactive.
2. status quo	ˈstāt-əs kwō	Latin. The way things are or their existing state at a given time.
3. award	ə-ˈwȯrd	To grant or to give. To decide or settle by law.
4. damages	ˈdam-ijs	An amount of money awarded by a court to one who was injured by another.
5. compensatory damages	kəm-ˈpen-sə-tōr-ē ˈdam-ijs	Damages awarded that are equal to and no more than the amount of the actual loss. The plaintiff would be awarded damages to compensate for the plaintiff's actual loss and nothing more.
6. redress	ri-ˈdres	To correct a wrong. To provide satisfaction or relief for one who has been injured by another.
7. injunction	in-ˈjəŋ-shən	A writ issued by a court commanding a person to do or not to do some act. If someone is using your property without your permission, you could get an injunction to prevent that person from using your property.

8. enjoin	in-ʹjoin	To require a person by a writ of injunction to do or not to do a specified act. If you get an injunction against a person to prevent him or her from using your property, then that person is enjoined from using your property.
9. stay	stā	A delay or stopping of a legal proceeding by the court.
10. supersedeas	sü-pər-ʹsēd-ē-əs	Latin. A writ issued by a judge to stay a legal proceeding. It supersedes a prior writ or order.
11. suppress	sə-ʹpres	To hold back or stop something. If the evidence or the outcome of a case is suppressed, it is not made known to the public.
12. conclusion of fact	kən-ʹklü-zhən əv fakt	An assumption or a conclusion based on the facts as presented in a case.
13. conclusion of law	kən-ʹklü-zhən əv lȯ	An assumption or a conclusion arrived at by applying the law to the facts as presented in a case.

Self-Evaluation A   TERMINOLOGY AND DEFINITION RECALL

Directions: In the Answers column at the right of each statement, write the letter that represents the word or group of words that correctly completes the statement. After you have completed this self-evaluation, check your answers with the key on page 495–496. If you have any incorrect answers, restudy the definitions for those terms before going on with this lesson. Then unless otherwise directed, submit this self-evaluation to your instructor.

Answers

1. An assumption or a conclusion arrived at by applying the law to the facts as presented in a case is a (a) conclusion of law, (b) conclusion of fact, (c) nunc pro tunc.   **1.** _____

2. A writ issued by a judge to stay a legal proceeding is a/an (a) injunction, (b) award, (c) supersedeas.   **2.** _____

3. A delay or stopping by the court of a legal proceeding is a/an (a) enjoin, (b) stay, (c) suppress.   **3.** _____

4. A writ issued by a judge commanding a person to do or not to do a specified act is a/an (a) stay, (b) redress, (c) injunction.   **4.** _____

5. The way things are or their existing state at a given time is (a) status quo, (b) supersedeas, (c) conclusion of fact.   **5.** _____

6. A decision or an order of the court that is retroactive and means now for then is (a) nunc pro tunc, (b) status quo, (c) supersedeas.   **6.** _____

7. To grant, to give, to decide or settle by law is to (a) nunc pro tunc, (b) award, (c) enjoin.   **7.** _____

8. An assumption or a conclusion based on the facts in a case is (a) conclusion of law, (b) redress, (c) conclusion of fact.   **8.** _____

9. To hold or stop something is to (a) stay, (b) suppress, (c) award.   **9.** _____

10. An amount of money awarded by a court to one who was injured by another is called (a) damages, (b) award, (c) redress.   **10.** _____

11. To require or forbid an act to be or not to be done is to (a) redress, (b) stay, (c) enjoin.   **11.** _____

12. To correct a wrong or to provide satisfaction or relief for one who has been injured by another is to (a) award, (b) redress, (c) enjoin.   **12.** _____

13. Damages that are equal to and no more than the amount of the actual loss are (a) supersedeas, (b) status quo, (c) compensatory damages.   **13.** _____

KEYING LEGAL TERMS

Directions: Unless otherwise instructed, use a 70-space line (typewriter) or 1-inch margins (computer) and double spacing. Correct all errors. Follow one of the procedures below.

WORDS

Keyboarding Procedure
On your typewriter or computer, key the following words at least two times, concentrating on the correct spelling and pronunciation.

Shorthand Procedure
On your typewriter or computer, key the following words once, concentrating on the correct spelling and pronunciation. Then write the shorthand outline for each word in your shorthand notebook or on your shorthand machine. Transcribe from the shorthand outlines one time on your typewriter or computer.

nunc pro tunc	status quo	award
damages	compensatory damages	redress
injunction	enjoin	stay
supersedeas	suppress	conclusion of fact
conclusion of law		

SENTENCES

Keyboarding Procedure
Key each of the following sentences one time on your typewriter or computer. Concentrate on the correct spelling and pronunciation of each underlined legal term.

Shorthand Procedure
Write the correct shorthand outlines for the following sentences in your shorthand notebook or on your shorthand machine. Transcribe from your shorthand outlines one time on your typewriter or computer.

These sentences will be used for practice dictation on the cassettes.

Nunc pro tunc is a Latin term meaning now for then. Nunc pro tunc applies to a decision or an order of the court that is retroactive. The Latin term referring to the way things are or their existing state at a given time is status quo. The status quo refers to the way things were preceding a cause of action.

Award means to grant, to give, or to decide by law. An amount of money awarded by a court to one who was injured by another is damages. Damages awarded that are equal to and no more than the amount of actual loss are called compensatory damages. Redress is to correct a wrong or to provide satisfaction or relief for one who has been injured by another. The awarding of compensatory damages by a jury is redress for the plaintiff.

A writ issued by a court commanding a person to do or not to do some act is an injunction. Enjoin means to require or forbid an act to be or not to be done. Therefore, a writ of injunction enjoins a person to perform or not to perform some act. A stay is a delay or a stopping by the court of a legal proceeding. For example, a stay of execution delays the execution of a person who is sentenced to death for a crime. Supersedeas is the Latin name for a writ issued by a judge to stay a legal proceeding.

To suppress something is to hold it back or to stop it. Evidence that is suppressed by the court cannot be used in a case. Also, evidence or the outcome of a case may be suppressed from the public. A conclusion of fact is an assumption or a conclusion based on the facts in a case, whereas a conclusion of law is an assumption or a conclusion arrived at by applying the law to the facts as presented in a case. For example, it is a conclusion of fact to state that an accident occurred, but it is a conclusion of law to state who was at fault.

TRANSCRIBING FROM DICTATION

Directions: This dictation emphasizes and reinforces the legal terms and definitions you have studied. Listen carefully to the pronunciation of each of the legal terms. Unless otherwise directed, use a 70-space line (typewriter) or 1-inch margins (computer) and double spacing. Correct all errors. Follow one of the procedures below.

Keyboarding Procedure
Using the cassette from Lesson 10, Part A, transcribe the dictation directly at your typewriter or computer.

Shorthand Procedure
Using the cassette from Lesson 10, Part A, take the dictation using your shorthand system and then transcribe from your shorthand notes on your typewriter or computer.

When you have finished transcribing Part A of the practice dictation, check your transcript with the printed copy. If you made any mistakes in the transcription, you should practice those words several times before going on.

Part B TERMINOLOGY AND DEFINITIONS

Directions: Study the terms, pronunciations, and definitions until you are thoroughly familiar with them. In order to complete this lesson successfully, you must understand the meaning and usage of all the legal terms presented. If you are using shorthand, write your shorthand outline for each legal term in your shorthand notebook or on your shorthand machine.

Legal Term	Pronunciation	Definition
1. appeal	ə-ˈpēl	To request an appellate court to review a case that was tried in a lower court.
2. appellant	ə-ˈpel-ənt	One who appeals a decision or verdict.
3. respondent	ri-ˈspän-dənt	The party who must contend against an appeal. Also known as an appellee.
4. brief	brēf	A statement filed with an appellate court that gives the facts and points of law on which the appeal is based.
5. review	rē-ˈvyü	An examination by an appellate court of a case that was tried in a lower court.
6. reverse	rē-ˈvərs	To repeal or change to the opposite. The appellate court may reverse the decision of a lower court.
7. abrogate	ˈab-rə-gāt	To abolish or do away with something, such as an order issued by a lower court.
8. remittitur	ri-ˈmit-ə-tər	Latin. The sending back of a case by the appellate court to a lower court. Also, the plaintiff returning damages awarded in a case that were in excess of what the plaintiff requested.
9. mandamus	ˈman-ˈdā-məs	Latin. A writ issued by a higher court to a lower court commanding or mandating that a certain thing be done.

10. rehearing	rē-'hir-iŋ	A retrial of a case in the court that heard it the first time in an effort to correct an error or omission.
11. trial de novo	trīl dē 'nō-vō	A new trial of a case conducted by an appellate court as though there had been no other trial.
12. certiorari	sər-shə-'rar-ē	Latin. An order or a writ of review or inquiry used in an appellate proceeding.
13. error coram vobis	'er-ər 'kō-ram 'vō-bis	Latin. A writ issued by an appellate court to a lower court stating that an error was made in the proceedings before you. An error coram vobis is a basis for an appellate court to reverse a decision made by a lower court.
14. error coram nobis	'er-ər 'kō-ram 'nō-bis	Latin. A writ issued by an appellate court stating that an error was committed in the proceeding before us. This writ directs the lower court to consider issues of fact that had not been considered before.

Self-Evaluation B   TERMINOLOGY AND DEFINITION RECALL

Directions: In the Answers column, write the letter from Column 1 that represents the word or phrase that best matches each item in Column 2. After you have completed this self-evaluation, check your answers with the key on page 496. If you have any incorrect answers, restudy the definitions for those terms before going on with this lesson. Then unless otherwise directed, submit this self-evaluation to your instructor.

Column 1	Column 2	Answers
a. abrogate	1. To repeal or change to the opposite.	1. _____
b. appeal	2. To abolish or do away with something, such as an order issued by a lower court.	2. _____
c. appellant		
d. brief	3. A writ issued by an appellate court stating that an error was committed in the proceeding before us.	3. _____
e. certiorari	4. An order or a writ of review or inquiry used in an appellate proceeding.	4. _____
f. error coram nobis		
g. error coram vobis	5. The party who must contend against an appeal.	5. _____
h. mandamus	6. A new trial of a case conducted by an appellate court as though there had been no other trial.	6. _____
i. rehearing		
j. remittitur	7. A writ issued by a higher court to a lower court commanding that a certain thing be done.	7. _____
k. respondent	8. The request for an appellate court to review a case that was tried in a lower court.	8. _____
l. reverse		
m. review	9. A retrial of a case in the court that heard it the first time in an effort to correct an error or omission.	9. _____
n. supersedeas	10. One who appeals a decision or verdict.	10. _____
o. trial de novo	11. The sending back of a case by the appellate court or the plaintiff returning damages awarded in a case that were in excess of what the plaintiff requested.	11. _____
	12. A statement filed with an appellate court that gives the facts and points of law on which the appeal is based.	12. _____
	13. An examination by an appellate court of a case that was tried in a lower court.	13. _____
	14. A writ issued by an appellate court to a lower court that states that an error was made in the proceedings before you.	14. _____

KEYING LEGAL TERMS

Directions: Unless otherwise instructed, use a 70-space line (typewriter) or 1-inch margins (computer) and double spacing. Correct all errors. Follow one of the procedures below.

WORDS

Keyboarding Procedure
On your typewriter or computer, key the following words at least two times, concentrating on the correct spelling and pronunciation.

Shorthand Procedure
On your typewriter or computer, key the following words once, concentrating on the correct spelling and pronunciation. Then write the shorthand outline for each word in your shorthand notebook or on your shorthand machine. Transcribe from the shorthand outlines one time on your typewriter or computer.

appeal	appellant	respondent
brief	review	reverse
abrogate	remittitur	mandamus
rehearing	trial de novo	certiorari
error coram vobis	error coram nobis	

SENTENCES

Keyboarding Procedure
Key each of the following sentences one time on your typewriter or computer. Concentrate on the correct spelling and pronunciation of each underlined legal term.

Shorthand Procedure
Write the correct shorthand outlines for the following sentences in your shorthand notebook or on your shorthand machine. Transcribe from your shorthand outlines one time on your typewriter or computer.

These sentences will be used for practice dictation on the cassettes.

An appeal is a request to an appellate court to review a case that was tried in a lower court. The party who appeals a decision or a verdict is called the appellant. The respondent is the party who must contend against an appeal. Each party in the case must file a brief with the appellate court. The appellant's brief gives the facts and points of law on which the appeal is based. The respondent's brief contests the facts and points of law stated in the appellant's brief. The appellate court will review, or reexamine, the case based upon the information filed in the brief by the appellant's counsel.

An appeals court may reverse a judgment, sentence, or decree of a lower court; or the appeals court may order a new trial. The appeals court may abrogate, or abolish, an order by a lower court. Remittitur means a remission or surrender. Remittitur is involved in cases that are sent back by an appellate court to a lower court. Remittitur also refers to the plaintiff returning damages awarded that were in excess of what the plaintiff requested. This is usually done upon an order by the court.

A mandamus is a writ issued by a higher court to a lower court commanding that a certain thing be done, such as a rehearing, or retrial, of the issues. A new trial held in an appellate court is called a trial de novo.

Certiorari is an order or a writ of review or inquiry used in an appellate proceeding. If the appellate court needs more information on a case, a writ of certiorari or review may be issued to the lower court to obtain the required information.

An error coram vobis is a writ of error issued by an appellate court that an error was made in the proceedings before you. An error coram nobis is a writ issued by an appellate court stating that an error was committed in the proceeding before us.

TRANSCRIBING FROM DICTATION

Directions: This dictation emphasizes and reinforces the legal terms and definitions you have studied. Listen carefully to the pronunciation of each of the legal terms. Unless otherwise directed, use a 70-space line (typewriter) or 1-inch margins (computer) and double spacing. Correct all errors. Follow one of the procedures below.

Keyboarding Procedure
Using the cassette from Lesson 10, Part B, transcribe the dictation directly at your typewriter or computer.

Shorthand Procedure
Using the cassette from Lesson 10, Part B, take the dictation using your shorthand system and then transcribe from your shorthand notes on your typewriter or computer.

When you have finished transcribing Part B of the practice dictation, check your transcript with the printed copy. If you made any mistakes in the transcription, you should practice those words several times before going on to Evaluation 5.

CHECKLIST
I have completed the following for Lesson 10:

	Part A, Date	Part B, Date	Submitted to Instructor Yes	No
Terminology and Definitions				
Self-Evaluation				
* Keying Legal Terms				
Words				
Sentences				
* Transcribing from Dictation				

When you have successfully completed all the exercises in this lesson and submitted to your instructor those requested, you are ready to proceed with Evaluation 5.

* If you are using a shorthand system, submit to your instructor your shorthand notes along with your transcript.

Evaluation No. 5 **SECTION A**

Directions: This dictation/transcription evaluation will test your transcription abilities on the legal terms that you studied in the two preceding lessons. Use a 5-space paragraph indention, a 70-space line (typewriter) or 1-inch margin (computer), and double spacing unless otherwise instructed. Correct all errors. Follow one of the procedures below.

Keyboarding Procedure

Using the cassette from Evaluation 5, transcribe the dictation directly at your typewriter or computer.

Shorthand Procedure

Using the cassette from Evaluation 5, take the dictation using your shorthand system and then transcribe from your shorthand notes on your typewriter or computer.

Sections B and C are available from your instructor.

Lesson 11

Civil Actions

"One must so use one's own rights as not to infringe upon the rights of another."

—Legal Maxim

A civil action involves a violation of an individual's legal rights. It includes all the fields of law that govern relationships between individuals, businesses, or institutions. Therefore, this lesson will cover terms that deal with civil actions in general, whereas the more specialized areas of civil actions will be presented in separate lessons. When you have successfully completed these exercises, you will be able to pronounce, define, spell, and transcribe correctly the civil law terms that are included.

Part A TERMINOLOGY AND DEFINITIONS

Directions: Study the terms, pronunciations, and definitions until you are thoroughly familiar with them. In order to complete this lesson successfully, you must understand the meaning and usage of all the legal terms presented. If you are using shorthand, write your shorthand outline for each legal term in your shorthand notebook or on your shorthand machine.

Legal Term	Pronunciation	Definition
1. civil law	′siv-əl lȯ	Law that deals with the private rights of individuals.
2. actio civilis	′ak-shē-ō si-′vil-əs	Latin. A civil action.
3. ex delicto	eks di-′likt-ō	Latin. A cause of action based on a civil wrong or tort.
4. tort	tȯrt	A civil wrong, other than a breach of contract, for which one has the right to bring a suit for recovery in a civil court.
5. tortious activity	′tȯr-shəs ak-′tiv-ət-ē	A wrongful or devious act. Tortious describes an act that results in a tort. For example, if you break someone's window, it would be a tortious activity because you could be sued to pay for the damages.
6. willful tort	′wil-fəl tȯrt	A tort that was committed intentionally and maliciously. If you intentionally damage someone's property, you have committed a willful tort.
7. tortfeasor	′tȯrt-fē-zer	One who commits a tort or a tortious activity. The person who commits a civil wrong against another is a tortfeasor.
8. replevin	ri-′plev-ən	An action to recover personal property that another is illegally possessing.
9. actio in personam	′ak-shē-ō in pər-′sän-əm	Latin. A civil action directed against a specific person.
10. grievance	′grē-vəns	A cause or basis for a complaint.
11. allegation	al-i-′gā-shən	A statement of the facts made in a pleading that one intends to prove.
12. intent	in-′tent	The purpose that one has for doing a certain thing.

Self-Evaluation A   TERMINOLOGY AND DEFINITION RECALL

Directions: In the Answers column at the right of each statement, write the letter that represents the word or group of words that correctly completes the statement. After you have completed this self-evaluation, check your answers with the key on page 496. If you have any incorrect answers, restudy the definitions for those terms before going on with this lesson. Then unless otherwise directed, submit this self-evaluation to your instructor.

Answers

1. The Latin term for a civil action is (a) ex delicto, (b) actio in personam, (c) actio civilis.   **1.** _____

2. One who commits a tortious activity is known as a/an (a) actio in personam, (b) tortfeasor, (c) ex delicto.   **2.** _____

3. A cause of action based on a civil wrong or tort is expressed in Latin as (a) ex delicto, (b) replevin, (c) actio civilis.   **3.** _____

4. An action to recover personal property that another is illegally possessing is known as (a) tortfeasor, (b) replevin, (c) intent.   **4.** _____

5. A statement of the facts made in a pleading that one intends to prove is a/an (a) intent, (b) tort, (c) allegation.   **5.** _____

6. A tort that was committed intentionally and maliciously is a/an (a) allegation, (b) tortious, (c) willful tort.   **6.** _____

7. The purpose that one has for doing a certain thing is referred to as (a) intent, (b) grievance, (c) tort.   **7.** _____

8. A wrongful or devious act is referred to as a/an (a) allegation, (b) tortious activity, (c) replevin activity.   **8.** _____

9. A cause or basis for a complaint is a/an (a) grievance, (b) actio civilis, (c) tort.   **9.** _____

10. A civil wrong, other than a breach of contract, for which one has the right to bring a suit for recovery in a civil court is a/an (a) tort, (b) allegation, (c) actio in personam.   **10.** _____

11. A Latin term that means a civil action directed against a specific person is (a) replevin, (b) actio civilis, (c) actio in personam.   **11.** _____

12. Law that deals with the private rights of individuals is called (a) ex delicto, (b) civil law, (c) replevin.   **12.** _____

KEYING LEGAL TERMS

Directions: Unless otherwise instructed, use a 70-space line (typewriter) or 1-inch margins (computer) and double spacing. Correct all errors. Follow one of the procedures below.

WORDS

Keyboarding Procedure
On your typewriter or computer, key the following words at least two times, concentrating on the correct spelling and pronunciation.

Shorthand Procedure
On your typewriter or computer, key the following words once, concentrating on the correct spelling and pronunciation. Then write the shorthand outline for each word in your shorthand notebook or on your shorthand machine. Transcribe from the shorthand outlines one time on your typewriter or computer.

civil law	actio civilis	ex delicto
tort	tortious activity	willful tort
tortfeasor	replevin	actio in personam
grievance	allegation	intent

SENTENCES

Keyboarding Procedure
Key each of the following sentences one time on your typewriter or computer. Concentrate on the correct spelling and pronunciation of each underlined legal term.

Shorthand Procedure
Write the correct shorthand outlines for the following sentences in your shorthand notebook or on your shorthand machine. Transcribe from your shorthand outlines one time on your typewriter or computer.

These sentences will be used for practice dictation on the cassettes.

Civil law is the law that deals with the private rights of individuals. Actio civilis means a civil action. An actio civilis is every action other than a criminal action. If a mechanic does not repair your car properly, you can start an actio civilis, or a civil action, against the mechanic.

Ex delicto is a cause of action based on a civil wrong or tort. An action ex delicto would be an action based upon a tort. A tort is a civil wrong, other than a breach of contract, for which one has the right to bring a suit for recovery in a civil court. A tortious activity is a wrongful or devious act. A willful tort is committed by a tortfeasor when the tortfeasor intentionally and maliciously injures another. A person who commits a tort is a tortfeasor.

Replevin is an action to recover personal property that another is illegally possessing. A replevin may be filed against a tortfeasor who takes another's property illegally. If a mechanic refuses to return your car to you, you may file a replevin against the mechanic because your car is being held illegally.

A civil action directed against a specific person is expressed in Latin as actio in personam. A civil action against a mechanic would be an actio in personam because the action is directed against a specific person. A grievance is a cause or basis for a complaint. A grievance may become the basis for an allegation in a civil action. An allegation is a statement of the facts made in a pleading that one intends to prove.

Intent is the purpose that one has for doing a certain thing. Intent is an element in the commission of a willful tort. For example, the mechanic must intend to deprive you of your car illegally to be guilty of a tort. A person committing a tortious activity has an intent of harming another and is liable to become the defendant in an actio civilis.

TRANSCRIBING FROM DICTATION

Directions: This dictation emphasizes and reinforces the legal terms and definitions you have studied. Listen carefully to the pronunciation of each of the legal terms. Unless otherwise directed, use a 70-space line (typewriter) or 1-inch margins (computer) and double spacing. Correct all errors. Follow one of the procedures below.

Keyboarding Procedure
Using the cassette from Lesson 11, Part A, transcribe the dictation directly at your typewriter or computer.

Shorthand Procedure
Using the cassette from Lesson 11, Part A, take the dictation using your shorthand system and then transcribe from your shorthand notes on your typewriter or computer.

When you have finished transcribing Part A of the practice dictation, check your transcript with the printed copy. If you made any mistakes in the transcription, you should practice those words several times before going on.

Part B TERMINOLOGY AND DEFINITIONS

Directions: Study the terms, pronunciations, and definitions until you are thoroughly familiar with them. In order to complete this lesson successfully, you must understand the meaning and usage of all the legal terms presented. If you are using shorthand, write your shorthand outline for each legal term in your shorthand notebook or on your shorthand machine.

Legal Term	Pronunciation	Definition
1. in forma pauperis	in ′fȯr-mə ′pȯ-pə-rəs	Latin. Permission granted by the court to a pauper, or poor person, to bring a suit without paying the court costs.
2. right	rīt	Something to which a person is legally entitled.
3. duty	′düt-ē	An obligation that one person has to another.
4. liability	lī-ə-′bil-ət-ē	Duty, obligation, or responsibility.
5. absolute liability	′ab-sə-lüt lī-ə-′bil-ət-ē	Liability without fault. Although due care is exercised, the nature of a person's activity may constitute a risk and harm to others. In such a case, that person would be liable for any injury and damages to another person even though no negligence was involved.
6. negligence	′neg-li-jəns	The want of due care or diligence. The failure to do something or the doing of something that an ordinary, reasonable person would or would not do.
7. contributory negligence	kən-′trib-yə-tȯr-ē ′neg-li-jəns	The negligence of the plaintiff that, together with the negligence of the defendant, caused the injury. In cases of contributory negligence, the plaintiff is not permitted to recover damages from the defendant.

8. comparative negligence	kəm-ʹpar-ət-iv ʹneg-li-jəns	A comparison of the negligence of the plaintiff and defendant. In some states, the plaintiff is permitted recovery when his or her negligence is less than that of the defendant. The amount of recovery may be decreased proportionately to the amount or degree of negligence.
9. culpable negligence	ʹkəl-pə-bəl ʹneg-li-jəns	Failure to act with due care. The person who commits culpable negligence is at fault or blamable for injuries or damages.
10. imputation of negligence	im-pyə-ʹtā-shən əv ʹneg-li-jəns	A negligent act committed by one person but chargeable to another who is responsible for the other person's acts. Thus, an employer may be held responsible for the negligence of an employee.
11. due care or diligence	dü ker ȯr ʹdil-ə-jens	As much care and attention as is required by the circumstances. The care that a reasonable person would have used in the same situation.
12. damnum absque injuria	ʹdam-nəm ʹabs-kwē in-ʹjür-ē-ə	Latin. Loss without injury. A loss that cannot be recovered in a court of law.
13. actio in rem	ʹak-shē-ō in rem	Latin. An action for the recovery of a thing possessed by another rather than an action against that person.

Self-Evaluation B   TERMINOLOGY AND DEFINITION RECALL

Directions: In the Answers column, write the legal term that is most representative of the corresponding statement. After you have completed this self-evaluation, check your answers with the key on page 496. If you have any incorrect answers, restudy the definitions for those terms before going on with this lesson. Then unless otherwise directed, submit this self-evaluation to your instructor.

Answers

1. Failure to act with due care is _____.

    1. _____

2. An obligation that one person has to another is a/an _____.

    2. _____

3. The failure to do something or the doing of something that an ordinary, reasonable person would or would not do is _____.

    3. _____

4. The care that a reasonable person would have used in the same situation or as much care and attention as is required by the circumstances is referred to as _____.

    4. _____

5. Permission granted by the court to a pauper, or poor person, to bring a suit without paying the court costs is expressed in Latin as _____.

    5. _____

6. A duty, an obligation, or a responsibility is a/an _____.

    6. _____

7. A loss that cannot be recovered in a court of law is referred to in Latin as a/an _____.

    7. _____

8. The negligence of the plaintiff that, together with the negligence of the defendant, caused the injury is _____.

    8. _____

9. An action for the recovery of a thing possessed by another rather than an action against that person is a/an _____.

    9. _____

10. A liability without fault is referred to as _____.

    10. _____

11. Something to which a person is legally entitled is a/an _____.

    11. _____

12. A comparison of the negligence of the plaintiff and defendant is _____.

    12. _____

13. A negligent act committed by one person but chargeable to another who is responsible for the other person's acts is _____.

    13. _____

KEYING LEGAL TERMS

Directions: Unless otherwise instructed, use a 70-space line (typewriter) or 1-inch margins (computer) and double spacing. Correct all errors. Follow one of the procedures below.

WORDS

Keyboarding Procedure
On your typewriter or computer, key the following words at least two times, concentrating on the correct spelling and pronunciation.

Shorthand Procedure
On your typewriter or computer, key the following words once, concentrating on the correct spelling and pronunciation. Then write the shorthand outline for each word in your shorthand notebook or on your shorthand machine. Transcribe from the shorthand outlines one time on your typewriter or computer.

in forma pauperis	right	duty
liability	absolute liability	negligence
contributory negligence	comparative negligence	culpable negligence
imputation of negligence	due care or diligence	damnum absque injuria
actio in rem		

SENTENCES

Keyboarding Procedure
Key each of the following sentences one time on your typewriter or computer. Concentrate on the correct spelling and pronunciation of each underlined legal term.

Shorthand Procedure
Write the correct shorthand outlines for the following sentences in your shorthand notebook or on your shorthand machine. Transcribe from your shorthand outlines one time on your typewriter or computer.

These sentences will be used for practice dictation on the cassettes.

In forma pauperis describes permission granted by the court to a pauper, or poor person, to bring a suit without paying the court costs. A right is something to which a person is legally entitled. A duty is an obligation that one person has to another. Right and duty are reciprocal terms when used within their legal meanings. Thus, if one person has a right, then another person has a duty. Liability is a duty, an obligation, or a responsibility. Absolute liability is liability without fault. Absolute liability applies to situations where one person is doing a legal but very risky act and another is injured as a result of the act, even though there was no negligence involved.

The want of due care or diligence is negligence. If a person fails to do something or does something that an ordinary, reasonable person would or would not do, he or she may be charged with negligence. In law, negligence may be more specifically defined as contributory, comparative, and culpable. Contributory negligence means that the complaining party contributed to the cause of the injury. Comparative negligence involves negligence on the part of both parties but permits a recovery if the plaintiff's negligence is considerably less than that of the defendant. Culpable negligence is the failure to act with due care and could result in a criminal action in addition to a civil action. Imputation of negligence is negligence attributed to one person but actually committed by another person for whom he or she may be responsible.

Due care or diligence means as much care and attention as is required by the circumstances. A loss that cannot be recovered in a court of law is expressed in Latin as **damnum absque injuria**. **Actio in rem** is an action for the recovery of something another is possessing.

TRANSCRIBING FROM DICTATION

Directions: This dictation emphasizes and reinforces the legal terms and definitions you have studied. Listen carefully to the pronunciation of each of the legal terms. Unless otherwise directed, use a 70-space line (typewriter) or 1-inch margins (computer) and double spacing. Correct all errors. Follow one of the procedures below.

Keyboarding Procedure

Using the cassette from Lesson 11, Part B, transcribe the dictation directly at your typewriter or computer.

Shorthand Procedure

Using the cassette from Lesson 11, Part B, take the dictation using your shorthand system and then transcribe from your shorthand notes on your typewriter or computer.

When you have finished transcribing Part B of the practice dictation, check your transcript with the printed copy. If you made any mistakes in the transcription, you should practice those words several times before going on to Lesson 12.

CHECKLIST
I have completed the following for Lesson 11:

	Part A, Date	Part B, Date	Submitted to Instructor Yes	No
Terminology and Definitions	_____	_____	_____	_____
Self-Evaluation	_____	_____	_____	_____
* **Keying Legal Terms**	_____	_____	_____	_____
Words	_____	_____	_____	_____
Sentences	_____	_____	_____	_____
* **Transcribing from Dictation**	_____	_____	_____	_____

When you have successfully completed all the exercises in this lesson and submitted to your instructor those requested, you are ready to proceed with Lesson 12.

* *If you are using a shorthand system, submit to your instructor your shorthand notes along with your transcript.*

Lesson 12

Civil Actions

This lesson continues the study of some of the general terms involved in civil law or civil actions. A knowledge and understanding of this terminology will assist you in applying the terms to various civil actions and procedures. Upon successful completion of these exercises, you will be able to spell, pronounce, define, and transcribe correctly the legal words presented.

"No one should suffer by the act of another."
—Legal Maxim

Part A   TERMINOLOGY AND DEFINITIONS

Directions: Study the terms, pronunciations, and definitions until you are thoroughly familiar with them. In order to complete this lesson successfully, you must understand the meaning and usage of all the legal terms presented. If you are using shorthand, write your shorthand outline for each legal term in your shorthand notebook or on your shorthand machine.

Legal Term	Pronunciation	Definition
1. misfeasance	mis-'fēz-ns	Improperly doing a legal act.
2. nonfeasance	nän-'fēz-ns	Failure to do an act that one has a duty to perform.
3. attractive nuisance doctrine	ə-'trak-tiv 'nüs-ns 'däk-trən	A doctrine applying to situations where something is on a person's property that will attract young children, and that person has a duty to exercise due care to prevent injury to them.
4. trespasser	'tres-pəs-ər	One who unlawfully enters or goes upon another's property.
5. licensee	līs-n-'sē	One who is on the premises of another for his or her own advantage and without any enticement from the owner. A salesperson would be a licensee.
6. invitee	in-və-'tē	One who enters the premises of another by express or implied invitation of the owner and whose purpose in being there is advantageous to the owner.
7. proximate cause	'präk-sə-mət kòz	The actual cause of an injury. Also referred to as the efficient cause.
8. intervening cause	int-ər-'vēn-iŋ kòz	A cause of injury that occurs after the negligent act of another and that could not have been expected to occur. One is not liable for an injury resulting from an intervening cause.

9. doctrine of last clear chance	'däk-trən əv last klir chans	A plaintiff who was contributorily negligent may recover for injuries if the defendant had a last clear chance to avoid the injury. For example, if a pedestrian is struck by a car while crossing a street against a red light and the car had ample time to stop and did not, the driver of the car may be held liable for the injury.
10. tangible damages	'tan-jə-bəl 'dam-ijs	Damages that are real or actual. An essential element of torts. There must have been real or actual damages for a tort to have been committed.
11. punitive or exemplary damages	'pyü-nət-iv ȯr ig-'zem-plə-rē 'dam-ijs	Damages that are awarded over and above the amount of the actual loss for mental anguish or the feelings of the one injured to serve as a punishment for the defendant or to set an example for others.
12. nominal damages	'näm-ən-l 'dam-ijs	A small amount of damages awarded in cases where an injury has occurred but tangible damages cannot be determined.
13. mental anguish	'ment-l 'aŋ-gwish	Suffering caused by emotional distress. In some states, damages may be awarded for mental anguish caused by an accident or injury.

Self-Evaluation A   TERMINOLOGY AND DEFINITION RECALL

Directions: In the Answers column, write the letter from Column 1 that represents the word or phrase that best matches each item in Column 2. After you have completed this self-evaluation, check your answers with the key on page 496. If you have any incorrect answers, restudy the definitions for those terms before going on with this lesson. Then unless otherwise directed, submit this self-evaluation to your instructor.

Column 1

a. attractive nuisance doctrine

b. intervening cause

c. invitee

d. doctrine of last clear chance

e. licensee

f. malfeasance

g. mental anguish

h. misfeasance

i. nominal damages

j. nonfeasance

k. proximate cause

l. punitive or exemplary damages

m. tangible damages

n. trespasser

Column 2

1. One who is on the premises of another for his or her own advantage and without any enticement from the owner.

2. A rule of law stating that a plaintiff who was contributorily negligent may recover for injuries if the defendant had an opportunity to avoid the injury just before it occurred.

3. A doctrine applying to situations where something is on a person's property that will attract young children and that requires that person to exercise due care to prevent injury to the children.

4. The actual cause of an injury or the efficient cause.

5. The failure to do an act that one has a duty to perform.

6. One who is upon the premises of another by express or implied invitation of the owner and whose purpose in being there is advantageous to the owner.

7. Improperly doing a legal act.

8. Damages that are awarded over and above the amount of the actual loss for mental anguish or the feelings of the one injured to serve as a punishment for the defendant or to set an example for others.

9. A cause of injury that occurs after the negligent act of another and that could not have been expected to occur.

10. One who unlawfully enters or goes upon another's property.

11. Damages that are real or actual and are an essential element of a tort.

12. Suffering that is caused by emotional distress.

13. A small amount of damages awarded in cases where an injury has occurred but tangible damages cannot be determined.

Answers

1. _____

2. _____

3. _____

4. _____

5. _____

6. _____

7. _____

8. _____

9. _____

10. _____

11. _____

12. _____

13. _____

KEYING LEGAL TERMS

Directions: Unless otherwise instructed, use a 70-space line (typewriter) or 1-inch margins (computer) and double spacing. Correct all errors. Follow one of the procedures below.

WORDS

Keyboarding Procedure
On your typewriter or computer, key the following words at least two times, concentrating on the correct spelling and pronunciation.

Shorthand Procedure
On your typewriter or computer, key the following words once, concentrating on the correct spelling and pronunciation. Then write the shorthand outline for each word in your shorthand notebook or on your shorthand machine. Transcribe from the shorthand outlines one time on your typewriter or computer.

misfeasance	nonfeasance	attractive nuisance doctrine
trespasser	licensee	invitee
proximate cause	intervening cause	doctrine of last clear chance
tangible damages	punitive or exemplary damages	nominal damages
mental anguish		

SENTENCES

Keyboarding Procedure
Key each of the following sentences one time on your typewriter or computer. Concentrate on the correct spelling and pronunciation of each underlined legal term.

Shorthand Procedure
Write the correct shorthand outlines for the following sentences in your shorthand notebook or on your shorthand machine. Transcribe from your shorthand outlines one time on your typewriter or computer.

These sentences will be used for practice dictation on the cassettes.

If one is accused of <u>misfeasance</u>, the person did a lawful act improperly; but if one is accused of <u>nonfeasance</u>, then the person failed to do an act that he or she had a duty to perform. If you were handling investments for another person and you did not make good decisions investing his or her money, you could be charged with misfeasance. However, if you did not invest the money and you were expected to do so, you could be charged with nonfeasance.

The <u>attractive nuisance doctrine</u> applies to situations where something is on a person's property that will attract young children, and that person has a duty to exercise due care to prevent an injury to them. <u>Trespasser</u>, <u>licensee</u>, and <u>invitee</u> are classifications of persons who enter or use another's premises. A trespasser is one who unlawfully enters or goes upon another's property; a licensee is there legally but for the licensee's own advantage; and the invitee is there for a reason that is advantageous to the owner. <u>Proximate cause</u> is the actual cause of an injury. A proximate cause is also referred to as an efficient cause. An <u>intervening cause</u> is a cause of injury that occurs after the negligent act and that could not have been expected to occur. One is not liable for an injury resulting from an intervening cause. The <u>doctrine of last clear chance</u> makes a person liable if there was a last clear chance to avoid injuring or damaging another.

Several types of damages may be awarded in a civil action. <u>Tangible damages</u> are an essential element of torts. Damages that are real or actual are tangible damages. <u>Punitive or exemplary damages</u> are damages that are awarded over and above the amount of the actual loss for mental anguish or the feelings of the one injured to serve as a punishment for the defendant or to set an example for others. <u>Nominal damages</u> are a small amount of damages awarded in cases where an injury has occurred but tangible damages cannot be determined. <u>Mental anguish</u> is suffering caused by emotional distress. In some states, damages may be awarded for mental anguish caused by an accident or injury.

TRANSCRIBING FROM DICTATION

Directions: This dictation emphasizes and reinforces the legal terms and definitions you have studied. Listen carefully to the pronunciation of each of the legal terms. Unless otherwise directed, use a 70-space line (typewriter) or 1-inch margins (computer) and double spacing. Correct all errors. Follow one of the procedures below.

Keyboarding Procedure
Using the cassette from Lesson 12, Part A, transcribe the dictation directly at your typewriter or computer.

Shorthand Procedure
Using the cassette from Lesson 12, Part A, take the dictation using your shorthand system and then transcribe from your shorthand notes on your typewriter or computer.

When you have finished transcribing Part A of the practice dictation, check your transcript with the printed copy. If you made any mistakes in the transcription, you should practice those words several times before going on.

Part B TERMINOLOGY AND DEFINITIONS

Directions: Study the terms, pronunciations, and definitions until you are thoroughly familiar with them. In order to complete this lesson successfully, you must understand the meaning and usage of all the legal terms presented. If you are using shorthand, write your shorthand outline for each legal term in your shorthand notebook or on your shorthand machine.

Legal Term	Pronunciation	Definition
1. act or omission	akt òr ō-'mish-ən	The doing or the failing to do something. The test is applied to determine whether a tort has been committed.
2. probable consequences	'präb-ə-bəl 'kän-sə-kwens-əs	Results that are most likely to follow a particular cause. If you drive in a reckless manner, then the probable consequence is that you will have an accident.
3. ordinary, reasonable person	'òrd-n-er-ē 'rēz-nə-bəl 'pərs-n	A normal, average person who has good judgment in everyday affairs. The standard for measuring whether or not someone acted in a negligent manner.
4. assumption of risk	ə-'səm-shən əv risk	If one voluntarily takes a chance and is injured as a result thereof, then that person is not considered to be injured in the eyes of the law.
5. foreseeability of injury	fōr-'sē-ə-bil-ət-ē əv 'inj-rē	The capability of seeing and knowing that an injury may result from certain acts or omissions.
6. knowledge of the peril	'näl-ij əv thə 'per-əl	When one has knowledge of something that may cause injury to another and fails to do something about it. An element that is essential to prove negligence.

7. implied or imputed knowledge	im-'plīd òr im-'pyüt-əd 'näl-ij	Knowledge that a person should have had or is responsible for having. Usually applies to an employer-employee relationship or an agency.
8. constructive notice	kən-'strək-tiv 'nōt-əs	Knowledge that one should have when a condition has existed for such a period of time that the person would have known of the condition had due care been exercised. If you own a building that has had a broken step for a period of time and you had a reasonable amount of time to discover it, you can be held liable if an injury results even though you had not actually seen the broken step.
9. wanton, reckless, and intentional	'wȯnt-n 'rek-ləs ən in-'tench-nəl	Willful misconduct that constitutes culpable negligence. Acts done with indifference and disregard of the consequences to others.
10. res ipsa loquitur	rēz 'ip-sə 'lō-kwə-tər	Latin. The thing speaks for itself. A presumption that the thing that happened does not normally happen unless there is negligence involved. It is a rebuttable presumption that may be proven otherwise by the facts.
11. Good Samaritan Statute	gu̇d sə-'mar-ət-n 'stach-üt	If one sees another in serious danger and tries to help the person, the one who gives assistance cannot be charged with contributory negligence. This doctrine varies from state to state.
12. sudden emergency doctrine	'səd-n i-'mər-jən-sē 'däk-trən	The degree of care required of a person in an emergency is less than would be required if the person had time to think before acting.
13. sovereign immunity	'säv-rən im-'yü-nət-ē	Protection from tort prosecution that is given to government units and officials in connection with the performance of their official duties.

Self-Evaluation B   TERMINOLOGY AND DEFINITION RECALL

Directions: In the Answers column, write the legal term that is most representative of the corresponding statement. After you have completed this self-evaluation, check your answers with the key on page 496. If you have any incorrect answers, restudy the definitions for those terms before going on with this lesson. Then unless otherwise directed, submit this self-evaluation to your instructor.

Answers

1. When one has knowledge of something that may cause injury to another and fails to do anything about it, it is called _____.

    1. _____

2. The capability of seeing or knowing that an injury may result from certain acts or omissions is _____.

    2. _____

3. The doing or the failure to do something and the test applied to determine whether a tort has been committed is referred to as _____.

    3. _____

4. Knowledge that a person should have had or is responsible for having is _____.

    4. _____

5. A doctrine stating that the degree of care required of a person in an emergency is less than would be required if the person had time to think before acting is the _____.

    5. _____

6. Willful misconduct that constitutes culpable negligence or acts done with indifference and disregard of the consequences to others are referred to as _____.

    6. _____

7. A presumption that the thing that happened does not normally happen unless there is negligence involved is _____.

    7. _____

8. A doctrine stating that if one sees another in serious danger and tries to help the person, the one giving the assistance cannot be charged with contributory negligence is the _____.

    8. _____

9. A situation in which one voluntarily takes a chance and is injured as a result thereof but is not considered to be injured in the eyes of the law is referred to as _____.

    9. _____

10. Knowledge that one should have when a condition has existed for such a period of time that the person would have known of the condition if due care had been exercised is called _____.

    10. _____

11. Protection from tort prosecution that is given to governmental units and officials in connection with the performance of their official duties is known as _____.

    11. _____

12. A result that is most likely to follow a particular cause is referred to as _____.

    12. _____

13. A normal, average person who has good judgment in everyday affairs is known as a/an _____.

    13. _____

KEYING LEGAL TERMS

Directions: Unless otherwise instructed, use a 70-space line (typewriter) or 1-inch margins (computer) and double spacing. Correct all errors. Follow one of the procedures below.

WORDS

Keyboarding Procedure
On your typewriter or computer, key the following words at least two times, concentrating on the correct spelling and pronunciation.

Shorthand Procedure
On your typewriter or computer, key the following words once, concentrating on the correct spelling and pronunciation. Then write the shorthand outline for each word in your shorthand notebook or on your shorthand machine. Transcribe from the shorthand outlines one time on your typewriter or computer.

act or omission	probable consequences	ordinary, reasonable person
assumption of risk	knowledge of the peril	foreseeability of injury
implied or imputed knowledge	res ipsa loquitur	constructive notice
wanton, reckless, and intentional	Good Samaritan Statute	sudden emergency doctrine
sovereign immunity		

SENTENCES

Keyboarding Procedure
Key each of the following sentences one time on your typewriter or computer. Concentrate on the correct spelling and pronunciation of each underlined legal term.

Shorthand Procedure
Write the correct shorthand outlines for the following sentences in your shorthand notebook or on your shorthand machine. Transcribe from your shorthand outlines one time on your typewriter or computer.

These sentences will be used for practice dictation on the cassettes.

The doing or the failure to do something is an <u>act or omission</u>. This is the test that is applied to determine whether or not a tort has been committed. Whenever you do something negligent, the results that are most likely to follow are called <u>probable consequences</u>.

An <u>ordinary, reasonable person</u> is one who is normal, average, and has good judgment in everyday affairs.

<u>Assumption of risk</u> means if one voluntarily takes a chance and is injured as a result thereof, then that person is not considered to be injured in the eyes of the law. <u>Knowledge of the peril</u> exists whenever one has the capability of seeing or knowing that an injury may result from certain acts or omissions. <u>Foreseeability of injury</u> is the ability to see or know in advance the probable consequences of an act or omission. <u>Implied or imputed knowledge</u> is knowledge that a person should have had or is responsible for having. Implied or imputed knowledge usually applies to an employer-employee relationship or an agency.

<u>Res ipsa loquitur</u> is a Latin phrase meaning the thing speaks for itself. Res ipsa loquitur is a presumption that something that happened would not normally happen unless there was negligence involved. If a person could have discovered a fact by exercising due care, he or she is said to have had <u>constructive notice</u> of the fact. <u>Wanton, reckless, and intentional</u> describe an act done with indifference and disregard of the consequences to others.

The **Good Samaritan Statute** protects one from contributory negligence if assistance is given to someone who is in danger, provided a certain degree of care is used. Under **the sudden emergency doctrine,** the degree of care required of a person in an emergency situation is less than that required if the person had time to think before acting. **Sovereign immunity** is protection from tort prosecution that is given to governmental units and officials in connection with the performance of their official duties.

TRANSCRIBING FROM DICTATION

Directions: This dictation emphasizes and reinforces the legal terms and definitions you have studied. Listen carefully to the pronunciation of each of the legal terms. Unless otherwise directed, use a 70-space line (typewriter) or 1-inch margins (computer) and double spacing. Correct all errors. Follow one of the procedures below.

Keyboarding Procedure

Using the cassette from Lesson 12, Part B, transcribe the dictation directly at your typewriter or computer.

Shorthand Procedure

Using the cassette from Lesson 12, Part B, take the dictation using your shorthand system and then transcribe from your shorthand notes on your typewriter or computer.

When you have finished transcribing Part B of the practice dictation, check your transcript with the printed copy. If you made any mistakes in the transcription, you should practice those words several times before going on to Evaluation 6.

CHECKLIST
I have completed the following for Lesson 12:

	Part A, Date	Part B, Date	Submitted to Instructor Yes	No
Terminology and Definitions				
Self-Evaluation				
* Keying Legal Terms				
Words				
Sentences				
* Transcribing from Dictation				

When you have successfully completed all the exercises in this lesson and submitted to your instructor those requested, you are ready to proceed with Evaluation 6.

* If you are using a shorthand system, submit to your instructor your shorthand notes along with your transcript.

Evaluation No. 6   **SECTION A**

Directions: This dictation/transcription evaluation will test your spelling and transcription abilities on the legal terms that you studied in the two preceding lessons. Use a 5-space paragraph indention, a 70-space line (typewriter) or 1-inch margins (computer), and double spacing unless otherwise instructed. Correct all errors. Follow one of the procedures below.

Keyboarding Procedure

Using the cassette from Evaluation 6, transcribe the dictation directly at your typewriter or computer.

Shorthand Procedure

Using the cassette from Evaluation 6, take the dictation using your shorthand system and then transcribe from your shorthand notes on your typewriter or computer.

Sections B and C are available from your instructor.

Lesson 13

Criminal Law

"An act does not make guilty unless there be a guilty intent."

—Legal Maxim

Criminal law deals with crimes committed in violation of a law. A crime is a public wrong and is prosecuted by the state or "the people." This lesson contains some of the basic terminology involved in criminal procedures. You should be able to spell, pronounce, define, and transcribe correctly the terms presented when you have successfully completed these exercises.

Part A   TERMINOLOGY AND DEFINITIONS

Directions: Study the terms, pronunciations, and definitions until you are thoroughly familiar with them. In order to complete this lesson successfully, you must understand the meaning and usage of all the legal terms presented. If you are using shorthand, write your shorthand outline for each legal term in your shorthand notebook or on your shorthand machine.

Legal Term	Pronunciation	Definition
1. crime	krīm	An illegal act that is punishable in a court of law.
2. corpus delicti	ˈkòr-pəs di-ˈlik-tī	Latin. The body of a crime. The material evidence that indicates a crime has been committed.
3. grand jury	grand ˈjùr-ē	A jury that makes inquiries into criminal cases and issues indictments when the evidence indicates that a crime has been committed.
4. indictment	in-ˈdīt-mənt	A written accusation issued by a grand jury charging that there is evidence that a crime has been committed and that the person so charged should be brought to trial.
5. information	in-fər-ˈmā-shən	A written accusation issued by a prosecuting attorney charging a person with a crime. (See Figure 13-1, page 181.)
6. offense	ə-ˈfens	A wrongdoing that is punishable by fine or imprisonment.
7. warrant	ˈwòr-ənt	A written order giving the authority to arrest a person or to search or seize property. (See Figure 13-2, page 182.)
8. arrest	ə-ˈrest	The act of taking a person into legal custody to answer to a criminal or civil charge.
9. arraignment	ə-ˈrān-mənt	To bring a person before a court of law to hear the charges in the indictment or information and to enter a plea of guilty or not guilty.
10. preliminary examination	pri-ˈlim-ə-ner-ē ig-zam-ə-ˈnā-shən	A hearing conducted by a judge to determine if there is enough evidence to hold for trial a person accused of a crime. Also referred to as a preliminary hearing.

11. felony	′fel-ə-nē	A crime of a serious nature that is punishable by imprisonment or death.
12. misdemeanor	mis-di-′mē-nər	Any crime that is not a felony. Usually punishable by fine or a short jail sentence.
13. habeas corpus	′hā-bē-əs ′kȯr-pəs	Latin. A writ requiring someone holding a person to bring that person into court to determine if he or she is being held justly or legally. (See Figure 13-3, page 183.)
14. extradition	ek-strə-′dish-ən	The delivery of a person from one state to another for trial or punishment.

FIGURE 13-1 An Information

Approved, SCAO

STATE OF MICHIGAN XXXXXXXXXXXX 30th JUDICIAL CIRCUIT	INFORMATION FELONY	CASE NO. XXXXXX CIRCUIT CT. 75-6482

District Court ORI: MI-   Circuit Court ORI: MI-

THE PEOPLE OF THE STATE OF MICHIGAN	Defendant name and address v. THORNE NATOLIE	Victim or complainant Roscoe Borg
		Complaining witness Roscoe Borg
Co-defendant(s)		Date: On or about August 13, 1997

City/Twp./Village Lansing	County in Michigan Ingham	Defendant CTN 76834	Defendant SID 10010	Defendant DOB 092239
Police agency report no. 6743	Charge Assault with intent to murder		Maximum penalty 20 years to life	
Witnesses Roscoe Borg			Defendant DLN M453-789-0003	

STATE OF MICHIGAN, COUNTY OF Ingham   .
IN THE NAME OF THE PEOPLE OF THE STATE OF MICHIGAN: The prosecuting attorney for this County
appears before the court and informs the court that on the date and at the location described, the defendant:

Assaulted the complaining witness, Roscoe Borg, with a deadly weapon,
to wit: a handgun.

and against the peace and dignity of the State of Michigan.

Prosecuting Attorney

August 14, 1997   By: Linda Soloman   (P 78833)
Date

MCLA 764.1 et seq.; MSA 28.860 et seq., MCLA 766.1 et seq.; MSA 28.919 et seq.; MCLA 767.1 et seq.; MSA 28.941 et seq.

MC 200 (3/87) FELONY SET, Information

CIRCUIT COURT

FIGURE 13-2   A Warrant

| | | | INFORMATION - CIRCUIT COURT
ORIGINAL COMPLAINT - COURT
WARRANT - COURT | | RETURN - CIRCUIT COURT
COMPLAINT COPY - PROSECUTOR
COMPLAINT COPY - DEFENDANT/ ATTORNEY |

Approved, SCAO

| STATE OF MICHIGAN
XXXXXXXXXXXX
30th JUDICIAL CIRCUIT | WARRANT
FELONY | CASE NO.
XXXXXX
CIRCUIT CT. 75-6482 |

District Court ORI: MI-   Circuit Court ORI: MI-

| THE PEOPLE OF THE STATE OF MICHIGAN | V. | Defendant name and address
THORNE NATOLIE | Victim or complainant
Roscoe Borg |
| | | | Complaining witness
Roscoe Borg |

Co-defendant(s)

Date: On or about
August 13, 1997

| City/Twp./Village
Lansing | County in Michigan
Ingham | Defendant CTN
76834 | Defendant SID
10010 | Defendant DOB
092239 |

| Police agency report no.
6743 | Charge
Assault with intent to murder | Maximum penalty
20 years to life |

| Witnesses
Roscoe Borg | Defendant DLN
M453-789-0003 |

STATE OF MICHIGAN, COUNTY OF Ingham   .

To any peace officer or court officer authorized to make arrest: The complaining witness has filed a sworn complaint in this court stating that on the date and the location described, the defendant, contrary to law,

Assaulted the complaining witness, Roscoe Borg, with a deadly weapon, to wit: a handgun.

Upon examination of the complaining witness, I find that the offense charged was committed and that there is probable cause to believe that defendant committed the offense. THEREFORE, IN THE NAME OF THE PEOPLE OF THE STATE OF MICHIGAN, I order you to arrest and bring defendant before the court immediately.

August 14, 1997   (SEAL)   *Stanford McClain*
Date   Judge/XXXXXXXX

RETURN   By virtue of this warrant the defendant has been taken into custody as commanded.

August 18, 1997   *Marcie Baker*
Date   Peace officer

MCLA 764.1 et seq.; MSA 28.860 et seq., MCLA 766.1 et seq.; MSA 28.919 et seq.; MCLA 767.1 et seq.; MSA 28.941 et seq.

MC 200 (3/87) **FELONY SET, Warrant**

COURT COPY

FIGURE 13-3 A Writ of Habeas Corpus

Approved, SCAO			ORIGINAL - COURT 1ST COPY - CUSTODIAL OFFICER 2ND COPY - TRANSPORT OFFICER	3RD COPY - PROSECUTOR 4TH COPY - RETURN

STATE OF MICHIGAN XXXXXXXXXXXX 30th **JUDICIAL CIRCUIT**	**WRIT OF HABEAS CORPUS**	**CASE NO.** 75-6482

Court address
2nd Floor, City Hall, Lansing, Michigan 48933   Court telephone no.
(517) 555-0650

IN THE NAME OF THE PEOPLE OF THE STATE OF MICHIGAN:

TO County of Cook, State of Illinois   THE AGENCY OR PERSON HAVING

CUSTODY OF   Thorne Natolie   785-643   9/22/39
               Name   I.D. no.   Date of birth

☒ To bring prisoner to court in the case of:
  People of the State of Michigan
       V.
  Thorne Natolie

☐ To inquire into detention/custody of:

YOU ARE ORDERED to:
1. ☐ Answer this writ, stating the authority under which you   ☐ restrain the named prisoner.
                                              ☐ exercise custody over the minor child.
   File your answer with the   ☐ court   by _____
                       ☐ judge   Date

2. ☒ Deliver the person named in this writ into the custody of Ingham County Sheriff
                                             Name/Title/Agency
   for the following purpose: to be held pending court appearance.
                     (To testify, for preliminary examination, trial, to be held pending court appearance, etc.)
   Immediately after the prisoner completes his/her appearance, the prisoner shall be returned to your custody.

3. ☐ Bring the person named in this writ before the Honorable _____

  at _____ , on _____ at _____ m.
    Location of court   Date   Time
  Bring this writ with you.

                         Clerk of the Court

August 18, 1997   By: *Corine Lin*
Date

CERTIFICATE OF ALLOWANCE OF WRIT

I, Stanford McClain _____ , p. 48921 , certify that the above writ of habeas corpus
  Name of Judge   Bar no.
was allowed by me on August 18, 1997 . ☒ Fees are allowed in the amount of $ 300.00 .
               Date

                     Stanford McClain
                     Judge

MC 203   (11/85)   **WRIT OF HABEAS CORPUS**   MCLA 600.4301 et seq.; MSA 27A.4301 et seq., MCR 3.303, 3.304

COURT

Self-Evaluation A   TERMINOLOGY AND DEFINITION RECALL

Directions: In the Answers column at the right of each statement, write the letter that represents the word or group of words that correctly completes the statement. After you have completed this self-evaluation, check your answers with the key on page 496. If you have any incorrect answers, restudy the definitions for those terms before going on with this lesson. Then unless otherwise directed, submit this self-evaluation to your instructor.

Answers

1. The act of taking a person into legal custody to answer to a criminal charge is a/an (a) offense, (b) preliminary examination, (c) arrest.

   1. _____

2. A jury that makes inquiries into criminal cases and issues indictments when the evidence indicates that a crime has been committed is a (a) grand jury, (b) corpus delicti, (c) preliminary examination.

   2. _____

3. A hearing conducted by a judge to determine if there is enough evidence to hold for trial a person accused of a crime is the (a) preliminary examination, (b) grand jury, (c) information.

   3. _____

4. Any crime that is not a felony and that is usually punishable by fine or a short jail sentence is a/an (a) arrest, (b) misdemeanor, (c) warrant.

   4. _____

5. The body of a crime or the material evidence indicating that a crime has been committed is expressed in Latin as (a) habeas corpus, (b) corpus delicti, (c) arraignment.

   5. _____

6. The process of bringing a person before a court of law to hear the charges in the indictment or information and to enter a plea of guilty or not guilty is the (a) indictment, (b) arraignment, (c) extradition.

   6. _____

7. A written accusation issued by a grand jury charging that there is evidence that a crime has been committed and that the person so charged should be brought to trial is a/an (a) warrant, (b) information, (c) indictment.

   7. _____

8. The delivery of a person from one state to another for trial or punishment is an (a) indictment, (b) arraignment, (c) extradition.

   8. _____

9. A written order giving the authority to arrest a person or to search or seize property is a/an (a) misdemeanor, (b) warrant, (c) offense.

   9. _____

10. An illegal act that is punishable in a court of law is a/an (a) crime, (b) arrest, (c) corpus delicti.

   10. _____

11. A writ requiring someone holding a person to bring that person into court to determine if he or she is being held justly or legally is a writ of (a) extradition, (b) arraignment, (c) habeas corpus.

   11. _____

12. A wrongdoing that is punishable by fine or imprisonment is a/an (a) habeas corpus, (b) corpus delicti, (c) offense.

   12. _____

13. A written accusation issued by a prosecuting attorney charging a person with a crime is a/an (a) warrant, (b) information, (c) indictment.

   13. _____

14. A crime of a serious nature that is punishable by imprisonment or death is a/an (a) felony, (b) misdemeanor, (c) extradition.

   14. _____

KEYING LEGAL TERMS

Directions: Unless otherwise instructed, use a 70-space line (typewriter) or 1-inch margins (computer) and double spacing. Correct all errors. Follow one of the procedures below.

WORDS

Keyboarding Procedure
On your typewriter or computer, key the following words at least two times, concentrating on the correct spelling and pronunciation.

Shorthand Procedure
On your typewriter or computer, key the following words once, concentrating on the correct spelling and pronunciation. Then write the shorthand outline for each word in your shorthand notebook or on your shorthand machine. Transcribe from the shorthand outlines one time on your typewriter or computer.

crime	offense	felony
indictment	warrant	misdemeanor
corpus delicti	arrest	habeas corpus
grand jury	arraignment	extradition
information	preliminary examination	

SENTENCES

Keyboarding Procedure
Key each of the following sentences one time on your typewriter or computer. Concentrate on the correct spelling and pronunciation of each underlined legal term.

Shorthand Procedure
Write the correct shorthand outlines for the following sentences in your shorthand notebook or on your shorthand machine. Transcribe from your shorthand outlines one time on your typewriter or computer.

These sentences will be used for practice dictation on the cassettes.

A crime is an illegal act that is punishable in a court of law. An indictment issued by a grand jury is based on the corpus delicti. Corpus delicti means the body of a crime or the material evidence indicating that a crime has been committed.

A grand jury is a jury that makes inquiries into criminal cases and issues indictments when the evidence indicates that a crime has been committed. An indictment is a written accusation issued by a grand jury charging that there is evidence that a crime has been committed and that the person so charged should be brought to trial. An information is a written accusation issued by a prosecuting attorney charging a person with committing a criminal offense. When a person has been charged with the commission of a crime, a warrant is issued requiring the arrest of that person. When a person is arrested, that person is taken into custody and held to answer the charge made against him or her.

At the arraignment, the prisoner is brought before the court to hear the reading of the indictment or the information and to enter a plea of guilty or not guilty. A preliminary examination is a hearing conducted by a judge to determine if there is enough evidence to hold for trial the person accused of a crime.

A crime is classified as a <u>felony</u> or a <u>misdemeanor</u>. A felony is a crime of a serious nature that is punishable by imprisonment or death. A misdemeanor is any crime that is not a felony and is usually punishable by fine or a short jail sentence. Committing murder is a felony, but jaywalking or parking violations are only misdemeanors.

A writ of <u>habeas corpus</u> requires someone holding a person to bring that person to court. If a person charged with a crime is arrested in a state other than the one in which the crime was committed, the person may be returned to the state in which the crime was committed by the process of <u>extradition</u>.

TRANSCRIBING FROM DICTATION

Directions: This dictation emphasizes and reinforces the legal terms and definitions you have studied. Listen carefully to the pronunciation of each of the legal terms. Unless otherwise directed, use a 70-space line (typewriter) or 1-inch margins (computer) and double spacing. Correct all errors. Follow one of the procedures below.

Keyboarding Procedure
Using the cassette from Lesson 13, Part A, transcribe the dictation directly at your typewriter or computer.

Shorthand Procedure
Using the cassette from Lesson 13, Part A, take the dictation using your shorthand system and then transcribe from your shorthand notes on your typewriter or computer.

When you have finished transcribing Part A of the practice dictation, check your transcript with the printed copy. If you made any mistakes in the transcription, you should practice those words several times before going on.

Part B TERMINOLOGY AND DEFINITIONS

Directions: Study the terms, pronunciations, and definitions until you are thoroughly familiar with them. In order to complete this lesson successfully, you must understand the meaning and usage of all the legal terms presented. If you are using shorthand, write your shorthand outline for each legal term in your shorthand notebook or on your shorthand machine.

Legal Term	Pronunciation	Definition
1. plea	plē	An answer made by a defendant at the arraignment for a criminal offense.
2. nolo contendre	′nō-lō kən-′ten-də-rē	Latin. I do not wish to contend. The plea of a defendant in a criminal action that means the punishment will be accepted but guilt will not be admitted.
3. defense	di-′fens	The defendant's denial to an accusation. The contesting of a lawsuit.
4. confession	kən-′fesh-ən	A statement made voluntarily by a person admitting that he or she committed a crime.
5. admission	əd-′mish-ən	A statement confirming that certain facts in a case are true. It is not a confession of guilt.
6. criminal intent	′krim-ən-l in-′tent	A plan or design to commit a crime.
7. sine qua non	′sin-i kwä nän	Latin. Something that is essential. An indispensible condition or requisite without which a thing cannot be.
8. scienter	sī-′en-tər	Latin. Knowingly, intent, or knowledge.

9. insanity	in-'san-ət-ē	A state of unsound mind in which a person does not know right from wrong and is, therefore, not responsible for any acts committed.
10. non compos mentis	nän 'käm-pəs 'ment-əs	Latin. Not of sound mind. Indicates that one is mentally unable to control one's own actions or to handle one's own affairs. Insanity.
11. Durham Rule	'dər-əm rül	A rule applied in some states that does not hold a person responsible for an act if it was done as the result of mental disease or defect.
12. M'Naghten Rule	mə-'nät-ən rül	A rule applied in some states that does not hold a person criminally responsible for an act if he or she does not have the mental capacity to know right from wrong.
13. irresistible impulse	ir-i-'zis-tə-bəl 'im-pəls	An uncontrollable urge to commit a crime due to insanity or a mental defect or disease.

Self-Evaluation B   TERMINOLOGY AND DEFINITION RECALL

Directions: In the Answers column, write the legal term that is most representative of the corresponding statement. After you have completed this self-evaluation, check your answers with the key on page 496. If you have any incorrect answers, restudy the definitions for those terms before going on with this lesson. Then unless otherwise directed, submit this self-evaluation to your instructor.

Answers

1. Something that is essential is _____.

   1. _____

2. The plan or design to commit a crime is _____.

   2. _____

3. An uncontrollable urge to commit a crime due to insanity or a mental defect or disease is a/an _____.

   3. _____

4. A state of unsound mind in which a person does not know right from wrong and is, therefore, not responsible for any acts committed is _____.

   4. _____

5. An answer made by a defendant at the arraignment for a criminal offense is a/an _____.

   5. _____

6. A rule applied in some states that does not hold a person responsible for an act if it was done as the result of mental disease or defect is the _____.

   6. _____

7. The plea of a defendant in a criminal action that means the punishment will be accepted but guilt will not be admitted is _____.

   7. _____

8. A Latin term indicating that one is mentally unable to control one's own actions or to handle one's own affairs is _____.

   8. _____

9. A statement made voluntarily by a person admitting that he or she committed a crime is a/an _____.

   9. _____

10. The defendant's denial to an accusation or the contesting of a lawsuit is the _____.

    10. _____

11. A Latin term that means knowingly, intent, or knowledge is _____.

    11. _____

12. A rule applied in some states that does not hold a person criminally responsible for an act if he or she does not have the mental capacity to know right from wrong is the _____.

    12. _____

13. A statement confirming that certain facts in a case are true is a/an _____.

    13. _____

KEYING LEGAL TERMS

Directions: Unless otherwise instructed, use a 70-space line (typewriter) or 1-inch margins (computer) and double spacing. Correct all errors. Follow one of the procedures below.

WORDS

Keyboarding Procedure
On your typewriter or computer, key the following words at least two times, concentrating on the correct spelling and pronunciation.

Shorthand Procedure
On your typewriter or computer, key the following words once, concentrating on the correct spelling and pronunciation. Then write the shorthand outline for each word in your shorthand notebook or on your shorthand machine. Transcribe from the shorthand outlines one time on your typewriter or computer.

plea	nolo contendere	defense
confession	admission	criminal intent
sine qua non	scienter	insanity
non compos mentis	Durham Rule	M'Naghten Rule
irresistible impulse		

SENTENCES

Keyboarding Procedure
Key each of the following sentences one time on your typewriter or computer. Concentrate on the correct spelling and pronunciation of each underlined legal term.

Shorthand Procedure
Write the correct shorthand outlines for the following sentences in your shorthand notebook or on your shorthand machine. Transcribe from your shorthand outlines one time on your typewriter or computer.

These sentences will be used for practice dictation on the cassettes.

A <u>plea</u> is an answer made by a defendant at an arraignment. The defendant will most likely plead guilty or not guilty. However, in some cases, the defendant may not enter a plea, which is referred to as standing mute before the court, or the defendant may plead <u>nolo contendere</u>. Nolo contendere is a Latin term meaning I do not wish to contend. Nolo contendere is a plea of a defendant in a criminal action that means the punishment will be accepted but guilt will not be admitted. A <u>defense</u> is the defendant's denial to an accusation or the contesting of a lawsuit.

A <u>confession</u> is a statement made voluntarily by a person admitting that he or she committed a crime. An <u>admission</u> is a statement confirming that certain facts in a case are true, but it is not a confession of guilt.

A <u>criminal intent</u> is a plan or design to commit a crime. Criminal intent is a <u>sine qua non</u>—an essential element—for one to be guilty of a crime. <u>Scienter</u> means knowingly and when used in a pleading means that the defendant was aware of what was being done.

As a defense in criminal law, <u>insanity</u> is a state of unsound mind in which a person does not know right from wrong and is, therefore, not responsible for any acts committed. The Latin term <u>non compos mentis</u> means not of sound mind. The <u>Durham Rule</u> and the <u>M'Naghten Rule</u> are sometimes applied to a defendant who pleads non compos mentis. The Durham Rule applies to persons who commit acts as a result of mental disease or defect, whereas the M'Naghten Rule applies to persons who do not have the mental capacity to know right from wrong. The Durham Rule is applied in some states as an <u>irresistible impulse</u> test. An irresistible impulse is an uncontrollable urge to commit a crime due to insanity or a mental defect or disease. The M'Naghten Rule is a right-wrong test of criminal responsibility that determines whether a person had sufficient understanding to know right from wrong.

TRANSCRIBING FROM DICTATION

Directions: This dictation emphasizes and reinforces the legal terms and definitions you have studied. Listen carefully to the pronunciation of each of the legal terms. Unless otherwise directed, use a 70-space line (typewriter) or 1-inch margins (computer) and double spacing. Correct all errors. Follow one of the procedures below.

Keyboarding Procedure
Using the cassette from Lesson 13, Part B, transcribe the dictation directly at your typewriter or computer.

Shorthand Procedure
Using the cassette from Lesson 13, Part B, take the dictation using your shorthand system and then transcribe from your shorthand notes on your typewriter or computer.

When you have finished transcribing Part B of the practice dictation, check your transcript with the printed copy. If you made any mistakes in the transcription, you should practice those words several times before going on to Lesson 14.

CHECKLIST
I have completed the following for Lesson 13:

	Part A, Date	Part B, Date	Submitted to Instructor Yes	No
Terminology and Definitions				
Self-Evaluation				
* Keying Legal Terms				
Words				
Sentences				
* Transcribing from Dictation				

When you have successfully completed all the exercises in this lesson and submitted to your instructor those requested, you are ready to proceed with Lesson 14.

* If you are using a shorthand system, submit to your instructor your shorthand notes along with your transcript.

Lesson 14

Criminal Law

"One who spares the guilty threatens the innocent."
—Legal Maxim

This lesson continues the study of some of the basic terms that are applicable to the field of criminal law. When you have successfully completed these exercises, you will be able to spell, define, pronounce, and transcribe correctly the legal terms presented that pertain to criminal law.

Part A TERMINOLOGY AND DEFINITIONS

Directions: Study the terms, pronunciations, and definitions until you are thoroughly familiar with them. In order to complete this lesson successfully, you must understand the meaning and usage of all the legal terms presented. If you are using shorthand, write your shorthand outline for each legal term in your shorthand notebook or on your shorthand machine.

Legal Term	Pronunciation	Definition
1. bail	bāl	Security placed with the court in order to obtain release until the time of the trial for a person being held in jail.
2. principal	′prin-sə-pəl	One who actually commits a crime or who actually or constructively aids and abets in its commission.
3. accomplice	ə-′käm-pləs	One who knowingly assists a principal in the commission of a crime.
4. accessory	ik-′ses-rē	One who aids the principal in the commission of a crime but is not present when the crime is actually committed. An accessory before the fact knowingly takes steps to effect the crime, whereas an accessory after the fact knowingly assists in concealing the crime and/or the offender.
5. aid and abet	ād ən ə-′bet	To assist in a criminal act by giving encouragement or support to its commission.
6. reasonable doubt	′rēz-nə-bəl daút	Doubt that is logical, credible, or plausible. It is not an imaginary or a fictitious doubt that one can have about anything. In a criminal case, proof must be beyond a reasonable doubt, not beyond all doubt.
7. conviction	kən-′vik-shən	The outcome of a criminal trial whereby a person is found guilty of the charges that were made.
8. sentence	′sent-ns	The punishment given by the court to one convicted of a crime.
9. imprisonment	im-′priz-ən-mənt	The act of placing a person in a prison or place of confinement.

10. incarcerate	in-ˈkär-sə-rāt	To imprison in a jail or penitentiary as a result of due legal process.
11. parole	pə-ˈrōl	The release of a person from prison before the end of the sentence. A parole is conditional in that if one violates the terms of the parole, the remainder of the sentence must be served.
12. pardon	ˈpärd-n	To release a person who has committed a crime from the punishment required by law. A pardon may be absolute or conditional.
13. reprieve	ri-ˈprēv	A delay or postponement of punishment.

Self-Evaluation A   TERMINOLOGY AND DEFINITION RECALL

Directions: In the Answers column, write the letter from Column 1 that represents the word or phrase that best matches each item in Column 2. After you have completed this self-evaluation, check your answers with the key on page 496. If you have any incorrect answers, restudy the definitions for those terms before going on with this lesson. Then unless otherwise directed, submit this self-evaluation to your instructor.

Column 1

a. accessory

b. accomplice

c. aid and abet

d. bail

e. conviction

f. imprisonment

g. incarcerate

h. pardon

i. parole

j. principal

k. reasonable doubt

l. replevin

m. reprieve

n. sentence

Column 2

1. The release of a person from prison before the end of the sentence on the condition that if he or she violates the terms of the release, the remainder of the sentence must be served.

2. An absolute or a conditional release from the punishment required by law of one who has committed a crime.

3. One who actually commits a crime or who actually or constructively aids and abets in its commission.

4. One who aids the principal in the commission of a crime.

5. A delay or postponement of punishment.

6. Doubt that is logical, credible, or plausible.

7. To assist in a criminal act by giving encouragement or support to its commission.

8. One who knowingly assists a principal in the commission of a crime.

9. The act of placing a person in a prison or place of confinement.

10. To imprison in a jail or penitentiary as a result of due legal process.

11. The outcome of a criminal trial whereby a person is found guilty of the charges that were made.

12. The punishment given by the court to one convicted of a crime.

13. Security placed with the court in order to obtain release for a person being held in jail until the time of the trial.

Answers

1. _____

2. _____

3. _____

4. _____

5. _____

6. _____

7. _____

8. _____

9. _____

10. _____

11. _____

12. _____

13. _____

KEYING LEGAL TERMS

Directions: Unless otherwise instructed, use a 70-space line (typewriter) or 1-inch margins (computer) and double spacing. Correct all errors. Follow one of the procedures below.

WORDS

Keyboarding Procedure
On your typewriter or computer, key the following words at least two times, concentrating on the correct spelling and pronunciation.

Shorthand Procedure
On your typewriter or computer, key the following words once, concentrating on the correct spelling and pronunciation. Then write the shorthand outline for each word in your shorthand notebook or on your shorthand machine. Transcribe from the shorthand outlines one time on your typewriter or computer.

bail	principal	accomplice
accessory	aid and abet	reasonable doubt
conviction	sentence	imprisonment
incarcerate	parole	pardon
reprieve		

SENTENCES

Keyboarding Procedure
Key each of the following sentences one time on your typewriter or computer. Concentrate on the correct spelling and pronunciation of each underlined legal term.

Shorthand Procedure
Write the correct shorthand outlines for the following sentences in your shorthand notebook or on your shorthand machine. Transcribe from your shorthand outlines one time on your typewriter or computer.

These sentences will be used for practice dictation on the cassettes.

A defendant may be released on bail prior to a trial, which means that security is placed with the court in order to obtain release for a person being held in jail until the time of the trial.

The parties to a crime may be a principal, an accomplice, and an accessory. One who actually commits a crime or who aids and abets in its commission is a principal. To aid and abet is to assist in a criminal act by giving encouragement or support to its commission. An accomplice is one who knowingly assists the principal in the commission of a crime. An accessory is one who aids the principal in the commission of a crime but is not present when the crime is actually committed. An accessory before the fact knows about the crime before it is committed and may have assisted in the planning of the crime. An accessory after the fact does not have any knowledge of the crime until after it is committed but helps conceal the known facts of the crime.

Reasonable doubt is a doubt that is logical, credible, or plausible. Reasonable doubt is not an imaginary or a fictitious doubt. A conviction is the outcome of a criminal trial whereby a person is found guilty of the charges that were made. Proof beyond a reasonable doubt is required for conviction in a criminal case. When one is convicted of a criminal offense, the sentence may be imprisonment in a jail or penitentiary. Incarcerate also means to imprison.

Parole, pardon, and reprieve all relate to the prisoner serving a lesser sentence than that given at the end of the trial. A reprieve is a delay or postponement of punishment. A parole is a conditional release of a person from prison before the end of the sentence. A pardon releases a person who has committed a crime from the punishment required by law.

TRANSCRIBING FROM DICTATION

Directions: This dictation emphasizes and reinforces the legal terms and definitions you have studied. Listen carefully to the pronunciation of each of the legal terms. Unless otherwise directed, use a 70-space line (typewriter) or 1-inch margins (computer) and double spacing. Correct all errors. Follow one of the procedures below.

Keyboarding Procedure
Using the cassette from Lesson 14, Part A, transcribe the dictation directly at your typewriter or computer.

Shorthand Procedure
Using the cassette from Lesson 14, Part A, take the dictation using your shorthand system and then transcribe from your shorthand notes on your typewriter or computer.

When you have finished transcribing Part A of the practice dictation, check your transcript with the printed copy. If you made any mistakes in the transcription, you should practice those words several times before going on.

Part B TERMINOLOGY AND DEFINITIONS

Directions: Study the terms, pronunciations, and definitions until you are thoroughly familiar with them. In order to complete this lesson successfully, you must understand the meaning and usage of all the legal terms presented. If you are using shorthand, write your shorthand outline for each legal term in your shorthand notebook or on your shorthand machine.

Legal Term	Pronunciation	Definition
1. homicide	′häm-ə-sīd	The killing of a human being by another, whether intentional or unintentional.
2. justifiable homicide	′jəs-tə-fī-ə-bəl ′häm-ə-sīd	The intentional killing of a human being that is done without any evil design. If a police officer kills someone to prevent the commission of a felony that could not otherwise be avoided, it would be a justifiable homicide.
3. excusable homicide	ik-′skyü-zə-bəl ′häm-ə-sīd	The killing of a human being that is the result of a person doing a legal act or of an act of self-defense.
4. felonious homicide	fə-′lō-nē-əs ′häm-ə-sīd	The wrongful killing of a human being without justification or excuse of law.
5. murder	′mərd-ər	The intentional killing of another human being with malice aforethought.
6. manslaughter	′man-slȯt-ər	The killing of another human being that is unlawful and done without malice aforethought. Manslaughter may be voluntary or involuntary. Voluntary manslaughter is a killing done in a heat of passion or on a provoked sudden impulse. Involuntary manslaughter is usually the result of negligence.

7. malice aforethought	'mal-əs ə-'fȯr-thȯt	The deliberate planning and intention to kill or seriously injure another person. An essential element that distinguishes murder from other types of homicide.
8. assault and battery	ə-'sȯlt ən 'bat-ə-rē	Assault is an actual threat to inflict bodily harm upon another, and battery is putting the threat into effect. Usually the two terms are used together in a charge because a battery is assumed, in law, to be preceded by an assault.
9. break and enter	brāk ən 'ent-ər	Forcible and unlawful entry, such as into a building, car, or boat, with the intent to commit a crime therein. A burglary. Sometimes called a B & E.
10. constructive breaking	kən-'strək-tiv 'brāk-iŋ	A breaking and entering that is accomplished by fraud, threats, or trickery rather than a forcible physical entry, such as the breaking of a lock or a window.
11. larceny	'lärs-nē	Illegally taking and carrying away personal property belonging to another with no intention of returning the property to the owner. The value of the goods stolen determines whether it is petit larceny or grand larceny. Same as burglary.
12. robbery	'räb-rē	A felony that is committed by one person taking property from another person or in the presence of that person by the use of force or violence and with no intention of returning the property to the owner.
13. animus furandi	'an-ə-məs 'fyu̇r-an-dī	Latin. The intent to steal the property of another and permanently deprive the owner of said property. An essential element of a larceny.
14. forgery	'fȯrj-rē	The alteration of anything in writing with the intention of defrauding another.
15. utter and publish	'ət-ər ən 'pəb-lish	The offering of a forged instrument with the intent to defraud. If you sign someone else's name to a check and try to cash it, you are guilty of uttering and publishing.

Self-Evaluation B   TERMINOLOGY AND DEFINITION RECALL

Directions: In the Answers column, write the legal term that is most representative of the corresponding statement. After you have completed this self-evaluation, check your answers with the key on page 496–497. If you have any incorrect answers, restudy the definitions for those terms before going on with this lesson. Then unless otherwise directed, submit this self-evaluation to your instructor.

Answers

1. The killing of a human being by another, whether intentional or unintentional is a/an _____.

   1. _____

2. The killing of another human being that is unlawful but done without malice aforethought is _____.

   2. _____

3. The intentional killing of another human being with malice aforethought is _____.

   3. _____

4. Illegally taking and carrying away personal property belonging to another with no intention of returning the property to the owner is _____.

   4. _____

5. The wrongful killing of another human being without justification or excuse of law is _____.

   5. _____

6. A Latin term meaning the intent to steal the property of another and permanently deprive the owner of said property is _____.

   6. _____

7. The offering of a forged instrument with the intent to defraud is to _____.

   7. _____

8. The alteration of anything in writing with the intention of defrauding another is _____.

   8. _____

9. An actual threat to inflict bodily harm upon another and putting the threat into effect is called _____.

   9. _____

10. The deliberate planning and intention to kill or seriously injure another person is _____.

    10. _____

11. A breaking and entering that is accomplished by fraud, threats, or trickery is a/an _____.

    11. _____

12. Forcible and unlawful entry, such as into a building, car, or boat, with the intent to commit a crime therein is referred to as _____.

    12. _____

13. The intentional killing of another human being that is done without any evil design is a/an _____.

    13. _____

14. The killing of another human being resulting from self-defense or from doing a legal act is _____.

    14. _____

15. A felony that is committed by one person taking property from another person or in the presence of that person by the use of force or violence and with no intention of returning the property to the owner is _____.

    15. _____

KEYING LEGAL TERMS

Directions: Unless otherwise instructed, use a 70-space line (typewriter) or 1-inch margins (computer) and double spacing. Correct all errors. Follow one of the procedures below.

WORDS

Keyboarding Procedure
On your typewriter or computer, key the following words at least two times, concentrating on the correct spelling and pronunciation.

Shorthand Procedure
On your typewriter or computer, key the following words once, concentrating on the correct spelling and pronunciation. Then write the shorthand outline for each word in your shorthand notebook or on your shorthand machine. Transcribe from the shorthand outlines one time on your typewriter or computer.

homicide	justifiable homicide	excusable homicide
felonious homicide	murder	malice aforethought
manslaughter	assault and battery	break and enter
constructive breaking	larceny	robbery
animus furandi	forgery	utter and publish

SENTENCES

Keyboarding Procedure
Key each of the following sentences one time on your typewriter or computer. Concentrate on the correct spelling and pronunciation of each underlined legal term.

Shorthand Procedure
Write the correct shorthand outlines for the following sentences in your shorthand notebook or on your shorthand machine. Transcribe from your shorthand outlines one time on your typewriter or computer.

These sentences will be used for practice dictation on the cassettes.

Homicide is the killing of a human being by another, whether intentional or unintentional. Homicide may be justifiable, excusable, or felonious. Justifiable homicide is an intentional killing without any evil design, such as a situation where a police officer kills someone to prevent the commission of a felony that could not otherwise be avoided. An excusable homicide is a death that results from an act of self-defense or an unintentional death resulting from someone doing a legal act. Felonious homicide is the wrongful killing of a human being without justification or excuse of law. Murder and manslaughter are the two types of felonious homicide.

Homicide is a necessary ingredient of the crimes of murder and manslaughter. Murder is the intentional killing of another human being with malice aforethought, which is the deliberate planning and intention to kill or seriously injure another person. Manslaughter is the killing of another human being that is unlawful but done without malice aforethought.

Assault and battery are two terms that are often combined. Assault is a threat to inflict bodily harm upon another, whereas battery is putting the threat into effect. Forcible and unlawful entry into a building with the intent to commit a crime therein is to break and enter. Breaking and entering is commonly referred to as a B & E. If a burglar gains entry into a house by fraud, threats, or trickery, the entry is referred to as constructive breaking.

Larceny and robbery are both felonies that involve the taking of another's personal property unlawfully. An essential element of larceny is <u>animus furandi</u>, which is the intent to steal the property of another and permanently deprive the owner of said property.

Forgery is the alteration of anything in writing with the intent to defraud. For instance, one might forge a signature on a check. The offering of a forged check for payment is to <u>utter and publish</u>.

TRANSCRIBING FROM DICTATION

Directions: This dictation emphasizes and reinforces the legal terms and definitions you have studied. Listen carefully to the pronunciation of each of the legal terms. Unless otherwise directed, use a 70-space line (typewriter) or 1-inch margins (computer) and double spacing. Correct all errors. Follow one of the procedures below.

Keyboarding Procedure
Using the cassette from Lesson 14, Part B, transcribe the dictation directly at your typewriter or computer.

Shorthand Procedure
Using the cassette from Lesson 14, Part B, take the dictation using your shorthand system and then transcribe from your shorthand notes on your typewriter or computer.

When you have finished transcribing Part B of the practice dictation, check your transcript with the printed copy. If you made any mistakes in the transcription, you should practice those words several times before going on to Evaluation 7.

CHECKLIST
I have completed the following for Lesson 14:

	Part A, Date	Part B, Date	Submitted to Instructor Yes	No
Terminology and Definitions	_____	_____	_____	_____
Self-Evaluation	_____	_____	_____	_____
* Keying Legal Terms	_____	_____	_____	_____
Words	_____	_____	_____	_____
Sentences	_____	_____	_____	_____
* Transcribing from Dictation	_____	_____	_____	_____

When you have successfully completed all the exercises in this lesson and submitted to your instructor those requested, you are ready to proceed with Evaluation 7.

* If you are using a shorthand system, submit to your instructor your shorthand notes along with your transcript.

Evaluation No. 7   SECTION A

Directions: This dictation/transcription evaluation will test your spelling and transcription abilities on the legal terms that you studied in the two preceding lessons. Use a 5-space paragraph indention, a 70-space line (typewriter) or 1-inch margins (computer), and double spacing unless otherwise instructed. Correct all errors. Follow one of the procedures below.

Keyboarding Procedure

Using the cassette from Evaluation 7, transcribe the dictation directly at your typewriter or computer.

Shorthand Procedure

Using the cassette from Evaluation 7, take the dictation using your shorthand system and then transcribe from your shorthand notes on your typewriter or computer.

Sections B and C are available from your instructor.

Lesson 15

Probate—Wills and Estates

"Every testament is perfected by death."

—Legal Maxim

When a person dies, his or her property must be distributed through probate procedures. State laws regarding probate procedures will vary considerably. However, the terminology and definitions in this lesson are standard in most jurisdictions. When you have satisfactorily completed the following exercises, you will be able to spell, define, pronounce, and transcribe correctly the terms that are related to probate procedures.

Part A TERMINOLOGY AND DEFINITIONS

Directions: Study the terms, pronunciations, and definitions until you are thoroughly familiar with them. In order to complete this lesson successfully, you must understand the meaning and usage of all the legal terms presented. If you are using shorthand, write your shorthand outline for each legal term in your shorthand notebook or on your shorthand machine.

Legal Term	Pronunciation	Definition
1. durable power of attorney	′dùr-ə-bəl paùr əv ə-′tər-nē	A written power of attorney giving someone the power to act for a person if he or she becomes disabled. To be valid, it must be signed prior to a person becoming disabled. The person appointed to act is sometimes referred to as an attorney in fact.
2. probate	′prō-bāt	The official proving of a will as being valid or genuine. In a broader sense, it refers to all matters over which a probate court has jurisdiction.
3. will	wil	A legal document that expresses how one wants property disposed of upon his or her death. Also referred to as a last will and testament or testament. (See Figure 15-1, page 211.)
4. petition for probate	pə-′tish-ən fər ′prō-bāt	A written application to a court that has jurisdiction over probate matters requesting that a will be admitted to probate.
5. attestation clause	a-tes-′tā-shən klòz	A clause at the end of a will by which witnesses verify or certify that the will was properly executed. (See Figure 15-2, page 212.)
6. codicil	′käd-ə-səl	Something added to a will that changes or modifies it in some way. A codicil may be added to change a part of a will so that the entire will does not have to be redone. (See Figure 15-3, page 213.)

7. nuncupative will	′nən-kyú-pat-iv wil	A will made in anticipation of immediate death that is stated orally before other persons and later put in written form.
8. holographic will	hō-lə-′graf-ik wil	A will that is in the handwriting of the one making it.
9. living will	′liv-iŋ wil	Commands an action while a person is still living. It is a means by which people can set limits on the efforts to keep them alive beyond the point they would choose themselves.
10. testator (male); testestatrix (female)	′tes-tāt-ər ′tes-tā-triks	A person who makes a will or a person who dies that has made a will.
11. testate	′tes-tāt	A person who dies leaving a legal and valid will. If one dies leaving a will, he or she is said to die testate.
12. intestate	in-′tes-tāt	A person who dies without a will. If one dies without a will, then he or she is said to have died intestate.
13. animus testandi	′an-ə-məs tes-′tan-dĭ	Latin. The intention to make a will. Essential to a valid will.
14. testamentary capacity	tes-tə-′ment-ə-rē kə-′pas-ət-ē	The mental ability and capacity required by law to be sufficient for one to make a valid will.

FIGURE 15-1 A Will

WILL (LONG FORM)   838

Be it Remembered, That I, DENNIS ASHTON GRIFFIN

of   54432 Westcox Drive, Paducah, Kentucky,

being of sound mind and memory, but knowing the uncertainties of this life, do hereby make,

execute and declare this to be My Last Will and Testament, in the manner following:

First, I will and direct that all my just debts and funeral expenses be paid in full.

Second, I give, devise and bequeath unto my wife, LESLIE ANN GRIFFIN, all

my tangible personalty and household effects of personal use, such

as clothing, jewelry, precious stones, books, pictures, vehicles,

hobby items, boats and pets of every kind and description and

wherever located, and any policies of insurance on any of said

property, the same to be hers absolutely. I do not intend hereby

to claim an interest in any such property which may already belong

to my wife, and I authorize my Executrix or Executor to honor in

her or his discretion any claim of ownership with reference to any

such property. If my said wife shall not survive me, I direct that

the foregoing property shall become a part of my residuary estate

and be distributed in the same manner as provided herein for the

disposition of my residuary estate.

THIRD: All of the rest, residue and remainder of my property

and estate, real, personal or mixed, now or hereafter acquired of

whatever nature and wherever situate to which I may be legally or

equitably entitled at the time of my death, I do give, devise and

bequeath to COMMONWEALTH BANK, a Kentucky Banking corporation of

Paducah, Kentucky, as Trustee, to be managed and administered and

the principal thereof and income therefrom held and distributed as

FIGURE 15-2 An Attestation Clause

FOURTEENTH: Although it is my understanding that my wife is or may be executing her Last Will and Testament at or about the time of the execution of this my Last Will and Testament, it is not my nor our intention that such Wills shall be construed or deemed to be mutual, reciprocal or dependent one upon the other, and such Wills are not executed pursuant to any contract or agreement.

I hereby appoint LESLIE ANN GRIFFIN of 54432 Westcox Drive, Paducah, Kentucky, executrix of this my Last Will and Testament.

Lastly, I do hereby revoke all former, any and every Will heretobefore made by me.

In Testimony Whereof, I have hereunto set my hand and seal, this sixth day of November in the year one thousand nine hundred and ninety-seven

Dennis Ashton Griffin (SEAL)

DENNIS ASHTON GRIFFIN

Attestation Clause

On this sixth day of November in the year one thousand nine hundred and ninety-seven, DENNIS ASHTON GRIFFIN of 54432 Westcox Drive in the County of McCracken and State of Kentucky signed the foregoing instrument in our presence, and declared it to be his Last Will and Testament, and we not being interested therein, at the request of said DENNIS ASHTON GRIFFIN in his presence, and in the presence of each other, and where he could see us sign our names, did thereupon, on said above mentioned day subscribe our names hereto as witnesses thereof.

Sandra Bright, residing at *849 Whitmore Drive*

Ralph Longshore, residing at *1740 Marigold Lane*

FIGURE 15-3 A Codicil

CODICIL

      I, DENNIS ASHTON GRIFFIN, of the City of Paducah, County of McCracken, State of Kentucky, do make, publish, and declare this to be the first codicil to my Last Will and Testament.

      In the event that my wife, LESLIE ANN GRIFFIN, should predecease me or die simultaneously as defined in my Last Will and Testament, I hereby bequeath my tangible personalty and household effects of personal use as defined in my Last Will and Testament to Habitat for Humanity, Inc., of Paducah, Kentucky, the same to belong to Habitat for Humanity absolutely.

      I hereby ratify, republish, and reaffirm said Last Will and Testament in all respects, except as modified by this Codicil thereto.

      In witness whereof, I have hereunto set my hand and seal this third day of December, 1997.

                        Dennis Ashton Griffin L.S.
                       DENNIS ASHTON GRIFFIN

Attestation Clause

      Signed, sealed, published, and declared by DENNIS ASHTON GRIFFIN the abovenamed testator, as and for a Codicil to his Last Will and Testament in the presence of us, who at his request and in his presence and in the presence of one another, have hereunto subscribed our names as witnesses, this third day of December, 1997.

Sandra Bright .... residing at *849 Whitmore Drive* ......

Ralph Longshore .... residing at *1740 Marigold Lane* ......

Self-Evaluation A   TERMINOLOGY AND DEFINITION RECALL

Directions: In the Answers column, write the letter from Column 1 that represents the word or phrase that best matches each item in Column 2. After you have completed this self-evaluation, check your answers with the key on page 497. If you have any incorrect answers, restudy the definitions for those terms before going on with this lesson. Then unless otherwise directed, submit this self-evaluation to your instructor.

Column 1

a. animus testandi

b. attestation clause

c. codicil

d. durable power of attorney

e. holographic will

f. intestate

g. living will

h. nuncupative will

i. petition for probate

j. power of attorney

k. probate

l. testate

m. testamentary capacity

n. testator/testatrix

o. will

Column 2

1. A person who dies without a will.

2. Commands an action while a person is still living.

3. A clause at the end of a will by which witnesses verify or certify that the will was properly executed.

4. The official proving of a will as being valid or genuine.

5. A will made in anticipation of immediate death that is stated orally before other persons and later put in written form.

6. A document giving someone the power to act for a person if he or she becomes disabled.

7. A Latin expression meaning the intention to make a will.

8. A written application to a court that has jurisdiction over probate matters requesting that a will be admitted to probate.

9. A word describing a deceased person who has left a legal and valid will.

10. A person who makes a will or a deceased person who has made a will.

11. Something added to a will that changes or modifies it in some way.

12. A will that is in the handwriting of the one making the will.

13. A legal document expressing how a person wants property disposed of upon his or her death.

14. The mental ability and capacity required by law to be sufficient for one to make a valid will.

Answers

1. _____

2. _____

3. _____

4. _____

5. _____

6. _____

7. _____

8. _____

9. _____

10. _____

11. _____

12. _____

13. _____

14. _____

KEYING LEGAL TERMS

Directions: Unless otherwise instructed, use a 70-space line (typewriter) or 1-inch margins (computer) and double spacing. Correct all errors. Follow one of the procedures below.

WORDS

Keyboarding Procedure
On your typewriter or computer, key the following words at least two times, concentrating on the correct spelling and pronunciation.

Shorthand Procedure
On your typewriter or computer, key the following words once, concentrating on the correct spelling and pronunciation. Then write the shorthand outline for each word in your shorthand notebook or on your shorthand machine. Transcribe from the shorthand outlines one time on your typewriter or computer.

durable power of attorney	probate	will
petition for probate	attestation clause	codicil
nuncupative will	holographic will	living will
testator	testatrix	testate
intestate	animus testandi	testamentary capacity

SENTENCES

Keyboarding Procedure
Key each of the following sentences one time on your typewriter or computer. Concentrate on the correct spelling and pronunciation of each underlined legal term.

Shorthand Procedure
Write the correct shorthand outlines for the following sentences in your shorthand notebook or on your shorthand machine. Transcribe from your shorthand outlines one time on your typewriter or computer.

These sentences will be used for practice dictation on the cassettes.

A durable power of attorney gives someone the power to act for you if you become disabled. However, a durable power of attorney must be signed prior to the person becoming disabled to be valid. A power of attorney that does not contain words stating that it shall not be affected by the person's disability is not valid after the person becomes disabled.

Probate is the official proving of a will as being valid or genuine. A will is a legal document that expresses how one wants property disposed of upon his or her death. A written application to a probate court requesting that a will be admitted to probate is a petition for probate.

An attestation clause is a clause at the end of a will by which witnesses verify or certify that the will was properly executed. A will may be added to or changed by a codicil. A will made in anticipation of immediate death that is stated orally before other persons and later put in written form is a nuncupative will. A holographic will is one that is in the handwriting of the person who makes it. A living will commands an action while a person is still living and is a means by which a person can set limits on the efforts to keep him or her alive. The intention of a living will is to assure that a patient's wishes regarding care during a terminal illness will be followed.

A testator or testatrix is a person who makes a will or one who dies who has made a will. If one dies leaving a will, then the person dies testate. However, if one dies without a will, he or she is said to have died intestate.

Animus testandi is essential to the making of a will. Animus testandi means the intention to make a will. Additionally, for a will to be valid, the testator or testatrix must have testamentary capacity. Testamentary capacity is the mental ability and capacity required by law to be sufficient for one to make a valid will. A will is also referred to as a last will and testament.

TRANSCRIBING FROM DICTATION

Directions: This dictation emphasizes and reinforces the legal terms and definitions you have studied. Listen carefully to the pronunciation of each of the legal terms. Unless otherwise directed, use a 70-space line (typewriter) or 1-inch margins (computer) and double spacing. Correct all errors. Follow one of the procedures below.

Keyboarding Procedure
Using the cassette from Lesson 15, Part A, transcribe the dictation directly at your typewriter or computer.

Shorthand Procedure
Using the cassette from Lesson 15, Part A, take the dictation using your shorthand system and then transcribe from your shorthand notes on your typewriter or computer.

When you have finished transcribing Part A of the practice dictation, check your transcript with the printed copy. If you made any mistakes in the transcription, you should practice those words several times before going on.

Part B TERMINOLOGY AND DEFINITIONS

Directions: Study the terms, pronunciations, and definitions until you are thoroughly familiar with them. In order to complete this lesson successfully, you must understand the meaning and usage of all the legal terms presented. If you are using shorthand, write your shorthand outline for each legal term in your shorthand notebook or on your shorthand machine.

Legal Term	Pronunciation	Definition
1. estate	is-'tāt	Property of any kind that one owns and can dispose of in a will.
2. publication	pəb-lə-'kā-shən	The formal declaration made by a testator or testatrix at the time a will is signed stating that it is his or her last will and testament.
3. bequest	bi-'kwest	Something that is given to another by a will. Usually money or personal property. A legacy.
4. bequeath	bi-'kwēth	The giving of something, such as personal property or money, to another by a will.
5. devise	di-'vīz	A bequest or to bequeath. Usually refers to real property that is given by will, but it may also refer to any property that is given by will or the giving of property by will.
6. abatement	ə-'bāt-mənt	A decrease in the bequests or legacies because there is not enough money in the estate to pay the full amount. The bequests or legacies are usually decreased proportionately.

7. residuary estate	ri-'zij-ə-wer-ē is-'tāt	The estate remaining after debts, expenses, and specific bequests have been settled.
8. creditor's claim	'kred-ət-ərs klām	A written request for the payment of a bill from the estate of the deceased.
9. hereditaments	her-ə-'dit-ə-mənts	Any kind of property that may be inherited.
10. tangible property	'tan-jə-bəl 'präp-ərt-ē	Any article of personal property. Does not include real estate. Also referred to as a chattel.
11. executor (male); executrix (female)	ig-'zek-ət-ər ig-'zek-ə-triks	A person named by a testator or testatrix to carry out the directions as stated in a will. Referred to in some states as a personal representative.
12. administrator (male); administratrix (female)	əd-'min-ə-strāt-ər əd-'min-ə-'strā-triks	A person who is appointed by the court to administer or take charge of an estate if the executor or executrix is unable or unwilling to serve or if a person dies intestate.
13. letters of authority	'let-ərs əv ə-'thär-ət-ē	A document issued by the probate court appointing a person as executor/executrix, or personal representative, of an estate. Also referred to in some states as letters testamentary. If the court document appoints a person as an administrator or administratrix, then the document is referred to as letters of administration. (See Figure 15-4, page 220.)

FIGURE 15-4   Letters of Authority

Approved, SCAO

STATE OF MICHIGAN PROBATE COURT COUNTY OF Ingham	LETTERS OF AUTHORITY	FILE NO. 789345-37

Estate of HEATHER CAROL BENNETT

TRAVIS WARD BENNETT
Name
789 Prescott Avenue, Holt, Michigan 48842
Address
has been appointed Administrator

of the estate and has filed an acceptance of trust or a bond which has been approved as required by law, and by this instrument is granted full power and authority to take possession, collect, preserve, manage and dispose of all the property of the estate according to law, and to perform all acts permitted or required by statute, court rule and orders and decrees of this court, unless limited below.

RESTRICTIONS: None

July 17, 1997
Date *Natalie Lee Lamont* (P 99905)
Judge of Probate   **Bar no.**

Morgan Renee Jeffery   (P 55217)
Attorney name   **Bar no.**
45 Edgewood Boulevard, Suite 17
Address
Lansing, Michigan 48910 (517) 555-7781
City, state, zip   **Telephone no.**

I certify that I have compared this copy with the original on file and that it is a correct copy of the whole of such original, and on this date, these letters are in full force and effect.

July 18, 1997   *Robert Lambropoulos*
Date   **Deputy Probate Register**

Do not write below this line - For court use only

PC 15 (1/85) **LETTERS OF AUTHORITY**   MCL 700.533, 700.534; MSA 27.5533, 27.5534, MCR 5.705

Self-Evaluation B   TERMINOLOGY AND DEFINITION RECALL

Directions: In the Answers column at the right of each statement, write the letter that represents the word or group of words that correctly completes the statement. After you have completed this self-evaluation, check your answers with the key on page 497. If you have any incorrect answers, restudy the definitions for those terms before going on with this lesson. Then unless otherwise directed, submit this self-evaluation to your instructor.

Answers

1. A proportional decrease in the bequests or legacies because there is not enough money in the estate to pay the full amount is known as (a) creditor's claim, (b) bequeath, (c) abatement.

    1. _____

2. The estate remaining after debts, expenses, and specific bequests have been settled is the (a) tangible property, (b) creditor's claim, (c) residuary estate.

    2. _____

3. Something that is given to another by a will is a/an (a) abatement, (b) bequest, (c) publication.

    3. _____

4. A document issued by a probate court appointing a person as administrator or administratrix of an estate is (a) creditor's claim, (b) publication, (c) letters of authority.

    4. _____

5. A written request for the payment of a bill from the estate of the deceased is a (a) bequest, (b) creditor's claim, (c) letters of authority.

    5. _____

6. A person named by a testator or testatrix in a will to carry out the directions as stated in the will is a/an (a) executor or executrix, (b) administrator or administratrix, (c) devise.

    6. _____

7. A bequest or to bequeath is (a) devise, (b) abatement, (c) hereditament.

    7. _____

8. Any kind of property that may be inherited is called (a) hereditaments, (b) bequest, (c) estate.

    8. _____

9. The formal declaration made by a testator or testatrix at the time of signing a will stating that it is his or her last will and testament is a/an (a) bequest, (b) abatement, (c) publication.

    9. _____

10. Any article of personal property is called (a) residuary estate, (b) tangible property, (c) devise.

    10. _____

11. A person who is appointed by the court to administer or take charge of an estate is referred to as a/an (a) executor or executrix, (b) testator or testatrix, (c) administrator or administratrix.

    11. _____

12. Property of any kind that one owns and can dispose of in a will is called (a) tangible property, (b) estate, (c) publication.

    12. _____

13. To give something, such as personal property or money, to another by a will is to (a) bequeath, (b) devise, (c) residuary estate.

    13. _____

KEYING LEGAL TERMS

Directions: Unless otherwise instructed, use a 70-space line (typewriter) or 1-inch margins (computer) and double spacing. Correct all errors. Follow one of the procedures below.

WORDS

Keyboarding Procedure
On your typewriter or computer, key the following words at least two times, concentrating on the correct spelling and pronunciation.

Shorthand Procedure
On your typewriter or computer, key the following words once, concentrating on the correct spelling and pronunciation. Then write the shorthand outline for each word in your shorthand notebook or on your shorthand machine. Transcribe from the shorthand outlines one time on your typewriter or computer.

estate	publication	bequest
bequeath	devise	abatement
residuary estate	creditor's claim	hereditaments
tangible property	executor	executrix
administrator	administratrix	letters of authority

SENTENCES

Keyboarding Procedure
Key each of the following sentences one time on your typewriter or computer. Concentrate on the correct spelling and pronunciation of each underlined legal term.

Shorthand Procedure
Write the correct shorthand outlines for the following sentences in your shorthand notebook or on your shorthand machine. Transcribe from your shorthand outlines one time on your typewriter or computer.

These sentences will be used for practice dictation on the cassettes.

An <u>estate</u> is property of any kind that a person owns and can dispose of in a will. <u>Publication</u> is the formal declaration made by a testator or testatrix at the time of signing a will stating that it is his or her last will and testament.

<u>Bequest</u> and <u>bequeath</u> are used in relation to personal property disposed of by a will. A bequest is money or personal property given to another by a will. Bequeath is the giving of something, such as personal property or money, to another by a will. <u>Devise</u> is a bequest, or it may also mean to bequeath. If the assets of an estate are not sufficient to pay the legacies in full, <u>abatement</u> results. Abatement is a proportional decrease of the legacies.

The <u>residuary estate</u> is what remains after all debts and expenses of a will have been settled. A written request for the payment of a bill from the estate of a deceased person is a <u>creditor's claim</u>.

Things or property that may be inherited are referred to as <u>hereditaments</u>. Hereditaments include <u>tangible property</u>, also called chattels, and real estate. Tangible property is any article of personal property but does not include real estate.

An <u>executor</u> or <u>executrix</u> is a person named by a <u>testator</u> or <u>testatrix</u> to carry out the directions as stated in a will after the testator's or testatrix's death. If a person dies intestate, the court will appoint an <u>administrator</u> or an <u>administratrix</u> to administer or take charge of the estate. If a testator or testatrix does not name an executor or executrix in a will or the persons named are incapable or unable to administer the will, the court will appoint an administrator or administratrix to handle the estate. A document issued by the probate court appointing a person as administrator or administratrix of an estate is referred to as <u>letters of authority</u>. This document gives the appointed person the authority to manage or dispose of the property in an estate.

TRANSCRIBING FROM DICTATION

Directions: This dictation emphasizes and reinforces the legal terms and definitions you have studied. Listen carefully to the pronunciation of each of the legal terms. Unless otherwise directed, use a 70-space line (typewriter) or 1-inch margins (computer) and double spacing. Correct all errors. Follow one of the procedures below.

Keyboarding Procedure

Using the cassette from Lesson 15, Part B, transcribe the dictation directly at your typewriter or computer.

Shorthand Procedure

Using the cassette from Lesson 15, Part B, take the dictation using your shorthand system and then transcribe from your shorthand notes on your typewriter or computer.

When you have finished transcribing Part B of the practice dictation, check your transcript with the printed copy. If you made any mistakes in the transcription, you should practice those words several times before going on to Lesson 16.

CHECKLIST
I have completed the following for Lesson 15:

	Part A, Date	Part B, Date	Submitted to Instructor Yes	No
Terminology and Definitions	_____	_____	_____	_____
Self-Evaluation	_____	_____	_____	_____
* Keying Legal Terms	_____	_____	_____	_____
Words	_____	_____	_____	_____
Sentences	_____	_____	_____	_____
* Transcribing from Dictation	_____	_____	_____	_____

When you have successfully completed all the exercises in this lesson and submitted to your instructor those requested, you are ready to proceed with Lesson 16.

* If you are using a shorthand system, submit to your instructor your shorthand notes along with your transcript.

Lesson 16

Probate—Wills and Estates

"No one can give what he or she has not."

—Legal Maxim

This lesson continues the study of some of the basic terms that are applicable to probate procedures. When you have successfully completed the following exercises, you will be able to spell, define, pronounce, and transcribe correctly the legal terms presented.

Part A TERMINOLOGY AND DEFINITIONS

Directions: Study the terms, pronunciations, and definitions until you are thoroughly familiar with them. In order to complete this lesson successfully, you must understand the meaning and usage of all the legal terms presented. If you are using shorthand, write your shorthand outline for each legal term in your shorthand notebook or on your shorthand machine.

Legal Term	*Pronunciation*	*Definition*
1. citation	sī-tā-'shən	A summons issued requiring a person to appear in court or risk losing a right to something. In probate matters, that right may be the right to inherit.
2. beneficiary	ben-ə-'fish-ē-er-ē	Anyone who is to receive benefit from a will.
3. cestui que trust	'ses-twē kē trəst	French. A beneficiary of a trust. A person who receives benefits from a trust.
4. heir	ar	A person who has a right by law to inherit the property of another.
5. pretermitted heir	prēt-ər-'mit-əd ar	A legal heir who is unintentionally omitted in the will by the testator or testatrix.
6. succession	sək-'sesh-ən	The right to an inheritance. The taking over of property that has been inherited.
7. legacy	'leg-ə-sē	A bequest. Usually money or personal property given to another by a will.
8. ademption	ə-'dem-shən	Revoking, recalling, or voiding a legacy. This can occur when a testator or testatrix disposes of property that is included in the will prior to the testator's or testatrix's death, thus voiding that part of the will.
9. escheat	is-'chēt	A reversion of property to the state if there is no individual competent to inherit it.
10. cy pres doctrine	sī 'prā 'däk-trən	French. As near as possible. The court will endeavor to carry out the testator's or testatrix's general intention as near as possible.

11. per stirpes	pər ´stər-pās	Latin. A method of dividing an estate. If an estate is to be divided between two persons and one has died leaving three heirs, then one half of the estate is given to the surviving person and the other half is divided among the heirs of the deceased person.
12. precatory words	´prek-ə-tōr-ē wərds	Words in a will that express a desire on the part of the testator or testatrix that are not binding upon the court.
13. ambulatory instrument	´am-byə-lə-tōr-ē ´in-strə-mənt	A legal document that can be changed. A will is an ambulatory instrument because it can be changed during the lifetime of the testator or testatrix.

Date _____   Name _____

Self-Evaluation A   TERMINOLOGY AND DEFINITION RECALL

Directions: In the Answers column at the right of each statement, write the letter that represents the word or group of words that correctly completes the statement. After you have completed this self-evaluation, check your answers with the key on page 497. If you have any incorrect answers, restudy the definitions for those terms before going on with this lesson. Then unless otherwise directed, submit this self-evaluation to your instructor.

Answers

1. A person who has a right by law to inherit the property of another is known as a/an (a) heir, (b) beneficiary, (c) legacy.

1. _____

2. A legal heir who is unintentionally omitted in the will by the testator or testatrix is a/an (a) legacy, (b) pretermitted heir, (c) escheat.

2. _____

3. Anyone who is to receive benefit from a will is known as a/an (a) heir, (b) legacy, (c) beneficiary.

3. _____

4. Words in a will expressing a desire on the part of the testator or testatrix that are not binding upon the courts are called (a) precatory words, (b) ambulatory instruments, (c) cy pres doctrines.

4. _____

5. A bequest that is usually money or personal property given to another by a will is a/an (a) legacy, (b) ademption, (c) cestui que trust.

5. _____

6. A reversion of property to the state if there is no individual competent to inherit it is known as (a) beneficiary, (b) escheat, (c) cestui que trust.

6. _____

7. A method of dividing an estate is (a) ademption, (b) succession, (c) per stirpes.

7. _____

8. A beneficiary of a trust or a person who receives benefits from a trust is expressed in French as (a) cestui que trust, (b) cy pres doctrine, (c) per stirpes.

8. _____

9. A doctrine indicating that the court will endeavor to carry out the testator's or testatrix's general intention as near as possible is the (a) ambulatory instrument, (b) cy pres doctrine, (c) precatory words.

9. _____

10. A legal document that can be changed, such as a will that can be changed during the lifetime of the testator or testatrix, is a/an (a) cy pres doctrine, (b) precatory words, (c) ambulatory instrument.

10. _____

11. A summons issued requiring a person to appear in court or risk losing a right to something, which in probate matters may be the right to inherit, is a/an (a) cy pres doctrine, (b) ambulatory instrument, (c) citation.

11. _____

12. Revoking, recalling, or voiding a legacy is (a) per stirpes, (b) ademption, (c) succession.

12. _____

13. The right to an inheritance or the taking over of property that has been inherited is (a) succession, (b) escheat, (c) legacy.

13. _____

KEYING LEGAL TERMS

Directions: Unless otherwise instructed, use a 70-space line (typewriter) or 1-inch margins (computer) and double spacing. Correct all errors. Follow one of the procedures below.

WORDS

Keyboarding Procedure
On your typewriter or computer, key the following words at least two times, concentrating on the correct spelling and pronunciation.

Shorthand Procedure
On your typewriter or computer, key the following words once, concentrating on the correct spelling and pronunciation. Then write the shorthand outline for each word in your shorthand notebook or on your shorthand machine. Transcribe from the shorthand outlines one time on your typewriter or computer.

citation	beneficiary	cestui que trust
heir	pretermitted heir	succession
legacy	ademption	escheat
cy pres doctrine	per stirpes	precatory words
ambulatory instrument		

SENTENCES

Keyboarding Procedure
Key each of the following sentences one time on your typewriter or computer. Concentrate on the correct spelling and pronunciation of each underlined legal term.

Shorthand Procedure
Write the correct shorthand outlines for the following sentences in your shorthand notebook or on your shorthand machine. Transcribe from your shorthand outlines one time on your typewriter or computer.

These sentences will be used for practice dictation on the cassettes.

A citation issued in probate matters requires a person to appear in court or risk losing a right to inherit something. A beneficiary is a person who is to receive benefit from a will. The person to whom a policy of insurance is payable is also a beneficiary. The beneficiary of a trust is also known as a cestui que trust. An heir is a person who has a right by law to inherit the property of another. An heir is appointed by the court to inherit an estate if there is no will or if a person died intestate. Thus, the difference between an heir and a beneficiary is that an heir is legally entitled to an estate if there is no will, whereas a beneficiary is named in a will to inherit an intestate.

A pretermitted heir is a legal heir who is unintentionally omitted in a will by the testator or testatrix. Succession involves the transfer of property according to law to the heirs when a person dies intestate. A legacy is a bequest, usually money or personal property, given to another by a will.

Ademption involves revoking, recalling, or voiding a legacy. Ademption occurs when a testator or testatrix disposes of property named in the will prior to death. Property disposed of by ademption makes it impossible to carry out the terms of the will. Escheat is a reversion of property to the state if there is no individual competent to inherit it.

The cy pres doctrine calls for the court to endeavor to carry out the testator's or testatrix's general intention as near as possible. If an estate is divided per stirpes, it is divided by representation or family groups instead of by individuals. Precatory words in a will express a desire or a wish rather than a command. Precatory words may not be legally binding.

An ambulatory instrument is a legal document that can be changed. A will is an ambulatory instrument because it can be changed during the lifetime of the testator or testatrix.

TRANSCRIBING FROM DICTATION

Directions: This dictation emphasizes and reinforces the legal terms and definitions you have studied. Listen carefully to the pronunciation of each of the legal terms. Unless otherwise directed, use a 70-space line (typewriter) or 1-inch margins (computer) and double spacing. Correct all errors. Follow one of the procedures below.

Keyboarding Procedure
Using the cassette from Lesson 16, Part A, transcribe the dictation directly at your typewriter or computer.

Shorthand Procedure
Using the cassette from Lesson 16, Part A, take the dictation using your shorthand system and then transcribe from your shorthand notes on your typewriter or computer.

When you have finished transcribing Part A of the practice dictation, check your transcript with the printed copy. If you made any mistakes in the transcription, you should practice those words several times before going on.

Part B TERMINOLOGY AND DEFINITIONS

Directions: Study the terms, pronunciations, and definitions until you are thoroughly familiar with them. In order to complete this lesson successfully, you must understand the meaning and usage of all the legal terms presented. If you are using shorthand, write your shorthand outline for each legal term in your shorthand notebook or on your shorthand machine.

Legal Term	Pronunciation	Definition
1. trust	trəst	Property that is placed in the care of one person for the benefit of another.
2. trust estate	trəst is-ʹtāt	Property that is held in trust for the benefit of another.
3. dower	daủr	The life estate to which every married woman is entitled upon her husband's death. Dower rights may vary from state to state.
4. reversion	ri-ʹvər-zhən	The future interest of the heirs of a testator or testatrix in property left to another for a specified period of time. At the end of the specified period, the property reverts back to the heirs of the testator or testatrix.
5. indefeasible	in-di-ʹfē-zə-bəl	Something that cannot be voided, annulled, or revoked. A right to an estate that cannot be defeated is said to be indefeasible.
6. revocation	rev-ə-ʹkā-shən	A voiding of a will by a testator or testatrix.
7. animus revocandi	ʹan-ə-məs rev-ə-ʹkan-dī	Latin. The intent to revoke.

8. guardian	'gärd-ē-ən	A person who is legally responsible for the care of a minor or an incompetent person and/or the estate of a minor or an incompetent person. The document issued by the court granting a guardian the power or authority to act on behalf of the ward is referred to as letters of guardianship.
9. guardian ad litem	'gärd-ē-ən ad 'lit-əm	Latin. A person designated by the court to conduct litigation on behalf of a minor.
10. ward	wȯrd	A person who has a legal guardian. A ward may be a minor or an incompetent person.
11. conservatorship	kən-'sər-vət-ər-ship	Created by law to care for the property of an incompetent person or a minor.
12. conservator	kən-'sər-vət-ər	One who is in charge of a conservatorship and manages the property of an incompetent person or a minor. Letters of conservatorship are issued by the court granting a conservator the power or authority to act on behalf of the conservatorship.
13. surrogate	'sər-ə-gāt	One appointed to act in the place of another. In some states, one who has jurisdiction over the probate of wills, guardianships, and conservatorships.

Self-Evaluation B   TERMINOLOGY AND DEFINITION RECALL

Directions: In the Answers column, write the legal term that is most representative of the corresponding statement. After you have completed this self-evaluation, check your answers with the key on page 497. If you have any incorrect answers, restudy the definitions for those terms before going on with this lesson. Then unless otherwise directed, submit this self-evaluation to your instructor.

Answers

1. A trust created by the court for the care of the property of an incompetent person or minor is a/an _____.

   1. _____

2. A person designated by the court to conduct litigation on behalf of a minor is a/an _____.

   2. _____

3. Something that cannot be voided, annulled, or revoked is said to be _____.

   3. _____

4. A person who is legally responsible for the care of a minor and/or the minor's estate is a/an _____.

   4. _____

5. A person who has a legal guardian is a/an _____.

   5. _____

6. One appointed to act in the place of another or, in some states, one who has jurisdiction over matters of probate, guardianships, and conservatorships is a/an _____.

   6. _____

7. Property that is placed in the care of one person for the benefit of another is a/an _____.

   7. _____

8. A voiding of a will by a testator or testatrix is a/an _____.

   8. _____

9. The future interest of the heirs in property left to another for a specified period of time after which the property reverts back to the heirs is _____.

   9. _____

10. One who is in charge of a conservatorship and manages the property of an incompetent person or a minor is a/an _____.

    10. _____

11. Property that is held in trust for the benefit of another is a/an _____.

    11. _____

12. The intent to revoke, as expressed in Latin, is _____.

    12. _____

13. The life estate to which every married woman is entitled upon her husband's death is a/an _____.

    13. _____

KEYING LEGAL TERMS

Directions: Unless otherwise instructed, use a 70-space line (typewriter) or 1-inch margins (computer) and double spacing. Correct all errors. Follow one of the procedures below.

WORDS

Keyboarding Procedure
On your typewriter or computer, key the following words at least two times, concentrating on the correct spelling and pronunciation.

Shorthand Procedure
On your typewriter or computer, key the following words once, concentrating on the correct spelling and pronunciation. Then write the shorthand outline for each word in your shorthand notebook or on your shorthand machine. Transcribe from the shorthand outlines one time on your typewriter or computer.

trust	**trust estate**	**dower**
reversion	**indefeasible**	**revocation**
animus revocandi	**guardian**	**guardian ad litem**
ward	**conservatorship**	**conservator**
surrogate		

SENTENCES

Keyboarding Procedure
Key each of the following sentences one time on your typewriter or computer. Concentrate on the correct spelling and pronunciation of each underlined legal term.

Shorthand Procedure
Write the correct shorthand outlines for the following sentences in your shorthand notebook or on your shorthand machine. Transcribe from your shorthand outlines one time on your typewriter or computer.

These sentences will be used for practice dictation on the cassettes.

A <u>trust</u> exists when real or personal property is held by one party for the benefit and use by a beneficiary or a cestui que trust. For example, property may be held in trust for minor children until they reach a specified age. A <u>trust estate</u> is property that is held in trust for the benefit of another.

<u>Dower</u> is the life estate to which every married woman is entitled upon her husband's death. Dower rights may vary from state to state. <u>Reversion</u> is the future interest of the heirs of a testator or testatrix in property left to another for a specified period of time after which the property reverts back to the heirs of the testator or testatrix.

An estate that cannot be defeated, revoked, or made void is <u>indefeasible</u>. <u>Revocation</u> is the voiding of a will by a testator or testatrix. The intent to revoke is expressed in Latin as <u>animus revocandi</u>. Animus revocandi is an element that must be present for a will to be revoked.

A <u>guardian</u> is legally responsible for the care of a minor and/or the minor's estate. A <u>guardian ad litem</u> is a person designated by the court to conduct litigation on behalf of a minor. However, a guardian ad litem has no responsibility for the minor personally or for the property that belongs to the minor. A person or an infant who has a legal guardian is called a <u>ward</u>. If a person is incompetent and cannot care for his or her own property, a <u>conservatorship</u> may be created by law to manage the property of that person. The person who manages a conservatorship is called the <u>conservator.</u>

A <u>surrogate</u> is one appointed to act in the place of another. Thus, a surrogate parent is one who has been appointed to act in the place of a natural parent. In some states, such as New York, a surrogate is one who has jurisdiction over the probate of wills.

TRANSCRIBING FROM DICTATION

Directions: This dictation emphasizes and reinforces the legal terms and definitions you have studied. Listen carefully to the pronunciation of each of the legal terms. Unless otherwise directed, use a 70-space line (typewriter) or 1-inch margins (computer) and double spacing. Correct all errors. Follow one of the procedures below.

Keyboarding Procedure
Using the cassette from Lesson 16, Part B, transcribe the dictation directly at your typewriter or computer.

Shorthand Procedure
Using the cassette from Lesson 16, Part B, take the dictation using your shorthand system and then transcribe from your shorthand notes on your typewriter or computer.

When you have finished transcribing Part B of the practice dictation, check your transcript with the printed copy. If you made any mistakes in the transcription, you should practice those words several times before going on to Evaluation 8.

CHECKLIST
I have completed the following for Lesson 16:

	Part A, Date	Part B, Date	Submitted to Instructor Yes	No
Terminology and Definitions				
Self-Evaluation				
* Keying Legal Terms				
Words				
Sentences				
* Transcribing from Dictation				

When you have successfully completed all the exercises in this lesson and submitted to your instructor those requested, you are ready to proceed with Evaluation 8.

* If you are using a shorthand system, submit to your instructor your shorthand notes along with your transcript.

Evaluation No. 8   SECTION A

Directions: This dictation/transcription evaluation will test your spelling and transcription abilities on the legal terms that you studied in the two preceding lessons. Use a 5-space paragraph indention, a 70-space line (typewriter) or 1-inch margins (computer), and double spacing unless otherwise instructed. Correct all errors. Follow one of the procedures below.

Keyboarding Procedure

Using the cassette from Evaluation 8, transcribe the dictation directly at your typewriter or computer.

Shorthand Procedure

Using the cassette from Evaluation 8, take the dictation using your shorthand system and then transcribe on your typewriter or computer from your shorthand notes.

Sections B and C are available from your instructor.

Lesson 17

Real Property

> *"One who possesses land, possesses also that which is above it."*
>
> —Legal Maxim

The area of law dealing with property governs the ownership and transfer of lands, tenements, and hereditaments. Many of the terms dealing with hereditaments (that which can be inherited) were covered in the lessons on probate. Also, terms involving leases are included in the lessons on contracts. Therefore, this lesson will include those terms that basically apply to the ownership and transfer of real property not involved in leases or probate. Upon successful completion of these exercises, you will be able to spell, pronounce, define, and transcribe correctly the basic real estate terms presented herein.

Part A TERMINOLOGY AND DEFINITIONS

Directions: Study the terms, pronunciations, and definitions until you are thoroughly familiar with them. In order to complete this lesson successfully, you must understand the meaning and usage of all the legal terms presented. If you are using shorthand, write your shorthand outline for each legal term in your shorthand notebook or on your shorthand machine.

Legal Term	Pronunciation	Definition
1. real property	rēl ′präp-ərt-ē	Land and everything that is built or growing on the land, such as buildings and trees. Also referred to as real estate.
2. realty	′rēl-tē	Real property.
3. premises	′prem-ə-sez	Generally means land that has a building on it.
4. title	′tīt-l	The ownership of real property. Also, the proof of the right to ownership in land or real property.
5. fee simple	fē ′sim-pəl	Absolute and unconditional ownership in land.
6. defeasible title	di-′fē-zə-bəl ′tīt-l	A title that can be voided or made invalid.
7. defective title	di-′fek-tiv ′tīt-l	A title that is deficient or incomplete in some aspect required by law.
8. freehold	′frē-hōld	A right of ownership to land for life.
9. title insurance	′tīt-l in-′shur-əns	Guarantees that a person has title to property. In case of a dispute in the title, the purchaser will be reimbursed for any loss up to the amount of the policy.
10. seisin (also seizin)	′sēz-n	Actual possession of real property with the intention of claiming title to said property.
11. deed	dēd	A document or an instrument that is used to convey a title to real property from one person to another. (See Figure 17-1, page 241.)

12. warranty deed	′wȯr-ənt-ē dēd	A deed guaranteeing that the person transferring real property has a good and complete title to said property.
13. quitclaim deed	′kwit-klām dēd	A deed that conveys only the person's interest in the property if any such interest exists. It does not warrant or guarantee the title, but it does give up any right or interest one might have in the property.
14. habendum clause	′ha-ben-dəm klȯz	A clause in a deed that clarifies the amount of ownership in the real property being transferred. Usually begins with the words "To have and to hold". (See Figure 17-1, page 241.)

FIGURE 17-1 A Deed

WARRANTY DEED—SHORT 891 (REV. 1967)
(PHOTO COPY FORM)   SPACE ABOVE FOR REAL ESTATE TRANSFER STAMP

This Indenture, made September 12   , 19 97
BETWEEN   KYLE RUSHING AND ABBY RUSHING, husband and wife, as tenants by the entirety, of 34550 Circle Way, Lansing, Michigan,
1   **parties** of the first part,
and   JANELLE ASHLEY MOORE, a single woman,

1   **party** of the second part,
whose address is 7885 Riverview Boulevard, Apt. 704, Lansing, Michigan
WITNESSETH, That the said party of the first part, for and in consideration of 2 Ninety-five thousand and No/100
Dollars------ ($95,000.00)------------------- ----------------------------------
to him in hand paid by the said party of the second part, the receipt whereof is hereby confessed and acknowledged, does by these presents, grant, bargain, sell, remise, release, alien and confirm unto the said party of the second part, 3 his heirs   and assigns,
FOREVER, all that certain piece or parcel of land situate and being in the   City
of   Lansing   County of   Ingham   and State of Michigan, and described as follows, to-wit:

Land Description

The South 41½ feet of the North 82½ feet of Lot 1, Block 12 of Green
Oak Addition to the City of Lansing. Also commencing 41½ feet South
of the Northeast corner of Lot 1, Block 12, said Green Oak Addition,
thence South 41½ feet, thence East 8'3", thence North 41½ feet of
Lot 1 and the East 33 feet of the North 82½ feet of Lot 2 of Block 12
of Green Oak Addition to the City of Lansing, Ingham County, Michigan;
also a strip of land described as commencing at the Northeast corner
of said Lot 1, and running thence South 41½ feet, thence East 8'3",
more or less, to East line of said Lot 1, place of beginning.

Habendum Clause

Together with all and singular the hereditaments and appurtenances thereunto belonging or in anywise appertaining: **To Have and to Hold** the said premises, as herein described, with the appurtenances, unto the said party of the second part and to 3 his heirs and assigns, FOREVER. And the said party of the first part, for himself, his heirs, executors and administrators, does covenant, grant, bargain and agree to and with the said party of the second part, 3 his heirs   and assigns, that at the time of the delivery of these presents he is well seized of the above granted premises in fee simple; that they are free from all incumbrances whatever, except such liens and encumbrances as may have accrued since the 10th day of January, 1997, the date of a certain executory land contract, in pursuance of and in fulfillment of which this conveyance is made.

and that he will, and his heirs, executors, and administrators shall **Warrant and Defend** the same against all lawful claims whatsoever,

When applicable, pronouns and relative words shall be read as plural, feminine or neuter.
In Witness Whereof, The said party of the first part has hereunto set his hand the day and year first above written.

Signed, and Delivered in Presence of   *Kyle Rushing*
                                                        * KYLE RUSHING
Bennie Andrews   *Abby Rushing*
* BENNIE ANDREWS   * ABBY RUSHING
Nina Joiner
* NINA JOINER   *

STATE OF MICHIGAN,   on September 12   , 19 97
                       ss. before me, a Notary Public, in and for said County, personally appeared
COUNTY OF Ingham   KYLE RUSHING AND ABBY RUSHING
to me known to be the same person S   described in and who executed the within instrument, who
acknowledged the same to be their   free act and deed.

4.   *Robert T Gates*
| Prepared by: David Turner (P56780)   * Robert T. Gates   Notary Public.
| 8546 East Michigan Avenue
| Lansing, Michigan 48912   Ingham   County, Michigan,
                                             My commission expires July 2   , 20 01

SEE FOOT NOTES ON OTHER SIDE

Self-Evaluation A   TERMINOLOGY AND DEFINITION RECALL

Directions: In the Answers column, write the letter from Column 1 that represents the word or phrase that best matches each item in Column 2. After you have completed this self-evaluation, check your answers with the key on page 497. If you have any incorrect answers, restudy the definitions for those terms before going on with this lesson. Then unless otherwise directed, submit this self-evaluation to your instructor.

Column 1

a. clear title

b. deed

c. defeasible title

d. defective title

e. fee simple

f. freehold

g. habendum clause

h. premises

i. quitclaim

j. real property

k. realty

l. seisin

m. title

n. title insurance

o. warranty deed

Column 2

1. A title that is deficient or incomplete in some aspect required by law.

2. Guarantees a title to property and provides reimbursement for any loss incurred because of a defective title.

3. The ownership of real property or the proof of the right of ownership in land or real property.

4. Land and everything that is built or growing on the land.

5. A deed guaranteeing that the person transferring real property has a good and complete title to said property.

6. A right of ownership to land for life.

7. Actual possession of real property with the intention of claiming title to said property.

8. A deed that conveys only the person's interest in the property if any such interest exists.

9. A word meaning real property.

10. Absolute and unconditional ownership in land.

11. A clause in a deed that clarifies the amount of ownership in the real property being transferred.

12. Generally means land that has a building on it.

13. A title that can be voided or made invalid.

14. A document or an instrument that is used to convey a title to real property from one person to another.

Answers

1. _____

2. _____

3. _____

4. _____

5. _____

6. _____

7. _____

8. _____

9. _____

10. _____

11. _____

12. _____

13. _____

14. _____

KEYING LEGAL TERMS

Directions: Unless otherwise instructed, use a 70-space line (typewriter) or 1-inch margins (computer) and double spacing. Correct all errors. Follow one of the procedures below.

WORDS

Keyboarding Procedure
On your typewriter or computer, key the following words at least two times, concentrating on the correct spelling and pronunciation.

Shorthand Procedure
On your typewriter or computer, key the following words once, concentrating on the correct spelling and pronunciation. Then write the shorthand outline for each word in your shorthand notebook or on your shorthand machine. Transcribe from the shorthand outlines one time on your typewriter or computer.

real property	realty	premises
title	fee simple	defeasible title
defective title	freehold	title insurance
seisin	deed	warranty deed
quitclaim deed	habendum clause	

SENTENCES

Keyboarding Procedure
Key each of the following sentences one time on your typewriter or computer. Concentrate on the correct spelling and pronunciation of each underlined legal term.

Shorthand Procedure
Write the correct shorthand outlines for the following sentences in your shorthand notebook or on your shorthand machine. Transcribe from your shorthand outlines one time on your typewriter or computer.

These sentences will be used for practice dictation on the cassettes.

Real property consists of land and everything that is built or growing on the land, such as buildings and trees. Realty is another term for real property. Premises generally means land that has a building on it. Title is the ownership of real property. Title may also be the proof of the right to ownership in land or real property.

A fee simple is an absolute and unconditional ownership in land. A defeasible title is one that is presently valid but could be voided or made invaild. A defective title is deficient or incomplete in some aspect required by law. Freehold is a right to ownership in land for life.

Title insurance guarantees that a person has a clear title to property. In case of a defective title, the title insurance company will reimburse the purchaser for any loss up to the value of the policy. Most property transfers are now being covered by title insurance. Seisin is the actual possession of real property with the intention of claiming title to said property. A deed is a document or an instrument that is used to convey a title to real property from one person to another. A warranty deed guarantees that the person transferring real property has a good and complete title to said property. The title to most property is transferred by a warranty deed. If you sell property to someone and you hold clear title to the property, you would give the buyer a warranty deed.

A **quitclaim deed** conveys only the person's interest in the property if any such interest exists. A quitclaim deed does not warrant or guarantee the title, but it does give up any right or interest one might have in the property. Thus, if you give a quitclaim deed to property, you have given up any right you might have to that property. The **habendum clause** in a deed clarifies the amount of ownership in the real property that is being transferred.

TRANSCRIBING FROM DICTATION

Directions: This dictation emphasizes and reinforces the legal terms and definitions you have studied. Listen carefully to the pronunciation of each of the legal terms. Unless otherwise directed, use a 70-space line (typewriter) or 1-inch margins (computer) and double spacing. Correct all errors. Follow one of the procedures below.

Keyboarding Procedure
Using the cassette from Lesson 17, Part A, transcribe the dictation directly at your typewriter or computer.

Shorthand Procedure
Using the cassette from Lesson 17, Part A, take the dictation using your shorthand system and then transcribe from your shorthand notes on your typewriter or computer.

When you have finished transcribing Part A of the practice dictation, check your transcript with the printed copy. If you made any mistakes in the transcription, you should practice those words several times before going on.

Part B TERMINOLOGY AND DEFINITIONS

Directions: Study the terms, pronunciations, and definitions until you are thoroughly familiar with them. In order to complete this lesson successfully, you must understand the meaning and usage of all the legal terms presented. If you are using shorthand, write your shorthand outline in your shorthand notebook or on your shorthand machine for each legal term.

Legal Term	Pronunciation	Definition
1. plat	plat	A map or plot showing how a certain piece of land is divided into lots.
2. abstract	′ab-strakt	A history of the title to realty that includes previous owners and any liens or encumbrances that may affect the title to the land.
3. land description	land di-′skrip-shən	A description or an identification of a specific parcel of land that may be the subject of a conveyance. Also known as a legal description or a property description. (See Figure 17-1, page 241.)
4. metes and bounds	mēts ən baúnds	A measurement of land indicating the boundary lines, points, and angles.
5. convey	kən-′vā	To transfer the title to property from one person to another.
6. conveyance	kən-′vā-əns	The instrument by which the title to property is transferred from one person to another.
7. tenancy in common	′ten-ən-sē in ′käm-ən	Title to land held by two or more persons who own the same land or property together, with each being entitled to a distinct but undivided interest.

8. joint tenancy	joint 'ten-ən-sē	Title to land held by two or more persons who have the same interest in the land with undivided possession. In case of death of one of the owners, the other owner or owners have full ownership of the property. Also called right to survivorship.
9. tenancy by the entirety	'ten-ən-sē bī the in-'tī-rət-ē	A husband and wife who own land together. Full ownership of the property will go to the survivor if one dies.
10. partition	pər-'tish-ən	The dividing of land held by joint tenants or tenants in common into distinct portions so that each may hold separate title to his or her portion.
11. homestead	'hōm-sted	A dwelling place and the land surrounding it that is occupied by a family and protected by law from the claims of creditors.
12. servitude	'sər-və-tüd	A right that an owner of property has in an adjoining property. For example, the owner of an adjoining property could not construct something on the property that would detract from or infringe on the neighbors' rightful use or enjoyment of their property.
13. easement	'ēz-ment	A right to use the land of another for a specified purpose. For example, a utility company may have a right to cross the property with electric wires and water or gas lines.

Self-Evaluation B   TERMINOLOGY AND DEFINITION RECALL

Directions: In the Answers column, write the legal term that is most representative of the corresponding statement. After you have completed this self-evaluation, check your answers with the key on page 497. If you have any incorrect answers, restudy the definitions for those terms before going on with this lesson. Then unless otherwise directed, submit this self-evaluation to your instructor.

Answers

1. A map or plot showing how a certain piece of land is divided into lots is a/an _____.

   1. _____

2. A dwelling place and the land surrounding it that is occupied by a family and protected by law from the claims of creditors is a/an _____.

   2. _____

3. Title to land held by two or more persons who have the same interest in land with undivided possession is known as a/an _____.

   3. _____

4. The dividing of land held by joint tenants or tenants in common into distinct portions so that each may hold separate title to his or her portion is known as _____.

   4. _____

5. A right to use the land of another for a specified purpose is referred to as a/an _____.

   5. _____

6. The instrument by which the title to property is transferred from one person to another is a/an _____.

   6. _____

7. Title to land held by two or more persons who own the same land or property together, with each being entitled to a distinct but undivided interest, is a/an _____.

   7. _____

8. A description or an identification of a specific parcel of land that may be the subject of a conveyance is a/an _____.

   8. _____

9. A right that an owner of property has in an adjoining property is called _____.

   9. _____

10. A husband and wife who own land together with full ownership of the property going to the survivor if one dies is a/an _____.

    10. _____

11. A measurement of land indicating the boundary lines, points, and angles is _____.

    11. _____

12. A history of the title to realty that includes previous owners and any liens or encumbrances that may affect the title to the land is a/an _____.

    12. _____

13. To transfer the title to property from one person to another is to _____ the title.

    13. _____

KEYING LEGAL TERMS

Directions: Unless otherwise instructed, use a 70-space line (typewriter) or 1-inch margins (computer) and double spacing. Correct all errors. Follow one of the procedures below.

WORDS

Keyboarding Procedure
On your typewriter or computer, key the following words at least two times, concentrating on the correct spelling and pronunciation.

Shorthand Procedure
On your typewriter or computer, key the following words once, concentrating on the correct spelling and pronunciation. Then write the shorthand outline for each word in your shorthand notebook or on your shorthand machine. Transcribe from the shorthand outlines one time on your typewriter or computer.

plat	abstract	land description
metes and bounds	convey	conveyance
tenancy in common	joint tenancy	tenancy by the entirety
partition	homestead	servitude
easement		

SENTENCES

Keyboarding Procedure
Key each of the following sentences one time on your typewriter or computer. Concentrate on the correct spelling and pronunciation of each underlined legal term.

Shorthand Procedure
Write the correct shorthand outlines for the following sentences in your shorthand notebook or on your shorthand machine. Transcribe from your shorthand outlines one time on your typewriter or computer.

These sentences will be used for practice dictation on the cassettes.

A map or a plot, usually drawn to a scale, showing how a certain piece of land is divided into lots is a plat. An abstract is a condensed history of the title to land consisting of a summary of all the conveyances, liens, or encumbrances that may affect the title to the land. A land description identifies or describes a specific parcel of land that may be the subject of a conveyance. Metes and bounds indicate the boundary lines, points, and angles of a parcel of land.

To convey the title to property is to transfer the title from one person to another. A conveyance is the instrument by which the title to property is transferred from one person to another.

When two or more persons own the same land or property together, with each being entitled to a distinct but undivided interest in the property, the ownership is a tenancy in common. Joint tenancy exists when two or more persons have the same interest in the land with undivided possession. Tenancy by the entirety refers to a husband and wife who own land together with full ownership going to the survivor if one dies. Land owned by tenancy in common or joint tenancy may be divided by partition. Land divided by partition gives each tenant a distinct portion that may be held separately by each tenant.

A homestead is a dwelling place and the land surrounding it that is occupied by a family and protected by law from the claims of creditors. Servitude is a right that the owner of property has in an adjoining property. For instance, something cannot be constructed on a property if it will interfere with the adjoining property. An <u>easement</u> is a right to use the land of another for a specified purpose.

TRANSCRIBING FROM DICTATION

Directions: This dictation emphasizes and reinforces the legal terms and definitions you have studied. Listen carefully to the pronunciation of each of the legal terms. Unless otherwise directed, use a 70-space line (typewriter) or 1-inch margins (computer) and double spacing. Correct all errors. Follow one of the procedures below.

Keyboarding Procedure

Using the cassette from Lesson 17, Part B, transcribe the dictation directly at your typewriter or computer.

Shorthand Procedure

Using the cassette from Lesson 17, Part B, take the dictation using your shorthand system and then transcribe from your shorthand notes on your typewriter or computer.

When you have finished transcribing Part B of the practice dictation, check your transcript with the printed copy. If you made any mistakes in the transcription, you should practice those words several times before going on to Lesson 18.

CHECKLIST
I have completed the following for Lesson 17:

	Part A, Date	Part B, Date	Submitted to Instructor Yes	No
Terminology and Definitions	_____	_____	_____	_____
Self-Evaluation	_____	_____	_____	_____
* Keying Legal Terms	_____	_____	_____	_____
Words	_____	_____	_____	_____
Sentences	_____	_____	_____	_____
* Transcribing from Dictation	_____	_____	_____	_____

When you have successfully completed all the exercises in this lesson and submitted to your instructor those requested, you are ready to proceed with Lesson 18.

* If you are using a shorthand system, submit to your instructor your shorthand notes along with your transcript.

Lesson 18

Real Property

"Everything built on the soil belongs to the soil."

—Legal Maxim

Additional terms that are applicable to the ownership and transfer of real property are given in this lesson. When you have successfully completed these exercises, you will be able to spell, define, pronounce, and transcribe correctly the legal terms presented herein.

Part A TERMINOLOGY AND DEFINITIONS

Directions: Study the terms, pronunciations, and definitions until you are thoroughly familiar with them. In order to complete this lesson successfully, you must understand the meaning and usage of all the legal terms presented. If you are using shorthand, write your shorthand outline for each legal term in your shorthand notebook or on your shorthand machine.

Legal Term	Pronunciation	Definition
1. possession	pə-ʹzesh-ən	The control or ownership of property for one's own use.
2. domain	dō-ʹmān	The ownership of real property.
3. eminent domain	ʹem-ə-nənt dō-ʹmān	The right or power of the government to purchase private property for public use such as the purchasing of private property for building a road.
4. condemnation	kän-dem-ʹnā-shən	The forced sale of private property to the government for public use. The government has the right to condemn private property that is needed for public use, such as the building of a road, and force the owner to sell the property to the government.
5. public domain	ʹpəb-lik dō-ʹmān	Property that is owned by the government.
6. adverse possession	ad-ʹvərs pə-ʹzesh-ən	The possession of another's land for a certain period of time, after which time the one in possession claims title to the land.
7. prescription	pri-ʹskrip-shən	The right or title to the use of another's property.
8. prescriptive rights	pri-ʹskrip-tiv rīts	Rights acquired by prescription.
9. reversionary interest	ri-ʹvər-zhə-ner-ē ʹin-trəst	The future interest one has in property that is presently in the possession of another. For example, the owner of property that is rented to another has a reversionary interest in the property.
10. riparian owner	rə-ʹper-ē-ən ʹo-nər	One who owns property adjoining a waterway and who has the right to use the waterway. The riparian owner's rights to the waterway are referred to as riparian rights.

11. ejectment	i-'jek-mənt	An action for the recovery of land that was unlawfully taken away.
12. fixture	'fiks-chər	Chattel, or personal property, that is attached to land or a building.
13. appurtenance	ə-'pərt-nəns	Something that is permanently attached to land.

Self-Evaluation A   TERMINOLOGY AND DEFINITION RECALL

Directions: In the Answers column, write the letter from Column 1 that represents the word or phrase that best matches each item in Column 2. After you have completed this self-evaluation, check your answers with the key on page 497. If you have any incorrect answers, restudy the definitions for those terms before going on with this lesson. Then unless otherwise directed, submit this self-evaluation to your instructor.

Column 1	Column 2	Answers
a. adverse possession	1. The possession of another's land for a certain period of time, after which time the one in possession claims title to the land.	1. _____
b. appurtenance		
c. condemnation	2. Chattel, or personal property, that is attached to land or a building.	2. _____
d. domain		
e. ejectment	3. Something that is permanently attached to land.	3. _____
f. eminent domain	4. The right or title to the use of another's property.	4. _____
g. fixture	5. One who owns property adjoining a waterway and has a right to use the waterway.	5. _____
h. possession		
i. prescription	6. The right or power of the government to purchase private property for public use.	6. _____
j. prescriptive rights	7. An action for the recovery of land that was unlawfully taken away.	7. _____
k. public domain		
l. reversionary interest	8. Property that is owned by the government.	8. _____
m. riparian owner	9. The control or ownership of property for one's own use.	9. _____
n. water rights	10. Rights acquired by having the right or title to the use of another's property.	10. _____
	11. The forced sale of private property to the government for public use.	11. _____
	12. The future interest one has in property that is presently in the possession of another.	12. _____
	13. The ownership of real property.	13. _____

KEYING LEGAL TERMS

Directions: Unless otherwise instructed, use a 70-space line (typewriter) or 1-inch margins (computer) and double spacing. Correct all errors. Follow one of the procedures below.

WORDS

Keyboarding Procedure
On your typewriter or computer, key the following words at least two times, concentrating on the correct spelling and pronunciation.

Shorthand Procedure
On your typewriter or computer, key the following words once, concentrating on the correct spelling and pronunciation. Then write the shorthand outline for each word in your shorthand notebook or on your shorthand machine. Transcribe from the shorthand outlines one time on your typewriter or computer.

possession	domain	adverse possession
condemnation	public domain	eminent domain
prescription	prescriptive rights	fixture
riparian owner	ejectment	reversionary interest
appurtenance		

SENTENCES

Keyboarding Procedure
Key each of the following sentences one time on your typewriter or computer. Concentrate on the correct spelling and pronunciation of each underlined legal term.

Shorthand Procedure
Write the correct shorthand outlines for the following sentences in your shorthand notebook or on your shorthand machine. Transcribe from your shorthand outlines one time on your typewriter or computer.

These sentences will be used for practice dictation on the cassettes.

Possession is the control or ownership of property for one's own use. Domain is the ownership of real property. Domain also refers to real estate that is owned. Eminent domain is the right or power of the government to purchase private property for public use, such as for the building of a highway. If a private owner refuses to sell property for public use, the government may take the property by condemnation. In a condemnation proceeding, the owner is paid just compensation for the forced sale of the property. Public domain is property that is owned by the government.

Adverse possession is the possession or use of another's land for a certain period of time, after which time the one possessing or using the land claims title to the land. Prescription is the right or title to the use of another's property. Rights acquired by prescription are called prescriptive rights. A reversionary interest is a future interest that one has in property that is presently in the possession of another. One who owns property adjoining a waterway and has a right to use the waterway is a riparian owner.

Ejectment is an action for the recovery of land that was unlawfully taken away. Ejectment has been modified in many states and may include the eviction of a tenant, such as for the enforcement of a sale contract for land. A <u>fixture</u> is chattel, or personal property, that is attached to land or a building. An <u>appurtenance</u> is something that is permanently attached to land. In some cases, fixtures may be removed from realty, but an appurtenance cannot be removed.

TRANSCRIBING FROM DICTATION

Directions: This dictation emphasizes and reinforces the legal terms and definitions you have studied. Listen carefully to the pronunciation of each of the legal terms. Unless otherwise directed, use a 70-space line (typewriter) or 1-inch margins (computer) and double spacing. Correct all errors. Follow one of the procedures below.

Keyboarding Procedure
Using the cassette from Lesson 18, Part A, transcribe the dictation directly at your typewriter or computer.

Shorthand Procedure
Using the cassette from Lesson 18, Part A, take the dictation using your shorthand system and then transcribe from your shorthand notes on your typewriter or computer.

When you have finished transcribing Part A of the practice dictation, check your transcript with the printed copy. If you made any mistakes in the transcription, you should practice those words several times before going on.

Part B   TERMINOLOGY AND DEFINITIONS

Directions: Study the terms, pronunciations, and definitions until you are thoroughly familiar with them. In order to complete this lesson successfully, you must understand the meaning and usage of all the legal terms presented. If you are using shorthand, write your shorthand outline for each legal term in your shorthand notebook or on your shorthand machine.

Legal Term	*Pronunciation*	*Definition*
1. land contract	land ′kän-trakt	A contract for the purchase of real property whereby the purchaser makes a down payment and specified payments thereafter, but the title to the property remains in the seller's name until the payments are made in full. (See Figure 18-1, pages 260-261.)
2. mortgage	′mȯr-gij	The pledging of property as security for a loan. In some states, a mortgage is a lien on the property; in others, it is a conditional conveyance of land. (See Figure 18-2, pages 262-263.)
3. lien	lēn	A legal claim on property for the payment of a debt, such as a mortgage. All liens on a property must be satisfied or released before the owner can transfer title to another party unless that party and the lienholder agree to the lien being assumed by the buyer.
4. encumbrance	in-′kəm-brəns	A lien. For example, if you mortgage property, the mortgage may be an encumbrance or a lien in some states.
5. hypothecate	hip-′äth-ə-kāt	To pledge property as security for a loan or mortgage without conveying the title or possession. If property is mortgaged but the title and possession stay with the person obtaining the mortgage, then the property is hypothecated. The creditor can force the sale of the property to satisfy the loan or mortgage.

6. collateral	kə-'lat-ə-rəl	Some security pledged in addition to the personal obligation of the borrower to insure repayment of a loan. When a person obtains a mortgage on real estate, the real estate is collateral for the mortgage.
7. recording	ri-'kȯrd-iŋ	The filing of a lien, mortgage, title, or other documents in the public records.
8. acceleration clause	ik-sel-ə-'rā-shən klȯz	A clause in a contract that requires immediate payment of the balance of the contract in the event that certain terms or conditions are not met, such as the failure to make payments when due. (See Figure 18-2, pages 262-263.)
9. foreclosure	fōr-'klō-zhər	Taking away the rights a mortgagor has in property that is mortgaged. Usually occurs when payments are not made or some other condition of the mortgage is not met.
10. release	ri-'lēs	The giving up of a right or claim against another person. Thus, a release of a lien means that the lien has been paid in full or satisfied.
11. escrow	'es-krō	Something that is delivered to a third party to be held by that party until certain conditions are met. Thus, a mortgagee may collect money and hold it in escrow for the payment of future taxes or insurance.
12. ad valorem	ad və-'lōr-əm	Latin. Taxes based upon the value of the thing being taxed. Also called a value added tax.
13. assessment	ə-'ses-mənt	The valuation, or appraisal, of property for the purpose of taxation.

FIGURE 18-1 A Land Contract

LAND CONTRACT—(GLEASON FORM)—INTEREST, INSURANCE AND TAX CLAUSES.   331

This Contract, Made the ___13th___ day of ___November___, A. D., 19_97_

BETWEEN _COREY ALLEN JOHNSON, R.R. #1, Box 350, Clarksville, Michigan_

_48815,_____ herein called first party,

and _KIPTON LYNN D'AMATO,_ 87 Main Street, Portland, Michigan 48875,

_____ herein called second party,

WITNESSETH, as follows:

1. Said first party, in consideration of the sum of _Seventy-five Thousand and No/100_ _———————($75,000.00)——————_Dollars to be paid by second party to first party, and of the covenants to be performed by second party, as hereinafter expressed, hereby agree_S_ to sell to second party, all that certain piece or parcel of land situate in the _Township_ of _Boston_ _____, in the County of _Ionia_____and State of Michigan, described as follows, viz: _Lot 136, Lot 137, and North one-half of Lot 135, Excelsior Land_ _Company's Addition, Township of Boston, County of Ionia, Michigan,_ _according to the recorded plat thereof._

2. Said second party, in consideration of the covenants herein made by first party, agree_S_ to purchase of first party, the above described premises, and to pay therefor to first party, or__his____legal representatives, at _Clarksville, Michigan_ the sum of _Seventy-five Thousand and_ _No/100——————($75,000.00)————————_ Dollars in manner as follows, viz: _Ten Thousand and No/100 Dollars ($10,000.00) at closing and payments_ _of Four Hundred and No/100 Dollars ($400.00) beginning on the 13th_ _day of December, 1997, and monthly thereafter_

together with interest on the whole sum that shall be from time to time unpaid, at the rate of _10_ per cent per annum, to be computed from _November 13, 1997_, and to be paid _monthly_ ~~annually~~. Principal or interest not paid when due shall bear interest until paid at _10_ per cent per annum.

3. Said second party shall keep all buildings now on, or that may hereafter be placed on said premises, insured in the name of, and in manner and amount and by insurers approved by first party, and leave the policy with first party, and in case of loss, the insurance, unless by mutual agreement used to repair or rebuild, shall be paid to first party and be endorsed on this contract to the extent of the amount unpaid thereon, and the balance, if any, shall belong and be paid to second party.

4. Said second party shall enter said premises for taxation in _her_ name and shall well and faithfully pay when due all taxes and assessments, ordinary and extraordinary, that may for any purpose be levied or assessed on said premises,_____and shall not commit or suffer any other person to commit any waste or damage to said premises or the appurtenances. Should second party fail to pay any tax or assessment when due, or to keep said buildings insured, first party may pay the same and have the buildings insured, and the amounts thus expended shall be a lien on said premises, be added to the amount then unpaid thereon, be due at once, and bear interest until paid at _10_ per cent per annum.

5. Said first party further agree_S_ that upon the full performance by second party of all covenants and agreements by second party to be performed, and upon the payment to first party of the several sums of money above mentioned, in time and manner and at the place mentioned, that thereupon first party will execute and deliver to second party a good and sufficient _warranty deed_ deed, and thereby convey to second party the premises above described free and clear of all incumbrance except taxes after date hereof, and claims and liens thereon due to any act or neglect of second party.

FIGURE 18-1 A Land Contract (continued)

6. All buildings and improvements now on, or that shall be placed or made on said premises, shall remain thereon as security for the performance by second party of this contract, and should default be made, and said contract be forfeited, said buildings and improvements and all payments made on said contract shall be forfeited to first party as stipulated damages for non-performance of this contract, or first party may at ___his___ option declare all sums unpaid immediately due and payable and enforce the collection thereof at law and make conveyance as aforesaid.

7. Said second party shall not assign or transfer this contract, or lease or sublet said premises, or the buildings thereon, or any part thereof, or add to or change said buildings without the previous written assent of first party thereto endorsed hereon.

8. It is further mutually agreed that second party may take possession of said premises.................... ....and remain thereon as long as ___she___ shall perform all the covenants and agreements herein mentioned on ___her___ part to be performed, and no longer; and that if ___she___ shall at any time hereafter, violate or neglect to fulfill any of said covenants or agreements ___she___ shall forfeit all right or claim under this contract, and be liable to be removed from said premises in the same manner as is provided by law for the removal of a tenant that holds over premises contrary to the terms of his lease and *notice to quit and of forfeiture are hereby waived.
And it shall be lawful for first party at any time after such default to sell and convey said premises, or any part thereof, to any other person without becoming liable to refund any part of the money received on this contract, or for any damages on account of such sale. And it is hereby expressly understood and agreed that **time** shall be deemed as of the very essence of this contract, and that unless the same shall, in all respects, be complied with by second party at the respective times, and in the manner above limited and specified, that second party shall lose and be debarred from all rights, remedies and actions, both at law and in equity, upon or under this contract.

IN WITNESS WHEREOF, The said parties have hereunto set their hands and seals the day and year first above written. (In duplicate).

Signed, Sealed and Delivered in Presence of

Nancy S. Woodford
Nancy S. Woodford

Todd M. Woodford
Todd M. Woodford

Corey Allen Johnson (L. S.)
COREY ALLEN JOHNSON, Seller

Kipton Lynn D'Amato (L. S.)
KIPTON LYNN D'AMATO, Buyer

_____ (L. S.)

*"INSERT" NOTICE TO QUIT AND OF FORFEITURE ARE EACH HEREBY WAIVED"

FIGURE 18-2 A Mortgage

CHATTEL MORTGAGE—For Individual, Partnership or
Corporation—(Short Form). 881

𝕶𝖓𝖔𝖜 𝕬𝖑𝖑 𝕸𝖊𝖓 𝕭𝖞 𝕿𝖍𝖊𝖘𝖊 𝕻𝖗𝖊𝖘𝖊𝖓𝖙𝖘, That SHELLEY D. EVERT

of the City   of East Lansing   County of Ingham

State of Michigan, part y   of the first part, being justly indebted unto SECURITY BANK AND TRUST

of the City   of East Lansing   County of Ingham

State of Michigan, part y   of the second part, in the sum of Five Thousand and No/100---
------------------($5,000.00)----------------------------- Dollars,

ha s   for the purpose of securing payment of said debt, and the interest thereof, granted, bargained,

sold and mortgaged, and by these presents do e s   grant, bargain, sell and mortgage unto the said

Security Bank and Trust

the following goods, chattels and personal property, to-wit:
   One Steinway Grand Piano, 7' Concert Model, Serial #2342.

which said above described goods, chattels and property, at the date hereof are the sole and absolute
property of the said first part y   and the said goods and chattels are now in the possession of the said
first part y   situated at 1504 Auburn Street   in the
     City   of East Lansing   County of Ingham
Michigan, are free and clear from all liens, conveyances, incumbrances and levies and are warranted and
will be defended against all lawful claims, liens and incumbrances of all persons whomsoever, and for a
valuable consideration said first part y   hereby warrants   the above representations to be true.

   That first part y   shall not attempt to sell, encumber, assign, dispose of or transfer any interest in
said property, or remove the same or any part thereof from the County of Ingham
State of Michigan without the written consent of the holder hereof.

   'That first part y   shall in all respects comply with the provisions of Act No. 167 of the Public Acts
of 1933 of the State of Michigan as amended. (Only applicable in the event that first part y   at the time
of execution of this instrument or any time thereafter is a tax payer as defined in said Public Acts and
subject to the provisions thereof).

   And the Further Condition of these Presents is Such, that if the said first part y   shall pay or
cause to be paid to the said second part y   the said sum of Five Thousand and No/100--
---------($5,000.00)--- Dollars,
being the debt aforesaid, with interest at the rate of Ten (10)   per cent. per annum, as follows:
Two Hundred and No/100 ($200.00) Dollars on the first day of each
month commencing October 24, 1997, until said principal and interest
are paid in full

according to a promissory note
                                        bearing even date herewith, executed by
said first part y   to said second party   and to which this Mortgage is collateral security, then this
Mortgage and said promissory note   shall be void and of no effect.
And the said first part y   agree s   to pay the same accordingly.

FIGURE 18-2 A Mortgage (continued)

That **Upon Default** in any of the terms and conditions hereof, the whole amount unpaid on the said note   shall thereupon become due and payable and the said second part y   is hereby authorized to take possession of any or all of the property above described and dispose of said property in accordance with the statute in such case made and provided.

2

In **Witness Whereof**, The said first part y____ha_s____hereunto set____his____hand____and seal_____ the ____24th____day of___September_____A. D., 19_97_.

Shelly D Evert
· SHELLY D. EVERT   (Name of Individual or Partnership)

By_____
·

3_____
·   (Name of Corporation)

By_____as its_____
·

By_____as its_____
·

STATE OF MICHIGAN, } ss.

County of____Ingham_____   SHELLY D. EVERT_____of

East Lansing, Michigan,_____being duly sworn, deposes and says, that____he is

4_himself_____the Mortgagor____named in the within and foregoing Chattel Mortgage, that the consideration of said Chattel Mortgage was actual and adequate, and that said Chattel Mortgage was given in good faith for the purpose therein set forth, and that this deponent has knowledge of these

Self-Evaluation B   TERMINOLOGY AND DEFINITION RECALL

Directions: In the Answers column at the right of each statement, write the letter that represents the word or group of words that correctly completes the statement. After you have completed this self-evaluation, check your answers with the key on page 497. If you have any incorrect answers, restudy the definitions for those terms before going on with this lesson. Then unless otherwise directed, sumbit this self-evaluation to your instructor.

Answers

1. Some security pledged in addition to the personal obligation of the borrower to insure repayment of a loan is (a) ad valorem, (b) collateral, (c) lien.

1. _____

2. Taking away the rights a mortgagor has in property that is mortgaged is known as (a) foreclosure, (b) escrow, (c) ad valorem.

2. _____

3. A lien is also referred to as a/an (a) acceleration clause, (b) foreclosure, (c) encumbrance.

3. _____

4. The giving up of a right or claim against another is a/an (a) release, (b) lien, (c) escrow.

4. _____

5. To pledge property as security for a loan is to (a) escrow, (b) foreclose, (c) mortgage.

5. _____

6. A contract for the purchase of real property whereby the purchaser makes a down payment and specified payments thereafter, but the title to the property remains in the seller's name until the property is paid for in full, is a/an (a) assessment, (b) land contract, (c) mortgage.

6. _____

7. Something that is delivered to a third party to be held by that party until certain conditions are met is said to be in (a) assessment, (b) escrow, (c) foreclosure.

7. _____

8. Value added taxes or taxes that are based upon the value of the thing being taxed are referred to as (a) collateral, (b) encumbrance, (c) ad valorem.

8. _____

9. The valuation, or appraisal, of property for the purpose of taxation is a/an (a) recording, (b) assessment, (c) release.

9. _____

10. A legal claim on property for the payment of a debt, such as a mortgage, is a/an (a) lien, (b) encumbrance, (c) land contract.

10. _____

11. To pledge property as security for a loan or mortgage without conveying the title or possession to the property is to (a) release, (b) hypothecate, (c) mortgage.

11. _____

12. A clause in a contract that requires immediate payment of the balance of the contract in the event that certain terms or conditions are not met is a/an (a) acceleration clause, (b) foreclosure, (c) collateral.

12. _____

13. Filing a lien, mortgage, title, or other documents in the public records is (a) accelerating, (b) hypothecating, (c) recording.

13. _____

KEYING LEGAL TERMS

Directions: Unless otherwise instructed, use a 70-space line (typewriter) or 1-inch margins (computer) and double spacing. Correct all errors. Follow one of the procedures below.

WORDS

Keyboarding Procedure
On your typewriter or computer, key the following words at least two times, concentrating on the correct spelling and pronunciation.

Shorthand Procedure
On your typewriter or computer, key the following words once, concentrating on the correct spelling and pronunciation. Then write the shorthand outline for each word in your shorthand notebook or on your shorthand machine. Transcribe from the shorthand outlines one time on your typewriter or computer.

land contract	mortgage	lien
encumbrance	hypothecate	collateral
recording	acceleration clause	foreclosure
release	escrow	ad valorem
assessment		

SENTENCES

Keyboarding Procedure
Key each of the following sentences one time on your typewriter or computer. Concentrate on the correct spelling and pronunciation of each underlined legal term.

Shorthand Procedure
Write the correct shorthand outlines for the following sentences in your shorthand notebook or on your shorthand machine. Transcribe from your shorthand outlines one time on your typewriter or computer.

These sentences will be used for practice dictation on the cassettes.

If property is purchased on a land contract, the purchaser makes a down payment followed by specified payments thereafter, but the title of the property remains in the seller's name until the balance of the land contract is paid in full. A mortgage is the pledging of property as security for a loan. In some states, a mortgage is a lien on the property; in others, it is a conditional conveyance of land.

A lien is a legal claim, or encumbrance, upon property. To hypothecate is to pledge property as security for a loan without conveying title or possession. Collateral is some security pledged in addition to the personal obligation of the borrower to insure repayment of a loan. When property is pledged as security for a loan, the property is referred to as collateral.

Recording is the filing of a lien, mortgage, title, or other documents in the public records. An acceleration clause in a contract requires immediate payment of the balance of the contract in the event that certain terms or conditions are not met.

A foreclosure is the taking away of the rights that a mortgagor has in property that is mortgaged. A foreclosure usually occurs when payments are not made or some other condition of the mortgage is not met. A release is the giving up of a right or claim against another person. A release of a lien means that it has been paid in full.

When something is delivered to a third party to be held by that party until certain conditions are met, it is in escrow. Thus, a mortgagee may collect money and hold it in escrow for the payment of future taxes or insurance. Ad valorem refers to taxes that are based upon the value of the thing being taxed. An assessment is the valuation, or appraisal, of property for the purpose of taxation.

TRANSCRIBING FROM DICTATION

Directions: This dictation emphasizes and reinforces the legal terms and definitions you have studied. Listen carefully to the pronunciation of each of the legal terms. Unless otherwise directed, use a 70-space line (typewriter) or 1-inch margins (computer) and double spacing. Correct all errors. Follow one of the procedures below.

Keyboarding Procedure
Using the cassette from Lesson 18, Part B, transcribe the dictation directly at your typewriter or computer.

Shorthand Procedure
Using the cassette from Lesson 18, Part B, take the dictation using your shorthand system and then transcribe from your shorthand notes on your typewriter or computer.

When you have finished transcribing Part B of the practice dictation, check your transcript with the printed copy. If you made any mistakes in the transcription, you should practice those words several times before going on to Evaluation 9.

CHECKLIST
I have completed the following for Lesson 18:

	Part A, Date	Part B, Date	Submitted to Instructor Yes	No
Terminology and Definitions				
Self-Evaluation				
* Keying Legal Terms				
Words				
Sentences				
* Transcribing from Dictation				

When you have successfully completed all the exercises in this lesson and submitted to your instructor those requested, you are ready to proceed with Evaluation 9.

* If you are using a shorthand system, submit to your instructor your shorthand notes along with your transcript.

Evaluation No. 9   **SECTION A**

Directions: This dictation/transcription evaluation will test your spelling and transcription abilities on the legal terms that you studied in the two preceding lessons. Use a 5-space paragraph indention, a 70-space line (typewriter) or 1-inch margins (computer), and double spacing unless otherwise instructed. Correct all errors. Follow one of the procedures below.

Keyboarding Procedure
Using the cassette from Evaluation 9, transcribe the dictation directly at your typewriter or computer.

Shorthand Procedure
Using the cassette from Evaluation 9, take the dictation using your shorthand system and then transcribe from your shorthand notes on your typewriter or computer.

Sections B and C are available from your instructor.

Lesson 19

Contracts

> "Equal knowledge on both sides makes the position of the contracting parties the same."
>
> —Legal Maxim

Contract law involves agreements between persons. Contracts must consist of persons competent to contract, a proper legal subject matter, an offer, an acceptance, and sufficient and legal consideration to be legally binding. Every person has the right to make a contract, regardless of the wisdom or desirability of the provisions. The terminology presented deals with that which is involved in legally binding contracts. When you have completed this lesson successfully, you will have a knowledge of some of the broad terminology of contract law.

Part A   TERMINOLOGY AND DEFINITIONS

Directions: Study the terms, pronunciations, and definitions until you are thoroughly familiar with them. In order to complete this lesson successfully, you must understand the meaning and usage of all the legal terms presented. If you are using shorthand, write your shorthand outline for each legal term in your shorthand notebook or on your shorthand machine.

Legal Term	Pronunciation	Definition
1. contract law	ʹkän-trakt lȯ	Law governing agreements made between individuals.
2. contract	ʹkän-trakt	An agreement whereby two or more persons promise to do or not to do certain things. (See Figure 19-1, pages 273-274.)
3. ex contractu	eks kän-ʹtrak-tü	Latin. Emerging or coming from a contract.
4. lex loci contractus	leks ʹlō-sī kän-ʹtrak-təs	Latin. The law of the place where a contract is made. For example, a contract made in Florida is subject only to the contract law for the state of Florida.
5. surety	ʹshu̇r-ət-ē	A person who agrees to be responsible for the debt of another in the event the other person fails to pay the debt.
6. bailment	ʹbāl-mənt	The delivery of personal property by the owner to another person for a specific purpose and period of time, after which time the property is to be returned to the owner. An example would be the delivery of an article for repair.
7. caveat emptor	ʹkav-ē-ät ʹem-tər	Latin. Let the buyer beware. A legal maxim meaning that a person is responsible for examining an article before purchasing it and is buying the article at his or her own risk.
8. parol evidence rule	ʹpar-əl ʹev-əd-əns rül	Once a contract is made in writing, it cannot be changed or altered by oral, or parol, evidence unless there was a mistake or fraud involved. If you make an oral agreement that is not included in the written agreement, then the oral agreement is not enforceable.

9. offer	'ȯf-ər	A proposal by one person to make an agreement or a contract with another person. One of the essential elements of a contract. (See Figure 19-2, page 275.)
10. acceptance	ik-'sep-təns	An agreement to an offer received from another. An essential element of a contract. (See Figure 19-2, page 275.)
11. counteroffer	'kau̇nt-ər-ȯf-ər	Changes made in an offer received from another. A counteroffer must be accepted by the person who made the original offer.
12. option	'äp-shən	An agreement whereby a person has the right to buy, sell, or lease certain property within a specified time. Thus, if a person has an option on land, he or she has the right to buy it within a certain time period. (See Figure 19-1, pages 273-274.)
13. binder	'bīn-der	Money or security given with an offer to insure the intentions of the person making the offer. May also be called earnest money or deposit money. Also refers to a temporary insurance agreement that provides coverage for property until a formal policy is issued.

FIGURE 19-1 An Option

OPTION FOR PURCHASE OF LAND.   580

This Contract, Made this............29th............day of

August............A. D. 19 97...., by and between....EVA J. JACKSON............

part...y......of the first part, and....DIRK L. WATSON............

part...y......of the second part.

WITNESSETH, That the said part y............of the first part, in consideration of the sum of

Three Thousand and No/100 ($3,000.00)............dollars to...her...in hand paid

by the said part y.....of the second part, do es....hereby agree that...she....shall and will at any time

within...six (6) months............from the date hereof, at the written request of the said
part...y.....of the second part, execute and deliver to him.., or to any person or persons as....agents....
the said part y......of the second part shall direct in writing, a good and sufficient Warranty Deed of the

following described land, situated in the....City............of...Lansing............

County of.....Ingham............, State of...Michigan............, to-wit:..Lot 74 of

Angels Subdivision, City of Lansing, County of Ingham, State of

Michigan,

for the sum of...Fifty-One Thousand and No/100 ($51,000.00)............Dollars
payable as follows:

In full upon closing.

And the said part...y.....of the first part do...es....hereby further agree that...she............shall and
will not within..six (6) months............from the date hereof, sell, convey, mortgage, or
otherwise encumber the said land, or any part thereof, or do, or permit to be done, any act or deed to
diminish or encumber the title to said land.

FIGURE 19-1 An Option (continued)

It is agreed by and between the parties hereto, that if the said part____Y____of the second part at the expiration of the aforesaid limited time shall have declined or omitted to make application for the purchase of said land at the price aforesaid, then this instrument shall be void, and the above sum of

Three Thousand and No/100 ($3,000.00)------------------------Dollars

so paid as aforesaid_on the 29th day of August, 1997,____shall be forfeited by the

said part__Y__of the second part, and the said part__Y____of the first part shall have the right to retain the same, as and for liquidated damages, and the said part__Y____of the second part shall relinquish to said part__Y__of the first part all claim to the said land, either in law or equity, and, also all claim to

the said sum of_Three Thousand and No/100 ($3,000.00)-------------Dollars,

so paid as aforesaid, and no claim of the said part__Y____of the second part under this Contract shall then be effectual.

In Witness Whereof, the said part_ies_____ha_ve__hereunto

set__their__hand_s__and seal_s__the day and year first above written.

IN PRESENCE OF

Randolph Myers
Randolph Myers

Robert T. Gates
Robert T. Gates

Eva J. Jackson
EVA J. JACKSON

Dirk L. Watson
DIRK L. WATSON

_____[SEAL]

State of_Michigan_____
County of_Ingham_____ } ss.

On this____29th____day of_August____A. D. 19_97

before me, the subscriber, a___Notary Public_____in and for said County

personally appeared___Eva J. Jackson and Dirk L. Watson_____

to me known to be the same person_s__described in and who executed the foregoing instrument, ~~on~~

~~behalf~~____, and acknowledged the same to be__their____free act and deed.

Robert T. Gates

My commission expires_July 2____20_01_____

FIGURE 19-2 An Offer to Purchase and Acceptance

AGREEMENT PROPOSITION ON THE SALE OF
REAL ESTATE.   118-A

Authorized Agreement through the office of .... Global Realty ....

.... Portland .... Mich., ... October 3 .... , 19 9 7

For a valuable consideration, I hereby agree to buy from .... Corey Allen Johnson
the property located and described as follows, namely:

Lot 136, Lot 137, and North one-half of Lot 135, Excelsior Land

Company's Addition, Township of Boston, County of Ionia, Michigan,

according to the recorded plat thereof.

in the Township of Boston .... , County of Ingham .... and State
of Michigan, for the sum of $75,000.00 ....

The terms of purchase to be as follows: $10,000.00 .... on delivery of land contract

and balance to be paid as follows: monthly principal and interest installments

of $400.00 or more including interest at 10 percent per annum, and

said contract shall be due and payable on or before 15 years after

closing date.
Interest to be computed at .... 10 .... per cent ~~PER ANNUM~~ to be included in said payments.

An abstract showing good title written up to date, also abstract of taxes, to be furnished me clear of expense.

Taxes assessed and unpaid to this date to be (paid) ~~(assumed)~~ by (seller) ~~(buyer)~~.

It is understood that any ~~(contract)~~ (mortgage) tax herein involved is payable by the seller.

I hereby agree to give .... seven (7) .... days to get the
owner's signature to the written acceptance of this proposition, appearing below, which, when signed,
will constitute a binding agreement between purchaser and seller, and herewith deposit $ 1,000.00
as earnest money to apply on the purchase price. If proposition is not accepted or the title is not good,
or cannot be made good, this amount to be refunded, otherwise to be retained.

Sale to be closed on or before .... January 2 .... , 19 9 7

Possession to be given .... at closing .... , 19 ....
Witnesses: Signed:

                                                                                   (Seal)
Nancy S. Woodford   *Kipton Lynn D'Amato* (Seal)

                                                                                   (Seal)
Todd M. Woodford   *Corey Allen Johnson* (Seal)
The above proposition.

I also agree to pay .... Statewide Realty .... a commission of $4,200.00
for negotiating this sale, but if not closed on account of purchaser's default the commission shall not exceed the amount of the deposit.
Witnesses: Signed:

Todd M. Woodford   *Corey Allen Johnson* (Seal)

                                                                                   (Seal)

.... Roberta Huggins .... Salesman.

Self-Evaluation A   TERMINOLOGY AND DEFINITION RECALL

Directions: In the Answers column at the right of each statement, write the letter that represents the word or group of words that correctly completes the statement. After you have completed this self-evaluation, check your answers with the key on page 497. If you have any incorrect answers, restudy the definitions for those terms before going on with this lesson. Then unless otherwise directed, submit this self-evaluation to your instructor.

Answers

1. A legal maxim meaning that a person is responsible for examining an article before purchasing it and is buying the article at his or her own risk is expressed in Latin as (a) ex contractu, (b) caveat emptor, (c) lex loci contractus.

   1. _____

2. An agreement whereby a person has the right to buy, sell, or lease certain property within a specified time is a/an (a) option, (b) offer, (c) contract.

   2. _____

3. The law of the place where a contract is made is expressed in Latin as (a) lex loci contractus, (b) caveat emptor, (c) ex contractu.

   3. _____

4. A person who agrees to be responsible for the debt of another in the event the other person fails to pay the debt is known as a (a) bailment, (b) surety, (c) binder.

   4. _____

5. A proposal of one person to make an agreement or a contract with another person is a/an (a) offer, (b) acceptance, (c) counteroffer.

   5. _____

6. An agreement whereby two or more persons promise to do or not to do certain things is a/an (a) bailment, (b) option, (c) contract.

   6. _____

7. Money or security given with an offer to insure the intentions of the person making the offer is a/an (a) option, (b) surety, (c) binder.

   7. _____

8. Law governing agreements made between individuals is (a) contract law, (b) ex contractu, (c) parol evidence rule.

   8. _____

9. When changes are made in an offer received from another, the offer is then referred to as a/an (a) contract, (b) option, (c) counteroffer.

   9. _____

10. An agreement to an offer received from another is called a/an (a) counteroffer, (b) acceptance, (c) binder.

    10. _____

11. Once a contract is made in writing, unless there was a mistake or fraud involved, it cannot be changed or altered by (a) bailment, (b) caveat emptor, (c) parol evidence.

    11. _____

12. The delivery of personal property by the owner to another person for a specific purpose and period of time, after which time the property is to be returned to the owner, is referred to as (a) option, (b) bailment, (c) surety.

    12. _____

13. A Latin term meaning emerging or coming from a contract is (a) ex contractu, (b) lex loci contractus, (c) caveat emptor.

    13. _____

KEYING LEGAL TERMS

Directions: Unless otherwise instructed, use a 70-space line (typewriter) or 1-inch margins (computer) and double spacing. Correct all errors. Follow one of the procedures below.

WORDS

Keyboarding Procedure
On your typewriter or computer, key the following words at least two times, concentrating on the correct spelling and pronunciation.

Shorthand Procedure
On your typewriter or computer, key the following words once, concentrating on the correct spelling and pronunciation. Then write the shorthand outline for each word in your shorthand notebook or on your shorthand machine. Transcribe from the shorthand outlines one time on your typewriter or computer.

contract law	contract	ex contractu
lex loci contractus	surety	bailment
caveat emptor	parol evidence rule	offer
acceptance	counteroffer	option
binder		

SENTENCES

Keyboarding Procedure
Key each of the following sentences one time on your typewriter or computer. Concentrate on the correct spelling and pronunciation of each underlined legal term.

Shorthand Procedure
Write the correct shorthand outlines for the following sentences in your shorthand notebook or on your shorthand machine. Transcribe from your shorthand outlines one time on your typewriter or computer.

These sentences will be used for practice dictation on the cassettes.

Contract law governs agreements made between individuals. A contract is an agreement whereby two or more persons promise to do or not to do certain things. Ex contractu means emerging or coming from a contract. Lex loci contractus is a Latin term meaning the law of the place where a contract is made.

A surety is a person who agrees to be responsible for the debt of another in the event the other person fails to pay the debt. Bailment is the delivery of personal property by the owner to another person for a specific purpose and period of time, after which time the property is to be returned to the owner. An example of a bailment would be the delivery of an article for repair.

Caveat emptor is Latin for let the buyer beware. Caveat emptor is a legal maxim meaning that a person is responsible for examining an article before purchasing it and that the purchase is made at his or her own risk. The parol evidence rule states that once a contract is made in writing, it cannot be changed by oral, or parol, evidence unless there was a mistake or fraud involved. An offer is a proposal by one person to make a contract with another person.

An acceptance is an agreement to an offer received by another. Offer and acceptance are two of the essential elements of a contract. If a party makes changes in an offer received from another party, it is then a counteroffer. An <u>option</u> is a continuing offer. If a person has an option on a property, he or she has the right to buy, sell, or lease it within a specified time. A <u>binder</u> is money or security presented with an offer to insure the intentions of the person making the offer.

TRANSCRIBING FROM DICTATION

Directions: This dictation emphasizes and reinforces the legal terms and definitions you have studied. Listen carefully to the pronunciation of each of the legal terms. Unless otherwise directed, use a 70-space line (typewriter) or 1-inch margins (computer) and double spacing. Correct all errors. Follow one of the procedures below.

Keyboarding Procedure
Using the cassette from Lesson 19, Part A, transcribe the dictation directly at your typewriter or computer.

Shorthand Procedure
Using the cassette from Lesson 19, Part A, take the dictation using your shorthand system and then transcribe from your shorthand notes on your typewriter or computer.

When you have finished transcribing Part A of the practice dictation, check your transcript with the printed copy. If you made any mistakes in the transcription, you should practice those words several times before going on.

Part B TERMINOLOGY AND DEFINITIONS

Directions: Study the terms, pronunciations, and definitions until you are thoroughly familiar with them. In order to complete this lesson successfully, you must understand the meaning and usage of all the legal terms presented. If you are using shorthand, write your shorthand outline for each legal term in your shorthand notebook or on your shorthand machine.

Legal Term	Pronunciation	Definition
1. consideration	kən-sid-ə-ˈrā-shən	The main reason for making a contract. An essential element of a contract. There must be consideration or benefit to both parties for a contract to be valid.
2. quid pro quo	kwid prō kwō	Latin. Something for something. The consideration in a contract.
3. mutual obligations	ˈmyüch-wəl äb-lə-ˈgā-shəns	A promise for a promise. Both parties to a legally binding contract must agree to do or not to do something.
4. competent parties	ˈkäm-pət-ənt ˈpärt-ēs	Persons who are legally qualified to make a contract. An essential element of a contract.
5. assumpsit	ə-ˈsəm-sət	Latin. A person promised. A written or oral promise made by one person to another.
6. condition	kən-ˈdish-ən	A provision in a contract pertaining to a future event that, if it occurs, would change the agreement.
7. performance	pə-ˈför-məns	The fulfillment of the terms of a contract.
8. pro tanto	prō ˈtan-tō	Latin. As far as it goes. One may recover on a contract that was not completely fulfilled for the value of his or her partial performance.
9. nudum pactum	ˈnü-dəm ˈpakt-əm	Latin. An agreement made without any consideration other than a promise.

10. quantum meruit	'kwänt-əm me-'rüit	Latin. As much as one deserves. One may recover the reasonable value of his or her performance on a contract.
11. assignable	ə-'sī-nə-bəl	That which may be assigned or transferred. A contract that is assignable may be transferred to another person.
12. assignment	ə-'sīn-mənt	A transfer of the title of property from one person to another.
13. subrogation	səb-rō-gā-shən	To stand in the place of the one who made the contract. A right of recovery granted to one for whose benefit a contract was made but who was not actually a party to the contract.
14. accord and satisfaction	e 'kòrd ən sat- əs 'fak-shən	An accord is an agreement between two persons whereby one agrees to accept an amount less than the full amount in satisfaction of the debt. Accord and satisfaction is when the agreement is made and the debt has been paid.

Self-Evaluation B   TERMINOLOGY AND DEFINITION RECALL

Directions: In the Answers column, write the legal term that is most representative of the corresponding statement. After you have completed this self-evaluation, check your answers with the key on page 497–498. If you have any incorrect answers, restudy the definitions for those terms before going on with this lesson. Then unless otherwise directed, submit this self-evaluation to your instructor.

Answers

1. A transfer of the title of property from one person to another is a/an _____.

   1. _____

2. The fulfillment of the terms of a contract is referred to as the _____.

   2. _____

3. A term meaning the agreement is made and the debt has been paid is _____.

   3. _____

4. A Latin phrase meaning as far as it goes, which applies to the recovery for the value of the partial performance on a contract that was not completely fulfilled, is _____.

   4. _____

5. A written or oral promise made by one person to another is _____.

   5. _____

6. A provision in a contract pertaining to a future event that, if it occurs, would change the agreement is a/an _____.

   6. _____

7. To stand in the place of the one who made the contract, or a right of recovery granted to one for whose benefit a contract was made but who was not actually a party to the contract, is referred to as _____.

   7. _____

8. An agreement made without any consideration other than a promise is expressed in Latin as a/an _____.

   8. _____

9. That which may be assigned or transferred is said to be _____.

   9. _____

10. A promise for a promise, or when both parties to a legally binding contract must agree to do or not to do something, is called _____.

    10. _____

11. A Latin term meaning something for something or the consideration in a contract, is _____.

    11. _____

12. Persons who are legally qualified to make a contract are said to be _____.

    12. _____

13. The main reason for making a contract is the _____.

    13. _____

14. A situation in which one may recover as much as one deserves or the reasonable value of the performance on a contract is expressed in Latin as _____.

    14. _____

KEYING LEGAL TERMS

Directions: Unless otherwise instructed, use a 70-space line (typewriter) or 1-inch margins (computer) and double spacing. Correct all errors. Follow one of the procedures below.

WORDS

Keyboarding Procedure
On your typewriter or computer, key the following words at least two times, concentrating on the correct spelling and pronunciation.

Shorthand Procedure
On your typewriter or computer, key the following words once, concentrating on the correct spelling and pronunciation. Then write the shorthand outline for each word in your shorthand notebook or on your shorthand machine. Transcribe from the shorthand outlines one time on your typewriter or computer.

consideration	quid pro quo	mutual obligations
competent parties	assumpsit	condition
performance	pro tanto	nudum pactum
quantum meruit	assignable	assignment
subrogation	accord and satisfaction	

SENTENCES

Keyboarding Procedure
Key each of the following sentences one time on your typewriter or computer. Concentrate on the correct spelling and pronunciation of each underlined legal term.

Shorthand Procedure
Write the correct shorthand outlines for the following sentences in your shorthand notebook or on your shorthand machine. Transcribe from your shorthand outlines one time on your typewriter or computer.

These sentences will be used for practice dictation on the cassettes.

Consideration is the main reason for making a contract. Consideration is an essential element of a contract, and there must be consideration or benefit to both parties for a contract to be valid. Quid pro quo means something for something. Quid pro quo is the consideration in a contract. Mutual obligations consist of a promise for a promise.

Competent parties are persons who are legally qualified to make a contract. Competent parties are an essential element of a contract. Assumpsit is a Latin term meaning a person promised. An assumpsit may be either a written or oral promise made by one person to another. A condition is a provision in a contract pertaining to a future event that, if it occurs, would change the agreement.

Performance refers to the fulfillment of the terms of a contract. Pro tanto means as far as it goes, or one may recover on a contract that was not completely fulfilled for the value of his or her partial performance. An agreement made without any consideration other than a promise is a nudum pactum. Quantum meruit refers to the amount one may recover for the reasonable value of his or her performance on a contract.

A contract that is assignable is one that may be transferred to another party. An assignment of a contract is the transfer or making over to another the title of any property or interest in a contract. Substituting a person in the place of the one who made the contract is called <u>subrogation</u>. When an agreement between two parties is made and the debt has been paid, the legal term is <u>accord and satisfaction</u>.

TRANSCRIBING FROM DICTATION

Directions: This dictation emphasizes and reinforces the legal terms and definitions you have studied. Listen carefully to the pronunciation of each of the legal terms. Unless otherwise directed, use a 70-space line (typewriter) or 1-inch margins (computer) and double spacing. Correct all errors. Follow one of the procedures below.

Keyboarding Procedure

Using the cassette from Lesson 19, Part B, transcribe the dictation directly at your typewriter or computer.

Shorthand Procedure

Using the cassette from Lesson 19, Part B, take the dictation using your shorthand system and then transcribe from your shorthand notes on your typewriter or computer.

When you have finished transcribing Part B of the practice dictation, check your transcript with the printed copy. If you made any mistakes in the transcription, you should practice those words several times before going on to Lesson 20.

CHECKLIST
I have completed the following for Lesson 19:

	Part A, Date	Part B, Date	Submitted to Instructor Yes	No
Terminology and Definitions				
Self-Evaluation				
***** **Keying Legal Terms**				
Words				
Sentences				
***** **Transcribing from Dictation**				

When you have successfully completed all the exercises in this lesson and submitted to your instructor those requested, you are ready to proceed with Lesson 20.

* If you are using a shorthand system, submit to your instructor your shorthand notes along with your transcript.

Lesson 20

Contracts and Leases

> "Whatsoever it is certain a person ought to do, the law will suppose the person to have promised to do."
>
> —Legal Maxim

Legal terms relating to contracts and leases are presented in the following exercises. Leases, which are a form of contract, involve the relationship between landlords and tenants. When you have satisfactorily completed this lesson, you should have a knowledge and understanding of the terminology involving contracts and leases.

Part A TERMINOLOGY AND DEFINITIONS

Directions: Study the terms, pronunciations, and definitions until you are thoroughly familiar with them. In order to complete this lesson successfully, you must understand the meaning and usage of all the legal terms presented. If you are using shorthand, write your shorthand outline for each legal term in your shorthand notebook or on your shorthand machine.

Legal Term	Pronunciation	Definition
1. bilateral contract	bī-ʹlat-ə-rəl ʹkän-trakt	A contract that involves mutual obligations for both sides of the contract.
2. unilateral contract	yü-ni-ʹlat-ə-rəl ʹkän-trakt	A contract in which a promise or an obligation exists only on one side. A unilateral contract is not enforceable until the specified act has been performed.
3. express contract	ik-ʹspres ʹkän-trakt	An actual agreement, not implied, that may be oral or written.
4. implied contract	im-ʹplīd ʹkän-trakt	An agreement arising from the actions or legal duties of the parties rather than from an actual contract. Implied contracts may be implied in fact or implied in law.
5. implied in fact	im-ʹplīd in fakt	An implied contract that is created by the actions of the parties.
6. implied in law	im-ʹplīd in lȯ	An implied contract that is based on obligations created by law.
7. escalator clause	ʹes-kə-lāt-ər klȯz	A clause in a contract stating that if costs increase or decrease, the payments may increase or decrease proportionately.
8. default	di-fȯlt	To fail to fulfill a legal duty.
9. breach of contract	brēch əv ʹkän-trakt	Failure to fulfill the terms of a contract.
10. privity of contract	ʹpriv-ət-ē əv ʹkän-trakt	The relationship of the parties to a contract. It is an essential element to recovery on a contract since only parties directly involved or with privity of contract have a right to sue.

11. rescind	ri-'sind	To cancel or void a contract and to treat it as though no contract had ever been made. Also referred to as recission or revocation of a contract.
12. vitiate	'vish-ē-āt	To destroy the legality of a contract.
13. inchoate	in-'kō-ət	Incomplete. Relates to valid contracts or instruments that are required by law to be recorded but have not been and are, therefore, called incomplete, or inchoate, instruments.

Date _____   Name _____

Self-Evaluation A   TERMINOLOGY AND DEFINITION RECALL

Directions: In the Answers column, write the legal term that is most representative of the corresponding statement. After you have completed this self-evaluation, check your answers with the key on page 498. If you have any incorrect answers, restudy the definitions for those terms before going on with this lesson. Then unless otherwise directed, submit this self-evaluation to your instructor.

Answers

1. An implied contract that is created by the actions of the parties is _____.

    1. _____

2. A contract that involves mutual obligations for both sides of the contract is a/an _____.

    2. _____

3. The relationship of the parties to a contract is known as _____.

    3. _____

4. A clause in a contract stating that if costs increase or decrease, the payments may increase or decrease proportionately is called a/an _____.

    4. _____

5. Failure to fulfill a legal duty is to _____.

    5. _____

6. To cancel or void a contract and to treat it as though no contract had ever been made is to _____.

    6. _____

7. To destroy the legality of a contract is to _____.

    7. _____

8. Instruments that are required by law to be recorded but have not been are referred to as _____.

    8. _____

9. An implied contract that is based on obligations created by law is _____.

    9. _____

10. An actual agreement, not implied, that may be oral or written is a/an _____.

    10. _____

11. The failure to fulfill the terms of a contract is known as _____.

    11. _____

12. A contract in which a promise or obligation exists only on one side is a/an _____.

    12. _____

13. An agreement arising from the actions or legal duties of the parties rather than from an actual contract is a/an _____.

    13. _____

KEYING LEGAL TERMS

Directions: Unless otherwise instructed, use a 70-space line (typewriter) or 1-inch margins (computer) and double spacing. Correct all errors. Follow one of the procedures below.

WORDS

Keyboarding Procedure
On your typewriter or computer, key the following words at least two times, concentrating on the correct spelling and pronunciation.

Shorthand Procedure
On your typewriter or computer, key the following words once, concentrating on the correct spelling and pronunciation. Then write the shorthand outline for each word in your shorthand notebook or on your shorthand machine. Transcribe from the shorthand outlines one time on your typewriter or computer.

bilateral contract	unilateral contract	express contract
implied contract	implied in fact	implied in law
escalator clause	default	breach of contract
privity of contract	rescind	vitiate
inchoate		

SENTENCES

Keyboarding Procedure
Key each of the following sentences one time on your typewriter or computer. Concentrate on the correct spelling and pronunciation of each underlined legal term.

Shorthand Procedure
Write the correct shorthand outlines for the following sentences in your shorthand notebook or on your shorthand machine. Transcribe from your shorthand outlines one time on your typewriter or computer.

These sentences will be used for practice dictation on the cassettes.

A <u>bilateral contract</u> involves mutual obligations for both parties of the contract. A <u>unilateral contract</u> is one in which a promise or an obligation exists only on one side. A unilateral contract is not enforceable until the specified act has been performed. An <u>express contract</u> is an actual agreement, not implied, that may be oral or written.

An <u>implied contract</u> is an agreement arising from the actions or legal duties of the parties rather than from an actual contract. Implied contracts may be <u>implied in fact</u> or <u>implied in law</u>. A contract implied in fact is created by the actions of the parties. A contract implied in law is based on obligations created by law. Thus, a legal maxim states, "Whatsoever it is certain a person ought to do, the law will suppose the person to have promised to do."

Some contracts or leases contain an <u>escalator clause</u> stating that if costs increase or decrease, the payment may increase or decrease proportionately. To fail to fulfill a legal duty is to <u>default</u>. If one defaults on a contract, he or she did not fulfill the terms of the agreement. A <u>breach of contract</u> involves the failure to fulfill the terms of a contract.

<u>Privity of contract</u> refers to the relationship of the parties to a contract. It is an essential element to recovery on a contract since only parties directly involved or with privity of contract have a right to sue.

To rescind a contract is to cancel or void it and to treat it as though no contract had ever been made. To vitiate a contract is to legally destroy it. Fraud will vitiate a contract. An inchoate contract is a valid contract or instrument that is required by law to be recorded but has not been.

TRANSCRIBING FROM DICTATION

Directions: This dictation emphasizes and reinforces the legal terms and definitions you have studied. Listen carefully to the pronunciation of each of the legal terms. Unless otherwise directed, use a 70-space line (typewriter) or 1-inch margins (computer) and double spacing. Correct all errors. Follow one of the procedures below.

Keyboarding Procedure
Using the cassette from Lesson 20, Part A, transcribe the dictation directly at your typewriter or computer.

Shorthand Procedure
Using the cassette from Lesson 20, Part A, take the dictation using your shorthand system and then transcribe from your shorthand notes on your typewriter or computer.

When you have finished transcribing Part A of the practice dictation, check your transcript with the printed copy. If you made any mistakes in the transcription, you should practice those words several times before going on.

Part B TERMINOLOGY AND DEFINITIONS

Directions: Study the terms, pronunciations, and definitions until you are thoroughly familiar with them. In order to complete this lesson successfully, you must understand the meaning and usage of all the legal terms presented. If you are using shorthand, write your shorthand outline for each legal term in your shorthand notebook or on your shorthand machine.

Legal Term	Pronunciation	Definition
1. inure	in-ʹür	To benefit or to have effect. In a contract, inure means that if benefits accrue, they will take effect for or come to the party.
2. execute	ʹek-si-kyüt	To carry out or put into effect. To execute a contract is to put it into effect by doing all the things that are necessary to make it valid and complete.
3. covenant	ʹkəv-nənt	An agreement between two or more persons that something will or will not be done.
4. lease	lēs	An agreement whereby a tenant or person has possession of property belonging to a landlord for a specified period of time. A landlord-tenant relationship. (See Figure 20-1, page 294.)
5. tenant	ʹten-ənt	One who leases property from a landlord. A lessee. (See Figure 20-1, page 294.)
6. landlord	ʹlan-lòrd	The owner of leased property. Another name for a lessor. (See Figure 20-1, page 294.)
7. lessee	le-ʹsē	One who leases the property of another and has possession of said property. (See Figure 20-1, page 294.)
8. lessor	ʹles-òr	One who owns property that is leased. (See Figure 20-1, page 294.)

9. demise	di-'mīz	A lease. When used in a lease, demise means that the lessee shall have full use and enjoyment of the leased premises. (See Figure 20-1, page 294.)
10. demised premises	di-'mīzd 'prem-ə-səz	Land and buildings that are leased. (See Figure 20-1, page 294.)
11. sublease	'səb-'lēs	A lease whereby the lessee lets another person who is called a sublessee occupy the leased premises either for a shorter period of time than for which the premises are leased or until the lease expires.
12. habitation	hab-ə-'tā-shən	The occupying of leased premises as a residence.
13. notice to quit	'nōt-əs tü kwit	A written notice to the tenant from the landlord stating that the tenant is to vacate the premises by a specified time if certain conditions are not met. (See Figure 20-2, page 295.)
14. eviction	i-'vik-shən	The legal removal of a tenant from leased property.
15. writ of restitution	rit əv res-tə-'tü-shən	A writ issued by the court to return to the previous condition. A tenant who does not move after the court has so ordered would be served with a writ of restitution that returns the property to the landlord. The sheriff can then physically remove the tenant and his or her possessions from the premises. (See Figure 20-3, page 296.)

FIGURE 20-1 A Lease

RENTAL AGREEMENT.   118-C

NOTICE: MICHIGAN LAW ESTABLISHES RIGHTS AND OBLIGATIONS FOR PARTIES TO RENTAL AGREEMENTS. THIS AGREEMENT IS REQUIRED TO COMPLY WITH THE TRUTH IN RENTING ACT. IF YOU HAVE A QUESTION ABOUT THE INTERPRETATION OR THE LEGALITY OF A PROVISION OF THIS AGREEMENT, YOU MAY WANT TO SEEK ASSISTANCE FROM A LAWYER OR OTHER QUALIFIED PERSON.

Office of Capitol Management Company   , Date October 17, 1997

This is an Agreement between   Capitol Management Company   as Landlord and
Daniel and Maria Spencer   as tenant, concerning tenancy of

premises known as Apartment 308
      4700 S. Cedar   XXXXX
in the   City   of Lansing   Street

Said tenancy shall be on a month to month basis with monthly rent of $ 450.00   , payable
in advance on the 1st   day of each month starting November   , 19 97 ,
upon which day said tenant shall be given possession of said premises. Both parties agree to give the other party thirty days notice in writing in case either party elects to terminate said tenancy and in such event rent shall be paid to the end of said thirty day period. Tenant agrees that said premises shall be used for residential purposes only, shall not be used for any unlawful purpose or in a manner contrary to law, and shall be occupied by not more than two (2)
adults and -0- children whose ages are

Tenant further agrees to maintain said premises in good repair and to deliver and surrender up the same upon termination of said tenancy in the same condition as when taken except for ordinary wear and tear.

The landlord or his authorized agents shall have the right to inspect said premises and repair and maintain the same, and may at any reasonable hour show the same and any part thereof to prospective purchasers, mortgagees, tenants, or agents thereof, and may, at any time, place and maintain one "for sale" sign thereon in event said property is now or hereafter for sale.

Tenant herewith deposits the sum of $ 250.00   with Community Management
Company   XXXXXXXXXX   , as renting agent of said landlord, to apply on the first
month's rent in event this agreement is signed by landlord or the agent thereof within 3 days from the date hereof, otherwise to be returned to tenant. The balance of said first month's rent shall be paid prior to Oct. 15, 1997
          and in any event before tenant occupies said premises or any part thereof.

Tenant further agrees to deposit one dollar to secure the return to the landlord of two (2)   keys
to said premises upon termination of said tenancy. Upon such return said sum is to be refunded to tenant.

Tenant makes the following representations of fact:
      Former landlord J & J Leasing Company
      Landlord's address 6850 N. Saginaw St.   Phone 555-6700
      Financial reference Federal Savings and Loan
      Occupation Mail Clerk   Employer Lansing Post Office
      Business address 315 West Allegan, Lansing, Michigan 48933
      Name and address of nearest relative Kenneth Spencer, 330 W. Maple,
East Lansing, Michigan 48823

Water bills are to be paid by { XXXX / landlord

Tenant agrees not to make any alterations or improvements to said premises without the written consent of the landlord, and that landlord shall have sole discretion as to the necessity of any repair, decorating or other work in and about said premises and as to the quality and cost thereof.

Tenant shall have no right to and shall not assign this agreement nor sublet said premises or any part thereof, and tenant agrees to immediately inform landlord of any future change in the above facts or in the number or identity of occupants of said premises, any such assignment, subletting or change shall be cause for the immediate termination of said tenancy at the option of landlord.

TRUTH IN RENTING ACT PROVISIONS: Landlord and Tenant specifically agree that this lease shall not, is not intended, nor shall it be construed, to violate any of the provisions of the Truth in Renting Act. If, however, any provision of this lease does in fact reach any such result, then such provision shall be null and void, but the other provisions of this lease shall continue to remain in full force and effect.

The address of the landlord for purposes of notice under the Truth in Renting Act and for all other purposes is 4700 S. Cedar Street, Lansing, Michigan 48910

IN WITNESS WHEREOF, The parties have hereunto set their hands and seals the day and year first above written.

Daniel Spencer *Maria Spencer*
                                    Tenant.

6850 N. Saginaw St., Apt. 605
                                    Present Address.

Abigail Cross
          Landlord.

FIGURE 20-2 A Notice to Quit

NOTICE TO QUIT

Termination Of Tenancy
Landlord - Tenant

To:

> Daniel and Maria Spencer
> 4700 S. Cedar Street, Apt. 30B
> Lansing, Michigan 48910

1. Your landlord/~~landlord~~ _Capitol Management Company_ _____ wants to evict you from:
   Name

   Address or description of premises rented (if different from mailing address):
   > Same

   for the reason that he/~~she~~ is terminating your tenancy.

2. You must move by ___January 17, 1998___ or your landlord/~~landlord~~ may take you to court to evict you.
   Date (*see note)

3. If your landlord/~~landlord~~ takes you to court to evict you, you will have the opportunity to present reasons why you believe you should not be evicted.

4. If you believe you have a good reason why you should not be evicted you may have a lawyer advise you. Call him or her soon.

___December 17, 1997___
Date

Abigail Cross
Signature of owner of premises, or agent

4700 S. Cedar Street
Address

Lansing, Michigan 48910   555-9920
City, state, zip   Telephone no.

*NOTE: if the lease agreement does not state otherwise, the landlord/~~landlord~~ must give notice equal in time to at least one rental period.

PROOF OF SERVICE

Abigail Cross _____ being duly sworn, says that on ___Dec. 17, 1997___ ~~he~~/she served the above notice on
Name   Date

Daniel and Maria Spencer _____
Name

by: ☒ personal service
     ☐ substitute service   _Abigail Cross_
     ☐ 1st class mail   Signature

Subscribed and sworn to before me on ___January 19, 1998___   Ingham _____ County, Michigan.
                                      Date

My commission expires: ___September 1, 2002___ Signature: _Michael Robins_ _____
                          Date   Deputy Clerk~~/Notary Public~~

(To be copied, if necessary, to attach to the complaint)

NOTICE TO QUIT, TERMINATION OF TENANCY, Landlord-Tenant, Form No. DCH100c, Revised 2/80
COURT COPY

FIGURE 20-3 A Writ of Restitution

ORIGINAL - OFFICER RETURN
1ST COPY - COURT
2ND COPY - DEFENDANT

STATE OF MICHIGAN 54th DISTRICT COURT	**WRIT OF RESTITUTION** LANDLORD/TENANT — LAND CONTRACT	CASE NO. 75-8001 LT

6th Floor, City Hall, Lansing, Michigan 48933   (517) 555-3445
Court address   Court telephone no.

Plaintiff name and address
Capitol Management Company
4700 S. Cedar Street
Lansing, Michigan 48910

Defendant name(s) and address(es)
Daniel and Maria Spencer
4700 S. Cedar Street, Apt. 308
Lansing, Michigan 48910

Plaintiff's attorney, bar no., address and telephone no.
in pro per

APPLICATION

The undersigned makes application for a writ of restitution and states:

1. On <u>January 28, 1998</u> judgment was entered against Defendant(s), and Plaintiff was awarded possession of the
   Date

   following described property: 4700 S. Cedar Street, Apt. 308, Lansing, Michigan

2. No payment has been made on the judgment and/or no rent has been received since the date of judgment, except the

   sum of $ _____ -0- _____ received under the following conditions: _____

3. The party awarded judgment has complied with its terms.
4. The time stated in the judgment to precede the issuance of a writ of restitution has elapsed.

I declare, under penalty of contempt of court, that to the best of my knowledge, information and belief, there is good
ground to support the contents of this pleading.

<u>February 9, 1998</u>
Date

Abigail Cross
Signature of Plaintiff/Attorney, Bar no.
4700 S. Cedar Street
Address
Lansing, Michigan 48910   555-9920
City, state, zip   Telephone no.

WRIT

IN THE NAME OF THE PEOPLE OF THE STATE OF MICHIGAN:
To the Court Officer: Based upon the facts set forth in the above application, you are commanded to remove the above-
named Defendant(s) and other occupants from the premises described, and to restore Plaintiff to peaceful possession.

SEAL   <u>February 9, 1998</u>   *Cecil Pulaski*
        Date issued   District Judge

NOTE: This writ must be served within 60 days of the issuance date.
COURT
WRIT OF RESTITUTION, LANDLORD-TENANT, LAND CONTRACT, Form No. DCH107, (3 part, pink) Revised 4/80

Self-Evaluation B   TERMINOLOGY AND DEFINITION RECALL

Directions: In the Answers column, write the letter from Column 1 that represents the word or phrase that best matches each item in Column 2. After you have completed this self-evaluation, check your answers with the key on page 498. If you have any incorrect answers, restudy the definitions for those terms before going on with this lesson. Then unless otherwise directed, submit this self-evaluation to your instructor.

Column 1	Column 2	Answers
a. covenant	1. A lease whereby the lessee lets another person occupy the leased premises.	1. _____
b. demise	2. Another name for a lessee.	2. _____
c. demised premises	3. A term used in a lease meaning that the lessee shall have full use and enjoyment of the leased premises.	3. _____
d. ejectment	4. The legal removal of a tenant from leased property.	4. _____
e. eviction	5. The occupying of leased premises as a residence.	5. _____
f. execute	6. A written notice to the tenant from the landlord stating that the tenant is to vacate the premises by a specified time if certain conditions are not met.	6. _____
g. habitation		
h. inure	7. To put a contract into effect by doing all the things that are necessary to make it valid and complete.	7. _____
i. landlord	8. An agreement whereby a tenant or person has possession of property belonging to a landlord for a specified period of time.	8. _____
j. lease		
k. lessee		
l. lessor	9. The owner of leased property; another name for a lessor.	9. _____
m. notice to quit	10. One who owns property that is leased.	10. _____
n. sublease	11. Land and buildings that are leased.	11. _____
o. tenant	12. An agreement between two or more persons that something will be or will not be done.	12. _____
p. writ of restitution	13. One who leases the property of another and has possession of said property.	13. _____
	14. A word used in a contract meaning that if benefits accrue, they will take effect for or come to the party.	14. _____
	15. A document issued by the court that means to return to the previous condition.	15. _____

KEYING LEGAL TERMS

Directions: Unless otherwise instructed, use a 70-space line (typewriter) or 1-inch margins (computer) and double spacing. Correct all errors. Follow one of the procedures below.

WORDS

Keyboarding Procedure
On your typewriter or computer, key the following words at least two times, concentrating on the correct spelling and pronunciation.

Shorthand Procedure
On your typewriter or computer, key the following words once, concentrating on the correct spelling and pronunciation. Then write the shorthand outline for each word in your shorthand notebook or on your shorthand machine. Transcribe from the shorthand outlines one time on your typewriter or computer.

inure	**execute**	**covenant**
lease	**tenant**	**landlord**
lessee	**lessor**	**demise**
demised premises	**sublease**	**habitation**
notice to quit	**eviction**	**writ of restitution**

SENTENCES

Keyboarding Procedure
Key each of the following sentences one time on your typewriter or computer. Concentrate on the correct spelling and pronunciation of each underlined legal term.

Shorthand Procedure
Write the correct shorthand outlines for the following sentences in your shorthand notebook or on your shorthand machine. Transcribe from your shorthand outlines one time on your typewriter or computer.

These sentences will be used for practice dictation on the cassettes.

<u>Inure</u> means to have effect or to benefit. Inure, when used in a contract, means that if benefits accrue, they will take effect for or come to the party. To <u>execute</u> means to carry out or put into effect. To execute a contract is to put it into effect by doing all the things that are necessary to make it valid and complete. A <u>covenant</u> is an agreement between two or more persons that something will be or will not be done.

A <u>lease</u> is an agreement whereby a <u>tenant</u> or person has possession of property belonging to a <u>landlord</u> for a specified period of time. A <u>lessee</u> is the one who leases the property from another, and the <u>lessor</u> is the one who owns the property that is leased. Thus, the tenant is the lessee, and the landlord is the lessor. The use of the term <u>demise</u> in a lease means that the lessee shall have full use and enjoyment of the leased premises. <u>Demised premises</u> are land and buildings that are leased.

A <u>sublease</u> is a lease whereby the lessee lets another person occupy the leased premises. A person who occupies leased premises as a residence has the right of <u>habitation</u>.

A <u>notice to quit</u> is a written notice to the tenant from the landlord stating that the tenant is to vacate the premises by a specified time if certain conditions are not met. If a tenant does not move from the demised premises after the landlord has served the notice to quit, the tenant is subject to <u>eviction</u>. Eviction is the legal removal of a tenant from leased property.

A <u>writ of restitution</u> means to return to the previous condition. If a tenant has been evicted from the premises and fails to move by the date ordered by the court, the landlord may have a writ of restitution issued. The writ of restitution gives the sheriff authority to remove physically the tenant and his or her possessions from the premises.

TRANSCRIBING FROM DICTATION

Directions: This dictation emphasizes and reinforces the legal terms and definitions you have studied. Listen carefully to the pronunciation of each of the legal terms. Unless otherwise directed, use a 70-space line (typewriter) or 1-inch margins (computer) and double spacing. Correct all errors. Follow one of the procedures below.

Keyboarding Procedure
Using the cassette from Lesson 20, Part B, transcribe the dictation directly at your typewriter or computer.

Shorthand Procedure
Using the cassette from Lesson 20, Part B, take the dictation using your shorthand system and then transcribe from your shorthand notes on your typewriter or computer.

When you have finished transcribing Part B of the practice dictation, check your transcript with the printed copy. If you made any mistakes in the transcription, you should practice those words several times before going on to Evaluation 10.

CHECKLIST
I have completed the following for Lesson 20:

	Part A, Date	Part B, Date	Submitted to Instructor Yes	No
Terminology and Definitions				
Self-Evaluation				
***Keying Legal Terms**				
Words				
Sentences				
***Transcribing from Dictation**				

When you have successfully completed all the exercises in this lesson and submitted to your instructor those requested, you are ready to proceed with Evaluation 10.

* If you are using a shorthand system, submit to your instructor your shorthand notes along with your transcript.

Evaluation No. 10   **SECTION A**

Directions: This dictation/transcription evaluation will test your spelling and transcription abilities on the legal terms that you studied in the two preceding lessons. Use a 5-space paragraph indention, a 70-space line (typewriter) or 1-inch margins (computer), and double spacing unless otherwise instructed. Correct all errors. Follow one of the procedures below.

Keyboarding Procedure

Using the cassette from Evaluation 10, transcribe the dictation directly at your typewriter or computer.

Shorthand Procedure

Using the cassette from Evaluation 10, take the dictation using your shorthand system and then transcribe from your shorthand notes on your typewriter or computer.

Sections B and C are available from your instructor.

Lesson 21

Domestic Relations—Marriage, Separation, and Divorce

"Between those who are equally in the right, or equally in the wrong, the law does not interpose."

—Legal Maxim

The area of domestic relations encompasses marriages, divorces, annulments, and separations. Most court actions in domestic relations involve divorce proceedings. Grounds and procedures for divorce actions vary widely from state to state. In this lesson, the terms presented are those that will generally be encountered, regardless of the jurisdiction. When you complete these exercises, you should have knowledge and an understanding of some of the terms used in reference to domestic relations.

Part A TERMINOLOGY AND DEFINITIONS

Directions: Study the terms, pronunciations, and definitions until you are thoroughly familiar with them. In order to complete this lesson successfully, you must understand the meaning and usage of all the legal terms presented. If you are using shorthand, write your shorthand outline for each legal term in your shorthand notebook or on your shorthand machine.

Legal Term	*Pronunciation*	*Definition*
1. domestic	də-ˈmes-tik	Refers to family affairs or to a home or household.
2. civil ceremony	ˈsiv-əl ˈser-ə-mō-nē	A ceremony that creates a valid marriage and is performed by a public official who is so authorized to perform marriages.
3. religious ceremony	ri-ˈlij-əs ˈser-ə-mō-nē	A ceremony that creates a valid marriage and is performed by a duly ordained minister or a member of the clergy of any recognized religion.
4. matrimony	ˈma-trə-mō-nē	The marriage relationship between husband and wife.
5. common-law marriage	ˈkäm-ən lȯ ˈmar-ij	A marriage that is not created by the usual ceremony required by law but exists between two people who agree to live together as husband and wife. It is not recognized as a valid marriage in some states.
6. valid marriage	ˈval-əd ˈmar-ij	A marriage that is created according to the requirements of the law.
7. voidable marriage	ˈvȯid-ə-bəl ˈmar-ij	A marriage that exists for all practical purposes but contains a legal imperfection that could void the relationship in a court of law.
8. void marriage	vȯid ˈmar-ij	A marriage that is not valid and does not meet the requirements established by law for a valid marriage.
9. monogamy	mə-ˈnäg-ə-mē	A marriage relationship between only one man and one woman at a time.

10. bigamy	'big-ə-mē	The state of having two husbands or two wives at any one time. A criminal offense in the United States.
11. annulment	ə-'nəl-mənt	The voiding of a marriage and treating it as though it never existed.
12. age of consent	āj əv kən-'sent	The age set by state law at which a person can marry without parental or guardian consent.
13. non-age	'nän-āj	Below the age of consent. In most states, non-age is a ground for obtaining an annulment.

Self-Evaluation A   TERMINOLOGY AND DEFINITION RECALL

Directions: In the Answers column, write the letter from Column 1 that represents the word or phrase that best matches each item in Column 2. After you have completed this self-evaluation, check your answers with the key on page 498. If you have any incorrect answers, restudy the definitions for those terms before going on with this lesson. Then unless otherwise directed, sumbit this self-evaluation to your instructor.

Column 1	**Column 2**	**Answers**
a. age of consent	1. A marriage relationship between only one man and one woman at a time.	1. i
b. annulment	2. A word meaning below the age of consent and a ground for annulment in most states.	2. j
c. bigamy	3. A marriage that is not valid and does not meet the requirements established by law for a valid marriage.	3. m
d. ceremony		
e. civil ceremony	4. The voiding of a marriage and treating it as though it never existed.	4. b
f. common-law marriage	5. The marriage relationship between a husband and wife.	5. h
g. domestic	6. A ceremony that creates a valid marriage and is performed by a duly ordained minister or member of the clergy of any recognized religion.	6. k
h. matrimony		
i. monogamy	7. A marriage that is not created by the usual ceremony required by law but exists between two people who live together as husband and wife.	7. f
j. non-age		
k. religious ceremony	8. A marriage that is created according to the requirements of the law.	8. l
l. valid marriage	9. A ceremony that creates a valid marriage and is performed by a public official who is authorized to perform marriages.	9. e
m. void marriage		
n. voidable marriage	10. The age set by state law at which a person can marry without parental or guardian consent.	10. a
	11. The state of having two husbands or two wives at any one time.	11. c
	12. A marriage that exists for all practical purposes but contains a legal imperfection that could void the relationship in a court of law.	12. n
	13. A term that refers to family affairs or to a home or household.	13. g

KEYING LEGAL TERMS

Directions: Unless otherwise instructed, use a 70-space line (typewriter) or 1-inch margins (computer) and double spacing. Correct all errors. Follow one of the procedures below.

WORDS

Keyboarding Procedure
On your typewriter or computer, key the following words at least two times, concentrating on the correct spelling and pronunciation.

Shorthand Procedure
On your typewriter or computer, key the following words once, concentrating on the correct spelling and pronunciation. Then write the shorthand outline for each word in your shorthand notebook or on your shorthand machine. Transcribe from the shorthand outlines one time on your typewriter or computer.

domestic	civil ceremony	valid marriage
religious ceremony	matrimony	common-law marriage
voidable marriage	void marriage	monogamy
bigamy	annulment	age of consent
non-age		

SENTENCES

Keyboarding Procedure
Key each of the following sentences one time on your typewriter or computer. Concentrate on the correct spelling and pronunciation of each underlined legal term.

Shorthand Procedure
Write the correct shorthand outlines for the following sentences in your shorthand notebook or on your shorthand machine. Transcribe from your shorthand outlines one time on your typewriter or computer.

These sentences will be used for practice dictation on the cassettes.

Domestic refers to family affairs or to a home or household. Domestic relations encompass the areas of marriages, divorces, annulments, and separations. A civil ceremony creates a valid marriage and is performed by a public official who is authorized to perform marriages. A marriage that is performed by a duly ordained minister or member of the clergy of any recognized religion is a religious ceremony. Matrimony is the marriage relation between a husband and wife. Matrimony does not refer to the ceremony itself.

A common-law marriage is one that is not created by the usual ceremony required by law but exists between two people who agree to live together as husband and wife. Common-law marriages are not recognized in many states.

A valid marriage is one that is created according to the requirements of the law. A voidable marriage is one that exists for all practical purposes but contains a legal imperfection that could void the relationship in a court of law. A void marriage is one that is not valid and does not meet the requirements established by law for a valid marriage.

Monogamy is a marriage relationship between only one man and one woman at a time. Bigamy is the state of having two husbands or two wives at the same time. Bigamy is a criminal offense in the United States.

An annulment voids a marriage and treats it as though it never existed. An annulment means in effect that there was no marriage at all. Each state sets the age at which a person may marry without parental or guardian consent. The age set by each state is referred to as the age of consent. Non-age is below the age of consent. In most states, non-age is a ground for obtaining an annulment.

TRANSCRIBING FROM DICTATION

Directions: This dictation emphasizes and reinforces the legal terms and definitions you have studied. Listen carefully to the pronunciation of each of the legal terms. Unless otherwise directed, use a 70-space line (typewriter) or 1-inch margins (computer) and double spacing. Correct all errors. Follow one of the procedures below.

Keyboarding Procedure
Using the cassette from Lesson 21, Part A, transcribe the dictation directly at your typewriter or computer.

Shorthand Procedure
Using the cassette from Lesson 21, Part A, take the dictation using your shorthand system and then transcribe from your shorthand notes on your typewriter or computer.

When you have finished transcribing Part A of the practice dictation, check your transcript with the printed copy. If you made any mistakes in the transcription, you should practice those words several times before going on.

Part B TERMINOLOGY AND DEFINITIONS

Directions: Study the terms, pronunciations, and definitions until you are thoroughly familiar with them. In order to complete this lesson successfully, you must understand the meaning and usage of all the legal terms presented. If you are using shorthand, write your shorthand outline for each legal term in your shorthand notebook or on your shorthand machine.

Legal Term	Pronunciation	Definition
1. premarital	prē-'mar-ət-l	Before the marriage.
2. antenuptial agreement	ant-i-'nəp-shəl ə-'grē-mənt	An agreement made between two people before they are married. Sometimes called a premarital agreement.
3. cohabitation	kō-hab-ə-'tā-shən	The state of living together as husband and wife.
4. consanguinity	kän-san-'gwin-ət-ē	A blood relationship between two people.
5. affinity	ə-'fin-ət-ē	The relationship of one spouse to the blood relatives of the other spouse because of marriage.
6. femme sole	fem sol	French. A woman who is not married. A woman who is single, divorced, or widowed.
7. separation	sep-ə-'rā-shən	A partial or qualified divorce where the parties may not live together but are otherwise legally bound as husband and wife.
8. a mensa et thoro	ā 'men-sə et 'thōr-ō	Latin. A legal separation.
9. separation agreement	sep-ə-'rā-shən ə-'grē-mənt	A contract between a husband and wife who are living separately that clarifies the property rights, custody, and support for each party.
10. separate maintenance	'sep-rət 'mānt-nəns	An amount granted by a court in a legal separation to one of the spouses for his or her support and for the support of the children.

| 11. privileged communications | ′priv-lijd kə-myü-nə-′kā-shəns | A spouse is not permitted to testify as a witness against the other spouse in regard to matters revealed to each other because of the confidence that exists between them as a result of the marital relation. |
| 12. counsel fee | ′kaủn-səl fē | A fee for legal counsel. In most states, the one filing for divorce is usually required to pay the counsel fees incurred by the other spouse in the divorce action. |

Self-Evaluation B   TERMINOLOGY AND DEFINITION RECALL

Directions: In the Answers column, write the legal term that is most representative of the corresponding statement. After you have completed this self-evaluation, check your answers with the key on page 498. If you have any incorrect answers, restudy the definitions for those terms before going on with this lesson. Then unless otherwise directed, submit this self-evaluation to your instructor.

Answers

1. A contract between a husband and wife who are living separately that clarifies the property rights, custody, and support for each party is a/an _____.

   1. *Separation agreement*

2. An agreement made between two people before they are married is a/an _____.

   2. *antinuptial agreement*

3. The relationship between husband and wife that prohibits one from testifying against the other about matters revealed to each other because of the confidence that exists between them as a result of the marital relationship is referred to as _____.

   3. *privileged communication*

4. A blood relationship between two people is referred to as _____.

   4. *Consanguinity*

5. The relationship of one spouse to the blood relatives of the other spouse because of the marriage is _____.

   5. *affinity*

6. The state of living together as husband and wife is referred to as _____.

   6. *cohabitation*

7. A Latin term meaning a legal separation is _____.

   7. *a mensa et thoro*

8. An amount granted by a court in a legal separation to one of the spouses for his or her support and for the support of the children is _____.

   8. *Separate maintenance*

9. A fee for legal counsel that is usually paid by the one filing for the divorce is referred to as the _____.

   9. *counsel fee*

10. A legal term that means before the marriage is _____.

    10. *premarital*

11. A partial or qualified divorce where the parties may not live together but are otherwise legally bound as husband and wife is a/an _____.

    11. *separation*

12. A French term for a woman who is not married is _____.

    12. *femme sole*

KEYING LEGAL TERMS

Directions: Unless otherwise instructed, use a 70-space line (typewriter) or 1-inch margins (computer) and double spacing. Correct all errors. Follow one of the procedures below.

WORDS

Keyboarding Procedure
On your typewriter or computer, key the following words at least two times, concentrating on the correct spelling and pronunciation.

Shorthand Procedure
On your typewriter or computer, key the following words once, concentrating on the correct spelling and pronunciation. Then write the shorthand outline for each word in your shorthand notebook or on your shorthand machine. Transcribe from the shorthand outlines one time on your typewriter or computer.

premarital	antenuptial agreement	cohabitation
consanguinity	affinity	femme sole
separation	a mensa et thoro	separation agreement
separate maintenance	privileged communications	counsel fee

SENTENCES

Keyboarding Procedure
Key each of the following sentences one time on your typewriter or computer. Concentrate on the correct spelling and pronunciation of each underlined legal term.

Shorthand Procedure
Write the correct shorthand outlines for the following sentences in your shorthand notebook or on your shorthand machine. Transcribe from your shorthand outlines one time on your typewriter or computer.

These sentences will be used for practice dictation on the cassettes.

Premarital means before the marriage. An antenuptial agreement, or a premarital agreement, is an agreement made between two people before they are married. An antenuptial agreement may also be referred to as a marriage contract, and it may detail how certain things will be handled during a marriage or if a marriage ends by divorce.

Cohabitation is the state of living together as husband and wife. Consanguinity is a blood relationship between two people. In most states, persons of the opposite sex are forbidden from living together unless they are related by consanguinity or marriage. Affinity is the relationship of one spouse to the blood relatives of the other spouse because of marriage. Femme sole is a French term referring to a single woman. Femme sole also includes those women who are divorced or widowed.

A partial or qualified divorce where the parties may not live together but are otherwise legally bound as husband and wife is a separation. A separation expressed in Latin is a mensa et thoro. A mensa et thoro usually involves a separation agreement between husband and wife that clarifies the property rights, custody, and support for each party. The separation agreement may contain provisions for separate maintenance, which is an allowance granted to one of the spouses for his or her support and for the support of the children.

Privileged communications exist between a husband and wife. Matters revealed to a spouse are privileged communications, and the spouse is not permitted to testify as a witness against the other spouse in regard to those matters. In most states, the one filing for a divorce is usually required to pay the counsel fee incurred by the spouse in the divorce action.

TRANSCRIBING FROM DICTATION

Directions: This dictation emphasizes and reinforces the legal terms and definitions you have studied. Listen carefully to the pronunciation of each of the legal terms. Unless otherwise directed, use a 70-space line (typewriter) or 1-inch margins (computer) and double spacing. Correct all errors. Follow one of the procedures below.

Keyboarding Procedure
Using the cassette from Lesson 21, Part B, transcribe the dictation directly at your typewriter or computer.

Shorthand Procedure
Using the cassette from Lesson 21, Part B, take the dictation using your shorthand system and then transcribe from your shorthand notes on your typewriter or computer.

When you have finished transcribing Part B of the practice dictation, check your transcript with the printed copy. If you made any mistakes in the transcription, you should practice those words several times before going on to Lesson 22.

CHECKLIST
I have completed the following for Lesson 21:

	Part A, Date	Part B, Date	Submitted to Instructor Yes	No
Terminology and Definitions				
Self-Evaluation				
* Keying Legal Terms				
Words				
Sentences				
* Transcribing from Dictation				

When you have successfully completed all the exercises in this lesson and submitted to your instructor those requested, you are ready to proceed with Lesson 22.

* If you are using a shorthand system, submit to your instructor your shorthand notes along with your transcript.

Lesson 22

Domestic Relations—Marriage, Separation, and Divorce

"One who consents to an act is not wronged by it."
—Legal Maxim

Many of the terms relating to the dissolution of marriage are introduced in this lesson. Divorce laws are changing rapidly and vary considerably from state to state. Therefore, the terms covered are those that are generally applicable to most states. For the successful completion of these exercises, you should be able to spell, pronounce, define, and transcribe correctly each of the terms that are presented.

Part A TERMINOLOGY AND DEFINITIONS

Directions: Study the terms, pronunciations, and definitions until you are thoroughly familiar with them. In order to complete this lesson successfully, you must understand the meaning and usage of all the legal terms presented. If you are using shorthand, write your shorthand outline for each legal term in your shorthand notebook or on your shorthand machine.

Legal Term	Pronunciation	Definition
1. divorce	də-'vōrs	The dissolving of a marriage legally by an action of the court. Also includes a legal separation. (See Figures 22-1 and 22-2, pages 317 and 318.)
2. dissolution of marriage	dis-ə-'lü-shən əv 'mar-ij	The termination of a marriage by divorce.
3. no-fault divorce	'nō-'fȯlt də-'vōrs	The divorce laws of several states that do not require the one filing for divorce to prove the spouse at fault on any grounds previously required for a divorce to be granted. Under no-fault law, neither party has to prove the other at fault in order to obtain a divorce.
4. grounds for divorce	graůnds fər də-'vōrs	The foundation or basis for the granting of a divorce. The grounds for divorce will vary from state to state. In states with no-fault divorce, grounds for divorce are no longer needed.
5. conciliation procedure	kən-sil-e-'a-shən prə-'sē-jər	A procedure whereby the judge meets with the parties to a divorce and attempts to work out their differences. The judge may recommend to the parties that they attempt to reconcile the marriage possibly through marital counseling before the divorce is granted.
6. corespondent	kō-ri-'spän-dənt	The person charged with committing adultery with the respondent in a divorce action for which the grounds are adultery.

7. desertion	di-'zər-shən	The refusal without just cause of a husband or wife to continue a marital relationship.
8. Enoch Arden Law	'ē-nək 'ärd-n lȯ	A law in some states specifying that the unexplained absence of a spouse for a lengthy and continuous period of time constitutes grounds for divorce.
9. limited divorce	'lim-ət-əd də-'vȯrs	A legal separation that does not totally dissolve the marriage.
10. absolute divorce	'ab-sə-lüt də-'vȯrs	The total dissolution of a marriage.
11. a vinculo matrimonii	ā vin-'kū-lō ma-trə-'mō-nē-ī	Latin. An absolute divorce.
12. contested divorce	kən-'test-əd də-'vȯrs	A divorce action in which one of the parties resists or opposes the granting of the divorce and challenges or defends the action.
13. uncontested divorce	ən-kən-'test-əd də-'vȯrs	A divorce action in which the party being sued for divorce does not resist or oppose the grounds for the divorce and makes no defense thereto.

FIGURE 22-1   A Complaint for Divorce

Approved, SCAO	Original - Court 1st copy - Friend of the Court	2nd copy - Defendant 3rd copy - Plaintiff

STATE OF MICHIGAN 30th JUDICIAL CIRCUIT Ingham COUNTY	COMPLAINT FOR DIVORCE Page 1 of 1 pages	CASE NO. 88521-D

Court address   Court telephone no.
2nd Floor, City Hall, Lansing, MI 48933   (517) 555-0650

Plaintiff Clara Annette Mills	☐ husband ☒ wife	v.	Defendant Scott Wendell Mills
Plaintiff's name before marriage Bolton			Defendant's name before marriage

1. Plaintiff's residence: at least   ☒ 180 days in Michigan
                                        ☒ 10 days in this county   immediately before filing of this complaint.

2. Defendant's residence: at least   ☒ 180 days in Michigan
                                        ☒ 10 days in this county   immediately before filing of this complaint.

3. Marriage: June 10, 1990   Lansing, Michigan
                 Date   Place

4. There has been a breakdown of the marriage relationship to the extent that the objects of matrimony have been
   destroyed and there remains no reasonable likelihood that the marriage can be preserved.

5. The wife ☒ is not pregnant.   ☐ is pregnant, and the estimated date of birth is _____ .

6. Complete names and dates of birth of children under 18 of the parties or born during this marriage:
        ☒ None   Attach a Uniform Child Custody Jurisdiction Act Affidavit

7. There   ☒ is   ☐ is no   property to be divided.

☐ 8. I request temporary support orders for the payment of the following: Attach a verified statement.
                                                                                Attach a motion when required.
   a. support for: ☐ child(ren)   ☐ plaintiff   ☐ defendant
   b. health care: ☐ expenses   ☐ insurance premiums   for ☐ child(ren)   ☐ spouse
   c. residence :   ☐ utilities   ☐ rent/mortgage/land contract   ☐ taxes   ☐ insurance
   d. other: Specify

☐ 9. Motion(s) are attached that request temporary restraining order(s) concerning:
   ☐ a. property
   ☐ b. domestic assault: ☐ civil   ☐ criminal
   ☐ c. other: Specify

10. I request a judgment of divorce, and:
   a. property: ☒ award to each party the property in their possession
                       ☐ divide
   ☒ b. change wife's last name to: Bolton
   ☐ c. legal custody to: ☐ plaintiff   ☐ defendant   ☐ joint/both parties
   ☐ d. physical custody to: ☐ plaintiff   ☐ defendant   ☐ joint/both parties
   ☐ e. visitation rights: ☐ reasonable   ☐ specific
   ☐ f. support money for: ☐ child(ren)   ☐ plaintiff   ☐ defendant
   ☐ g. other: Specify

January 3, 1997   _Clara Annette Mills_
Date   Plaintiff signature
January 3, 1997   _Jill F. Sinclair_   P 54079
Date   Plaintiff attorney signature   Bar no.
CC 415   (11/86)   COMPLAINT FOR DIVORCE (page 1)   MCLA 552.6; MSA 25.86, MCR 3.204

FIGURE 22-2 A Judgment of Divorce

Approved, SCAO

Original - Court
1st copy - Friend of the Court

2nd copy - Defendant
3rd copy - Plaintiff

STATE OF MICHIGAN 30th JUDICIAL CIRCUIT Ingham COUNTY	JUDGMENT OF DIVORCE Page 1 of 1 pages	CASE NO. 88521-D

Court address
2nd Floor, City Hall, Lansing, MI 48933

Court telephone no.
(517) 555-0650

Plaintiff's name, address, and social security number

Clara Annette Mills
6090 Sundown Avenue, Apt. 106
Lansing, MI 48933
SS# 404-39-8786

v.

Defendant's name, address, and social security number

Scott Wendell Mills
7110 Hickory Lane
Lansing, MI 48912
SS# 783-00-3221

Plaintiff's attorney, bar no., address, and telephone no.
Jill F. Sinclair   (P 70030)
700 Larch Street, Suite 17
Lansing, MI 48910
(517) 555-8890

Defendant's attorney, bar no., address, and telephone no.
Patrick B. Harvey   (P 34789)
845 Wastenau Avenue, Suite 206
Lansing, MI 48906
(517) 555-5454

☐ After trial   ☐ Default   ☒ Consent

Date of hearing: February 17, 1998   Judge: *Marsha Sanders*   P 52901
Bar no.

IT IS ORDERED:

1. **DIVORCE:** The parties are divorced.

2. **PROPERTY DIVISION:**   ☐ There is no property to be divided.
   ☒ Each party is awarded the property in their possession.
   ☐ Property is divided elsewhere in this judgment.

3. **MINOR CHILDREN:** There   ☐ are
   ☒ are not   children under 18 of the parties or born during this marriage.
   (Custody, visitation, support, and/or other required provisions are attached.)

☐ 4. **NAME CHANGE:**   Wife's last name is changed to ___ Bolton ___ .

5. **ALIMONY:** Alimony is   ☒ not granted for   ☒ wife.   ☒ husband.
   ☐ reserved for   ☐ wife.   ☐ husband.
   ☐ granted elsewhere in this judgment for   ☐ wife.   ☐ husband.

6. **STATUTORY RIGHTS:** All interests of the parties in the property of the other, now owned or later acquired, arising under MCL 700.281 – 700.291, are extinguished.

7. **BENEFICIARY RIGHTS:** The rights each party has to the proceeds of policies or contracts of life insurance, endowments, or annuities upon the life of the other as a named beneficiary or by assignment during or in anticipation of marriage, are   ☒ extinguished.   ☐ provided for elsewhere in this judgment.

8. **PENSION RIGHTS:** Any rights of either party in any pension, annuity, or retirement plan benefit of the other, whether vested or unvested, accumulated or contingent, are
   ☒ extinguished.   ☐ provided for elsewhere in this judgment.

9. **JOINT REAL ESTATE:** All real estate owned by the parties as joint tenants or as tenants by the entireties is
   ☒ converted to a tenancy in common.   ☐ provided for elsewhere in this judgment.

10. **DOCUMENTATION:** Each party shall promptly and properly execute and deliver to the other appropriate documents required to carry out the terms of this judgment. A certified copy of this judgment may be recorded with the register of deeds in any county of this state where property may be located.

11. **INTERIM ORDERS:** Except as otherwise provided in this judgment, all interim orders and injunctions entered in this action are terminated.

MCLA 552.6; MSA 25.86, MCLA 552.18; MSA 25.98, MCLA 552.101; MSA 25.131
MCLA 552.102; MSA 25.132, MCLA 552.104; MSA 25.134, MCLA 552.402; MSA 25.137
MCLA 700.281 - 700.291; MSA 27.5281 - 27.5291, MCR 3.209

CC 427a (11/86) **JUDGMENT OF DIVORCE, page 1**

Self-Evaluation A   TERMINOLOGY AND DEFINITION RECALL

Directions: In the Answers column, write the legal term that is most representative of the corresponding statement. After you have completed this self-evaluation, check your answers with the key on page 498. If you have any incorrect answers, restudy the definitions for those terms before going on with this lesson. Then unless otherwise directed, submit this self-evaluation to your instructor.

Answers

1. The total dissolution of a marriage is a/an _____.

   1. *absolute divorce*

2. The person charged with committing adultery with the respondent in a divorce action for which the grounds are adultery is called a/an _____.

   2. *corespondent*

3. An absolute divorce is expressed in Latin as _____.

   3. *a vinculo matrimonii*

4. A legal separation that does not totally dissolve the marriage is a/an _____.

   4. *limited divorce*

5. A divorce in which the one filing for the divorce does not have to prove that the spouse is at fault on grounds previously required in most states for a divorce to be granted is a/an _____.

   5. *nofault divorce*

6. A divorce action in which one of the parties resists or opposes the granting of the divorce and challenges or defends the action is a/an _____.

   6. *contested divorce*

7. A divorce action in which the party being sued for divorce does not resist or oppose the grounds for the divorce and makes no defense thereto is a/an _____.

   7. *uncontested divorce*

8. The dissolving of a marriage legally by an action of a court is a/an _____.

   8. *divorce*

9. Termination of a marriage by divorce is a/an _____.

   9. *dissolution of marriage*

10. The foundation or basis for the granting of a divorce is referred to as _____.

    10. *grounds for divorce*

11. A procedure whereby the judge meets with the parties to a divorce and endeavors to reconcile them is a/an _____.

    11. *conciliation procedure*

12. A law in some states specifying that the unexplained absence of a spouse for a lengthy and continuous period of time constitutes grounds for divorce is the _____.

    12. *Enoch Arden law*

13. The refusal without just cause of a husband or wife to continue a marital relationship is _____.

    13. *desertion*

KEYING LEGAL TERMS

Directions: Unless otherwise instructed, use a 70-space line (typewriter) or 1-inch margins (computer) and double spacing. Correct all errors. Follow one of the procedures below.

WORDS

Keyboarding Procedure
On your typewriter or computer, key the following words at least two times, concentrating on the correct spelling and pronunciation.

Shorthand Procedure
On your typewriter or computer, key the following words once, concentrating on the correct spelling and pronunciation. Then write the shorthand outline for each word in your shorthand notebook or on your shorthand machine. Transcribe from the shorthand outlines one time on your typewriter or computer.

divorce	dissolution of marriage	no-fault divorce
grounds for divorce	conciliation procedure	corespondent
desertion	Enoch Arden Law	limited divorce
absolute divorce	a vinculo matrimonii	contested divorce
uncontested divorce		

SENTENCES

Keyboarding Procedure
Key each of the following sentences one time on your typewriter or computer. Concentrate on the correct spelling and pronunciation of each underlined legal term.

Shorthand Procedure
Write the correct shorthand outlines for the following sentences in your shorthand notebook or on your shorthand machine. Transcribe from your shorthand outlines one time on your typewriter or computer.

These sentences will be used for practice dictation on the cassettes.

A divorce is the dissolving of a marriage legally by an action of the court. A dissolution of marriage is the act of terminating a marriage by divorce.

Most states have now enacted no-fault divorce laws. A no-fault divorce does not require the one filing for divorce to prove the spouse at fault on grounds that were previously required for a divorce action. Grounds for divorce are the foundation or basis for the granting of a divorce as required by state law.

If a judge feels that the marriage might possibly be reconciled, a conciliation procedure may be recommended. The judge may make several recommendations to the parties that they attempt to reconcile the marriage before a divorce is granted.

A corespondent is a person charged with committing adultery with the respondent in a divorce action for which the grounds are adultery. Desertion is the refusal without just cause to continue a marital relationship. The Enoch Arden Law in some states permits divorce on the grounds of desertion.

A divorce may be either limited or absolute. A limited divorce is a legal separation of husband and wife that does not totally dissolve the marriage. An absolute divorce is the total dissolution of the marriage. An absolute divorce expressed in Latin terms is a vinculo matrimonii.

A divorce action may be either contested or uncontested by the party against whom it is filed. In a contested divorce, the party against whom it is filed resists or opposes the granting of the divorce and challenges or defends the action. An uncontested divorce is one in which the party being sued for divorce does not resist or oppose the divorce and makes no defense thereto.

TRANSCRIBING FROM DICTATION

Directions: This dictation emphasizes and reinforces the legal terms and definitions you have studied. Listen carefully to the pronunciation of each of the legal terms. Unless otherwise directed, use a 70-space line (typewriter) or 1-inch margins (computer) and double spacing. Correct all errors. Follow one of the procedures below.

Keyboarding Procedure

Using the cassette from Lesson 22, Part A, transcribe the dictation directly at your typewriter or computer.

Shorthand Procedure

Using the cassette from Lesson 22, Part A, take the dictation using your shorthand system and then transcribe from your shorthand notes on your typewriter or computer.

When you have finished transcribing Part A of the practice dictation, check your transcript with the printed copy. If you made any mistakes in the transcription, you should practice those words several times before going on.

Part B TERMINOLOGY AND DEFINITIONS

Directions: Study the terms, pronunciations, and definitions until you are thoroughly familiar with them. In order to complete this lesson successfully, you must understand the meaning and usage of all the legal terms presented. If you are using shorthand, write your shorthand outline for each legal term in your shorthand notebook or on your shorthand machine.

Legal Term	Pronunciation	Definition
1. domicile	′däm-ə-sīl	The legal place where a person or family resides.
2. community property	kə-′myü-nət-ē ′präp-ərt-ē	Any property that is acquired by husband and wife during the marriage.
3. property settlement	′präp-ərt-ē ′set-l-ment	An agreement between the parties of a divorce action as to the division of property owned or acquired during the marriage.
4. earning capacity	′ər-niŋ kə-′pas-ət-ē	The capacity or capability of one to earn money. A consideration in the awarding of alimony in a divorce action.
5. custody	′kəs-təd-ē	The care and possession of minor children of a marriage that is in a state of separation or divorce.
6. adoption	ə-′däp-shən	The taking of another person's child and giving the child all the rights and duties of one's own child.
7. alimony	′al-ə-mō-nē	A provision for the support and maintenance of a wife by her divorced husband. In recent years, some states have ruled that a wife who is financially able has to pay alimony to the husband.
8. permanent alimony	′pərm-nənt ′al-ə-mō-nē	Alimony that is to continue during the lifetime of the spouse.

9. temporary alimony	′tem-pə-rer-ē ′al-ə-mō-nē	An amount paid to the wife or husband while the divorce suit is pending.
10. alimony pendente lite	′al-ə-mō-nē pen-′den-tē ′lī-tē	Latin. Temporary alimony paid while the divorce action is pending.
11. necessaries	′nes-ə-ser-ēs	Generally means food, clothing, shelter, and medicines. Creditors who provide necessaries can file a claim for a judgment against alimony payments.
12. support	sə-′pōrt	The payment of money in a divorce action that will provide the necessaries or maintain the lifestyle for the spouse and children.
13. nonsupport	nän-sə-′pōrt	In some states, nonsupport is grounds for a divorce if the husband has the ability to support his wife but fails to do so. A husband's actual inability to provide for his wife is generally not sufficient grounds for divorce.

Self-Evaluation B   TERMINOLOGY AND DEFINITION RECALL

Directions: In the Answers column at the right of each statement, write the letter that represents the word or group of words that correctly completes the statement. After you have completed this self-evaluation, check your answers with the key on page 498. If you have any incorrect answers, restudy the definitions for those terms before going on with this lesson. Then unless otherwise directed, submit this self-evaluation to your instructor.

Answers

1. The capability of an individual to earn that is considered in the awarding of alimony in a divorce action is called the (a) earning capacity, (b) nonsupport, (c) necessaries.

1. _A_____

2. The legal place where a person or family resides is called the (a) community property, (b) domicile, (c) property settlement.

2. _b_____

3. Food, clothing, shelter, and medicines are generally referred to as (a) alimony pendente lite, (b) necessaries, (c) domicile.

3. _B_____

4. The care and possession of minor children of a marriage that is in a state of separation or divorce is (a) adoption, (b) custody, (c) domicile.

4. _B_____

5. An agreement between the parties of a divorce action as to the division of property owned or acquired during the marriage is the (a) property settlement, (b) earning capacity, (c) community property.

5. _A_____

6. An amount paid to the wife or husband while the divorce suit is pending is referred to as (a) permanent alimony, (b) alimony pendente lite, (c) temporary alimony.

6. _B_____

7. Temporary alimony paid while the divorce action is pending is expressed in Latin as alimony (a) domicile, (b) custody, (c) pendente lite.

7. _C_____

8. A provision for the support and maintenance of a husband or wife by the divorced spouse is (a) support, (b) alimony, (c) necessaries.

8. _B_____

9. The payment of money in a divorce action that will provide the necessaries or maintain the lifestyle for the spouse and children is (a) support, (b) alimony, (c) property settlement.

9. _A_____

10. The act of taking another's child into one's own family, treating the child as one's own, and giving the child all the rights and duties of one's own child is called (a) adoption, (b) custody, (c) support.

10. _A_____

11. Any property that is acquired by husband and wife during the marriage is referred to as (a) pendente lite, (b) property settlement, (c) community property.

11. _C_____

12. Alimony that is to continue during the lifetime of the spouse is (a) temporary alimony, (b) support, (c) permanent alimony.

12. _C_____

13. If a husband has the ability to support his wife but fails to do so, it is grounds for divorce in some states and is referred to as (a) nonsupport, (b) earning capacity, (c) necessaries.

13. _A_____

KEYING LEGAL TERMS

Directions: Unless otherwise instructed, use a 70-space line (typewriter) or 1-inch margins (computer) and double spacing. Correct all errors. Follow one of the procedures below.

WORDS

Keyboarding Procedure
On your typewriter or computer, key the following words at least two times, concentrating on the correct spelling and pronunciation.

Shorthand Procedure
On your typewriter or computer, key the following words once, concentrating on the correct spelling and pronunciation. Then write the shorthand outline for each word in your shorthand notebook or on your shorthand machine. Transcribe from the shorthand outlines one time on your typewriter or computer.

domicile	community property	property settlement
earning capacity	custody	adoption
alimony	permanent alimony	temporary alimony
alimony pendente lite	necessaries	support
nonsupport		

SENTENCES

Keyboarding Procedure
Key each of the following sentences one time on your typewriter or computer. Concentrate on the correct spelling and pronunciation of each underlined legal term.

Shorthand Procedure
Write the correct shorthand outlines for the following sentences in your shorthand notebook or on your shorthand machine. Transcribe from your shorthand outlines one time on your typewriter or computer.

These sentences will be used for practice dictation on the cassettes.

A domicile is the legal place where a person or family resides. Community property is acquired by husband and wife during the marriage. In community property states, the property belongs equally to both husband and wife without regard to who paid for it or whether the property is in only one party's name. The parties to a divorce must come to an agreement as to a property settlement. A property settlement is an agreement as to the division of property owned or acquired during the marriage.

Earning capacity, which affects the amount of alimony payments, is the capability or capacity of a person to earn money. Thus, the earning capacity of each spouse is taken into consideration to determine how much alimony and child support one spouse will have to pay to the other spouse.

Custody relates to the care and possession of minor children after a divorce. Usually the parent receiving custody of the minor children will receive support payments for their care from the other parent. The taking of another person's child and giving the child all the rights and duties of one's own child is called adoption.

Alimony is a provision for the support and maintenance of a wife by her divorced husband. In recent years, some states have ruled that a wife who is financially able has to pay alimony to her husband. Alimony may be either permanent or temporary. Permanent alimony is to continue during the lifetime of the spouse. Temporary alimony is an amount paid while the divorce suit is pending. Temporary alimony is referred to in Latin as alimony pendente lite.

Necessaries are generally food, clothing, shelter, medicines. Creditors who provide necessaries can file a claim for a judgment against alimony payments. Support is the payment of money in a divorce action that will provide the necessaries or maintain the lifestyle for the spouse and children. In some states, a husband failing to provide necessaries for a wife is called nonsupport and is grounds for divorce.

TRANSCRIBING FROM DICTATION

Directions: This dictation emphasizes and reinforces the legal terms and definitions you have studied. Listen carefully to the pronunciation of each of the legal terms. Unless otherwise directed, use a 70-space line (typewriter) or 1-inch margins (computer) and double spacing. Correct all errors. Follow one of the procedures below.

Keyboarding Procedure
Using the cassette from Lesson 22, Part B, transcribe the dictation directly at your typewriter or computer.

Shorthand Procedure
Using the cassette from Lesson 22, Part B, take the dictation using your shorthand system and then transcribe from your shorthand notes on your typewriter or computer.

When you have finished transcribing Part B of the practice dictation, check your transcript with the printed copy. If you made any mistakes in the transcription, you should practice those words several times before going on to Evaluation 11.

CHECKLIST
I have completed the following for Lesson 22:

	Part A, Date	Part B, Date	Submitted to Instructor Yes	No
Terminology and Definitions				
Self-Evaluation				
* Keying Legal Terms				
Words				
Sentences				
* Transcribing from Dictation				

When you have successfully completed all the exercises in this lesson and submitted to your instructor those requested, you are ready to proceed with Evaluation 11.

* If you are using a shorthand system, submit to your instructor your shorthand notes along with your transcript.

Evaluation No. 11   **SECTION A**

Directions: This dictation/transcription evaluation will test your spelling and transcription abilities on the legal terms that you studied in the two preceding lessons. Use a 5-space paragraph indention, a 70-space line (typewriter) or 1-inch margins (computer), and double spacing unless otherwise instructed. Correct all errors. Follow one of the procedures below.

Keyboarding Procedure

Using the cassette from Evaluation 11, transcribe the dictation directly at your typewriter or computer.

Shorthand Procedure

Using the cassette from Evaluation 11, take the dictation using your shorthand system and then transcribe from your shorthand notes on your typewriter or computer.

Sections B and C are available from your instructor.

Lesson 23

Commercial Paper

"Time does not confirm a void act."

—Legal Maxim

The extensive use of commercial paper in our society has resulted in uniform laws regulating commercial paper. The Uniform Commercial Code has been adopted in all states. This area of law affects the daily lives of individuals and businesses, and almost everyone has direct contact with commercial paper of some type. The terminology taught in the following exercises deals with the various trends of commercial paper. When you have satisfactorily completed the lesson, you will be able to spell, pronounce, define, and transcribe correctly each of the terms presented in the area of commercial paper.

Part A TERMINOLOGY AND DEFINITIONS

Directions: Study the terms, pronunciations, and definitions until you are thoroughly familiar with them. In order to complete this lesson successfully, you must understand the meaning and usage of all the legal terms presented. If you are using shorthand, write your shorthand outline for each legal term in your shorthand notebook or on your shorthand machine.

Legal Term	*Pronunciation*	*Definition*
1. Uniform Commercial Code (UCC)	′yü-nə-fòrm kə-′mər-shəl kōd	Adopted by all states to govern and define commercial paper.
2. commercial paper	kə-′mər-shəl ′pā-per	A written promise that is capable of being transferred or assigned to another.
3. negotiable	ni-′gō-shə-bel	Capable of being transferred or assigned to another. Cash, checks, money orders, and cashier's checks are examples of negotiable instruments.
4. legal tender	′lē-gəl ′ten-dər	An accepted form of exchange that, according to law, must be accepted in the payment of a debt.
5. promissory note	′präm-ə-sòr-ē nōt	An unconditional written commercial paper by which one promises to pay a certain amount of money to another at a definite time. (See Figure 23-1, page 333.)
6. demand note	di-′mand nōt	A promissory note that has no specific payment date but must be paid upon demand.
7. time note	tīm nōt	A promissory note that specifies the date on which it must be paid.
8. collateral note	kə-′lat-ə-rəl nōt	A note for which one has pledged security other than one's own promise to pay.
9. judgment note	′jəj-mənt nōt	A promissory note in which the maker authorizes that a judgment may be made against the maker if the note is not paid when due.

10. cognovit note	′käg-nō-vit nōt	Same as a judgment note.
11. check	chek	A commercial paper that is used to transfer money from a person's bank account to another person. (See Figure 23-2, page 333.)
12. cashier's check	ka-′shirs chek	A check issued by a bank that promises to make payment on demand. An individual can go to a bank and give the bank cash, and the bank will then draw a cashier's check on its own funds.
13. certificate of deposit	sər-′tif-i-kət əv di-′päz-ət	An instrument issued by a bank acknowledging the deposit of a specific sum of money and promising to pay the holder of the certificate that amount of money.

FIGURE 23-1 A Promissory Note

Payee	NOTE. A-1
	$5,000.00 March 7 , 19 97
	Ninety days -------------------------------- after date I promise to pay to the order of
	Michelle Faye Wells --
	Five thousand and 00/100--- Dollars
	At Southfield, Michigan
	Value received with interest at 7 per cent per annum.
Marker/ Payer	No. 1 Due June 5, 1997 Oliver N. Redman

FIGURE 23-2 A Check

Self-Evaluation A   TERMINOLOGY AND DEFINITION RECALL

Directions: In the Answers column at the right of each statement, write the letter that represents the word or group of words that correctly completes the statement. After you have completed this self-evaluation, check your answers with the key on page 498. If you have any incorrect answers, restudy the definitions for those terms before going on with this lesson. Then unless otherwise directed, submit this self-evaluation to your instructor.

Answers

1. An act that has been adopted by all states to govern and define commercial paper is the (a) collateral, (b) Uniform Commercial Code, (c) certificate of deposit.

   1. _____

2. An instrument issued by a bank acknowledging the deposit of a specific sum of money and promising to pay the holder of the instrument that amount of money is a (a) promissory note, (b) cashier's check, (c) certificate of deposit.

   2. _____

3. A promissory note in which the maker authorizes that a judgment may be made against him or her if the note is not paid when due is a (a) collateral note, (b) judgment note, (c) certificate of deposit.

   3. _____

4. A promissory note that has no specific payment date but must be paid upon demand is a (a) demand note, (b) judgment note, (c) cognovit note.

   4. _____

5. An accepted form of exchange that, according to law, must be accepted in the payment of a debt is a (a) check, (b) legal tender, (c) commercial paper.

   5. _____

6. Something that is capable of being transferred or assigned to another is referred to as being (a) negotiable, (b) legal tender, (c) certificate of deposit.

   6. _____

7. A written promise that is capable of being transferred or assigned to another is a (a) promissory note, (b) check, (c) commercial paper.

   7. _____

8. A note for which one pledges security other than one's promise to pay is a (a) demand note, (b) collateral note, (c) judgment note.

   8. _____

9. Another name for a judgment note is (a) cognovit note, (b) collateral note, (c) demand note.

   9. _____

10. A commercial paper that is used to transfer money from a person's bank account to another person is a (a) cashier's check, (b) commercial paper, (c) check.

    10. _____

11. A check issued by a bank that promises to make payment on demand is a (a) cashier's check, (b) collateral note, (c) demand note.

    11. _____

12. An unconditional commercial paper by which one promises to pay a certain amount of money to another at a given time is a (a) demand note, (b) time note, (c) cognovit note.

    12. _____

13. A promissory note that specifies the date on which it must be paid is a (a) cognovit note, (b) collateral note, (c) time note.

    13. _____

KEYING LEGAL TERMS

Directions: Unless otherwise instructed, use a 70-space line (typewriter) or 1-inch margins (computer) and double spacing. Correct all errors. Follow one of the procedures below.

WORDS

Keyboarding Procedure
On your typewriter or computer, key the following words at least two times, concentrating on the correct spelling and pronunciation.

Shorthand Procedure
On your typewriter or computer, key the following words once, concentrating on the correct spelling and pronunciation. Then write the shorthand outline for each word in your shorthand notebook or on your shorthand machine. Transcribe from the shorthand outlines one time on your typewriter or computer.

Uniform Commercial Code	commercial paper	negotiable
legal tender	promissory note	demand note
time note	collateral note	judgment note
cognovit note	check	cashier's check
certificate of deposit		

SENTENCES

Keyboarding Procedure
Key each of the following sentences one time on your typewriter or computer. Concentrate on the correct spelling and pronunciation of each underlined legal term.

Shorthand Procedure
Write the correct shorthand outlines for the following sentences in your shorthand notebook or on your shorthand machine. Transcribe from your shorthand outlines one time on your typewriter or computer.

These sentences will be used for practice dictation on the cassettes.

The requirements of commercial paper are defined under the Uniform Commercial Code, which has been adopted by all states. Commercial paper is a written promise that is capable of being transferred or assigned to another. Negotiable means capable of being transferred or assigned to another. Legal tender is an accepted form of exchange, usually money, that, according to law, must be accepted in the payment of a debt.

A promissory note is a written commercial paper by which one promises to pay a certain amount of money to another at a definite time. A demand note is a promissory note that has no specific payment date but must be paid upon demand. A promissory note that specifies the date on which it must be paid is a time note. If security other than a promise to pay has been pledged, the note is referred to as a collateral note. A judgment note is a promissory note authorizing that a judgment may be made against the maker if the note is not paid when due. A cognovit note is the same as a judgment note.

A check is a commercial paper that is used to transfer money from a person's bank account to another person. A cashier's check is a check issued by a bank with a guarantee of payment on demand.

A certificate of deposit is an instrument issued by a bank acknowledging the deposit of a specific sum of money and promising to pay the holder of the certificate that amount.

TRANSCRIBING FROM DICTATION

Directions: This dictation emphasizes and reinforces the legal terms and definitions you have studied. Listen carefully to the pronunciation of each of the legal terms. Unless otherwise directed, use a 70-space line (typewriter) or 1-inch margins (computer) and double spacing. Correct all errors. Follow one of the procedures below.

Keyboarding Procedure

Using the cassette from Lesson 23, Part A, transcribe the dictation directly at your typewriter or computer.

Shorthand Procedure

Using the cassette from Lesson 23, Part A, take the dictation using your shorthand system and then transcribe from your shorthand notes on your typewriter or computer.

When you have finished transcribing Part A of the practice dictation, check your transcript with the printed copy. If you made any mistakes in the transcription, you should practice those words several times before going on.

Part B TERMINOLOGY AND DEFINITIONS

Directions: Study the terms, pronunciations, and definitions until you are thoroughly familiar with them. In order to complete this lesson successfully, you must understand the meaning and usage of all the legal terms presented. If you are using shorthand, write your shorthand outline for each legal term in your shorthand notebook or on your shorthand machine.

Legal Term	Pronunciation	Definition
1. payee	′pā-ē	The person to whom a check, promissory note, or draft is payable. (See Figures 23-1 and 23-2, page 333.)
2. payer	′pā-ər	The one who pays a check, promissory note, or draft. (See Figures 23-1 and 23-2, page 333.)
3. maker	′mā-kər	The one who orders payment on a check or draft or who makes a promissory note. (See Figures 23-1 and 23-2, page 333.)
4. comaker	′kō-mā-kər	One who signs a commercial paper with others and is also responsible for its payment.
5. holder in due course	′hōl-dər in dü kōrs	One who has accepted a commercial paper for value on the condition that it is valid and not overdue.
6. bearer	′bar-ər	A person who is holding or in possession of a commercial paper that is made payable to bearer.
7. draft	draft	A bill of exchange. A written order drawn by one person upon another requiring that person to pay a certain amount of money to a third party on demand or at a definite time. A check is a draft.
8. bill of exchange	bil əv iks-′chānj	A draft.
9. trade acceptance	trād ik-′sep-təns	A time draft drawn on the purchaser of goods by the one selling the goods and accepted by the purchaser.
10. draft-varying acceptance	draft-′ver-ē-iŋ ik-′sep-təns	A draft in which the order of the instrument varies from the acceptor's agreement.
11. qualified acceptance	′kwäl-ə-fĭd ik-′sep-təns	An acceptance that is only partial in that it varies the order of the draft in some way.

| 12. accommodation paper | ə-käm-ə-ʹdā-shən ʹpā-pər | A paper, bill, or note signed by a person without consideration to accommodate another party to enable that party to obtain credit based on the paper. |
| 13. carte blanche | kärt blänsh | French. A blank instrument that is signed with the intention that it is to be filled in by another person without restriction. |

Self-Evaluation B   TERMINOLOGY AND DEFINITION RECALL

Directions: In the Answers column, write the legal term that is most representative of the corresponding statement. After you have completed this self-evaluation, check your answers with the key on page 498. If you have any incorrect answers restudy the definitions for those terms before going on with this lesson. Then unless otherwise directed, submit this self-evaluation to your instructor.

Answers

1. The person to whom a check, promissory note, or draft is payable is the _____.

   1. _____

2. A written order drawn by one person upon another requiring that person to pay a certain amount of money to a third party on demand or at a definite time is a/an _____.

   2. _____

3. A person who is holding or in possession of a commercial paper that is made payable to bearer is a/an _____.

   3. _____

4. A draft, or bill of exchange, in which the order of the instrument varies from the acceptor's agreement is a/an _____.

   4. _____

5. One who signs a commercial paper with others and is also responsible for its payment is a/an _____.

   5. _____

6. A time draft drawn on the purchaser of goods by the one selling the goods and accepted by the purchaser is a/an _____.

   6. _____

7. A paper, bill, or note signed by a person without consideration to accommodate another party to enable that party to obtain credit based on the paper is a/an _____.

   7. _____

8. One who has accepted a commercial paper for value on the condition that it is valid and not overdue is a/an _____.

   8. _____

9. The one who orders payment of a check or draft or who makes a promissory note is the _____.

   9. _____

10. An acceptance that is only partial in that it varies the order of the draft in some way is a/an _____.

    10. _____

11. A blank instrument that is signed with the intention that it is to be filled in by another person without restriction is a/an _____.

    11. _____

12. Another name for a draft is _____.

    12. _____

13. The one who pays a check, promissory note, or draft is the _____.

    13. _____

KEYING LEGAL TERMS

Directions: Unless otherwise instructed, use a 70-space line (typewriter) or 1-inch margins (computer) and double spacing. Correct all errors. Follow one of the procedures below.

WORDS

Keyboarding Procedure
On your typewriter or computer, key the following words at least two times, concentrating on the correct spelling and pronunciation.

Shorthand Procedure
On your typewriter or computer, key the following words once, concentrating on the correct spelling and pronunciation. Then write the shorthand outline for each word in your shorthand notebook or on your shorthand machine. Transcribe from the shorthand outlines one time on your typewriter or computer.

payee	payer	maker
comaker	holder in due course	bearer
draft	bill of exchange	trade acceptance
draft-varying acceptance	qualified acceptance	accommodation paper
carte blanche		

SENTENCES

Keyboarding Procedure
Key each of the following sentences one time on your typewriter or computer. Concentrate on the correct spelling and pronunciation of each underlined legal term.

Shorthand Procedure
Write the correct shorthand outlines for the following sentences in your shorthand notebook or on your shorthand machine. Transcribe from your shorthand outlines one time on your typewriter or computer.

These sentences will be used for practice dictation on the cassettes.

The person to whom a check, promissory note, or bill of exchange is payable is the payee. If you receive a check made out to you, you are the payee. The payer is the one who pays. In other words, the payer is the one who pays the amount of money for which the check is written. The one who makes or executes a promissory note is called the maker. If you give someone a promissory note, you are the maker. A comaker is one who signs a commercial paper with others and is also responsible for its payment. If another person cosigns a promissory note or other commercial paper with you, that person is the comaker and is also responsible for payment of the commercial paper.

A holder in due course is one who accepts a commercial paper for value on the condition that it is valid and not overdue. A bearer is a person who is holding or in possession of a commercial paper that is payable to bearer.

A draft is a written order drawn by one person upon another requiring that person to pay a certain amount of money to a third party on demand. The common term for a bill of exchange is draft.

A trade acceptance is a draft, or bill of exchange, drawn on the purchaser of goods by the one selling the goods and accepted by the purchaser. If the instrument varies from the acceptor's agreement, it is called a draft-varying acceptance. A qualified acceptance is an acceptance that is only partial in that it varies the order of the draft in some way.

An accommodation paper is a paper, bill, or note signed by a person without consideration to accommodate another party to enable that party to obtain credit based on the paper. Carte blanche is a blank instrument that is signed with the intention that it is to be filled in by another person without restriction.

TRANSCRIBING FROM DICTATION

Directions: This dictation emphasizes and reinforces the legal terms and definitions you have studied. Listen carefully to the pronunciation of each of the legal terms. Unless otherwise directed, use a 70-space line (typewriter) or 1-inch margins (computer) and double spacing. Correct all errors. Follow one of the procedures below.

Keyboarding Procedure
Using the cassette from Lesson 23, Part B, transcribe the dictation directly at your typewriter or computer.

Shorthand Procedure
Using the cassette from Lesson 23, Part B, take the dictation using your shorthand system and then transcribe from your shorthand notes on your typewriter or computer.

When you have finished transcribing Part B of the practice dictation, check your transcript with the printed copy. If you made any mistakes in the transcription, you should practice those words several times before going on to Lesson 24.

CHECKLIST
I have completed the following for Lesson 23:

	Part A, Date	Part B, Date	Submitted to Instructor Yes	No
Terminology and Definitions				
Self-Evaluation				
* Keying Legal Terms				
Words				
Sentences				
* Transcribing from Dictation				

When you have successfully completed all the exercises in this lesson and submitted to your instructor those requested, you are ready to proceed with Lesson 24.

* If you are using a shorthand system, submit to your instructor your shorthand notes along with your transcript.

Lesson 24

Commercial Paper

"One who grants a thing is presumed to grant also whatever is essential to its use."

—Legal Maxim

Additional terms that relate to the area of commercial paper are presented in this lesson. The Federal Reserve System requirements that govern the placement of indorsements on checks are also covered. Upon satisfactory completion of the following exercises, you will be able to spell, pronounce, define, and transcribe correctly each of the terms introduced pertaining to commercial paper.

Part A TERMINOLOGY AND DEFINITIONS

Directions: Study the terms, pronunciations, and definitions until you are thoroughly familiar with them. In order to complete this lesson successfully, you must understand the meaning and usage of all the legal terms presented. If you are using shorthand, write your shorthand outline for each legal term in your shorthand notebook or on your shorthand machine.

Legal Term	Pronunciation	Definition
1. delivery	di-'liv-rē	The act of transferring or placing a commercial paper in the possession or control of another person.
2. maturity	mə-'tùr-ət-ē	The date or time on which a commercial paper comes due and is payable. (See Figure 24-1, page 347.)
3. presentment	pri-'zent-mənt	The presentation of a commercial paper for payment to the one who has the responsibility for making such payment.
4. dishonor	dis-'än-ər	To refuse to pay a commercial paper when it is due or to refuse to accept a commercial paper.
5. without recourse	with-'aùt 'rē-kōrs	A phrase used in an indorsement of a commercial paper meaning that the indorser cannot be held liable if the original makers of the instrument fail to make payment when due.
6. protest	'prō-test	A written notarized statement certifying that a commercial paper was presented for payment and refused. Also refers to the payment of a debt that one does not feel he or she owes with the intention of recovering the amount later. Such a debt is paid under protest.
7. grace period	grās 'pir-ē-əd	An extension of time after the due date for the payment of a commercial paper without defaulting on the obligation.
8. postdate	pōs-'dāt	To put a future date on a commercial paper instead of the date on which it is actually made.

9. value	'val-yü	The consideration involved in a contract. It may also be an abbreviation for valuable consideration.
10. interest	'in-trəst	An amount of money paid for the use of money belonging to another person. (See Figure 24-1, page 347.)
11. usury	'yüzh-rē	An illegal amount of interest charged for the use of money. Most states have usury laws that regulate the amount of interest that can be charged for certain types of loans.
12. accrue	ə-'krü	To be added to or to increase. Interest on a note accrues to, or is added to, the principal of the note.

FIGURE 24-1 A Promissory Note

Interest

Maturity

Self-Evaluation A

TERMINOLOGY AND DEFINITION RECALL

Directions: In the Answers column, write the letter from Column 1 that represents the word or phrase that best matches each item in Column 2. After you have completed this self-evaluation, check your answers with the key on page 498–499. If you have any incorrect answers, restudy the definitions for those terms before going on with this lesson. Then unless otherwise directed, submit this self-evaluation to your instructor.

Column 1

a. accrue

b. delivery

c. dishonor

d. grace period

e. interest

f. maturity

g. payment date

h. postdate

i. presentment

j. protest

k. usury

l. value

m. without recourse

Column 2

1. A term that means to be added to or to increase, such as when interest on a note is added to the principal of the note.

2. The presentation of a commercial paper for payment to the one who has the responsibility for making such payment.

3. The act of transferring or placing an instrument in the possession or control of another person.

4. To put a future date on a commercial paper instead of the date on which it is actually made.

5. An amount of money paid for the use of money belonging to another person.

6. To refuse to pay a commercial paper when it is due or to refuse to accept a commercial paper.

7. The consideration involved in a contract.

8. The date or time on which a commercial paper comes due and is payable.

9. A phrase used in an indorsement of a commercial paper meaning that the indorser cannot be held liable if the original makers of the instrument fail to make payment when due.

10. An extension of time after the due date for the payment of a commercial paper without defaulting on the obligation.

11. A written notarized statement certifying that a commercial paper was presented for payment and refused.

12. An illegal amount of interest charged for the use of money.

Answers

1. _____

2. _____

3. _____

4. _____

5. _____

6. _____

7. _____

8. _____

9. _____

10. _____

11. _____

12. _____

KEYING LEGAL TERMS

Directions: Unless otherwise instructed, use a 70-space line (typewriter) or 1-inch margins (computer) and double spacing. Correct all errors. Follow one of the procedures below.

WORDS

Keyboarding Procedure
On your typewriter or computer, key the following words at least two times, concentrating on the correct spelling and pronunciation.

Shorthand Procedure
On your typewriter or computer, key the following words once, concentrating on the correct spelling and pronunciation. Then write the shorthand outline for each word in your shorthand notebook or on your shorthand machine. Transcribe from the shorthand outlines one time on your typewriter or computer.

delivery	maturity	presentment
dishonor	without recourse	protest
grace period	postdate	value
interest	usury	accrue

SENTENCES

Keyboarding Procedure
Key each of the following sentences one time on your typewriter or computer. Concentrate on the correct spelling and pronunciation of each underlined legal term.

Shorthand Procedure
Write the correct shorthand outlines for the following sentences in your shorthand notebook or on your shorthand machine. Transcribe from your shorthand outlines one time on your typewriter or computer.

These sentences will be used for practical dictation on the cassettes.

Delivery is the act of transferring or placing an instrument in the possession or control of another person. Delivery is usually a requirement for the legal transfer of a commercial paper. Maturity is the date or time on which a commercial paper comes due and is payable. On the maturity date, a commercial paper may be presented to the maker for payment. Presentment is the presentation of a commercial paper for payment to the one who has the responsibility for making such payment.

Dishonor is to refuse to pay a commercial paper when it is due or to refuse to accept a commercial paper. When an indorser writes without recourse when endorsing an instrument, the indorser cannot be held liable if the original makers of the instrument fail to make payment when due. A protest is a written notarized statement certifying that a commercial paper was presented for payment and refused. A debt paid under protest is the payment of a debt that one feels is not owed with the intention of recovering the amount later.

An extension of time after the due date of the payment of a commercial paper without defaulting on the obligation is called a grace period. To put a future date on a commercial paper instead of the date on which it is actually made is to postdate.

Value is the consideration involved in a contract. Value is also an abbreviation for valuable consideration.

Interest is an amount of money paid for the use of money belonging to another person. Usury is an illegal amount of interest charged for the use of money. Accrue means to be added to or to increase.

> Interest on a note accrues to, or is added to, the principal. Most states have usury laws that set a limit on the amount of interest that can be charged for different types of loans.

TRANSCRIBING FROM DICTATION

Directions: This dictation emphasizes and reinforces the legal terms and definitions you have studied. Listen carefully to the pronunciation of each of the legal terms. Unless otherwise directed, use a 70-space line (typewriter) or 1-inch margins (computer) and double spacing. Correct all errors. Follow one of the procedures below.

Keyboarding Procedure
Using the cassette from Lesson 24, Part A, transcribe the dictation directly at your typewriter or computer.

Shorthand Procedure
Using the cassette from Lesson 24, Part A, take the dictation using your shorthand system and then transcribe from your shorthand notes on your typewriter or computer.

When you have finished transcribing Part A of the practice dictation, check your transcript with the printed copy. If you made any mistakes in the transcription, you should practice those words several times before going on.

Part B TERMINOLOGY AND DEFINITIONS

Directions: Study the terms, pronunciations, and definitions until you are thoroughly familiar with them. In order to complete this lesson successfully, you must understand the meaning and usage of all the legal terms presented. If you are using shorthand, write your shorthand outline for each legal term in your shorthand notebook or on your shorthand machine.

Legal Term	Pronunciation	Definition
1. bona fide	′bō-nə fīd	Latin. Genuine or real. In good faith without deceit or fraud.
2. bogus	′bō-gəs	Not genuine. Counterfeit.
3. kite	kīt	To secure the temporary use of money by issuing worthless paper. Also refers to the worthless paper itself. Writing a check on an account before depositing money in the account is called kiting.
4. spoliation	spō-lē-′ā-shən	An alteration, or change, made on a commercial paper by one who is not a party to the instrument. It does not affect the validity of the instrument if the terms can be determined.
5. indorsement	in-′dȯr-smənt*	The signing of one's name on the back of a commercial paper with the purpose of transferring or assigning it to another person. Under Federal Reserve System requirements, a bank does not have to accept a check that does not have the indorsement in the proper place. (See Figure 24-2, page 354.)
6. special or full indorsement	′spesh-əl ȯr fu̇l in-′dȯr-smənt	An indorsement that specifically names the person to whom the instrument is being transferred. (See Figure 24-3, page 355.)

* The form *indorse* is used in the UCC. The form *endorse* is commonly used in business.

7. restrictive indorsement	ri-'strik-tiv in-'dòr-smənt	An indorsement that contains restrictions as to any further transfer of a commercial paper. For example, if you indorse a check with "For deposit only," the check can only be deposited and cannot be transferred to another party. (See Figure 24-4, page 355.)
8. qualified indorsement	'kwäl-ə-fīd in-'dòr-smənt	An indorsement that qualifies, or restricts, the liability of the indorser. Includes an indorsement that contains the words "without recourse." If the maker of the commercial paper does not pay it, the indorser will not be responsible for payment. (See Figure 24-5, page 356.)
9. blank indorsement	blaŋk 'in-'dòr-smənt	An indorsement that consists of only the indorser's name. Anyone holding a commercial paper with a blank indorsement can receive the funds for it. (See Figure 24-6, page 356.)
10. successive indorsement	sək-'ses-iv in-'dòr-smənt	A series of indorsements following one after another on a commercial paper. (See Figure 24-7, page 357.)
11. allonge	a-'lōnzh	A piece of paper attached to a commercial paper to provide space for the indorsements when there is not enough space on the instrument itself.

FIGURE 24-2 Indorsement Requirements

Trailing Edge

FRONT

PAY TO THE ORDER OF—

AMY JO WILSON
JOSEPH R. WILSON
34 ELM STREET
OAKS, NY 11004

Fifty and 00/100

FIRST CITY BANK
100 MAIN STREET
OAKS, NEW YORK, 11004

MEMO

NON-NEGOTIABLE May 5 19 97

$ 50.00

01-1234
D210

DOLLARS

Amy Jo Wilson

June K. Newman

Signature must be in black or blue ink and must be within 1½ inches from the trailing edge so as not to interfere with indorsements from the bank.

June K. Newman

Reserved for indorsement by the bank at which the check is deposited.

Leading Edge

BACK

FIGURE 24-3 A Special or Full Indorsement

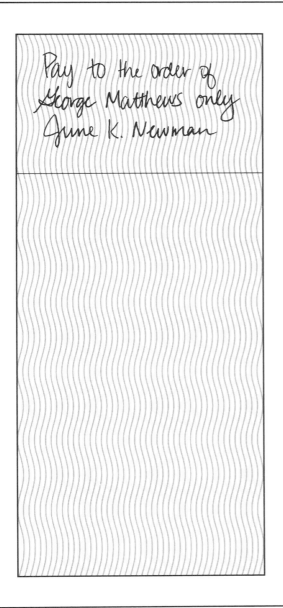

Pay to the order of
George Matthews only
June K. Newman

FIGURE 24-4 A Restrictive Indorsement

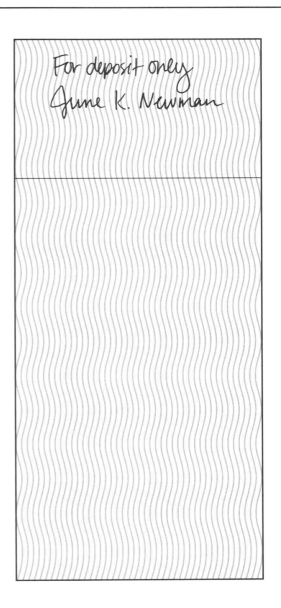

For deposit only
June K. Newman

FIGURE 24-5 A Qualified Indorsement

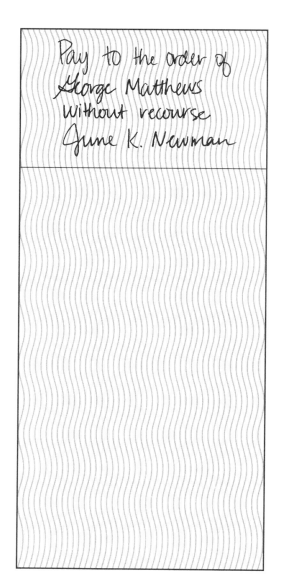

FIGURE 24-6 A Blank Indorsement

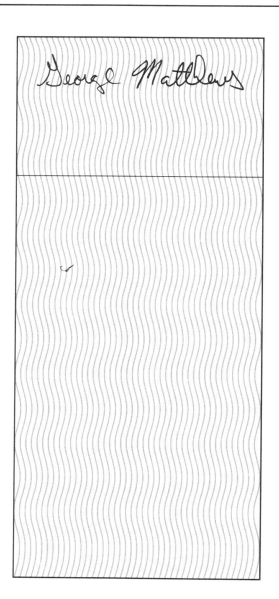

FIGURE 24-7 A Successive Indorsement

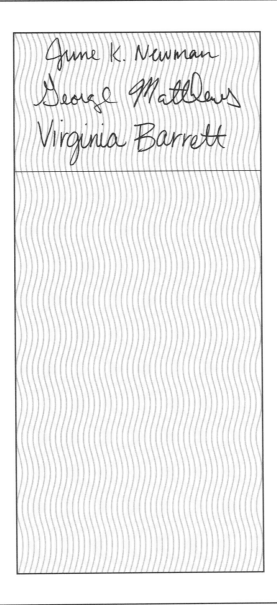

Self-Evaluation B   TERMINOLOGY AND DEFINITION RECALL

Directions: In the Answers column, write the legal term that is most representative of the corresponding statement. After you have completed this self-evaluation, check your answers with the key on page 499. If you have any incorrect answers, restudy the definitions for those terms before going on with this lesson. Then unless otherwise directed, submit this self-evaluation to your instructor.

Answers

1. A word meaning not genuine, or counterfeit, is _____.

   1. _____

2. An indorsement that contains restrictions as to any further transfer of a commercial paper is a/an _____.

   2. _____

3. One's name signed on the back of a commercial paper with the purpose of transferring or assigning it to another person is a/an _____.

   3. _____

4. A piece of paper attached to a commercial paper to provide space for the indorsements when there is not enough space on the instrument itself is a/an _____.

   4. _____

5. An indorsement that specifically names the person to whom the instrument is being transferred is a/an _____.

   5. _____

6. Securing the temporary use of money by issuing worthless paper is to _____.

   6. _____

7. A series of indorsements following one after another on a commercial paper is a/an _____.

   7. _____

8. An indorsement that qualifies, or restricts, the liability of the indorser and includes the words "without recourse" is a/an _____.

   8. _____

9. A word meaning genuine or real or in good faith without deceit or fraud is _____.

   9. _____

10. An indorsement that consists of only the indorser's name is a/an _____.

    10. _____

11. An alteration, or change, made on a commercial paper by one who is not a party to the instrument is called _____.

    11. _____

KEYING LEGAL TERMS

Directions: Unless otherwise instructed, use a 70-space line (typewriter) or 1-inch margins (computer) and double spacing. Correct all errors. Follow one of the procedures below.

WORDS

Keyboarding Procedure
On your typewriter or computer, key the following words at least two times, concentrating on the correct spelling and pronunciation.

Shorthand Procedure
On your typewriter or computer, key the following words once, concentrating on the correct spelling and pronunciation. Then write the shorthand outline for each word in your shorthand notebook or on your shorthand machine. Transcribe from the shorthand outlines one time on your typewriter or computer.

bona fide	bogus	kite
spoliation	indorsement	special or full indorsement
restrictive indorsement	qualified indorsement	blank indorsement
successive indorsement	allonge	

SENTENCES

Keyboarding Procedure
Key each of the following sentences one time on your typewriter or computer. Concentrate on the correct spelling and pronunciation of each underlined legal term.

Shorthand Procedure
Write the correct shorthand outlines for the following sentences in your shorthand notebook or on your shorthand machine. Transcribe from your shorthand outlines one time on your typewriter or computer.

These sentences will be used for practice dictation on the cassettes.

Bona fide means genuine or real or in good faith and without deceit or fraud. A commercial paper that is not genuine, or is a counterfeit, is called a bogus instrument. Kite is worthless paper used to secure the temporary use of money. Kite also refers to the worthless paper itself. Writing a check on an account before depositing money in that account is referred to as kiting.

Spoliation is an alteration, or change, made on a commercial paper by one who is not a party to the instrument. Spoliation does not affect the validity of the instrument if the terms can be determined.

An indorsement is the signing of one's name on the back of a commercial paper with the purpose of transferring or assigning it to another person. Under new Federal Reserve System requirements, a bank does not have to accept a check for deposit that does not have the indorsement in the proper place. An indorsement that specifically names the person to whom the instrument is being transferred is a special or full indorsement. An indorsement that contains restrictions as to any further transfer of the instrument is a restrictive indorsement. "For deposit only" is an example of a restrictive indorsement. If one wishes to qualify, or restrict, his or her liability for the instrument, a qualified indorsement would be used. A qualified indorsement contains the words "without recourse" and usually means that the indorser will not be responsible for payment of the instrument if the maker does not pay it.

A blank indorsement consists only of the indorser's name. A successive indorsement is a series of indorsements that follow one after the other on a commercial paper. If there is not enough space on the instrument for the indorsements, an allonge, or a piece of paper, may be attached to the instrument to accommodate the indorsements.

TRANSCRIBING FROM DICTATION

Directions: This dictation emphasizes and reinforces the legal terms and definitions you have studied. Listen carefully to the pronunciation of each of the legal terms. Unless otherwise directed, use a 70-space line (typewriter) or 1-inch margins (computer) and double spacing. Correct all errors. Follow one of the procedures below.

Keyboarding Procedure
Using the cassette from Lesson 24, Part B, transcribe the dictation directly at your typewriter or computer.

Shorthand Procedure
Using the cassette from Lesson 24, Part B, take the dictation using your shorthand system and then transcribe from your shorthand notes on your typewriter or computer.

When you have finished transcribing Part B of the practice dictation, check your transcript with the printed copy. If you made any mistakes in the transcription, you should practice those words several times before going on to Evaluation 12.

CHECKLIST
I have completed the following for Lesson 24:

	Part A, Date	Part B, Date	Submitted to Instructor Yes	No
Terminology and Definitions				
Self-Evaluation				
* Keying Legal Terms				
Words				
Sentences				
* Transcribing from Dictation				

When you have successfully completed all the exercises in this lesson and submitted to your instructor those requested, you are ready to proceed with Evaluation 12.

* If you are using a shorthand system, submit to your instructor your shorthand notes along with your transcript.

Evaluation No. 12   SECTION A

Directions: This dictation/transcription evaluation will test your spelling and transcription abilities on the legal terms that you studied in the two preceding lessons. Use a 5-space paragraph indention, a 70-space line (typewriter) or 1-inch margins (computer), and double spacing unless otherwise instructed. Correct all errors. Follow one of the procedures below.

Keyboarding Procedure

Using the cassette from Evaluation 12, transcribe the dictation directly at your typewriter or computer.

Shorthand Procedure

Using the cassette from Evaluation 12, take the dictation using your shorthand system and then transcribe from your shorthand notes on your typewriter or computer.

Sections B and C are available from your instructor.

Lesson 25

Bankruptcy

Due to changes in society and economic conditions, bankruptcy law is affecting more and more individuals and businesses. Bankruptcy proceedings are under the jurisdiction of the federal courts rather than the state courts. A person cannot be sent to jail for failure to pay his or her debts; however, the person's property may be taken to satisfy those debts. Bankruptcy is a branch of equity jurisprudence, but, because of its increased importance, this lesson is devoted exclusively to the terms relating to bankruptcy. When you have satisfactorily completed these exercises, you will be able to spell, pronounce, define, and transcribe correctly each of the terms presented that relate to the area of bankruptcy law.

Part A   TERMINOLOGY AND DEFINITIONS

Directions: Study the terms, pronunciations, and definitions until you are thoroughly familiar with them. In order to complete this lesson successfully, you must understand the meaning and usage of all the legal terms presented. If you are using shorthand, write your shorthand outline for each legal term in your shorthand notebook, or on your shorthand machine.

Legal Term	Pronunciation	Definition
1. bankruptcy court	'baŋ-krəp-sē kōrt	Federal courts that are established to administer the bankruptcy laws.
2. petition for bankruptcy	pə-'tish-ən fər 'baŋ-krəp-sē	The document filed in a court requesting that bankruptcy proceedings be started against a certain person. May be filed by the person declaring bankruptcy or by the creditors. (See Figure 25-1, page 367.)
3. bankrupt	'baŋ-krəpt	A person who is declared by a court to be unable or unwilling to pay his or her debts.
4. bankruptcy	'baŋ-krəp-sē	The process of declaring a person bankrupt and then taking the person's assets and distributing them among the creditors.
5. creditors	'kred-ət-ərs	Person or persons to whom a debt is owed.
6. voluntary bankruptcy	'väl-ən-ter-ē 'baŋ-krəp-sē	A bankruptcy proceeding that is started by the person who is bankrupt.
7. debtor's petition	'det-ərs pə-'tish-ən	A petition filed by the debtor requesting the benefit of the bankruptcy laws. A petition for voluntary bankruptcy.
8. involuntary bankruptcy	in-'väl-ən-ter-ē 'baŋ-krəp-sē	A bankruptcy proceeding that is started by the creditors of the bankrupt person.
9. solvent	'säl-vənt	The ability or capacity of a person to pay his or her debts.

10. insolvency	in-'säl-vən-sē	The inability of a person to pay his or her debts.
11. ex parte application	eks 'pärt-ē ap-lə-'kā-shən	Latin. An application filed by one side or one party. It is made by a creditor who is not a party to the bankruptcy proceeding but who has an interest in it.
12. referee	ref-ə-'rē	An officer serving as the trial judge of a bankruptcy court who is in charge of the proceedings in that court in accordance with federal bankruptcy laws.
13. receiver	ri-'sē-vər	An impartial person appointed by the court to take charge of property involved in a bankruptcy proceeding and to follow the directions of the court in disposing of the property.
14. trustee	trəs-'tē	A person who holds the property of a bankrupt for the benefit of the creditors.

FIGURE 25-1 A Bankruptcy Petition (cover sheet)

B-103 (Rev. 5/87)	**BANKRUPTCY PETITION COVER SHEET**	CASE NUMBER (Court Use Only) 34987–VB–33

INSTRUCTIONS: This form must be completed by the debtor or the debtor's attorney and submitted to the clerk of court upon the filing of the petition.

NAME OF DEBTOR (Last, First, Middle) Findley, Anna Marie	NAME OF JOINT DEBTOR (Spouse) (Last, First, Middle) Collins, Richard Lee
ALL OTHER NAMES, INCLUDING TRADE NAMES, USED BY THE DEBTOR IN THE LAST 6 YEARS F & C Enterprises	ALL OTHER NAMES, INCLUDING TRADE NAMES, USED BY THE JOINT DEBTOR IN THE LAST 6 YEARS F & C Enterprises
SOCIAL SECURITY NO. AND/OR EMPLOYER'S TAX ID NO. 000-01-0000	SOCIAL SECURITY NO. AND/OR EMPLOYER'S TAX ID NO. 000-02-0000
ADDRESS OF DEBTOR (Street, City, State, and Zip Code) 7320 Sandstone Drive Lansing, Michigan 48906	ADDRESS OF JOINT DEBTOR (Street, City, State, and Zip Code) 7320 Sandstone Drive Lansing, Michigan 48906
NAME OF COUNTY Ingham	NAME OF COUNTY Ingham

CHECK PROPER BOXES

TYPE OF PETITION
☒ Voluntary Petition ☐ Involuntary Petition

NATURE OF DEBT
☒ Business – Complete A, B, C below ┐ ☐ Non-business/Consumer

A. FORM OF ORGANIZATION (Check One Box)
☒ Individual ☐ Partnership
☐ Corporation Publicly Held ☐ Corporation Closely Held

CHAPTER OF THE BANKRUPTCY CODE UNDER WHICH THE PETITION IS FILED (Check One Box)

☐ Chapter 7 ☐ Chapter 11 Railroad
☐ Ch. 7 Broker ☐ Chapter 12
☐ Ch. 9 ☒ Chapter 13
☐ Chapter 11 ☐ Sec. 304

B. TYPE OF BUSINESS (Check One Box)
☐ Farmer ☐ Transportation ☐ Construction
☐ Professional ☐ Manufacture/Mining ☐ Real Estate
☒ Retail/Wholesale ☐ Other Business

C. BRIEFLY DESCRIBE NATURE OF BUSINESS

Accounting Services

DEBTOR'S ESTIMATES

ESTIMATED NUMBER OF CREDITORS

1-15	16-49	50-99	100-999	1000-over
☒	☐	☐	☐	☐

☒ No assets will be available for distribution to creditors
☐ Assets will be available for distribution to creditors

ESTIMATED ASSETS (IN THOUSANDS OF DOLLARS)

Under 50	50-99	100-499	500-999	1000-over
☒	☐	☐	☐	☐

ESTIMATED NUMBER OF EMPLOYEES—CHAPTER 11 AND 12 ONLY

0	1-19	20-99	100-999	1000-over
☐	☐	☐	☐	☐

ESTIMATED LIABILITIES (IN THOUSANDS OF DOLLARS)

Under 50	50-99	100-499	500-999	1000-over
☐	☒	☐	☐	☐

ESTIMATED NO. OF EQUITY SECURITY HOLDERS—CH. 11 & 12 ONLY

0	1-19	20-99	100-999	1000-over
☐	☐	☐	☐	☐

ATTORNEY FOR THE DEBTOR (Firm Name, Address, Tel. No.) ☒ No Attorney	ATTORNEY FOR THE PETITIONER (IF INVOLUNTARY PETITION) (Firm Name, Address, Tel. No.)

FILING FEE (Check One Box) ☒ Filing Fee Attached ☐ Filing fee to be paid in installments by individuals only. Must attach signed application for the court's consideration indicating that the debtor is unable to pay fee except in installments. Rule 1006 (b).

RELATED BANKRUPTCY CASE (IF ANY)

DEBTOR	CASE NO.
DISTRICT	DIVISIONAL OFFICE	NAME OF JUDGE

DATE 12-20-97	PRINT NAME Richard Lee Collins	SIGNATURE OF ATTORNEY (OR DEBTOR) Richard Lee Collins

Self-Evaluation A   TERMINOLOGY AND DEFINITION RECALL

Directions: In the Answers column at the right of each statement, write the letter that represents the word or group of words that correctly completes the statement. After you have completed this self-evaluation, check your answers with the key on page 499. If you have any incorrect answers, restudy the definitions for those terms before going on with this lesson. Then, unless otherwise directed, submit this self-evaluation to your instructor.

Answers

1. Federal courts that are established to administer the bankruptcy laws are (a) bankruptcy courts, (b) ex parte courts, (c) receiver courts.

   1. _____

2. A person who holds the property of a bankrupt for the benefit of the creditors is a (a) creditor, (b) referee, (c) trustee.

   2. _____

3. The document filed in a bankruptcy court requesting that bankruptcy proceedings be started against a certain person is called a/an (a) petition for bankruptcy, (b) ex parte application, (c) debtor's petition.

   3. _____

4. The inability of a person to pay his or her debts is referred to as (a) solvent, (b) trustee, (c) insolvency.

   4. _____

5. An impartial person appointed by the court to take charge of property involved in a bankruptcy proceeding and to follow the directions of the court in disposing of the property is a (a) trustee, (b) receiver, (c) referee.

   5. _____

6. A petition filed by the debtor requesting the benefit of the bankruptcy laws is a/an (a) petition for bankruptcy, (b) debtor's petition, (c) ex parte application.

   6. _____

7. The process of declaring a person bankrupt and then taking the person's assets and distributing them among the creditors is (a) bankruptcy, (b) insolvency, (c) petition for bankruptcy.

   7. _____

8. A person who is declared by a court to be unable or unwilling to pay his or her debts is a (a) creditor, (b) referee, (c) bankrupt.

   8. _____

9. An officer serving as the trial judge of a bankruptcy court who is in charge of the proceedings in that court is a (a) creditor, (b) referee, (c) trustee.

   9. _____

10. One to whom a debt is owed is a (a) debtor, (b) creditor, (c) receiver.

    10. _____

11. When a person has the ability or capacity to pay his or her debts, he or she is (a) solvent, (b) insolvent, (c) bankrupt.

    11. _____

12. A bankruptcy proceeding that is started by the person who is bankrupt is referred to as (a) involuntary bankruptcy, (b) debtor's petition, (c) voluntary bankruptcy.

    12. _____

13. An application filed by one side or one party that is made by a creditor who is not a party to the bankruptcy proceeding but has an interest in it is a/an (a) ex parte application, (b) petition for bankruptcy, (c) debtor's petition.

    13. _____

14. A bankruptcy proceeding that is started by the creditors of the bankrupt person is called (a) voluntary bankruptcy, (b) involuntary bankruptcy, (c) petition for bankruptcy.

    14. _____

KEYING LEGAL TERMS

Directions: Unless otherwise instructed, use a 70-space line (typewriter) or 1-inch margins (computer) and double spacing. Correct all errors. Follow one of the procedures below.

WORDS

Keyboarding Procedure
On your typewriter or computer, key the following words at least two times, concentrating on the correct spelling and pronunciation.

Shorthand Procedure
On your typewriter or computer, key the following words once, concentrating on the correct spelling and pronunciation. Then write the shorthand outline for each word in your shorthand notebook or on your shorthand machine. Transcribe from the shorthand outlines one time on your typewriter or computer.

bankruptcy court	petition for bankruptcy	bankrupt
bankruptcy	creditors	voluntary bankruptcy
debtor's petition	involuntary bankruptcy	solvent
insolvency	ex parte application	referee
receiver	trustee	

SENTENCES

Keyboarding Procedure
Key each of the following sentences one time on your typewriter or computer. Concentrate on the correct spelling and pronunciation of each underlined legal term.

Shorthand Procedure
Write the correct shorthand outlines for the following sentences in your shorthand notebook or on your shorthand machine. Transcribe from your shorthand outlines one time on your typewriter or computer.

These sentences will be used for practice dictation on the cassettes.

The bankruptcy laws are administered in a federal court called a bankruptcy court. A petition for bankruptcy is the document filed in a bankruptcy court requesting that bankruptcy proceedings be started against a certain person. A bankrupt is a person who is declared by a court to be unable or unwilling to pay his or her debts. Bankruptcy is the process of declaring a person bankrupt and then taking the person's assets and distributing them among the creditors. A creditor is a person to whom a debt is owed.

If a debtor initiates a bankruptcy proceeding, the proceeding is called voluntary bankruptcy. A debtor's petition is one filed by the debtor requesting the benefit of the bankruptcy laws. A petition for voluntary bankruptcy is a debtor's petition. However, if one is forced into bankruptcy by the petition of creditors, the proceeding is called involuntary bankruptcy.

If a person is solvent, that person has the ability or capacity to pay his or her debts. Insolvency is the inability of a person to pay his or her debts. Insolvency exists when one's liabilities exceed one's assets.

A petition for bankruptcy filed by a creditor for involuntary bankruptcy of a debtor is called an ex parte application. In bankruptcy courts, a referee is appointed by the court to assist in the bankruptcy proceedings. A referee is an officer of the bankruptcy court and serves as the trial judge in charge of the proceedings in that court in accordance with federal bankruptcy laws.

A receiver is an impartial person appointed by the court to take charge of and dispose of the property involved in a bankruptcy proceeding under the direction of the court. A trustee is a person who holds the property of a bankrupt for the benefit of the creditors.

TRANSCRIBING FROM DICTATION

Directions: This dictation emphasizes and reinforces the legal terms and definitions you have studied. Listen carefully to the pronunciation of each of the legal terms. Unless otherwise directed, use a 70-space line (typewriter) or 1-inch margins (computer) and double spacing. Correct all errors. Follow one of the procedures below.

Keyboarding Procedure
Using the cassette from Lesson 25, Part A, transcribe the dictation directly at your typewriter or computer.

Shorthand Procedure
Using the cassette from Lesson 25, Part A, take the dictation using your shorthand system and then transcribe from your shorthand notes on your typewriter or computer.

When you have finished transcribing Part A of the practice dictation, check your transcript with the printed copy. If you made any mistakes in the transcription, you should practice those words several times before going on.

Part B TERMINOLOGY AND DEFINITIONS

Directions: Study the terms, pronunciations, and definitions until you are thoroughly familiar with them. In order to complete this lesson successfully, you must understand the meaning and usage of all the legal terms presented. If you are using shorthand, write your shorthand outline for each legal term in your shorthand notebook or on your shorthand machine.

Legal Term	Pronunciation	Definition
1. insolvent debtor	in-'säl-vənt 'det-ər	A person who cannot pay his or her debts.
2. account stated	ə-'kaủnt 'stāt-əd	An agreement between a debtor and creditor that the amount stated as being owed to the creditor is accurate.
3. account current	ə-'kaủnt 'kər-ənt	An open or unsettled account between a debtor and creditor. The opposite of account stated.
4. summary of debts and assets	'səm-ə-rē əv dets ən 'as-ets	A listing provided to the court containing all the debts and assets of the debtor in a bankruptcy proceeding.
5. assets	'as-ets	The property owned by a bankrupt that may be applied to pay his or her debts.
6. liabilities	lī-ə-'bil-ət-ēs	Something that one owes to another and has an obligation to pay.
7. composition	käm-pə-'zish-ən	An agreement between a debtor and creditor in which the creditor agrees to accept less than the amount of the debt in settlement for the entire debt.
8. secured debts	si-'kyủrd dets	Debts that are guaranteed by pledged collateral, such as a mortgage.
9. balance of funds	'bal-əns əv fənds	The amount remaining after the secured debts are paid that is to be divided among the other creditors.
10. liquidate	'lik-wə-dāt	To convert assets into cash to be used to pay the amount owed to creditors.

11. deficiency decree	di-'fish-ən-sē di-'krē	A judgment for a portion of a secured debt for which the sale of the property does not pay in full.
12. discharge	'dis-chärj	The release of a bankrupt from the obligation of paying his or her former debts.
13. after-acquired property	'af-tər ə-'kwĭrd 'präp-ərt-ē	Property acquired after a person has filed for bankruptcy. After-acquired property is not subject to the claims of bankruptcy creditors.

Self-Evaluation B   TERMINOLOGY AND DEFINITION RECALL

Directions: In the Answers column, write the legal term that is most representative of the corresponding statement. After you have completed this self-evaluation, check your answers with the key on page 499. If you have any incorrect answers, restudy the definitions for those terms before going on with this lesson. Then unless otherwise directed, submit this self-evaluation to your instructor.

Answers

1. The amount remaining after the secured debts are paid that is to be divided among the other creditors is the _____.

    1. _____

2. An open or unsettled account between a debtor and creditor is a/an _____.

    2. _____

3. The release of a bankrupt from the obligation of paying former debts is a/an _____.

    3. _____

4. Debts that are guaranteed by pledged collateral, such as a mortgage, are called _____.

    4. _____

5. An agreement between a debtor and creditor in which the creditor agrees to accept less than the amount of the debt in settlement for the entire debt is referred to as _____.

    5. _____

6. An agreement between a debtor and creditor that the amount stated as being owed to the creditor is accurate is a/an _____.

    6. _____

7. A listing provided to the court containing all the debts and assets of the debtor in a bankruptcy proceeding is a/an _____.

    7. _____

8. A person who cannot pay his or her debts is a/an _____.

    8. _____

9. A judgment for a portion of a secured debt for which the sale of the property does not pay in full is a/an _____.

    9. _____

10. Property acquired after a person has filed for bankruptcy is called _____.

    10. _____

11. The property owned by a bankrupt that may be applied to pay his or her debts is referred to as _____.

    11. _____

12. To convert assets into cash to be used to pay the amounts owed to creditors is to _____.

    12. _____

13. Something that one owes to another and has an obligation to pay is called _____.

    13. _____

KEYING LEGAL TERMS

Directions: Unless otherwise instructed, use a 70-space line (typewriter) or 1-inch margins (computer) and double spacing. Correct all errors. Follow one of the procedures below.

WORDS

Keyboarding Procedure
On your typewriter or computer, key the following words at least two times, concentrating on the correct spelling and pronunciation.

Shorthand Procedure
On your typewriter or computer, key the following words once, concentrating on the correct spelling and pronunciation. Then write the shorthand outline for each word in your shorthand notebook or on your shorthand machine. Transcribe from the shorthand outlines one time on your typewriter or computer.

insolvent debtor	account stated	account current
summary of debts and assets	assets	liabilities
composition	secured debts	balance of funds
liquidate	deficiency decree	discharge
after-acquired property		

SENTENCES

Keyboard Procedures
Key each of the following sentences one time on your typewriter or computer. Concentrate on the correct spelling and pronunciation of each underlined legal term.

Shorthand Procedure
Write the correct shorthand outlines for the following sentences in your shorthand notebook or on your shorthand machine. Transcribe from your shorthand outlines one time on your typewriter or computer.

These sentences will be used for practice dictation on the cassettes.

An <u>insolvent debtor</u> is a person who cannot pay his or her debts. <u>Account stated</u> refers to an agreement between a debtor and creditor that the amount stated as being owed to the creditor is accurate. However, an open or unsettled account between a debtor and creditor is referred to as an <u>account current</u>.

When a petition for bankruptcy is filed, a <u>summary of debts and assets</u> of the debtor must be provided to the bankruptcy court. A summary of debts and assets is a list containing all that a debtor owes and owns. <u>Assets</u> are the property owned by a bankrupt that may be applied to pay his or her debts. Those debts are called <u>liabilities</u>.

If the creditors agree to accept less than the total amount owed as settlement for the entire debt, the agreement is called <u>composition</u>. Debts that are guaranteed by pledged collateral, such as a mortgage, are called <u>secured debts</u>. <u>Balance of funds</u> is the amount remaining after the secured debts are paid that is to be divided among the other creditors. To <u>liquidate</u> is to convert assets into cash to be used to pay the amounts owed to creditors.

A <u>deficiency decree</u> may be entered for the portion of a secured debt for which the sale of the property does not pay in full. A <u>discharge</u> releases a bankrupt from the obligation or liability of paying former debts. Property that a bankrupt acquires after filing for bankruptcy is referred to as <u>after-acquired property</u> and is not subject to the claims of the bankruptcy creditors.

TRANSCRIBING FROM DICTATION

Directions: This dictation emphasizes and reinforces the legal terms and definitions you have studied. Listen carefully to the pronunciation of each of the legal terms. Unless otherwise directed, use a 70-space line (typewriter) or 1-inch margins (computer) and double spacing. Correct all errors. Follow one of the procedures below.

Keyboarding Procedure
Using the cassette from Lesson 25, Part B, transcribe the dictation directly at your typewriter or computer.

Shorthand Procedure
Using the cassette from Lesson 25, Part B, take the dictation using your shorthand system and then transcribe from your shorthand notes on your typewriter or computer.

When you have finished transcribing Part B of the practice dictation, check your transcript with the printed copy. If you made any mistakes in the transcription, you should practice those words several times before going on to Lesson 26.

CHECKLIST
I have completed the following for Lesson 25:

	Part A, Date	Part B, Date	Submitted to Instructor Yes	No
Terminology and Definitions				
Self-Evaluation				
* Keying Legal Terms				
Words				
Sentences				
* Transcribing from Dictation				

When you have successfully completed all the exercises in this lesson and submitted to your instructor those requested, you are ready to proceed with Lesson 26.

* If you are using a shorthand system, submit to your instructor your shorthand notes along with your transcript.

Lesson 26

Agency

> "No one can do that by another which one cannot do of oneself."
>
> —Legal Maxim

In an agency relationship, a person grants another the authority to act for him or her in the commission of certain acts. Generally an agency relationship may exist for the doing of any lawful act unless the law deems such an act as so personal that another person cannot do it, such as the making of a will. Agency relationships affect many day-to-day business transactions, including activities involving brokers, attorneys, and bankers. When you have satisfactorily completed this lesson, you should be able to pronounce, define, spell, and transcribe correctly the terms applicable to the principles of an agency.

Part A TERMINOLOGY AND DEFINITIONS

Directions: Study the terms, pronunciations, and definitions until you are thoroughly familiar with them. In order to complete this lesson successfully, you must understand the meaning and usage of all the legal terms presented. If you are using shorthand, write your shorthand outline for each legal term in your shorthand notebook or on your shorthand machine.

Legal Term	Pronunciation	Definition
1. agency	′ā-jən-sē	A relationship whereby one person gives permission to another person to act for or represent him or her.
2. principal	′prin-spəl	The one who gives permission to another person to act for or represent him or her.
3. undisclosed principal	ən-dis-′klōzd ′prin-spəl	A principal who is not known to the party with whom an agent transacts business.
4. power of attorney	paˑur əv ə-′tər-nē	The instrument by which the principal gives the agent the authority to represent or act for him or her. If the principal becomes incapacitated or disabled, the power of attorney is no longer valid; however, a durable power of attorney would be valid. (See Figure 26-1, page 381.)
5. agent	′ā-jənt	The one who acts for or represents a principal with the principal's permission.
6. plenipotentiary	plen-ə-pə-′tench-rē	A person who has complete authority to do a certain thing or act for another person.
7. general agent	′jen-rəl ′ā-jənt	An agent who has permission to transact any and all affairs of a particular business for a principal.
8. special agent	′spesh-əl ′ā-jənt	An agent who has permission to transact a specified act for a principal.
9. universal agent	yü-nə-′vər-səl ′ā-jənt	An agent who has the authority to transact any and all business for a principal.

10. primary agent	′prī-mer-ē ′ā-jənt	An agent who is given direct and first authority by a principal to act as an agent.
11. subagent	səb-′ā-jənt	An agent who is given permission by a primary agent to transact business for the principal.
12. exclusive or irrevocable agency	iks-′klü-siv ər ir-′əv-ə-kə-bəl ′ā-jən-sē	An agency that cannot be revoked by the principal while the agency contract or agreement is in effect.
13. implied agency	im-′plīd ′ā-jən-sē	An agency that is created by the actions of the parties in a particular situation.
14. del credere agent	del kred-′ər-ē ′ā-jənt	Latin. An agent who guarantees or acts as a surety for the principal against the default of persons with whom the agent conducts business on behalf of the principal.

FIGURE 26-1 A Power of Attorney

POWER OF ATTORNEY.   24

Know All Men By These Presents, That I, George S. Bartlett

have made, constituted and appointed, and By THESE PRESENTS, do make, constitute and appoint

Ronald F. Bartlett ----------------------------- true and lawful ATTORNEY for

me   and in my   name, place and stead, to purchase a parcel of real

estate located in the City of Lansing, County of Ingham, State of

giving and granting unto Ronald F. Bartlett   said Attorney, full power and
authority to do and perform all and every act and thing whatsoever requisite and necessary to be done in

and about the premises, as fully to all intents and purposes, as I
might or could do if personally present, with full power of substitution and revocation hereby ratifying

Self-Evaluation A   TERMINOLOGY AND DEFINITION RECALL

Directions: In the Answers column, write the legal term that is most representative of the corresponding statement. After you have completed this self-evaluation, check your answers with the key on page 499. If you have any incorrect answers, restudy the definitions for those terms before going on with this lesson. Then unless otherwise directed, submit this self-evaluation to your instructor.

Answers

1. An agent who guarantees or acts as a surety for the principal against the default of persons with whom the agent conducts business on behalf of the principal is a/an _____.

    1. _____

2. A relationship whereby one person gives permission to another person to act for or represent him or her is a/an _____.

    2. _____

3. The one who gives permission to another person to act for or represent him or her is a/an _____.

    3. _____

4. A principal who is not known to the party with whom an agent transacts business is a/an _____.

    4. _____

5. An agent who has the authority to transact any or all business for a principal is a/an _____.

    5. _____

6. An agency that cannot be revoked by the principal while the agency contract or agreement is in effect is a/an _____.

    6. _____

7. An agency that is created by the actions of the parties in a particular situation is a/an _____.

    7. _____

8. The one who acts for or represents a principal with the principal's permission is a/an _____.

    8. _____

9. The instrument by which the principal gives the agent the authority to represent or act for him or her is a/an _____.

    9. _____

10. An agent who has permission to transact a specified act for a principal is a/an _____.

    10. _____

11. The one who is given direct and first authority by a principal to act as an agent is a/an _____.

    11. _____

12. An agent who is given permission by a primary agent to transact business for the principal is a/an _____.

    12. _____

13. A person who has complete authority to do a certain thing or to act for another person is a/an _____.

    13. _____

14. An agent who has permission to transact any and all affairs of a particular business for the principal is a/an _____.

    14. _____

KEYING LEGAL TERMS

Directions: Unless otherwise instructed, use a 70-space line (typewriter) or 1-inch margins (computer) and double spacing. Correct all errors. Follow one of the procedures below.

WORDS

Keyboarding Procedure
On your typewriter or computer, key the following words at least two times, concentrating on the correct spelling and pronunciation.

Shorthand Procedure
On your typewriter or computer, key the following words once, concentrating on the correct spelling and pronunciation. Then write the shorthand outline for each word in your shorthand notebook or on your shorthand machine. Transcribe from the shorthand outlines one time on your typewriter or computer.

agency	principal	undisclosed principal
power of attorney	agent	plenipotentiary
general agent	special agent	universal agent
primary agent	subagent	exclusive or irrevocable agency
implied agency	del credere agent	

SENTENCES

Keyboarding Procedure
Key each of the following sentences one time on your typewriter or computer. Concentrate on the correct spelling and pronunciation of each underlined legal term.

Shorthand Procedure
Write the correct shorthand outlines for the following sentences in your shorthand notebook or on your shorthand machine. Transcribe from your shorthand outlines one time on your typewriter or computer.

These sentences will be used for practice dictation on the cassettes.

An <u>agency</u> is a relationship whereby one person gives permission to another person to act for or represent him or her. A <u>principal</u> is the person who gives permission to another person to act for or represent him or her. If a third party does not know who the principal is at the time a transaction is conducted by an agent, the principal is referred to as an <u>undisclosed principal</u>.

A <u>power of attorney</u> is the instrument by which a principal gives an agent the authority to act for him or her. If the principal becomes incapacitated or disabled, the power of attorney is no longer valid. To act for a disabled principal, the agent must have a durable power of attorney.

The person who acts for or represents a principal with the principal's permission is an <u>agent</u>. A <u>plenipotentiary</u> is one who has authority to do a certain thing or to act for another person.

A <u>general agent</u> is one who has authorization to transact any or all affairs of a particular business for a principal, whereas a <u>special agent</u> is one who has permission to transact only an act specified for the principal. A <u>universal agent</u> is one who has the authority to transact any and all business for the principal. A <u>primary agent</u> is one who is given direct and first authority by a principal to act as an agent. A primary agent may give a <u>subagent</u> the authority to transact business for the primary agent's principal.

An **exclusive or irrevocable agency** is an agency that cannot be revoked by the principal while the agency contract or agreement is in effect. An **implied agency** is one that is created by the actions of the parties in the situation. A **del credere agent** is one who guarantees or acts as a surety for the principal against the default of persons with whom the agent conducts business on behalf of the principal.

TRANSCRIBING FROM DICTATION

Directions: This dictation emphasizes and reinforces the legal terms and definitions you have studied. Listen carefully to the pronunciation of each of the legal terms. Unless otherwise directed, use a 70-space line (typewriter) or 1-inch margins (computer) and double spacing. Correct all errors. Follow one of the procedures below.

Keyboarding Procedure
Using the cassette from Lesson 26, Part A, transcribe the dictation directly at your typewriter or computer.

Shorthand Procedure
Using the cassette from Lesson 26, Part A, take the dictation using your shorthand system and then transcribe from your shorthand notes on your typewriter or computer.

When you have finished transcribing Part A of the practice dictation, check your transcript with the printed copy. If you made any mistakes in the transcription, you should practice those words several times before going on.

Part B TERMINOLOGY AND DEFINITIONS

Directions: Study the terms, pronunciations, and definitions until you are thoroughly familiar with them. In order to complete this lesson successfully, you must understand the meaning and usage of all the legal terms presented. If you are using shorthand, write your shorthand outline for each legal term in your shorthand notebook or on your shorthand machine.

Legal Term	Pronunciation	Definition
1. delegation of authority	del-i-ˈgā-shən əv ə-ˈthär- ət-ē	One person giving or transferring his or her authority to another person.
2. mutual consent	ˈmyüch-wəl kən-ˈsent	Agreement by both parties to the agent/principal relationship. An essential element of an agency.
3. third party	thord ˈpärt-ē	The party with whom an agent transacts the business for a principal.
4. fiduciary relationship	fə-ˈdü-shē-er-ē ri-ˈlā-shən-ship	A relationship that exists when one person trusts and relies upon another.
5. implied ratification	im-ˈplīd rat-ə-fə-ˈkā-shən	The presumed acceptance by the principal, because of the principal's actions, of the things done on his or her behalf by an agent.
6. estoppel	e-ˈstäp-əl	A situation that arises when a principal is forbidden by law from alleging or denying certain things done by an agent because of the principal's action or lack of action in the past.
7. ratification	rat-ə-fə-ˈkā-shən	The acceptance by a principal of the acts performed on the principal's behalf by an agent or another person.
8. respondeat superior	ri-ˈspän-dē-at sù-ˈpir-ē-ər	Latin. Let the master answer. A principal is responsible for the wrongful acts that the agent does for him or her.

9. factor	′fak-tər	An agent who is employed by a principal to sell goods for the principal. The factor usually has possession of said goods and sells them in his or her own name.
10. nonfeasance	nän-′fēz-ns	The failure of an agent to perform the acts that the agent agreed to do for the principal.
11. ostensible authority or apparent authority	ä-′sten-sə-bəl ə-′thär-ət-ē ər ə-′par-ənt ə-′thär-ət-ē	The authority that a principal, either intentionally or by want of due care, leads a third party to believe the agent possesses.
12. implied authority	im-′plĭd ə-′thär-ət-ē	Authority of an agent that is implied by the actions of a principal.
13. incidental authority	in-sə-′dent-l ə-′thär-ət-ē	The authority that an agent must have in order to perform the business authorized by a principal.
14. express authority	ik-′spres ə-′thär-ət-ē	Authority, either oral or written, that is definitely and explicitly given to an agent.

Self-Evaluation B   TERMINOLOGY AND DEFINITION RECALL

Directions: In the Answers column, write the letter from Column 1 that represents the word or phrase that best matches each item in Column 2. After you have completed this self-evaluation, check your answers with the key on page 499. If you have any incorrect answers, restudy the definitions for those terms before going on with this lesson. Then unless otherwise directed, submit this self-evaluation to your instructor.

Column 1

a. delegation of authority

b. estoppel

c. express authority

d. factor

e. fiduciary relationship

f. implied authority

g. implied ratification

h. incidental authority

i. mutual consent

j. nonfeasance

k. ostensible or apparent authority

l. plenipotentiary

m. ratification

n. respondeat superior

o. third party

Column 2

1. Agreement by both parties to the agent/principal relationship.

2. Authority of an agent that is implied by the actions of a principal.

3. The authority that an agent must have in order to perform the business authorized by a principal.

4. The party with whom an agent transacts the business for a principal.

5. A Latin phrase meaning that a principal is responsible for the wrongful acts of an agent.

6. An agent who is employed by a principal to sell goods for the principal.

7. The failure of an agent to perform the acts that the agent agreed to do for the principal.

8. A relationship that exists when one person trusts and relies upon another.

9. The presumed acceptance by the principal, because of the principal's actions, of the things done on his or her behalf by an agent.

10. The acceptance by a principal of the acts performed on the principal's behalf by an agent or another person.

11. A situation that arises when a principal is forbidden by law from alleging or denying certain things done by an agent because of the principal's action or lack of action in the past.

12. The authority that a principal, either intentionally or by want of due care, leads a third party to believe the agent possesses.

13. Authority, either oral or written, that is definitely and explicitly given to an agent.

14. The giving or transferring of authority from one person to another.

Answers

1. _____

2. _____

3. _____

4. _____

5. _____

6. _____

7. _____

8. _____

9. _____

10. _____

11. _____

12. _____

13. _____

14. _____

KEYING LEGAL TERMS

Directions: Unless otherwise instructed, use a 70-space line (typewriter) or 1-inch margins (computer) and double spacing. Correct all errors. Follow one of the procedures below.

WORDS

Keyboarding Procedure
On your typewriter or computer, key the following words at least two times, concentrating on the correct spelling and pronunciation.

Shorthand Procedure
On your typewriter or computer, key the following words once, concentrating on the correct spelling and pronunciation. Then write the shorthand outline for each word in your shorthand notebook or on your shorthand machine. Transcribe from the shorthand outlines one time on your typewriter or computer.

delegation of authority	mutual consent	third party
fiduciary relationship	implied ratification	estoppel
ratification	respondeat superior	factor
nonfeasance	ostensible authority or apparent authority	implied authority
incidental authority		express authority

SENTENCES

Keyboarding Procedure
Key each of the following sentences one time on your typewriter or computer. Concentrate on the correct spelling and pronunciation of each underlined legal term.

Shorthand Procedure
Write the correct shorthand outlines for the following sentences in your shorthand notebook or on your shorthand machine. Transcribe from your shorthand outlines one time on your typewriter or computer.

These sentences will be used for practice dictation on the cassettes.

One person giving or transferring his or her authority to another person is <u>delegation of authority</u>. <u>Mutual consent</u> is essential in a principal/agent relationship. Mutual consent is the agreement by both parties to the agency relationship. A <u>third party</u> in an agency relationship is the one with whom an agent transacts the business for a principal.

A relationship that exists when one person trusts and relies upon another is a <u>fiduciary relationship</u>. <u>Implied ratification</u> is the presumed acceptance by the principal, because of the principal's actions, of the things done on his or her behalf by an agent.

An <u>estoppel</u> arises when a principal is forbidden by law from alleging or denying certain things that have been done because of the principal's action or lack of action in the past. The acceptance by a principal of the acts performed on the principal's behalf by an agent or another person is called <u>ratification</u>. <u>Respondeat superior</u> is a Latin phrase for let the master answer. Respondeat superior means that a principal is responsible for the wrongful acts of an agent acting for him or her.

A <u>factor</u> is an agent who is employed by a principal to sell goods for the principal. The failure of an agent to perform the acts that the agent agreed to do for the principal is called <u>nonfeasance</u>.

Ostensible authority or apparent authority is the authority that a principal, either intentionally or by want of due care, leads a third party to believe the agent possesses. **Implied authority** is the authority of an agent that is implied by the principal's actions. **Incidental authority** is the authority that an agent must have in order to perform the business authorized by a principal. **Express authority** is authority, either oral or written, that is definitely and explicitly given to an agent.

TRANSCRIBING FROM DICTATION

Directions: This dictation emphasizes and reinforces the legal terms and definitions you have studied. Listen carefully to the pronunciation of each of the legal terms. Unless otherwise directed, use a 70-space line (typewriter) or 1-inch margins (computer) and double spacing. Correct all errors. Follow one of the procedures below.

Keyboarding Procedure
Using the cassette from Lesson 26, Part B, transcribe the dictation directly at your typewriter or computer.

Shorthand Procedure
Using the cassette from Lesson 26, Part B, take the dictation using your shorthand system and then transcribe from your shorthand notes on your typewriter or computer.

When you have finished transcribing Part B of the practice dictation, check your transcript with the printed copy. If you made any mistakes in the transcription, you should practice those words several times before going on to Evaluation 13.

CHECKLIST
I have completed the following for Lesson 26:

	Part A, Date	Part B, Date	Submitted to Instructor Yes	No
Terminology and Definitions				
Self-Evaluation				
* Keying Legal Terms				
Words				
Sentences				
* Transcribing from Dictation				

When you have successfully completed all the exercises in this lesson and submitted to your instructor those requested, you are ready to proceed with Evaluation 13.

* If you are using a shorthand system, submit to your instructor your shorthand notes along with your transcript.

Evaluation No. 13 SECTION A

Directions: This dictation/transcription evaluation will test your spelling and transcription abilities on the legal terms that you studied in the two preceding lessons. Use a 5-space paragraph indention, a 70-space line (typewriter) or 1-inch margins (computer), and double spacing unless otherwise instructed. Correct all errors. Follow one of the procedures below.

Keyboarding Procedure

Using the cassette from Evaluation 13, transcribe the dictation directly at your typewriter or computer.

Shorthand Procedure

Using the cassette from Evaluation 13, take the dictation using your shorthand system and then transcribe from your shorthand notes on your typewriter or computer.

Sections B and C are available from your instructor.

Lesson 27

Equity

Equity law is based on rules of morality rather than on judicial laws. If there is no legal remedy available, relief may be granted under equity law. Equity is flexible and may be changed to meet the needs of each individual case. Since equity is administered in the same courts as common law, many of the terms dealing with equity are presented in other lessons. This lesson introduces terms relevant to equity that have not been taught in other areas of law. When you have successfully completed these exercises, you should be able to pronounce, spell, define, and transcribe correctly the terms that are applicable to the principles of the law of equity.

Part A   TERMINOLOGY AND DEFINITIONS

Directions: Study the terms, pronunciations, and definitions until you are thoroughly familiar with them. In order to complete this lesson successfully, you must understand the meaning and usage of all the legal terms presented. If you are using shorthand, write your shorthand outline for each legal term in your shorthand notebook or on your shorthand machine.

Legal Term	Pronunciation	Definition
1. maxims of equity	′mak-səms əv ′ek-w ət-ē	General rules of conduct based upon reason and justice.
2. equity	′ek-wət-ē	A system of law that is based on good conscience, justice, honesty, and right rather than common law.
3. chancery	′chans-rē	Another word for equity.
4. chancery law	′chans-rē lȯ	The basis for equity law in the United States.
5. chancery court	′chans-rē kȯrt	A court of equity. Administers justice according to the rules of conscience and provides remedy for things not covered by common law.
6. preventive jurisdiction	pri-′vent-iv jür- əs-′dik-shən	Jurisdiction that a court of equity has in order to prevent future wrongs from being committed, as compared to courts of law that are concerned with wrongs that have already been committed.
7. concurrent jurisdiction	kən-′kər-ənt jür- əs-′dik-shən	Jurisdiction that exists when a court of law or a court of equity can try both common law cases and equity cases.
8. bill of interpleader	bil əv int-ər-′plēd-ər	A bill that provides that all persons who are interested in the same action will be joined together in a single lawsuit so as to prevent multiple suits for the same cause.
9. bill quia timet	bil ′kwē-ə ′tĭm-et	A bill filed with a court of equity that requests the court to exercise its preventive jurisdiction.

10. laches (plural, laches)	'lach-əz	An unreasonable delay on the part of a plaintiff in asserting a right. A delay that causes a disadvantage to another and for which the court will not grant relief.
11. framed questions of fact	frāmd 'kwes-chəns əv fakt	Questions that a judge gives to a jury in an equity case for their determination.
12. advisory jury	əd-'vīz-rē 'jur-ē	A jury to which framed questions of fact are presented for their determination in an equity suit. The findings of an advisory jury are not binding on the court of equity.
13. mistake of fact	mə-'stāk əv fakt	A mistake that occurs unintentionally as to what the true facts are. A court of equity will grant relief on a mistake of fact.
14. mistake of law	mə-'stāk əv lȯ	A mistake that occurs when one who knows all the facts makes an error as to their legal effect. A court of equity will not usually grant relief on a mistake of law.

Self-Evaluation A   TERMINOLOGY AND DEFINITION RECALL

Directions: In the Answers column at the right of each statement, write the letter that represents the word or group of words that correctly completes the statement. After you have completed this self-evaluation, check your answers with the key on page 499. If you have any incorrect answers, restudy the definitions for those terms before going on with this lesson. Then unless otherwise directed, submit this self-evaluation to your instructor.

Answers

1. Jurisdiction that exists when a court of law or a court of equity can try both common law cases and equity cases is referred to as (a) concurrent jurisdiction, (b) preventive jurisdiction, (c) maxims of equity.

1. _____

2. An unreasonable delay on the part of a plaintiff in asserting a right that causes a disadvantage to another and for which the court will not grant relief is referred to as (a) chancery, (b) advisory, (c) laches.

2. _____

3. A bill filed with a court of equity that requests the court to exercise its preventive jurisdiction is a (a) bill of interpleader, (b) bill quia timet, (c) framed questions of fact.

3. _____

4. Questions that a judge gives to a jury in an equity case for their determination are (a) laches, (b) framed questions of fact, (c) maxims of equity.

4. _____

5. A court of equity that administers justice according to the rules of conscience and provides remedy for things not covered by common law is a/an (a) preventive jurisdiction, (b) advisory court, (c) chancery court.

5. _____

6. A system of law that is based on good conscience, justice, honesty, and right rather than common law is (a) interpleader, (b) equity, (c) laches.

6. _____

7. A bill that provides that all persons who are interested in the same action will be joined together in a single lawsuit so as to prevent multiple suits for the same cause is a (a) bill of interpleader, (b) bill quia timet, (c) preventive jurisdiction.

7. _____

8. Another word for equity is (a) chancery, (b) advisory, (c) laches.

8. _____

9. A mistake that occurs when one who knows all the facts makes an error as to their legal effect is a (a) mistake of fact, (b) framed question of fact, (c) mistake of law.

9. _____

10. A jury to which framed questions of fact are presented for their determination in an equity suit is a/an (a) preventive jurisdiction, (b) advisory jury, (c) concurrent jurisdiction.

10. _____

11. The basis for equity law in the United States is (a) maxims of equity, (b) chancery law, (c) laches.

11. _____

12. General rules of conduct based upon reason and justice are (a) maxims of equity, (b) framed questions of fact, (c) bills of interpleader.

12. _____

13. Jurisdiction that a court of equity has in order to prevent future wrongs from being committed, as compared to courts of law that are concerned with wrongs that have already been committed, is (a) advisory, (b) concurrent jurisdiction, (c) preventive jurisdiction.

13. _____

14. A mistake that occurs unintentionally as to what the true facts are is called a (a) mistake of fact, (b) mistake of law, (c) bill quia timet.

14. _____

KEYING LEGAL TERMS

Directions: Unless otherwise instructed, use a 70-space line (typewriter) or 1-inch margins (computer) and double spacing. Correct all errors. Follow one of the procedures below.

WORDS

Keyboarding Procedure
On your typewriter or computer, key the following words at least two times, concentrating on the correct spelling and pronunciation.

Shorthand Procedure
On your typewriter or computer, key the following words once, concentrating on the correct spelling and pronunciation. Then write the shorthand outline for each word in your shorthand notebook or on your shorthand machine. Transcribe from the shorthand outlines one time on your typewriter or computer.

maxims of equity	equity	chancery
chancery law	chancery court	preventive jurisdiction
concurrent jurisdiction	bill of interpleader	bill quia timet
laches	framed questions of fact	advisory jury
mistake of fact	mistake of law	

SENTENCES

Keyboarding Procedure
Key each of the following sentences one time on your typewriter or computer. Concentrate on the correct spelling and pronunciation of each underlined legal term.

Shorthand Procedure
Write the correct shorthand outlines for the following sentences in your shorthand notebook or on your shorthand machine. Transcribe from your shorthand outlines one time on your typewriter or computer.

These sentences will be used for practice dictation on the cassettes.

Maxims of equity are general rules of conduct that are based upon reason and justice. Equity is a system of law that is based on good conscience, justice, honesty, and rights rather than common law. Chancery is another term meaning equity. Chancery law is the basis for equity law in the United States. A chancery court administers justice according to the rules of conscience and provides a remedy for things not covered by common law.

Preventive jurisdiction is the jurisdiction that a court of equity has in order to prevent future wrongs from being committed. Concurrent jurisdiction exists when courts of law and courts of equity can try both common law cases and equity cases.

When two or more persons are interested in the same action, a bill of interpleader may be filed to join them together in one lawsuit so as to prevent multiple suits for the same cause. Bill quia timet is a bill filed with a court of equity that requests the court to exercise its preventive jurisdiction.

Laches is an unreasonable delay on the part of the plaintiff in asserting a right. Framed questions of fact are questions that a judge gives to an advisory jury in an equity case for their determination. A jury in an equity suit serves only as an advisory jury to the judge, and its findings are not binding on the court.

> A **mistake of fact** is one that occurs unintentionally as to what the true facts are, and relief on a mistake of fact may be sought in a court of equity. A **mistake of law** occurs when one knows all the facts but makes an error as to their legal effect for which relief cannot be sought in a court of equity.

TRANSCRIBING FROM DICTATION

Directions: This dictation emphasizes and reinforces the legal terms and definitions you have studied. Listen carefully to the pronunciation of each of the legal terms. Unless otherwise directed, use a 70-space line (typewriter) or 1-inch margins (computer) and double spacing. Correct all errors. Follow one of the procedures below.

Keyboarding Procedure
Using the cassette from Lesson 27, Part A, transcribe the dictation directly at your typewriter or computer.

Shorthand Procedure
Using the cassette from Lesson 27, Part A, take the dictation using your shorthand system and then transcribe from your shorthand notes on your typewriter or computer.

When you have finished transcribing Part A of the practice dictation, check your transcript with the printed copy. If you made any mistakes in the transcription, you should practice those words several times before going on.

Part B TERMINOLOGY AND DEFINITIONS

Directions: Study the terms, pronunciations, and definitions until you are thoroughly familiar with them. In order to complete this lesson successfully, you must understand the meaning and usage of all the legal terms presented. If you are using shorthand, write your shorthand outline for each legal term in your shorthand notebook or on your shorthand machine.

Legal Term	Pronunciation	Definition
1. consent decree	kən-'sent di-'krē	A decree entered by consent of the parties under the sanction of the court. Both parties coming to an agreement before the case is tried is a consent decree.
2. finding of fact	'fīn-diŋ əv fakt	A statement made by the court pertaining to the conclusions reached that are based on the evidence in an equity case.
3. declaratory judgment	di-'klar-ə-tōr-ē 'jəj-mənt	A judgment that declares the existence of a right but does not provide any measure for enforcement.
4. waiver	'wā-vər	The intentional giving up of a right that one has.
5. reformation	ref-ər-'ma-shən	An equity remedy that provides for the amending or correcting of a written document so that it conforms with the intentions of the parties.
6. in pari delicto	in 'par-ī di-'likt-ō	Latin. In equal fault. Equity relief will not be granted if both parties are at fault.
7. sua sponte	swä 'spän-tə	Latin. Of one's own will, or voluntarily.
8. de minimis non curat lex	dā 'min-ə-mēs nōn kü-'rät leks	Latin. The law is not concerned with trifles. For example, an error involving a few cents will not be considered.
9. matter in pais	'mat-er in pā	French. A matter of fact that is oral and not in writing. It is an estoppel that is created by the conduct of a party.

10. estoppel in pais	e-'stäp-əl in pā	French. An estoppel that arises from the conduct of a party, laches, or negligence.
11. remedial	ri-'mēd-ē-əl	Providing a remedy.
12. right and duty	rīt ən 'düt-ē	The foundation of equity jurisprudence.
13. rule of morality	rül əv mə-'ral-ət-ē	The rule of right and wrong conduct that forms the basis of the standards that people should follow in dealing with others.
14. clean hands doctrine	klēn hands 'däk-trən	An equity maxim that states that one who comes into equity must come with clean hands. The one filing for equity must not be guilty of any wrongdoing.
15. doctrine of doing complete justice	'däk-trən əv 'dü-iŋ kəm-'plēt 'jəs-təs	The broad power of an equity court to dispose of all issues existing between the parties that are related to the main purpose of the suit.

Self-Evaluation B   TERMINOLOGY AND DEFINITION RECALL

Directions: In the Answers column, write the legal term that is most representative of the corresponding statement. After you have completed this self-evaluation, check your answers with the key on page 499. If you have any incorrect answers, restudy the definitions for those terms before going on with this lesson. Then unless otherwise directed, submit this self-evaluation to your instructor.

Answers

1. The rule of right and wrong conduct that forms the basis of the standards that people should follow in dealing with others is the _____.

    1. _____

2. The foundation of equity jurisprudence is _____.

    2. _____

3. A decree that is entered by agreement between the parties under the sanction of the court is a/an _____.

    3. _____

4. An estoppel that arises from the conduct of a party, laches, or negligence is a/an _____.

    4. _____

5. A Latin phrase meaning of one's own will, or voluntarily, is _____.

    5. _____

6. A Latin phrase meaning the law is not concerned with trifles is _____.

    6. _____

7. The broad power of an equity court to dispose of all issues existing between the parties that are related to the main purpose of the suit is the _____.

    7. _____

8. An equity maxim that states that one who comes into equity must not be guilty of any wrongdoing is _____.

    8. _____

9. A matter of fact that is oral and not in writing that creates an estoppel based on the conduct of a party is a/an _____.

    9. _____

10. A judgment that declares the existence of a right but does not provide any measure for enforcement is a/an _____.

    10. _____

11. A statement made by the court pertaining to the conclusions reached that are based on the evidence in an equity case is a/an _____.

    11. _____

12. The intentional giving up of a right that one has is a/an _____.

    12. _____

13. An equity remedy that provides for the amending or correcting of a written document so that it conforms with the intentions of the parties is _____.

    13. _____

14. A Latin phrase meaning in equal fault and for which equity will not be granted is _____.

    14. _____

15. A term that means providing a remedy is _____.

    15. _____

KEYING LEGAL TERMS

Directions: Unless otherwise instructed, use a 70-space line (typewriter) or 1-inch margins (computer) and double spacing. Correct all errors. Follow one of the procedures below.

WORDS

Keyboarding Procedure
On your typewriter or computer, key the following words at least two times, concentrating on the correct spelling and pronunciation.

Shorthand Procedure
On your typewriter or computer, key the following words once, concentrating on the correct spelling and pronunciation. Then write the shorthand outline for each word in your shorthand notebook or on your shorthand machine. Transcribe from the shorthand outlines one time on your typewriter or computer.

consent decree	finding of fact	eclaratory judgment
waiver	reformation	in pari delicto
sua sponte	de minimis non curat lex	matter in pais
estoppel in pais	remedial	right and duty
rule of morality	clean hands doctrine	doctrine of doing complete justice

SENTENCES

Keyboarding Procedure
Key each of the following sentences one time on your typewriter or computer. Concentrate on the correct spelling and pronunciation of each underlined legal term.

Shorthand Procedure
Write the correct shorthand outlines for the following sentences in your shorthand notebook or on your shorthand machine. Transcribe from your shorthand outlines one time on your typewriter or computer.

These sentences will be used for practice dictation on the cassettes.

If the parties come to an agreement under the sanction of the court prior to trial, a consent decree is entered. A finding of fact is a statement by the court pertaining to the conclusions reached that are based on the evidence in an equity case. A declaratory judgment declares the existence of a right but does nothing to enforce it.

A waiver is the intentional giving up of a right. Reformation is a remedy that provides for the amending or correcting of a written document so that it conforms with the intentions of the parties.

In pari delicto is a Latin phrase meaning in equal fault. When both parties are in pari delicto, equity relief will not be granted. Sua sponte is a Latin phrase meaning of one's own will, or voluntarily. De minimis non curat lex is a Latin phrase meaning the law is not concerned with trifles. A matter in pais is a matter of fact not in writing. An estoppel in pais is an estoppel that arises from the conduct of a party, laches, or negligence.

Remedial means providing a remedy. Right and duty form the foundation of equity jurisprudence. Whenever a right exists, there is also a duty. The rule of morality is a rule of right and wrong conduct that forms the basis of the standards that people should follow in dealing with others. The clean hands doctrine is an equity maxim that states that one who comes into equity must not be guilty of any wrongdoing. The doctrine of doing complete justice is the broad power of an equity court to dispose of all issues existing between the parties that are related to the main purpose of the suit.

TRANSCRIBING FROM DICTATION

Directions: This dictation emphasizes and reinforces the legal terms and definitions you have studied. Listen carefully to the pronunciation of each of the legal terms. Unless otherwise directed, use a 70-space line (typewriter) or 1-inch margins (computer) and double spacing. Correct all errors. Follow one of the procedures below.

Keyboarding Procedure
Using the cassette from Lesson 27, Part B, transcribe the dictation directly at your typewriter or computer.

Shorthand Procedure
Using the cassette from Lesson 27, Part B, take the dictation using your shorthand system and then transcribe from your shorthand notes on your typewriter or computer.

When you have finished transcribing Part B of the practice dictation, check your transcript with the printed copy. If you made any mistakes in the transcription, you should practice those words several times before going on to Lesson 28.

CHECKLIST
I have completed the following for Lesson 27:

	Part A, Date	Part B, Date	Submitted to Instructor Yes	No
Terminology and Definitions				
Self-Evaluation				
* Keying Legal Terms				
Words				
Sentences				
* Transcribing from Dictation				

When you have successfully completed all the exercises in this lesson and submitted to your instructor those requested, you are ready to proceed with Lesson 28.

* If you are using a shorthand system, submit to your instructor your shorthand notes along with your transcript.

Lesson 28

Partnerships

> "One who can and does not forbid that which is done on his or her behalf, is deemed to have bidden it."
>
> —Legal Maxim

The sole proprietorship, the partnership, and the corporation are the three most common types of business organizations. Partnerships and corporations involve more legalities than single proprietorships; therefore, the terms in this lesson will deal mainly with partnerships, and the next two lessons will deal with corporations. When you complete these exercises, you should be able to spell, pronounce, define, and transcribe correctly the terms that are introduced herein.

Part A TERMINOLOGY AND DEFINITIONS

Directions: Study the terms, pronunciations, and definitions until you are thoroughly familiar with them. In order to complete this lesson successfully, you must understand the meaning and usage of all the legal terms presented. If you are using shorthand, write your shorthand outline for each legal term in your shorthand notebook or on your shorthand machine.

Legal Term	*Pronunciation*	*Definition*
1. sole proprietorship	sōl prə-'prī-ət-ər-ship	A business owned by one person who has the legal right to the business.
2. proprietor	prə-'prī-ət-ər	One who is the sole owner of something, such as a business.
3. severalty	'sev-rəl-tē	Sole ownership of property. Owned by one person.
4. Uniform Partnership Act	'yü-nə-fòrm 'pärt-nər-ship akt	Uniform laws adopted by most states to define the legalities and requirements for the formation and operation of partnerships.
5. partnership	'pärt-nər-ship	A business owned by two or more persons who share in the profits and losses for their common benefit.
6. articles of partnership	'ärt-i-kəls əv 'pärt-nər-ship	An agreement that contains the terms of a partnership. (See Figure 28-1, page 409.)
7. Uniform Limited Partnership Act	'yü-nə-fòrm 'lim-ət-əd 'pärt-nər-ship akt	Uniform laws that have been adopted in most states to define the legalities and requirements for the formation and operation of limited partnerships.
8. limited partnership	'lim-ət-əd 'pärt-nər-ship	A partnership that consists of a general partner, who conducts the business, and one or more limited partners, who contribute capital and share in profits.
9. general partner	'jen-rəl 'pärt-nər	One who conducts the business of a partnership and has unlimited liability.

10. limited partner	'lim-ət-əd 'pärt-nər	One who contributes capital and shares in the profits of a limited partnership but whose liability is limited to the amount of his or her investment.
11. senior partner	'sē-nyər 'pärt-nər	Usually one who has a greater investment, seniority, and role in the management of the business.
12. junior partner	'jün-yər 'pärt-nər	Usually one who has a lesser investment, seniority, and role in the management of the business than the senior partner.
13. silent partner	'sī-lənt 'pärt-nər	One who is not publicly known as being a partner but who shares in the profits. Sometimes called a dormant or sleeping partner.

FIGURE 28-1 Articles of Partnership

Articles of Agreement, Made the 11th day of July
in the year one thousand nine hundred and ninety-seven
BETWEEN COLLEEN J. SUMMERS and STEWART K. ROSS

Witnesseth as follows:

1. The said parties above named have agreed to become co-partners in business, and by these presents do agree to become co-partners together under the firm and partnership name of

SUMMERS AND ROSS

in the business of retail sales of office supplies

the said partnership to commence on the 1st day of August 19 97 and to continue for five (5) years thereafter.

2. To that end and purpose the said Colleen J. Summers has contributed in cash the sum of Twenty-five thousand and 00/100 dollars ($25,000.00)

and the said Stewart K. Ross has contributed in cash the sum of Twenty-five thousand and 00/100 dollars ($25,000.00) to

the capital stock so formed to be used and employed in common between them, for the support and management of the said business, to their mutual benefit and advantage.

3. It is Agreed by and between the parties hereto that at all times during the continuance of their co-partnership, they and each of them shall and will give their personal attention to the said business, and will to the utmost of their skill and power exert themselves for their joint interest, profit, benefit and advantage, in the said business.

Self-Evaluation A   TERMINOLOGY AND DEFINITION RECALL

Directions: In the Answers column, write the legal term that is most representative of the corresponding statement. After you have completed this self-evaluation, check your answers with the key on page 499. If you have any incorrect answers, restudy the definitions for those terms before going on with this lesson. Then unless otherwise directed, submit this self-evaluation to your instructor.

Answers

1. One who conducts the business of a partnership and has unlimited liability is a/an _____.

   1. _____

2. One who is the sole owner of something, such as a business, is a/an _____.

   2. _____

3. Sole ownership of property is referred to as _____.

   3. _____

4. Uniform laws adopted by most states to define the legalities and requirements for the formation and operation of limited partnerships are referred to as the _____.

   4. _____

5. Usually one who has a lesser investment, seniority, and role in the management of the business than the senior partner is a/an _____.

   5. _____

6. One who contributes capital and shares in the profits of a limited partnership but whose liability is limited to the amount of his or her investment is a/an _____.

   6. _____

7. A business owned by two or more persons who share in the profits and losses for their common benefit is called a/an _____.

   7. _____

8. Uniform laws adopted by most states to define the legalities and requirements for the formation and operation of partnerships are referred to as _____.

   8. _____

9. A partnership that consists of a general partner, who conducts the business, and one or more limited partners, who contribute capital and share in profits, is a/an _____.

   9. _____

10. One who is not publicly known as being a partner but who shares in the profits is a/an _____.

    10. _____

11. A business owned by one person who has the legal right to the business is a/an _____.

    11. _____

12. Usually one who has a greater investment, seniority, and role in the management of the business is a/an _____.

    12. _____

13. An agreement that contains the terms of a partnership is a/an _____.

    13. _____

KEYING LEGAL TERMS

Directions: Unless otherwise instructed, use a 70-space line (typewriter) or 1-inch margins (computer) and double spacing. Correct all errors. Follow one of the procedures below.

WORDS

Keyboarding Procedure
On your typewriter or computer, key the following words at least two times, concentrating on the correct spelling and pronunciation.

Shorthand Procedure
On your typewriter or computer, key the following words once, concentrating on the correct spelling and pronunciation. Then write the shorthand outline for each word in your shorthand notebook or on your shorthand machine. Transcribe from the shorthand outlines one time on your typewriter or computer.

sole proprietorship	articles of partnership	limited partner
proprietor	Uniform Limited Partnership Act	senior partner
severalty	limited partnership	junior partner
Uniform Partnership Act	general partner	silent partner
partnership		

SENTENCES

Keyboarding Procedure
Key each of the following sentences one time on your typewriter or computer. Concentrate on the correct spelling and pronunciation of each underlined legal term.

Shorthand Procedure
Write the correct shorthand outlines for the following sentences in your shorthand notebook or on your shorthand machine. Transcribe from your shorthand outlines one time on your typewriter or computer.

These sentences will be used for practice dictation on the cassettes.

A sole proprietorship is a business owned by one person who has the legal right to the business. A proprietor is one who is the sole owner of something. Sole ownership of property is also called severalty.

The Uniform Partnership Act consists of uniform laws that have been adopted by most states to define the legalities and requirements for the formation and operation of partnerships. A partnership is a business owned by two or more persons for their common benefit and who share in the profits and losses. When parties enter into a partnership, the written agreement stating the terms and conditions is called the articles of partnership.

Most states have adopted the Uniform Limited Partnership Act to define the legalities and requirements for the formation and operation of limited partnerships. A limited partnership is a partnership that consists of a general partner, who conducts the business, and one or more limited partners, who contribute capital and share in profits.

A general partner is one who conducts the business of a partnership and has unlimited liability, whereas a limited partner is one who contributes capital and shares in the profits but whose liability is limited to the amount of his or her investment. The senior partner has a greater investment, seniority, and role in the management of the business than the junior partner. A silent partner is one whose name is not publicly known as being a partner but who shares in the profits.

TRANSCRIBING FROM DICTATION

Directions: This dictation emphasizes and reinforces the legal terms and definitions you have studied. Listen carefully to the pronunciation of each of the legal terms. Unless otherwise directed, use a 70-space line (typewriter) or 1-inch margins (computer) and double spacing. Correct all errors. Follow one of the procedures below.

Keyboarding Procedure
Using the cassette from Lesson 28, Part A, transcribe the dictation directly at your typewriter or computer.

Shorthand Procedure
Using the cassette from Lesson 28, Part A, take the dictation using your shorthand system and then transcribe from your shorthand notes on your typewriter or computer.

When you have finished transcribing Part A of the practice dictation, check your transcript with the printed copy. If you made any mistakes in the transcription, you should practice those words several times before going on.

Part B TERMINOLOGY AND DEFINITIONS

Directions: Study the terms, pronunciations, and definitions until you are thoroughly familiar with them. In order to complete this lesson successfully, you must understand the meaning and usage of all the legal terms presented. If you are using shorthand, write your shorthand outline for each legal term in your shorthand notebook or on your shorthand machine.

Legal Term	*Pronunciation*	*Definition*
1. secret partner	′sē-krət ′pärt-nər	A dormant or silent partner.
2. nominal partner	′näm-ən-l ′pärt-nər	One who permits his or her name to be used as though the person were a partner but who really has no financial interest in the business.
3. joint venture	jȯint ′ven-chər	Two or more persons joined together in a business venture without forming an actual partnership or corporation.
4. assumed name	ə-′sümd nām	A name other than one's own under which business is transacted. The law usually requires the name to be filed so that the persons operating under the assumed name are known. (See Figure 28-2, page 416.)
5. D/B/A	′dü-iŋ ′biz-nəs əz	Abbreviation for doing business as. Used when identifying a person who is doing business under an assumed name.
6. Securities and Exchange Commission	si-′kyůr-ət-ēs ən iks-′chānj kə-′mish-ən	A commission formed to regulate the exchange of securities. Stocks, securities, and shares in limited partnerships must comply with SEC requirements.
7. syndicate	′sin-di-kət	A joint venture composed of individuals who have the purpose of conducting a specific business transaction.
8. underwriting syndicate	′ən-də-rīt-iŋ ′sin-di-kət	A joint venture that consists of investment banking companies and whose purpose is to sell large issues of stocks and bonds.
9. capital	′kap-ət-l	The assets of a company or corporation. The money that partners are required to invest in a business venture.
10. commingle	kə-′miŋ-gəl	To put two different persons' money together into one account.

| 11. prospectus | prə-ˈspek-təs | A printed document issued by a company or corporation that describes a proposed business venture, such as a limited partnership. |
| 12. subscription | səb-ˈskrip-shən | A written contract by which one agrees to purchase shares, debentures, or other securities issued by a company or corporation. (See Figure 28-3, page 417.) |

FIGURE 28-2 An Assumed Name Certificate

CERTIFICATE OF PERSONS CONDUCTING BUSINESS
UNDER ASSUMED NAME—Act No. 151, P. A. 1949. M310 (REVISED 1978)

Certificate of Persons Conducting Business Under Assumed Name

STATE OF MICHIGAN, }ss.   FILING FEE $10.00
COUNTY OF Ingham

The undersigned hereby certifies that they (it) now own (or) intend to own, conduct or transact
business at 7320 Sandstone Drive
(Street and No.)

in the City of Lansing   of   Ingham
(City, Village or Township)

County, Michigan, under the assumed name, designation and style of
F & C Enterprises

The undersigned further certifies that the true or real full name and the address of the person[1] owning,
conducting or transacting said business is:

PRINT OR TYPE NAMES AND ADDRESS

NAME	STREET ADDRESS	CITY OR TOWN
Anna Marie Findley	7320 Sandstone Drive	Lansing, Michigan
Richard Lee Collins	7320 Sandstone Drive	Lansing, Michigan

In Witness Whereof, I/We have this 3rd day of January 1997,
made and signed this certificate.

SIGNATURES OF PERSONS CONDUCTING BUSINESS UNDER ASSUMED NAME

Anna Marie Findley
Richard Lee Collins

STATE OF MICHIGAN, }ss.
COUNTY OF Ingham   On   3rd   , 19 97, before
me, a Notary Public, personally appeared the above named person or persons, whose signatures appear above,
and who executed the foregoing instrument, and they acknowledged to me that they executed the
same, and that they are all of the persons now owning, conducting and transacting or who intend to own,
conduct and transact the business under the above name, style and designation.

FIGURE 28-3 A Subscription

ZENITH OIL AND GAS CORP.
1997 DRILLING PROGRAM
SUBSCRIPTION

The undersigned prospective Limited Partner ("Subscriber") hereby offers to purchase a Limited Partnership interest in the Zenith Oil and Gas Corp. 1997 Drilling Program Limited Partnership No. 2 and encloses herewith the entire purchase price of Five thousand and 00/100 Dollars ($ 5,000.00) for 1 Limited partnership Unit(s) at $5,000 each.

The Subscriber acknowledges receipt of the Prospectus containing the Limited Partnership Agreement relating to this offering and agrees to be bound and governed by the provisions of the Limited Partnership Agreement of which this Subscription shall become a part upon its execution. The Subscriber states that he has relied solely upon the Prospectus in making his investment decision. The Subscriber understands the speculative nature of this Program and the risks involved in said offering, including the possible loss of his entire investment; the lack of liquidity of the Units offered and the restrictions on their transferability; the tax consequences of his investment; and the background and qualifications of Zenith Oil and Gas Corp. as sponsor of this offering. The Subscriber hereby represents that the prospective purchase is for his own account and that he is not subscribing with the present intention of reselling such securities. The Subscriber agrees that this offer shall remain irrevocable for a period of six (6) months.

The Subscriber hereby represents that: (a) he has a net worth of not less than $200,000 (exclusive of home, furnishings and automobiles); or (b) he has a net worth of not less than $50,000 (exclusive of home, furnishings and automobiles) and some portion of his taxable income for the previous year was, or some portion of his estimated taxable income for the current year will be, subject to Federal income tax at a rate of less than 50%; and (c) he is a citizen of the United States of America.

Zenith Oil and Gas Corp., upon the acceptance of this Subscription will forward to the Subscriber a notice of acceptance in the Zenith Oil and Gas Corp. 1997 Drilling Program Limited Partnership No. 2 .

California: The issuance of any Limited Partnership interests resulting from any offer and/or sale in the State of California of the Limited Partnership interests is subject to the following legend condition restricting transfer.

CALIFORNIA: IT IS UNLAWFUL TO CONSUMMATE A SALE OR TRANSFER OF THIS SECURITY OR ANY INTEREST THEREIN, OR TO RECEIVE ANY CONSIDERATION THERE-FOR, WITHOUT THE PRIOR WRITTEN CONSENT OF THE COMMISSIONER OF CORPORATIONS OF THE STATE OF CALIFORNIA, EXCEPT AS PERMITTED IN THE COMMISSIONER'S RULES.

Dated this 17th day of October 1997

Social Security No. or 000-00-0001
Federal Identification No.

Mailing Address: 2660 Columbia St.
Holt, Michigan

Occupation: Investor

Marion O. Klotz
Signature

_____
Signature

Marion O. Klotz
Please Print Name(s)

☐ Tenants in common (each person must sign)
☐ Joint tenants with right of survivorship, and not as tenants in common
☐ Tenants by the entirety
☐ _____, as Custodian for
_____ under the _____
Uniform Gifts to Minors Act   (State)

Dealer Name: Hartman, Inc.

Dealer Branch Office: Lansing, MI

Representative: Manuel Hartman

Representative Number: 00910

MAIL THE ORIGINAL EXECUTED SUBSCRIPTION AND ONE COPY WITH CHECK PAYABLE TO "ZENITH OIL AND GAS CORP., GENERAL PARTNER" TO ZENITH PROGRAMS, INC., P.O. BOX 1000, BLOOMFIELD HILLS, MICHIGAN 48013. THE SUBSCRIBER AND THE SELLING BROKER-DEALER EACH RETAIN ONE COPY.

Self-Evaluation B   TERMINOLOGY AND DEFINITION RECALL

Directions: In the Answers column, write the letter from Column 1 that represents the word or phrase that best matches each item in Column 2. After you have completed this self-evaluation, check your answers with the key on page 499. If you have any incorrect answers, restudy the definitions for those terms before going on with this lesson. Then unless otherwise directed, submit this self-evaluation to your instructor.

Column 1	Column 2	Answers
a. assumed name	1. A dormant or silent partner.	1. _____
b. capital	2. A joint venture that consists of investment banking companies and whose purpose is to sell large issues of stocks and bonds.	2. _____
c. commingle		
d. D/B/A	3. A printed document issued by a company or corporation that describes a proposed business venture, such as a limited partnership.	3. _____
e. joint venture		
f. nominal partner	4. A name other than one's own under which business is transacted.	4. _____
g. prospectus		
h. secret partner	5. One who permits his or her name to be used as though the person were a partner but who really has no financial interest in the business.	5. _____
i. Securities and Exchange Commission		
	6. To put two different persons' money together into one account.	6. _____
j. silent partner		
k. subscription	7. A joint venture composed of individuals who have the purpose of conducting a specific business transaction.	7. _____
l. syndicate		
m. underwriting syndicate	8. The assets of a company or corporation or the money that partners are required to invest in a business venture.	8. _____
	9. An abbreviation used when identifying a person who is doing business under an assumed name.	9. _____
	10. A commission formed to regulate the exchange of securities.	10. _____
	11. A written contract by which one agrees to purchase shares, debentures, or other securities issued by a company or corporation.	11. _____
	12. Two or more persons joined together in a business venture without forming an actual partnership or corporation.	12. _____

KEYING LEGAL TERMS

Directions: Unless otherwise instructed, use a 70-space line (typewriter) or 1-inch margins (computer) and double spacing. Correct all errors. Follow one of the procedures below.

WORDS

Keyboarding Procedure
On your typewriter or computer, key the following words at least two times, concentrating on the correct spelling and pronunciation.

Shorthand Procedure
On your typewriter or computer, key the following words once, concentrating on the correct spelling and pronunciation. Then write the shorthand outline for each word in your shorthand notebook or on your shorthand machine. Transcribe from the shorthand outlines one time on your typewriter or computer.

secret partner	nominal partner	joint venture
assumed name	D/B/A	Securities and Exchange Commission
syndicate	underwriting syndicate	prospectus
capital	commingle	
subscription		

SENTENCES

Keyboarding Procedure
Key each of the following sentences one time on your typewriter or computer. Concentrate on the correct spelling and pronunciation of each underlined legal term.

Shorthand Procedure
Write the correct shorthand outlines for the following sentences in your shorthand notebook or on your shorthand machine. Transcribe from your shorthand outlines one time on your typewriter or computer.

These sentences will be used for practice dictation on the cassettes.

A secret partner is a dormant or silent partner. A nominal partner permits one's name to be used as though he or she were a partner but who really has no financial interest in the business.

A joint venture is where two or more persons join together in a business venture without forming an actual partnership or corporation.

An assumed name is a name other than one's own under which business is transacted. The abbreviation for doing business as is D/B/A and is used to identify a person who is doing business under an assumed name; for example, Sally and Jerry Bates D/B/A Bates Enterprises.

The Securities and Exchange Commission regulates the exchange of securities. Stocks, securities, and shares in limited partnerships must comply with SEC requirements.

A syndicate is a joint venture composed of individuals who have the purpose of conducting a specific business transaction. An underwriting syndicate is a group of investment banking companies who enter into a joint venture for the purpose of selling large issues of stocks and bonds.

The assets of a corporation or company are referred to as capital. Capital is also the money required of partners when entering into a business arrangement. To commingle is to put two different persons' money into one account.

> A company or corporation that invites the public to subscribe to shares, debentures, or other securities publishes a <u>prospectus</u>. The prospectus describes the proposed business venture. A <u>subscription</u> is a written contract by which one agrees to purchase shares, debentures, or other securities issued by a company or corporation.

TRANSCRIBING FROM DICTATION

Directions: This dictation emphasizes and reinforces the legal terms and definitions you have studied. Listen carefully to the pronunciation of each of the legal terms. Unless otherwise directed, use a 70-space line (typewriter) or 1-inch margins (computer) and double spacing. Correct all errors. Follow one of the procedures below.

Keyboarding Procedure
Using the cassette from Lesson 28, Part B, transcribe the dictation directly at your typewriter or computer.

Shorthand Procedure
Using the cassette from Lesson 28, Part B, take the dictation using your shorthand system and then transcribe from your shorthand notes on your typewriter or computer.

When you have finished transcribing Part B of the practice dictation, check your transcript with the printed copy. If you made any mistakes in the transcription, you should practice those words several times before going on to Evaluation 14.

CHECKLIST
I have completed the following for Lesson 28:

	Part A, Date	Part B, Date	Submitted to Instructor Yes	No
Terminology and Definitions				
Self-Evaluation				
* Keying Legal Terms				
Words				
Sentences				
* Transcribing from Dictation				

When you have successfully completed all the exercises in this lesson and submitted to your instructor those requested, you are ready to proceed with Evaluation 14.

* If you are using a shorthand system, submit to your instructor your shorthand notes along with your transcript.

Evaluation No. 14   SECTION A

Directions: This dictation/transcription evaluation will test your spelling and transcription abilities on the legal terms that you studied in the two preceding lessons. Use a 5-space paragraph indention, a 70-space line (typewriter) or 1-inch margins (computer), and double spacing unless otherwise instructed. Correct all errors. Follow one of the procedures below.

Keyboarding Procedure
Using the cassette from Evaluation 14, transcribe the dictation directly at your typewriter or computer.

Shorthand Procedure
Using the cassette from Evaluation 14, take the dictation using your shorthand system and then transcribe from your shorthand notes on your typewriter or computer.

Sections B and C are available from your instructor.

Lesson 29

Corporations

> "The law respects form less than substance."
> —Legal Maxim

Of the three types of businesses, corporations are the most legally complex. Corporate law is a specialty for some law firms and involves many different legal activities. Even though corporate law varies from state to state, most of the terminology presented is used in most states. When you have satisfactorily completed the following exercises, you will be able to spell, pronounce, define, and transcribe correctly the terms that are introduced relating to the field of corporate law.

Part A TERMINOLOGY AND DEFINITIONS

Directions: Study the terms, pronunciations, and definitions until you are thoroughly familiar with them. In order to complete this lesson successfully, you must understand the meaning and usage of all the legal terms presented. If you are using shorthand, write your shorthand outline for each legal term in your shorthand notebook or on your shorthand machine.

Legal Term	Pronunciation	Definition
1. legal entity	ˈlē-gəl ˈen-ət-ē	Legal being or existence.
2. corporation	kȯr-pə-ˈrā-shən	An artificial being created by law.
3. articles of incorporation	ˈärt-i-kəls əv in-kȯr-pə-ˈrā-shən	The instrument that provides for the organization of a corporation (See Figure 29-1, pages 427-428.)
4. charter	ˈchärt-ər	The authority granted by a legislature that gives a corporation the right to exist. (See Figure 29-2, page 429.)
5. franchise	ˈfran-chīz	A special privilege that does not belong to the general public but is granted by the government to an individual or a corporation. A corporation is a franchise.
6. domestic corporation	də-ˈmes-tik kȯr-pə-ˈrā-shən	A corporation created by or organized under the laws of the state in which it is transacting business.
7. foreign corporation	ˈfȯr-ən kȯr-pə-ˈrā-shən	A corporation created by or under the laws of another state, government, or country other than the one in which it is transacting business.
8. de jure corporation	dē ˈjùr-ē kȯr-pə-ˈrā-shən	A corporation that is created in total compliance with the laws of the state in which it is organized.
9. de facto corporation	di ˈfak-tō kȯr-pə-ˈrā-shən	A corporation existing in fact and that, in good faith, has made an effort to comply with state law but has failed to meet one or more of the requirements of the law.

10. eleemosynary corporation	el-i-'mäs-ən-er-ē kȯr-pə-'rā-shən	A corporation organized for a charitable or benevolent purpose. In many states, an eleemosynary corporation is now referred to as a charitable or nonprofit or not-for-profit corporation.
11. subsidiary corporation	səb-'sid-ē-er-ē kȯr-pə-'rā-shən	A corporation that is under the control of another corporation that owns a majority of the shares.
12. board of directors	bōrd əv də-'rek-tərs	The group of persons who is responsible for governing a corporation.
13. chairperson	'cher-pərs-n	The presiding officer of the board of directors of a corporation.
14. president	'prez-əd-ənt	The chief officer of a corporation who implements the policies established by the board of directors.

FIGURE 29-1 Articles of Incorporation

MICHIGAN DEPARTMENT OF COMMERCE — CORPORATION AND SECURITIES BUREAU

(FOR BUREAU USE ONLY)

Date Received

EFFECTIVE DATE:

CORPORATION IDENTIFICATION NUMBER —

ARTICLES OF INCORPORATION
For use by Domestic Profit Corporations
(Please read instructions and Paperwork Reduction Act notice on last page)

Pursuant to the provisions of Act 284, Public Acts of 1972, as amended, the undersigned corporation executes the following Articles:

Article I

The name of the corporation is:

COLLIER PLASTICS CORPORATION

Article II

The purpose or purposes for which the corporation is organized is to engage in any activity within the purposes for which corporations may be organized under the Business Corporation Act of Michigan.

Manufacturing of plastic products.

Article III

The total authorized capital stock is:

1. Common Shares _____100_____ Par Value Per Share $1.00_____

   Preferred Shares _____-0-_____ Par Value Per Share $_____

and/or shares without par value as follows:

2. Common Shares _____ Stated Value Per Share $_____

   Preferred Shares _____ Stated Value Per Share $_____

3. A statement of all or any of the relative rights, preferences and limitations of the shares of each class is as follows: None

FIGURE 29-1 Articles of Incorporation (continued)

Article IV

1. The address of the registered office is:

9001 Okemos Road, Okemos , Michigan 48864
(Street Address) (City) (ZIP Code)

2. The mailing address of the registered office if different than above:

Same , Michigan
(P.O. Box) (City) (ZIP Code)

3. The name of the resident agent at the registered office is:

Article V

The name(s) and address(es) of the incorporator(s) is (are) as follows:

Name	Residence or Business Address
John D. Mazzo	9001 Okemos Road, Okemos, MI 48864
Silvia P. Hatcher	9001 Okemos Road, Okemos, MI 48864
Alfred J. Jennings	9001 Okemos Road, Okemos, MI 48864
Teresa L. Canton	9001 Okemos Road, Okemos, MI 48864

Article VI   (Optional. Delete if not applicable)

When a compromise or arrangement or a plan of reorganization of this corporation is proposed between this corporation and its creditors or any class of them or between this corporation and its shareholders or any class of them, a court of equity jurisdiction within the state, on application of this corporation or of a creditor or shareholder thereof, or on application of a receiver appointed for the corporation, may order a meeting of the creditors or class of creditors or of the shareholders or class of shareholders to be affected by the proposed compromise or arrangement or reorganization, to be summoned in such manner as the court directs. If a majority in number representing ¾ in value of the creditors or class of creditors, or of the shareholders or class of shareholders to be affected by the proposed compromise or arrangement or a reorganization, agree to a compromise or arrangement or a reorganization of this corporation as a consequence of the compromise or

FIGURE 29-2 A Charter

UNITED STATES OF AMERICA

The State of Michigan

TUEBOR

CIRCUMSPICE

Michigan Department of Commerce

Lansing, Michigan

This is to Certify That Articles of Incorporation of

COLLIER PLASTICS CORPORATION

were duly filed in this office on the   19TH   day of   MARCH   ,19 97 ,
in conformity with Act 284, Public Acts of 1972, as amended.

In testimony whereof, I have her to set my
hand and affixed the Seal of the Department,
in the City of Lansing, this   19TH   day
of   MARCH   ,19 97

Edith M. Craig   Director

C & S–175

Date _____   Name _____

Self-Evaluation A   TERMINOLOGY AND DEFINITION RECALL

Directions: In the Answers column at the right of each statement, write the letter that represents the word or group of words that correctly completes the statement. After you have completed this self-evaluation, check your answers with the key on page 500. If you have any incorrect answers, restudy the definitions for those terms before going on with this lesson. Then unless otherwise directed, submit this self-evaluation to your instructor.

Answers

1. A corporation that is under the control of another corporation that owns a majority of the shares is a (a) foreign corporation, (b) domestic corporation, (c) subsidiary corporation.

   1. _____

2. A special privilege that does not belong to the general public but is granted by the government to an individual or a corporation is a (a) franchise, (b) charter, (c) legal entity.

   2. _____

3. A corporation created by or under the laws of a state, government, or country other than the one in which it is transacting business is a/an (a) eleemosynary corporation, (b) foreign corporation, (c) subsidiary corporation.

   3. _____

4. An artificial being created by law is a (a) corporation, (b) legal entity, (c) franchise.

   4. _____

5. The instrument that provides for the organization of a corporation is referred to as the (a) articles of incorporation, (b) franchise, (c) charter.

   5. _____

6. A legal being or existence is referred to as a (a) franchise, (b) charter, (c) legal entity.

   6. _____

7. The chief officer of a corporation who implements the policies established by the board of directors is the (a) president, (b) chairperson, (c) legal entity.

   7. _____

8. A corporation organized for a charitable or benevolent purpose is a/an (a) subsidiary corporation, (b) de jure corporation, (c) eleemosynary corporation.

   8. _____

9. The group of persons who is responsible for governing a corporation is the (a) chairperson, (b) board of directors, (c) president.

   9. _____

10. A corporation that exists in fact and that has made an effort to comply with state law but has failed to meet one or more of the requirements of the law is a (a) de jure corporation, (b) de facto corporation, (c) foreign corporation.

    10. _____

11. A corporation that is organized in total compliance with the laws of the state in which it is organized is a/an (a) de facto corporation, (b) eleemosynary corporation, (c) de jure corporation.

    11. _____

12. The presiding officer of the board of directors of a corporation is the (a) president, (b) chairperson, (c) franchise.

    12. _____

13. The authority granted by a legislature that gives a corporation the right to exist is a/an (a) franchise, (b) charter, (c) articles of incorporation.

    13. _____

14. A corporation created by or organized under the laws of the state in which it is transacting business is a (a) de facto corporation, (b) de jure corporation, (c) domestic corporation.

    14. _____

KEYING LEGAL TERMS

Directions: Unless otherwise instructed, use a 70-space line (typewriter) or 1-inch margins (computer) and double spacing. Correct all errors. Follow one of the procedures below.

WORDS

Keyboarding Procedure
On your typewriter or computer, key the following words at least two times, concentrating on the correct spelling and pronunciation.

Shorthand Procedure
On your typewriter or computer, key the following words once, concentrating on the correct spelling and pronunciation. Then write the shorthand outline for each word in your shorthand notebook or on your shorthand machine. Transcribe from the shorthand outlines one time on your typewriter or computer.

legal entity	corporation	articles of incorporation
charter	franchise	domestic corporation
foreign corporation	de jure corporation	de facto corporation
eleemosynary corporation	subsidiary corporation	board of directors
chairperson	president	

SENTENCES

Keyboarding Procedure
Key each of the following sentences one time on your typewriter or computer. Concentrate on the correct spelling and pronunciation of each underlined legal term.

Shorthand Procedure
Write the correct shorthand outlines for the following sentences in your shorthand notebook or on your shorthand machine. Transcribe from your shorthand outlines one time on your typewriter or computer.

These sentences will be used for practice dictation on the cassettes.

A legal entity refers to a legal being or existence. A corporation is an artificial being created by law. The instrument that provides for the organization of a corporation is called articles of incorporation. A charter is the authority granted by a legislature that gives a corporation the right to exist.

A special privilege that does not belong to the general public but is granted by the government to an individual or a corporation is a franchise. A corporation is a franchise.

A domestic corporation is a corporation created by the laws of the state in which it is transacting business; whereas a foreign corporation is a corporation created by the laws of another state, government, or country other than the one in which it is transacting business.

A corporation that is in total compliance with the laws of the state in which it is organized is a de jure corporation. A corporation that exists in fact and has made a good faith effort to comply with the state laws but has failed to meet one or more of the requirements of the law is called a de facto corporation.

An eleemosynary corporation is a corporation that organized for a charitable or benevolent purpose. In many states, an eleemosynary corporation is now referred to as a charitable or nonprofit corporation. A subsidiary corporation is one that is under the control of another corporation that owns a majority of the shares.

A private corporation is governed by a <u>board of directors</u>. The presiding officer of the board of directors of a corporation is the <u>chairperson</u>. The <u>president</u> is the chief officer of a corporation who implements the policies established by the board of directors.

TRANSCRIBING FROM DICTATION

Directions: This dictation emphasizes and reinforces the legal terms and definitions you have studied. Listen carefully to the pronunciation of each of the legal terms. Unless otherwise directed, use a 70-space line (typewriter) or 1-inch margins (computer) and double spacing. Correct all errors. Follow one of the procedures below.

Keyboarding Procedure
Using the cassette from Lesson 29, Part A, transcribe the dictation directly at your typewriter or computer.

Shorthand Procedure
Using the cassette from Lesson 29, Part A, take the dictation using your shorthand system and then transcribe from your shorthand notes on your typewriter or computer.

When you have finished transcribing Part A of the practice dictation, check your transcript with the printed copy. If you made any mistakes in the transcription, you should practice those words several times before going on.

Part B TERMINOLOGY AND DEFINITIONS

Directions: Study the terms, pronunciations, and definitions until you are thoroughly familiar with them. In order to complete this lesson successfully, you must understand the meaning and usage of all the legal terms presented. If you are using shorthand, write your shorthand outline for each legal term in your shorthand notebook or on your shorthand machine.

Legal Term	Pronunciation	Definition
1. share	sher	A specific part or portion of the capital of a company or corporation. (See Figure 29-3, page 435.)
2. stock	stäk	Shares of ownership in a corporation.
3. common stock	′käm-ən stäk	The ordinary stock of a corporation that has no preference or special rights.
4. preferred stock	pri-′ferd stäk	Stock that has priority as to dividends over the common stock of the corporation.
5. par value	pär ′val-yü	Face value of all shares of stock in a particular class.
6. book value	bük ′val-yü	The net worth of a share of stock.
7. shareholder (stockholder)	′sher-hōl-dər ′stäk-hōl-dər	A person who owns shares of stock in a corporation. (See Figure 29-3, page 435.)
8. stock certificate	stäk sər-′tif-i-kət	A written document stating that the named person owns a certain number of shares of stock in a corporation. (See Figure 29-3, page 435.)
9. promoters	prə-′mōt-ərs	The persons who organize a corporation.
10. transfer agent	′trans-fər ′ā-jənt	A bank or other institution that handles the transfer of stock for a corporation.
11. treasury stock	′trezh-rē stäk	Stock that belongs to a corporation.
12. watered stock	′wȯt-ərd stäk	Stock that is issued as paid-up stock, but is not, and that is issued below par value.

FIGURE 29-3 A Stock Certificate

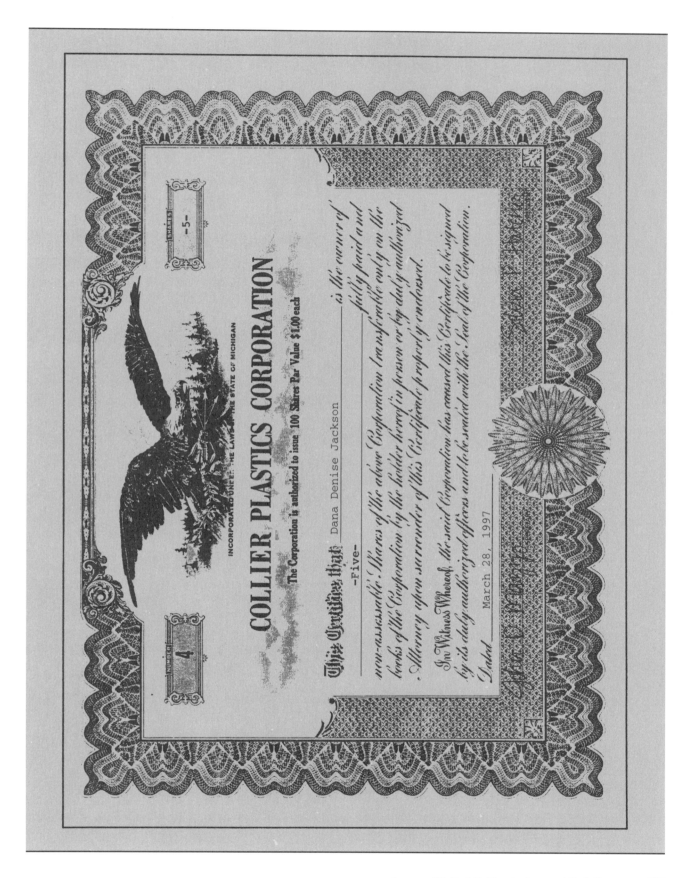

Self-Evaluation B   TERMINOLOGY AND DEFINITION RECALL

Directions: In the Answers column, write the legal term that is most representative of the corresponding statement. After you have completed this self-evaluation, check your answers with the key on page 500. If you have any incorrect answers, restudy the definitions for those terms before going on with this lesson. Then unless otherwise directed, submit this self-evaluation to your instructor.

Answers

1. The net worth of a share of stock is the _____.

   1. _____

2. Stock that is issued as paid-up stock, but is not, and that is issued below par value is _____.

   2. _____

3. A person who owns shares of stock in a corporation is a/an _____.

   3. _____

4. Stock that has priority as to dividends over other stock of the corporation is _____.

   4. _____

5. A bank or other institution that handles the transfer of stock for a corporation is a/an _____.

   5. _____

6. A written document stating or acknowledging that the named person is owner of a designated number of shares of stock in a corporation is a/an _____.

   6. _____

7. The face value of all shares of stock in a particular class is the _____.

   7. _____

8. A specific part or portion of the capital of a company or corporation is called a/an _____.

   8. _____

9. The ordinary stock of a corporation that has no preference or special rights is _____.

   9. _____

10. The persons who organize a corporation are known as the _____.

    10. _____

11. Shares of ownership in a corporation are referred to as _____.

    11. _____

12. Stock that belongs to a corporation is _____.

    12. _____

.

KEYING LEGAL TERMS

Directions: Unless otherwise instructed, use a 70-space line (typeriter) or 1-inch margins (computer) and double spacing. Correct all errors. Follow one of the procedures below.

WORDS

Keyboarding Procedure
On your typewriter or computer, key the following words at least two times, concentrating on the correct spelling and pronunciation.

Shorthand Procedure
On your typewriter or computer, key the following words once, concentrating on the correct spelling and pronunciation. Then write the shorthand outline for each word in your shorthand notebook or on your shorthand machine. Transcribe from the shorthand outlines one time on your typewriter or computer.

share	stock	common stock
preferred stock	par value	book value
shareholder (stockholder)	stock certificate	promoters
transfer agent	treasury stock	watered stock

SENTENCES

Keyboarding Procedure
Key each of the following sentences one time on your typewriter or computer. Concentrate on the correct spelling and pronunciation of each underlined legal term.

Shorthand Procedure
Write the correct shorthand outlines for the following sentences in your shorthand notebook or on your shorthand machine. Transcribe from your shorthand outlines one time on your typewriter or computer.

These sentences will be used for practice dictation on the cassettes.

A share is a specific part or portion of the capital of a company or corporation. Shares of ownership in a corporation are called stock.

The ordinary stock of a corporation that has no preference or special rights is known as common stock. Preferred stock is a stock that has priority as to dividends over the common stock of the corporation.

Par value is the face value of all shares of stock in a particular class. Par value is the value of the stock listed on the stock certificate regardless of the amount actually paid for the stock. The net worth of a share of stock is the book value. The book value is determined by deducting the liabilities from the assets.

One who owns shares of stock in a corporation is called a shareholder, or stockholder. A stock certificate is a written document stating that the named person owns a certain number of shares of stock in a corporation.

Promoters are persons who organize a corporation. A transfer agent is a bank or other institution that handles the transfer of stock for a corporation.

Stock that is owned by a corporation is referred to as treasury stock. Stock that is issued by a corporation as fully paid-up stock when in fact it is not and is sold below par value is called watered stock.

TRANSCRIBING FROM DICTATION

Directions: This dictation emphasizes and reinforces the legal terms and definitions you have studied. Listen carefully to the pronunciation of each of the legal terms. Unless otherwise directed, use a 70-space line (typewriter) or 1-inch margins (computer) and double spacing. Correct all errors. Follow one of the procedures below.

Keyboarding Procedure
Using the cassette from Lesson 29, Part B, transcribe the dictation directly at your typewriter or computer.

Shorthand Procedure
Using the cassette from Lesson 29, Part B, take the dictation using your shorthand system and then transcribe from your shorthand notes on your typewriter or computer.

When you have finished transcribing Part B of the practice dictation, check your transcript with the printed copy. If you made any mistakes in the transcription, you should practice those words several times before going on to Lesson 30.

CHECKLIST
I have completed the following for Lesson 29:

	Part A, Date	Part B, Date	Submitted to Instructor Yes	No
Terminology and Definitions				
Self-Evaluation				
***Keying Legal Terms**				
Words				
Sentences				
***Transcribing from Dictation**				

When you have successfully completed all the exercises in this lesson and submitted to your instructor those requested, you are ready to proceed with Lesson 30.

* If you are using a shorthand system, submit to your instructor your shorthand notes along with your transcript.

Lesson 30

Corporations

"Acquiescence in error takes away the right of objecting to it."
—Legal Maxim

This lesson continues the study of some of the terms relating to corporate law. A knowledge of these terms will assist your understanding of corporations and the laws that govern them. You will be able to spell, define, pronounce, and transcribe correctly the legal terms presented in the following exercises when you have satisfactorily completed the lesson.

Part A   TERMINOLOGY AND DEFINITIONS

Directions: Study the terms, pronunciations, and definitions until you are thoroughly familiar with them. In order to complete this lesson successfully, you must understand the meaning and usage of all the legal terms presented. If you are using shorthand, write your shorthand outline for each legal term in your shorthand notebook or on your shorthand machine.

Legal Term	Pronunciation	Definition
1. ultra vires	′əl-trə ′vī-rēz	Latin. Acts that are not within the powers of a corporation as defined in its charter.
2. blue-sky laws	′blü-′skī lòs	Laws to protect persons from investing in fraudulent companies.
3. antitrust acts	ant-i-′trəst akts	Laws to prevent monopolies. A corporation cannot own or control so much of a market as to eliminate competition.
4. merger	′mər-jər	The joining of one corporation with another that continues in existence as one corporation.
5. bylaws	′bī-lòs	The rules or regulations by which a corporation is managed. (See Figure 30-1, pages 443-444.)
6. minutes	′min-əts	A written record of the proceedings that took place at a board of directors' or shareholders' meeting.
7. quorum	′kwōr-əm	A majority. The number of members required to be present at a meeting for business to be transacted.
8. proxy	′präk-sē	A person who is designated to represent or act for another in a meeting. Also refers to the instrument that gives the authority.
9. annual report	′an-yəl ri-′pōrt	A report to the shareholders of a corporation at the end of a fiscal year that presents financial statements and operational information for the corporation for the preceding year.

10. goodwill	′gu̇d-′wil	The favorable reputation of an established business with its customers.
11. dissolution	dis-ə-′lü-shən	The termination of the legal existence of a corporation.
12. liquidation	lik-wə-′dā-shən	The distribution of the assets of a business to settle accounts with creditors.

FIGURE 30-1 Bylaws

```
                        BYLAWS OF

                COLLIER PLASTICS CORPORATION

        Incorporated under the Laws of the State of Michigan

Registered office address: 9001 Okemos Road, Okemos, MI 48864

Annual meeting time: Month  December  Day  2nd Monday  Hour  10:00 a.m.

Fiscal year begins:  Month  November  Day  1st
```

ARTICLE I - OFFICES

The address of the registered office of the corporation in Michigan is stated at the beginning of these bylaws. The corporation may have other offices or branches as determined by the board of directors.

ARTICLE II - FISCAL YEAR

The date on which the fiscal year of the corporation begins each year is stated at the beginning of these bylaws.

ARTICLE III - MEETINGS OF SHAREHOLDERS

1.   PLACE

Shareholders' meetings shall be held at the registered office of the corporation or at another location determined by the board of directors and stated in the notice of the meeting.

2.   TIME

The time of the annual meeting of shareholders is stated at the beginning of these bylaws. If this date falls on a legal holiday then the annual meeting shall be held on the next business day.

3.   PURPOSE

The purpose of the annual meeting shall be to elect a board of directors and transact other business as may come before the meeting.

4.   SPECIAL MEETINGS

Special meetings of the shareholders may be called by the president, two directors or by the holders of at least 10% of the shares entitled to vote at a meeting. A special meeting may be called anytime for any business purpose, unless otherwise prohibited by statute and shall be held at the registered office of the corporation.

5.   NOTICE

Written notice stating the place, day, and time of the meeting and, in case of a special meeting, the purpose or purposes for which the meeting is called shall be delivered not less than 10 nor more than 60 days before the date of the meeting. If mailed, such notice shall be considered to be delivered when deposited in the United States Postal Service, addressed to the shareholder at his/her address as it appears on the share transfer books of the corporation, with the correct amount of postage on it.

6.   FIXING RECORD DATE

For the purpose of determining the shareholders entitled to notice of or to vote at any meeting of shareholders or for the purpose of any other action, the board of directors shall fix in advance a date as a record date. The date shall not be more than 60 nor less than 10 days before the meeting, nor more than 60 days prior to any other action.

FIGURE 30-1 Bylaws (continued)

7. QUORUM

At any meeting of shareholders a majority of the outstanding shares of the corporation entitled to vote, represented in person or by proxy, shall constitute a quorum. The shareholders present in person or by proxy at such meeting may continue to do business until adjournment even if this means the withdrawal of enough shareholders to leave less than a quorum. If a quorum is not present, the shareholders present in person or by proxy may adjourn to a date they agree upon.

8. PROXIES

At all meetings of shareholders, a shareholder may vote by proxy executed in writing by the shareholder or his/her duly authorized attorney in fact. A proxy is not valid after the expiration of 3 years from its date unless otherwise provided in the proxy. A proxy is not invalidated by the death or incompetency of the shareholder, unless, before the authority is exercised, written notice of such an adjudication is received by the corporate office responsible for maintaining the list of shareholders.

9. VOTING

Each outstanding share is entitled to 1 vote on each matter submitted to a vote. A vote may be cast either orally or in writing in

Self-Evaluation A   TERMINOLOGY AND DEFINITION RECALL

Directions: In the Answers column, write the letter from Column 1 that represents the word or phrase that best matches each item in Column 2. After you have completed this self-evaluation, check your answers with the key on page 500.
If you have any incorrect answers, restudy the definitions for those terms before going on with this lesson. Then unless otherwise directed, submit this self-evaluation to your instructor.

Column 1	**Column 2**	**Answers**
a. annual report	1. The termination of the legal existence of a corporation.	1. _____
b. antitrust acts	2. The joining of one corporation with another that continues in existence as one corporation.	2. _____
c. blue-sky laws		
d. bylaws	3. The rules or regulations by which a corporation is managed.	3. _____
e. charter	4. Laws that are for the purpose of preventing monopolies.	4. _____
f. dissolution	5. A majority or the number of members required to be pre-sent at a meeting for business to be transacted.	5. _____
g. goodwill	6. Laws that are designed to protect persons from investing in fraudulent companies.	6. _____
h. liquidation		
i. merger	7. A written record of the proceedings that took place at a board of directors' or shareholders' meeting.	7. _____
j. minutes		
k. proxy	8. The distribution of the assets of a business to settle accounts with creditors.	8. _____
l. quorum	9. The Latin term for acts that are not within the powers of a corporation as defined in its charter.	9. _____
m. ultra vires		
	10. The favorable reputation of an established business with its customers.	10. _____
	11. A report to the shareholders of a corporation at the end of a fiscal year that presents financial statements and opera-tional information for the corporation for the preceding year.	11. _____
	12. A person who is designated to represent or act for another in a meeting or the instrument that gives a person authori-ty to act for another in a meeting.	12. _____

KEYING LEGAL TERMS

Directions: Unless otherwise instructed, use a 70-space line (typewriter) or 1-inch margins (computer) and double spacing. Correct all errors. Follow one of the procedures below.

WORDS

Keyboarding Procedure
On your typewriter or computer, key the following words at least two times, concentrating on the correct spelling and pronunciation.

Shorthand Prodedure
On your typewriter or computer, key the following words once, concentrating on the correct spelling and pronunciation. Then write the shorthand outline for each word in your shorthand notebook or on your shorthand machine. Transcribe from the shorthand outlines one time on your typewriter or computer.

ultra vires	blue-sky laws	antitrust acts
merger	bylaws	minutes
quorum	proxy	annual report
goodwill	dissolution	liquidation

SENTENCES

Keyboarding Procedure
Key each of the following sentences one time on your typewriter or computer. Concentrate on the correct spelling and pronunciation of each underlined legal term.

Shorthand Procedure
Write the correct shorthand outlines for the following sentences in your shorthand notebook or on your shorthand machine. Transcribe from your shorthand outlines one time on your typewriter or computer.

These sentences will be used for practice dictation on the cassettes.

Ultra vires is a Latin term referring to acts that are not within the powers of a corporation as defined in its charter. Blue-sky laws are designed to protect persons from investing in fraudulent companies. Antitrust acts are laws to prevent monopolies. The antitrust acts prevent a corporation from controlling so much of a market as to eliminate competition. The joining of two or more corporations into one corporation is a merger.

The rules and regulations that govern the operations of a corporation are the bylaws. The written record of the proceedings that took place at a board of directors' or shareholders' meeting is the minutes. A quorum is a majority or the number of members required to be present at a meeting for business to be transacted. A proxy is a person who is designated to represent or act for another in a meeting. A proxy is also the instrument that gives such authority.

A corporation makes an annual report to its shareholders at the end of a fiscal year that presents financial statements and operational information for the corporation for the preceding year.

Goodwill refers to the favorable reputation of an established business with its customers. The dissolution of a corporation is the termination of its legal existence. Liquidation is the distribution of the assets of a business to settle accounts with creditors.

TRANSCRIBING FROM DICTATION

Directions: This dictation emphasizes and reinforces the legal terms and definitions you have studied. Listen carefully to the pronunciation of each of the legal terms. Unless otherwise directed, use a 70-space line (typewriter) or 1-inch margins (computer) and double spacing. Correct all errors. Follow one of the procedures below.

Keyboarding Procedure
Using the cassette from Lesson 30, Part A, transcribe the dictation directly at your typewriter or computer.

Shorthand Procedure
Using the cassette from Lesson 30, Part A, take the dictation using your shorthand system and then transcribe from your shorthand notes on your typewriter or computer.

When you have finished transcribing Part A of the practice dictation, check your transcript with the printed copy. If you made any mistakes in the transcription, you should practice those words several times before going on.

Part B TERMINOLOGY AND DEFINITIONS

Directions: Study the terms, pronunciations, and definitions until you are thoroughly familiar with them. In order to complete this lesson successfully, you must understand the meaning and usage of all the legal terms presented. If you are using shorthand, write your shorthand outline for each legal term in your shorthand notebook or on your shorthand machine.

Legal Term	Pronunciation	Definition
1. dividend	′div-ə-dend	A portion of the profits of a corporation that is to be divided among the shareholders.
2. earnings per share	′ər-niŋz pər sher	The average earnings based on the number of shares of stock issued by the corporation.
3. working capital	wərk-iŋ ′kap-ət-l	Cash or other assets that are readily available for the use of a corporation.
4. sinking fund	′siŋk-iŋ fənd	A sum of money set aside by a corporation to pay off a debt.
5. financial reports	fə-′nan-chəl ri-′pōrts	Statements of the financial condition of a company or corporation that include the balance sheet, the income statement, the statement of retained earnings, and other statements relating to the financial condition of a corporation. (See Figures 30-2, 30-3, and 30-4, pages 450 and 451.)
6. balance sheet	′bal-ens shēt	A statement that summarizes the net worth of a business at the end of a fiscal period and shows the assets and liabilities of the company. (See Figure 30-2, page 450.)
7. income statement	′in-kəm ′stāt-mənt	A statement showing the income of the business, the cost of goods sold, the expenses, and the net income that resulted from the operation of the business for a specified fiscal period.
8. retained earnings	ri-′tānd ′ər-niŋz	That portion of the earnings that a company keeps for operations or additional capital investments.
9. net worth	net wərth	The worth of a business after deducting the liabilities from the assets.

10. auditor	ˊȯd-ət-ər	A person who examines the financial accounts and statements of a corporation or company and verifies their accuracy.
11. liability	li̱-ə-ˊbil-ət-e̱	A debt or an obligation of a business or company. That which is owed.
12. debenture	di-ˊben-chər	An instrument that acknowledges a debt of a corporation.

FIGURE 30-2 Financial Reports (Balance Sheet)

FINANCIAL REPORTS
CONSOLIDATED BALANCE SHEET
December 31, 1996 and 1997

ASSETS

	1996	1997
	(In thousands of dollars)	
Current assets:		
Cash and cash equivalents	$ 7,984	$ 6,767
Receivables—		
Joint operations, net of allowance for doubtful accounts of $1,009,000 and $567,000	9,188	9,449
Oil and gas sales	12,782	9,085
Notes	891	1,741
Windfall profit tax refund	3,771	—
Equity in net current assets of, and advances to, managed partnerships	1,318	—
Tubular inventories, at lower of cost or market	838	1,324
Prepaid expenses and other	1,153	507
Total current assets	37,925	28,873

FIGURE 30-3 Financial Reports (Statement of Changes in Financial Position)

FINANCIAL REPORTS
CONSOLIDATED STATEMENT OF CHANGES IN FINANCIAL POSITION
For the years ended December 31, 1997, 1996 and 1995
(In thousands of dollars)

	1997	1996	1995
Source of funds:			
Net income	$ 4,218	$ 5,165	$ 9,653
Items not affecting working capital in the current year:			
Depreciation, depletion and amortization	20,309	16,341	20,581
Deferred income taxes	2,802	3,599	9,547
Litigation settlement	1,537	—	—
Other	546	1,847	526
Funds provided by operations	29,412	26,952	40,307
Proceeds from sales of oil and gas properties	3,011	8,156	5,825
Benefit from utilization of tax loss of acquired entity	1,649	—	—
Long-term borrowings, including capital lease of geothermal equipment	19,682	3,018	11,000
Common stock issued in merger with Integrated Energy Inc., net of direct acquisition costs	13,006	—	—
Other, net	150	1,207	1,461
Total source of funds	66,910	39,333	58,593

FIGURE 30-4 Financial Reports (Statement of Operations)

FINANCIAL REPORTS
CONSOLIDATED STATEMENT OF OPERATIONS
For the years ended December 31, 1997, 1996, and 1995
(In thousands of dollars, except per share amounts)

	1997	1996	1995
Revenues:			
Oil and gas	$56,811	$60,374	$77,377
Other, primarily interest income	3,619	699	2,665
	60,430	61,073	80,042
Costs and expenses:			
Oil and gas production	16,546	17,999	19,099
Windfall profit tax refund	(5,517)	—	—
General and administrative	13,778	12,112	13,710
Depreciation, depletion and amortization	20,309	16,341	20,581
Interest and other	6,197	5,627	7,252
	51,313	52,079	60,642
Income before income taxes	9,117	8,994	19,400
Provision for income taxes	4,899	3,829	9,747
Net income	4,218	5,165	9,653

Self-Evaluation B   TERMINOLOGY AND DEFINITION RECALL

Directions: In the Answers column, write the legal term that is most representative of the corresponding statement. After you have completed this self-evaluation, check your answers with the key on page 500. If you have any incorrect answers, restudy the definitions for those terms before going on with this lesson. Then unless otherwise directed, submit this self-evaluation to your instructor.

Answers

1. A portion of the profits of a corporation that is to be divided among the shareholders is referred to as a/an _____.

    1. _____

2. A sum of money set aside by a corporation to pay off a debt is a/an _____.

    2. _____

3. Cash or other assets that are readily available for the use of a corporation are referred to as _____.

    3. _____

4. A person who examines the financial accounts and statements of a corporation or company and verifies their accuracy is a/an _____.

    4. _____

5. An instrument that acknowledges a debt of a corporation is a/an _____.

    5. _____

6. A statement showing the income of the business, the cost of goods sold, the expenses, and the net income that resulted from the operation of the business for a specified fiscal period is a/an _____.

    6. _____

7. Statements of the financial condition of a company or corporation are referred to as _____.

    7. _____

8. That portion of the earnings that a company keeps for operations or additional capital investments is _____.

    8. _____

9. The average earnings of a corporation based on the number of shares of stock issued by the corporation are _____.

    9. _____

10. The worth of a business after deducting the liabilities from the assets is the _____.

    10. _____

11. A debt or an obligation of a business or company or that which is owed is a/an _____.

    11. _____

12. A statement that summarizes the net worth of a business at the end of a fiscal period and shows the assets and liabilities of the company is a/an _____.

    12. _____

KEYING LEGAL TERMS

Directions: Unless otherwise instructed, use a 70-space line (typewriter) or 1-inch margins (computer) and double spacing. Correct all errors. Follow one of the procedures below.

WORDS

Keyboarding Procedure
On your typewriter or computer, key the following words at least two times, concentrating on the correct spelling and pronunciation.

Shorthand Procedure
On your typewriter or computer, key the following words once, concentrating on the correct spelling and pronunciation. Then write the shorthand outline for each word in your shorthand notebook or on your shorthand machine. Transcribe from the shorthand outlines one time on your typewriter or computer.

dividend	earnings per share	working capital
sinking fund	financial reports	balance sheet
income statement	retained earnings	net worth
auditor	liability	debenture

SENTENCES

Keyboarding Procedure
Key each of the following sentences one time on your typewriter or computer. Concentrate on the correct spelling and pronunciation of each underlined legal term.

Shorthand Procedure
Write the correct shorthand outlines for the following sentences in your shorthand notebook or on your shorthand machine. Transcribe from your shorthand outlines one time on your typewriter or computer.

These sentences will be used for practice dictation on the cassettes.

A dividend is a portion of the profits of a corporation that is to be divided among the shareholders. The average earnings of a corporation based on the number of shares of stock issued by the corporation are referred to as earnings per share. Working capital is cash and other assets that a corporation has readily available for use. A sinking fund is a sum of money set aside by a corporation to pay off a debt.

Financial reports consist of statements of the financial condition of a company or corporation. Financial reports include the balance sheet, the income statement, the statement of retained earnings, and other statements relating to the financial condition of a corporation. A balance sheet summarizes the net worth of a business at the end of a fiscal period and shows the assets and liabilities of the company. Net worth is the worth of a business after deducting the liabilities from the assets. An income statement shows the income of the business, the cost of goods sold, the expenses, and the net income that resulted from the operation of the business for a specified period of time. Retained earnings is that portion of the earnings that the company keeps for operations or additional capital investments.

A person who examines the financial accounts and financial statements of a corporation or company and verifies their accuracy is an auditor. A liability is a debt or an obligation of a business or company. A debenture is an instrument that acknowledges a debt of a corporation.

TRANSCRIBING FROM DICTATION

Directions: This dictation emphasizes and reinforces the legal terms and definitions you have studied. Listen carefully to the pronunciation of each of the legal terms. Unless otherwise directed, use a 70-space line (typewriter) or 1-inch margins (computer) and double spacing. Correct all errors. Follow one of the procedures below.

Keyboarding Procedure
Using the cassette from Lesson 30, Part B, transcribe the dictation directly at your typewriter or computer.

Shorthand Procedure
Using the cassette from Lesson 30, Part B, take the dictation using your shorthand system and then transcribe from your shorthand notes on your typewriter or computer.

When you have finished transcribing Part B of the practice dictation, check your transcript with the printed copy. If you made any mistakes in the transcription, you should practice those words several times before going on to Evaluation 15.

CHECKLIST
I have completed the following for Lesson 30:

	Part A, Date	Part B, Date	Submitted to Instructor Yes	No
Terminology and Definitions				
Self-Evaluation				
* Keying Legal Terms				
Words				
Sentences				
* Transcribing from Dictation				

When you have successfully completed all the exercises in this lesson and submitted to your instructor those requested, you are ready to proceed with Evaluation 15.

* If you are using a shorthand system, submit to your instructor your shorthand notes along with your transcript.

Evaluation No. 15   SECTION A

Directions: This dictation/transcription evaluation will test your spelling and transcription abilities on the legal terms that you studied in the two preceding lessons. Use a 5-space paragraph indention, a 70-space line (typewriter) or 1-inch margins (computer), and double spacing unless otherwise instructed. Correct all errors. Follow one of the procedures below.

Keyboarding Procedure
Using the cassette from Evaluation 15, transcribe the dictation directly at your typewriter or computer.

Shorthand Procedure
Using the cassette from Evaluation 15, take the dictation using your shorthand system and then transcribe from your shorthand notes on your typewriter or computer.

Sections B and C are available from your instructor.

Lesson 31

Additional Legal Terms— General and Real Property

"Extreme law is the greatest injury; strict law is great punishment."

—Legal Maxim

This lesson consists of additional general legal terms and terms relating to real property that were not presented in earlier lessons. When you complete these exercises, you should have knowledge and an understanding of more general legal terms and terms that are used in reference to real property.

Part A TERMINOLOGY AND DEFINITIONS

Directions: Study the terms, pronunciations, and definitions until you are thoroughly familiar with them. In order to complete this lesson successfully, you must understand the meaning and usage of all the legal terms presented. If you are using shorthand, write your shorthand outline for each legal term in your shorthand notebook or on your shorthand machine.

Legal Term	Pronunciation	Definition
1. clerk of the court	klərk əv thə kōrt	An officer of the court whose duties include issuing the process or docket of the court, filing of court documents, issuing summonses, and keeping the seal of the court and records of court proceedings.
2. docket	′däk-ət	The schedule of cases to be tried by a court. When a case is filed, the clerk of the court assigns a number to the case which is called the docket, file, or case number.
3. joinder	′join-dər	The joining or uniting with others in a litigation. For example, a new party may be brought in to join with the plaintiff or the defendant in a lawsuit. Two or more matters may also be combined in the same suit.
4. cross-complaint	kròs kəm-′plānt	A complaint brought by a defendant against a co-defendant. For example, if you and your roommate are sued by your landlord for damages and you feel that your roommate was responsible, then you may file a cross-complaint against your roommate.
5. certificate of service	sər-′tif-i-kət əv ′sər-vəs	A statement that avers that the opposing party has been given a copy of a designated document. Also, referred to as proof of service. (See Figure 31-1, page 461.)
6. alias summons	′ā-lē-əs ′səm-ənz	When the first summons is returned because it could not be served due to a defect or manner of service, a second summons is issued with the defect, such as an incorrect address, corrected.

7. pluries summons	'plùr-ēz 'səm-ənz	A third and subsequent summonses issued when the first two summonses have not been effective.
8. disclosure statement	dis-'klō-zhər 'stāt-mənt	A statement that makes known or reveals information. For example, a party who owes money to another party may be forced to reveal to the court the location of all of his or her assets. In real estate law, a seller may be required to provide a statement to the buyer which reveals the condition of the property. Also, the Truth in Lending Act requires a mortgagee to issue a disclosure statement to the mortgagor that states the annual percentage rate of the mortgage (APR).
9. certificate of readiness	sər-'tif-i-kat əv 'red-ē-nəs	A document filed with the court in some states that specifies that all the parties are ready for trial.
10. discovery	dis-'kəv-rē	The gathering of information about a case prior to trial. Interrogatories and depositions are part of the discovery process. Also attorneys may be required to provide any relevant items to the opposing party.
11. proffer	'präf-ər	To offer or propose. An avowel or offer of proof that is usually made out of the presence of the jury which may have an effect on an appeal.
12. sidebar	'sīd-bär	A conference held in the courtroom between the judge and counsel out of the hearing of the jury.
13. realtime	'rēl-tīm	A computer-aided transcript produced instantaneously as the court reporter records the proceedings. A realtime transcript is not edited or certified but is used by the judge and attorneys as reference notes for the proceedings.
14. undue influence	ən-'dü 'in-flü-əns	Improperly putting pressure on a person so as to affect that person's free will, acts, or decisions.
15. chose in possession	'shōz in pə-'zesh-ən	Personal property of which one has possession.
16. perfect	pər-'fekt	To make complete, without defect or enforceable. For example, when a document such as a deed is recorded, it is said to become enforceable or perfect.

FIGURE 31-1 A Certificate of Service

Self-Evaluation A   TERMINOLOGY AND DEFINITION RECALL

Directions: In the Answers column, write the legal term that is most representative of the corresponding statement. After you have completed this self-evaluation, check your answers with the key on page 500. If you have any incorrect answers, restudy the definitions for those terms before going on with this lesson. Then unless otherwise directed, submit this self-evaluation to your instructor.

Answers

1. A third and subsequent summonses that are issued when the first two have not been effective is called a/an_____.

    1. _____

2. A statement that makes known or reveals information is a/an _____.

    2. _____

3. A conference held in the courtroom between the judge and counsel out of the hearing of the jury is referred to as a/an _____.

    3. _____

4. To offer or propose is called _____.

    4. _____

5. A computer-aided transcipt produced instantaneously as the court reporter records the proceedings is referred to as _____.

    5. _____

6. The gathering of information about a case prior to trial is called _____.

    6. _____

7. A document filed with the court in some states that specifies that all the parties are ready for trial is a/an _____.

    7. _____

8. To make complete, without defect, or enforceable is referred to as to _____.

    8. _____

9. Improperly putting pressure on a person so as to affect that person's free will, acts, or decisions is called _____.

    9. _____

10. Personal property of which one has possession is referred to as _____.

    10. _____

11. A complaint brought by a defendant against a co-defendant is a/an _____.

    11. _____

12. A statement that avers that the opposing party has been given a copy of a designated document is a/an _____.

    12. _____

13. The second summons that is issued when the first summons cannot be delivered is called a/an _____.

    13. _____

14. An officer of the court whose duties include issuing the process or docket of the court, filing of court documents, issuing summonses, and keeping the seal of the court and records of court proceedings is the _____.

    14. _____

15. A schedule of cases to be tried by a court is a/an _____.

    15. _____

16. The joining or uniting with others in a litigation is referred to as _____.

    16. _____

KEYING LEGAL TERMS

Directions: Unless otherwise instructed, use a 70-space line (typewriter) or 1-inch margins (computer) and double spacing. Correct all errors. Follow one of the procedures below.

WORDS

Keyboarding Procedure
On your typewriter or computer, key the following words at least two times, concentrating on the correct spelling and pronunciation.

Shorthand Procedure
On your typewriter or computer, key the following words once, concentrating on the correct spelling and pronunciation. Then write the shorthand outline for each word in your shorthand notebook or on your shorthand machine. Transcribe from the shorthand outlines one time on your typewriter or computer.

clerk of the court	docket	joinder
cross-complaint	certificate of service	alias summons
pluries summons	disclosure statement	certificate of readiness
discovery	proffer	sidebar
realtime	undue influence	chose in possession
perfect		

SENTENCES

Keyboarding Procedure
Key each of the following sentences one time on your typewriter or computer. Concentrate on the correct spelling and pronunciation of each underlined legal term.

Shorthand Procedure
Write the correct shorthand outlines for the following sentences in your shorthand notebook or on your shorthand machine. Transcribe from your shorthand outlines one time on your typewriter or computer.

These sentences will be used for practice dictation on the cassettes.

The clerk of the court is a court officer who is responsible for issuing the process or docket of the court, filing of court documents, issuing summonses, and keeping the seal of the court and records of court proceedings. The schedule of cases to be tried by a court is called the docket. When a case is filed, the clerk of the court assigns a number to the case which is called the docket, file, or case number.

When a new party is brought in to join with the plaintiff or the defendant in a lawsuit or two or more matters are combined in the same suit, it is called joinder. Joinder means joining or uniting with others in a litigation. If a defendant brings a complaint against a co-defendant, it is called a cross-complaint. If you and your roommate are sued by your landlord for damages and you feel that your roommate was responsible, then you may file a cross-complaint against your roommate.

A certificate of service is a statement that avers that the opposing party has been given a copy of a designated document. A certificate of service may also be called a proof of service. An alias summons is issued when the first summons is returned because it could not be served due to a defect or manner of service. If a third and subsequent summonses have to be issued because the first two are not effective, they are called a pluries summons.

A disclosure statement makes known or reveals information. A party who owes money to another party may be required to come into court and reveal the location of his or her assets in a disclosure statement. A seller of real property may be required to give the buyer a disclosure statement which reveals the condition of the property. Also, the Truth in Lending Act requires a mortgagee to issue a disclosure statement which states the annual percentage rate of the mortgage.

In some states when both parties to a lawsuit are ready to proceed to trial, a certificate of readiness is filed with the court. A certificate of readiness is filed when discovery or the gathering of information about a case prior to trial is completed. To offer or propose is referred to as proffer. A proffer is usually made out of the presence of the jury and may have an effect on an appeal. During the trial, the judge and the attorneys may have a conference out of the hearing of the jury which is called a sidebar. When the court reporter produces a transcript instantaneously as the proceedings are recorded, it is referred to as realtime.

Undue influence is improperly putting pressure on a person so as to affect that person's free will, acts, or decisions. Personal property which one has in their possession is called chose in possession. To make complete, without defect, or enforceable is to perfect. When a document such as a deed is recorded, it is said to be perfected or enforceable.

TRANSCRIBING FROM DICTATION

Directions: This dictation emphasizes and reinforces the legal terms and definitions you have studied. Listen carefully to the pronunciation of each of the legal terms. Unless otherwise directed, use a 70-space line (typewriter) or 1-inch margins (computer) and double spacing. Correct all errors. Follow one of the procedures below.

Keyboarding Procedure
Using the cassette from Lesson 31, Part A, transcribe the dictation directly at your typewriter or computer.

Shorthand Procedure
Using the cassette from Lesson 31, Part A, take the dictation using your shorthand system and then transcribe from your shorthand notes on your typewriter or computer.

When you have finished transcribing Part A of the practice dictation, check your transcript with the printed copy. If you made any mistakes in the transcription, you should practice those words several times before going on.

Part B   TERMINOLOGY AND DEFINITIONS

Directions: Study the terms, pronunciations, and definitions until you are thoroughly familiar with them. In order to complete this lesson successfully, you must understand the meaning and usage of all the legal terms presented. If you are using shorthand, write your shorthand outline for each legal term in your shorthand notebook or on your shorthand machine.

Legal Term	Pronunciation	Definition
1. grantor	′grant-ər	The person who transfers the title to real property.
2. grantee	grant-′ē	The person to whom the title to real property is transferred.

3. purchase-money mortgage	'pər-chəs-'mən-ē 'mòr-gij	A realty property mortgage which is held by the seller of the real property. Differs from a land contract in that the title passes at the time of the sale and the purchase-money mortgage is a lien on the property.
4. mortgagor	mòr-gi-'jòr	One who pledges his or her property as security for a debt. For example, if you borrow money from a bank and pledge your ownership in your home as collateral or security for the loan, you are a mortgagor.
5. mortgagee	mòr-gi-'jē	One who takes or receives a mortgage as security or collateral for a loan. For example, if you borrow money from a bank and the bank holds your home as collateral or security for the loan, the bank is the mortgagee.
6. sales or purchase agreement	sālz ər 'pər-chəs ə-'grē-mənt	An agreement between two parties whereby the seller is obligated to sell and the buyer is obligated to purchase specified real property under the terms specified in the agreement.
7. deed of trust	dēd əv trəst	Differs from a mortgage in that the title to real property is placed in the name of a third party or trustee who holds title until the mortgage is paid or other specified conditions are met.
8. derivation clause	der-ə-'vā-shən klòz	A clause in a deed of trust that names the parties from whom the current owner purchased the real property. It also provides information regarding the recording of that transfer.
9. affidavit of value	af-ə-'dā-vət əv 'val-yü	Some states require an affidavit as to the sale price or value of the real property, whichever is greater, to be included in the deed. Other states require that a separate affidavit of value be filed with the tax assessor's office.
10. amortization	am-ərt-ə-'zā-shən	The paying of an obligation by installments. For example, if you mortgage your home, each month you will be required to pay a specified amount for principal and interest for a definite number of years after which the mortgage will be paid in full.
11. Mechanic's Lien	mi-'kan-iks lēn	A claim that a worker or contractor has against real property for work performed or materials used on the property.
12. waiver of lien	'wā-vər əv lēn	A release of any and all claims relating to Mechanic's Liens that a worker or contractor has against real property. (See Figure 31-2, page 468.)
13. tax sale	taks sāl	A sale of land for unpaid taxes. If real property taxes are not paid by a date determined by state law, the property is sold, usually at auction, for the amount of the unpaid taxes.
14. tax certificate	taks sər-'tif-i-kat	At a tax sale, some states sell only a tax certificate which gives the purchaser the right to receive a deed (title) for the property if the owner does not redeem the certificate by paying the taxes within a specified period of time.
15. tax deed	taks dēd	A deed that conveys title to the purchaser for real property sold at a tax sale.

FIGURE 31-2 A Waiver of Lien

WAIVER OF LIEN—MATERIAL OR LABOR

PARTIAL ☐
COMPLETE ☒

State of ___Illinois___ } ss.

County of ___DuPage___

_____ July 18 ___ 19 XX

TO ALL WHOM IT MAY CONCERN:

Whereas __I__ the undersigned __Sarkis Tajari__

have been employed by __Gates Construction Company__

to furnish __materials and labor__

for the Building known as __7849 Marissa Avenue__

City of __Wheaton__

Lot No. __64__   Section __768__   Township __Monroe__   Range __41__

County of __DuPage__   State of __Illinois__

NOW, THEREFORE, KNOW YE, That __Sarkis Tajari__   the undersigned

for and in consideration of the sum of __One and 00/100__   Dollars

and other good and valuable considerations, the receipt whereof is hereby acknowledged, do hereby waive and release any and all lien, or

claim or right to lien on said above described building and premises under the Statutes of the State of __Illinois__

relating to Mechanics' Liens, on account of labor or materials, or both, furnished or which may be furnished, by the undersigned to or on

account of the said __Gates Construction Company__

_____ for said building or premises.

Given under __my__ hand____ and seal ____ this __18th__   Day of __July__   A.D., 19__XX__

Witness: _Terri F. Thurmond_   _Sarkis Tajari_   (SEAL)

_____   _____ (SEAL)

Self-Evaluation B   TERMINOLOGY AND DEFINITION RECALL

Directions: In the Answers column, write the letter from Column 1 that represents the word or phrase that best matches each item in Column 2. After you have completed this self-evaluation, check your answers with the key on page 500. If you have any incorrect answers, restudy the definitions for those terms before going on with this lesson. Then unless otherwise directed, submit this self-evaluation to your instructor.

Column 1	Column 2	Answers
a. affidavit of value	1. The person to whom the title to real property is transferred.	1. _____
b. amortization	2. One who pledges his or her real property as security for a debt.	2. _____
c. deed of trust		
d. derivation clause	3. A document that places the title to real property in the name of a third party or trustee who holds title until the mortgage is paid or other specific conditions are met.	3. _____
e. grantee		
f. grantor	4. A statement that verifies the value or sales price of real property.	4. _____
g. Mechanic's Lien	5. The paying of an obligation by installments.	5. _____
h. mortgage	6. A release of any and all claims relating to Mechanic's Liens that a worker or contractor may have against a real property.	6. _____
i. mortgagee		
j. mortgagor		
k. purchase-money mortgage	7. A document that gives the purchaser the right to receive title to property if the owner does not pay the taxes within a specified period of time.	7. _____
l. sales or purchase agreement	8. A realty property mortgage that is held by the seller of the property.	8. _____
m. tax certificate	9. The person who transfers the title to real property.	9. _____
n. tax deed	10. One who takes or receives a mortgage as security or collateral for a loan.	10. _____
o. tax sale		
p. waiver of lien	11. An agreement between two parties whereby the seller is obligated to sell and the buyer is obligated to purchase specified real property under the terms of the agreement.	11. _____
	12. A portion of a deed of trust that names the parties from whom the current owner purchased the real property.	12. _____
	13. A sale of land for unpaid taxes.	13. _____
	14. A claim that a worker or contractor has against real property for work performed or materials used on the property.	14. _____
	15. Conveys title to the purchaser for real property that is sold at a tax sale.	15. _____

KEYING LEGAL TERMS

Directions: Unless otherwise instructed, use a 70-space line (typewriter) or 1-inch margins (computer) and double spacing. Correct all errors. Follow one of the procedures below.

WORDS

Keyboarding Procedure
On your typewriter or computer, key the following words at least two times, concentrating on the correct spelling and pronunciation.

Shorthand Procedure
On your typewriter or computer, key the following words once, concentrating on the correct spelling and pronunciation. Then write the shorthand outline for each word in your shorthand notebook or on your shorthand machine. Transcribe from the shorthand outlines one time on your typewriter or computer.

grantor	grantee	purchase-money mortgage
mortgagor	mortgagee	sales or purchase agreement
deed of trust	derivation clause	affidavit of value
amortization	Mechanic's Lien	waiver of lien
tax sale	tax certificate	tax deed

SENTENCES

Keyboarding Procedure
Key each of the following sentences one time on your typewriter or computer. Concentrate on the correct spelling and pronunciation of each underlined legal term.

Shorthand Procedure
Write the correct shorthand outlines for the following sentences in your shorthand notebook or on your shorthand machine. Transcribe from your shorthand outlines one time on your typewriter or computer.

These sentences will be used for practice dictation on the cassettes.

A grantor is the person who transfers the title to real property. A grantee is the person to whom the title to real property is transferred. A realty property mortgage which is held by the seller of the real property is called a purchase-money mortgage. A purchase-money mortgage differs from a land contract in that the title passes at the time of the sale and the mortgage is a lien on the property.

A person who pledges his or her property as security for a debt is referred to as a mortgagor. A mortgagee is the one who takes or receives a mortgage as security or collateral for a loan. Therefore, if you borrow money from a bank and pledge your ownership in your home as collateral or security for the loan, you are the mortgagor and the bank is the mortgagee.

An agreement between two parties whereby the seller is obligated to sell and the buyer is obligated to purchase specified real property under the terms specified in the agreement is a sales or purchase agreement. When a deed of trust is used in a real estate transaction, the title to real property is placed in the name of a third party who holds title until the mortgage is paid or other specified conditions are met. The derivation clause in a deed of trust names the parties from whom the current owner purchased the real property and also provides information regarding the recording of that transfer. An affidavit of value stating the price or value of the real property may also be included in the deed or filed with the tax assessor's office.

Amortization refers to the paying of an obligation by installments. A **Mechanic's Lien** is a claim that a worker or contractor has against real property for work performed or materials used on the property. A **waiver of lien** is used to release any and all claims that a worker or contractor has against real property.

If real property taxes are not paid by a date determined by state law, the property is sold at a **tax sale**, usually at auction, for the amount of the unpaid taxes. At a tax sale, some states sell only a **tax certificate** which gives the purchaser the right to receive a **tax deed** or title for the property if the owner does not redeem the tax certificate within a specified period of time.

TRANSCRIBING FROM DICTATION

Directions: This dictation emphasizes and reinforces the legal terms and definitions you have studied. Listen carefully to the pronunciation of each of the legal terms. Unless otherwise directed, use a 70-space line (typewriter) or 1-inch margins (computer) and double spacing. Correct all errors. Follow one of the procedures below.

Keyboarding Procedure
Using the cassette from Lesson 31, Part B, transcribe the dictation directly at your typewriter or computer.

Shorthand Procedure
Using the cassette from Lesson 31, Part B, take the dictation using your shorthand system and then transcribe from your shorthand notes on your typewriter or computer.

When you have finished transcribing Part B of the practice dictation, check your transcript with the printed copy. If you made any mistakes in the transcription, you should practice those words several times before going on to Lesson 32.

CHECKLIST
I have completed the following for Lesson 31:

	Part A, Date	Part B, Date	Submitted to Instructor Yes	No
Terminology and Definitions				
Self-Evaluation				
* Keying Legal Terms				
Words				
Sentences				
* Transcribing from Dictation				

When you have successfully completed all the exercises in this lesson and submitted to your instructor those requested, you are ready to proceed with Lesson 32.

* If you are using a shorthand system, submit to your instructor your shorthand notes along with your transcript.

Lesson 32

Additional Legal Terms—Domestic Relations, Corporations, Probate, Bankruptcy, and Contracts and Leases

"Suppression of the truth is equivalent to the expression of what is false."

—Legal Maxim

This lesson consists of additional legal terms relating to domestic relations, corporations, probate, bankruptcy, and contracts and leases that were not presented in earlier lessons. When you complete these exercises, you should have knowledge and an understanding of more terms that are used in reference to these areas of law.

Part A   TERMINOLOGY AND DEFINITIONS

Directions: Study the terms, pronunciations, and definitions until you are thoroughly familiar with them. In order to complete this lesson successfully, you must understand the meaning and usage of all the legal terms presented. If you are using shorthand, write your shorthand outline for each legal term in your shorthand notebook or on your shorthand machine.

Legal Term	Pronunciation	Definition
		Domestic Relations:
1. irreconcilable differences	ir-ek-ən-′sī-lə-bəl ′dif-ərn-səz	Unspecified differences which cannot be reconciled that parties to a divorce action have. A ground for divorce in states that have no-fault divorce laws.
2. stalking laws	′stȯ-kiŋ lȯz	Laws in some states that prevent a person from following or harassing another person.
3. alleged father	ə-′lejd ′fäth-ər	One who is assumed to be the natural father of a child.
4. paternity test	pə-′tər-nət-ē test	A comparison of genetic traits called blood groups that is used to determine if a given man could be the biological father of a given child.
5. adoptee	ə-däp-′tē	One who is adopted.
6 issue of marriage	′ish-ü əv ′mar-ij	Children who are born to the parties of a marriage. Generally, the term is used to apply only to legitimate children.
7. sole custody	sōl ′kəs-təd-ē	Custody in which the total care and responsibility for the care of a minor child of a marriage that is in a state of separation or divorce is placed with one parent.
8. joint custody	jȯint ′kəs-təd-ē	Custody in which the care and responsibility for the care of a minor child of a marriage that is in a state of separation or divorce is placed equally with both parents.

9. split custody	split 'kəs-təd-ē	Custody in which the child spends part of the time with one parent and part of the time with the other parent. One parent is designated as the custodial parent who makes the decisions regarding the care of the child.
10. noncustodial parent	nän-kəs-'tōd-ē-əl 'par-ənt	The parent who is not responsible for the care of a minor child of a marriage that is in a state of separation or divorce. A noncustodial parent may have visitation rights.

Corporations:

11. corporate resolution	'kòr-prət rez-ə-'lü-shən	A motion or intention adopted by a corporate board of directors directing that a certain thing be done. For example, a corporate resolution may be passed giving the officers the authority to open a bank account in the corporation's name. (See Figure 32-1, page 475.)
12. corporate seal	'kòr-prət sēl	An official seal used by a corporation to imprint the corporation's legal documents.
13. subscription right	səb-'skrip-shən rīt	A right of shareholders to purchase additional shares of stock when new stock is issued by the corporation.
14. public corporation	'pəb-lik kòr-pə-'rā-shən	One that is created by the state to act as an agency in administrating civil government such as a county, city, town, or school district.
15. professional corporation	prə-'fesh-nəl kòr-pə-'rā-shən	One that is formed by one or more licensed professionals such as doctors, lawyers, or accountants.

FIGURE 32-1 A Corporate Resolution

ACTION BY WRITTEN CONSENT OF

THE BOARD OF DIRECTORS

OF

LAMBDA OMEGA CORPORATION, INC.

The undersigned, being a Director of Lambda Omega Corporation, Inc., (hereinafter referred to as the "Corporation"), a Michigan non-profit corporation, hereby authorizes the following action by written consent, pursuant to the Michigan Business Corporation Act, as amended:

1. <u>PURCHASE OF REAL PROPERTY:</u> The Directors hereby resolve that the Corporation purchase by Land Contract certain real property commonly known as 1600 Perry Street, East Lansing, Michigan.

2. <u>DESIGNATION OF AGENTS:</u> The Directors hereby resolve that Benjamin Klotz be authorized to execute, on behalf of the Corporation, a Promissory Note in connection with the aforesaid purchase in a principal amount not to exceed Five Thousand and 00/100 Dollars ($5,000.00). The Directors further authorize Casey Ginovelli, the Corporation's attorney, to execute all necessary or reasonably desirable documents of conveyance in connection with the aforesaid acquisition.

DATED: December 30, 1997   BY: _Cyrus Schevenko_____
                                 Cyrus Schevenko

Self-Evaluation A   TERMINOLOGY AND DEFINITION RECALL

Directions: In the Answers column at the right of each statement, write the letter that represents the word or group of words that correctly completes the statement. After you have completed this self-evaluation, check your answers with the key on page 500. If you have any incorrect answers, restudy the definitions for those terms before going on with this lesson. Then unless otherwise directed, submit this self-evaluation to your instructor.

Answers

1. The parent who is not responsible for the care of a minor child of a marriage that is in a state of separation or divorce is a/an (a) adoptee, (b) alleged father, (c) noncustodial parent.

   1. _____

2. When the parties to a divorce action have unspecified differences that cannot be reconciled, it is referred to as (a) issue of marriage, (b) irreconcilable differences, (c) split custody.

   2. _____

3. A comparison of genetic traits called blood groups which is used to determine if a given man could be the biological father of a given child is (a) a paternity test, (b) subscription rights, (c) stalking laws.

   3. _____

4. A corporation that is created by the state to act as an agency in administrating civil government such as a county, city, town, or school district is a (a) public corporation, (b) professional corporation, (c) corporate seal.

   4. _____

5. A right of shareholders to purchase additional shares of stock when new stock is issued by a corporation is (a) corporate seal, (b) corporate resolution, (c) subscription rights.

   5. _____

6. Laws in some states that prevent a person from following or harassing another person are (a) stalking laws, (b) paternity test, (c) subscription rights.

   6. _____

7. Custody in which the care and responsibility for the care of a minor child of a marriage that is in a state of separation or divorce is placed with both parents is (a) sole custody, (b) split custody, (c) joint custody.

   7. _____

8. One who is adopted is a/an (a) issue of marriage, (b) alleged father, (c) adoptee.

   8. _____

9. Custody in which the total care and responsibility for the care of a minor child of a marriage that is in a state of separation or divorce is placed with one parent is (a) sole custody, (b) joint custody, (c) split custody.

   9. _____

10. A corporation that is formed by one or more licensed professionals, such as doctors, lawyers, or accountants, is a (a) public corporation, (b) professional corporation, (c) joint custody.

    10. _____

11. Custody in which the child spends part of the time with one parent and part of the time with the other parent, but one parent is designated as the custodial parent who makes the decisions regarding the care of the child, is (a) split custody, (b) joint custody, (c) sole custody.

    11. _____

12. A motion or intention adopted by a corporate board of directors directing that a certain thing be done is a (a) corporate seal, (b) subscription right, (c) corporate resolution.

    12. _____

13. One who is assumed to be the natural father of a child is a/an (a) noncustodial parent, (b) alleged father, (c) adoptee.

    13. _____

14. Children who are born to the parties of a marriage are referred to as (a) issue of marriage, (b) adoptee, (c) paternity test.

    14. _____

15. An official seal used by a corporation to imprint the corporation's legal documents is a (a) corporate resolution, (b) corporate seal, (c) subscription right.

    15. _____

KEYING LEGAL TERMS

Directions: Unless otherwise instructed, use a 70-space line (typewriter) or 1-inch margins (computer) and double spacing. Correct all errors. Follow one of the procedures below.

WORDS

Keyboarding Procedure
On your typewriter or computer, key the following words at least two times, concentrating on the correct spelling and pronunciation.

Shorthand Procedure
On your typewriter or computer, key the following words once, concentrating on the correct spelling and pronunciation. Then write the shorthand outline for each word in your shorthand notebook or on your shorthand machine. Transcribe from the shorthand outlines one time on your typewriter or computer.

irreconcilable differences	**stalking laws**	**alleged father**
paternity test	**adoptee**	**issue of marriage**
sole custody	**joint custody**	**split custody**
noncustodial parent	**corporate resolution**	**corporate seal**
subscription rights	**public corporation**	**professional corporation**

SENTENCES

Keyboarding Procedure
Key each of the following sentences one time on your typewriter or computer. Concentrate on the correct spelling and pronunciation of each underlined legal term.

Shorthand Procedure
Write the correct shorthand outlines for the following sentences in your shorthand notebook or on your shorthand machine. Transcribe from your shorthand outlines one time on your typewriter or computer.

These sentences will be used for practice dictation on the cassettes.

Parties to a divorce action may have <u>irreconcilable differences</u>, which are unspecified differences that cannot be reconciled. Irreconcilable differences are a ground for divorce in states that have no-fault divorce laws. Some states have passed <u>stalking laws</u> that prevent a person from following or harassing another person.

An <u>alleged father</u> is one who is assumed to be the natural father of a child. A <u>paternity test</u>, a comparison of genetic traits called blood groups, may be used to determine if a given man could be the biological father of a given child. A child who is adopted is referred to as an <u>adoptee</u>, but children who are born to the parties of a marriage are referred to as <u>issue of marriage</u>. Generally, issue of marriage applies only to legitimate children.

Custody in which the total care and responsibility for the care of a minor child of a marriage that is in a state of separation or divorce is placed with one parent is <u>sole custody</u>. <u>Joint custody</u> is custody in which the care and responsibility for the care of a minor child of a marriage that is in a state of separation or divorce is placed equally with both parents. If the child spends part of the time with one parent and part of the time with the other parent, and one parent is designated as the custodial parent who makes the decisions regarding the care of the child, it is called <u>split custody</u>. The parent who is not responsible for the care of a minor child of a marriage that is in a state of separation or divorce is a <u>noncustodial parent</u>.

A motion or intention adopted by a corporate board of directors directing that a certain thing be done is a corporate resolution. A corporate seal is an official seal used by a corporation to imprint the corporation's legal documents. A subscription right is a right of shareholders to purchase additional shares of stock when new stock is issued by the corporation.

A public corporation is one that is created by the state to act as an agency in administrating civil government such as a county, city, town, or school district. If one or more licensed professionals such as doctors, lawyers, or accountants, form a corporation, it is called a professional corporation.

TRANSCRIBING FROM DICTATION

Directions: This dictation emphasizes and reinforces the legal terms and definitions you have studied. Listen carefully to the pronunciation of each of the legal terms. Unless otherwise directed, use a 70-space line (typewriter) or 1-inch margins (computer) and double spacing. Correct all errors. Follow one of the procedures below.

Keyboarding Procedure
Using the cassette from Lesson 32, Part A, transcribe the dictation directly at your typewriter or computer.

Shorthand Procedure
Using the cassette from Lesson 32, Part A, take the dictation using your shorthand system and then transcribe from your shorthand notes on your typewriter or computer.

When you have finished transcribing Part A of the practice dictation, check your transcript with the printed copy. If you made any mistakes in the transcription, you should practice those words several times before going on.

Part B TERMINOLOGY AND DEFINITIONS

Directions: Study the terms, pronunciations, and definitions until you are thoroughly familiar with them. In order to complete this lesson successfully, you must understand the meaning and usage of all the legal terms presented. If you are using shorthand, write your shorthand outline for each legal term in your shorthand notebook or on your shorthand machine.

Legal Term	Pronunciation	Definition
		Probate:
1. legatee	leg-ə-'tē	The person to whom a legacy is given.
2. declarant	di-'klar-ənt	In probate, a declarant is a person who signs a living will. In general, a declarant is a person who makes an unsworn statement of facts in a case.
3. decedant	di-'sēd-nt	Refers to a deceased person whether they died testate or intestate.
4. devise	dev-ə-'zē	The person to whom real property is given by will.
5. testamentary instrument	tes-tə-'ment-ə-rē 'in-strə-mənt	A written document that is in the nature of a will although it is not formally a will. Upon court approval, a testamentary instrument will have the same effect as a will.
6. testamentary trust	tes-tə-'ment-ə-rē trəst	A trust that is set up by the terms of a will and which does not come into being until the death of the person making the will.

7. life estate	līf is-'tāt	One's right to the lifetime use and enjoyment of property that is owned by another. For example, a person may pass ownership of his or her home to children or other heirs but retain the right to live there until his or her death.
8. succession	sək-'sesh-ən	That which is established by law as to the rights of heirs to inherit property of a person who dies intestate. For example, if a person dies without a will, the laws of succession determine how the property is to be divided and who is the heir at law.
9. distribute	dis-'trib-yət	If a person dies intestate, the estate is divided equally among the legal heirs. Also, referred to as per capita which is the opposite of per stirpes.
10. exception	ik-'sep-shən	The excluding or intentionally leaving someone out of a will. Also, may refer to a document filed with the court which disputes the claim of a creditor against an estate.
11. age of majority	āj əv mə-'jör-ət-ē	The age established by law at which a person is entitled to manage his or her own affairs. Eighteen is the age of majority in most states.

Bankruptcy:

12. statutory lien	'stach-ə-tōr-ē lēn	An encumbrance imposed on property by law. For example, if you do not pay your property taxes, they become a lien on your property as specified by law.
13. secured claim	si-'kyùrd klām	An indebtedness for which property was pledged as security. If the debt is not paid, the property can be sold to satisfy the claim. A mortgage on real property is an example of a secured claim.
14. exempt property	ig-'zemt 'präp-ərt-ē	Property as defined by federal or state statutes that is exempt from bankruptcy proceedings and that can, therefore, be retained by the person filing for bankruptcy.

Contracts and Leases:

15. lawful purpose	'lò-fəl 'pər-pəs	An essential element of a legal contract. For example, a contract cannot be enforced if it involves committing a crime, harming someone, or committing fraud.
16. security deposit	si-'kyùr-ət-ē di-'päz-ət	Money paid by a tenant to a landlord as security for the tenant's performance in fulfilling the terms of the lease. State laws vary as to the amount of deposit that can be collected and under what conditions it can be retained by the landlord.

Self-Evaluation B   TERMINOLOGY AND DEFINITION RECALL

Directions: In the Answers column, write the legal term that is most representative of the corresponding statement. After you have completed this self-evaluation, check your answers with the key on page 500. If you have any incorrect answers, restudy the definitions for those terms before going on with this lesson. Then unless otherwise directed, submit this self-evaluation to your instructor.

Answers

1. That which is established by law as the rights of heirs to inherit property of a person who dies intestate is referred to as _____.

   1. _____

2. A written document that is in the nature of a will although it is not formally a will is called a/an _____.

   2. _____

3. An encumbrance imposed on property by law is a/an _____.

   3. _____

4. The age established by law at which a person is entitled to manage his or her own affairs is the _____.

   4. _____

5. The term _____ refers to a deceased person whether they died testate or intestate.

   5. _____

6. The person to whom a legacy is given is a/an _____.

   6. _____

7. Property that is defined by federal or state statutes that is exempt from bankruptcy proceedings and that can, therefore, be retained by the person filing for bankruptcy is known as _____.

   7. _____

8. Money paid by a tenant to a landlord as security for the tenant's performance in fulfilling the terms of the lease is a/an _____.

   8. _____

9. An essential element of a legal contract that means that a contract cannot be enforced if it involves committing a crime is _____.

   9. _____

10. In probate, a person who signs a living will is a/an _____.

    10. _____

11. An indebtedness for which property was pledged as security is referred to as a/an _____.

    11. _____

12. The excluding or intentionally leaving someone out of a will is called _____.

    12. _____

13. The person to whom real property is given by will is a/an _____.

    13. _____

14. The term _____ refers to the equal division of an estate among the legal heirs of a person who dies intestate.

    14. _____

15. A trust that is set up by the terms of a will and which does not come into being until the death of the person making the will is a/an _____.

    15. _____

16. One's right to the lifetime use and enjoyment of property that is owned by another is a/an _____.

    16. _____

KEYING LEGAL TERMS

Directions: Unless otherwise instructed, use a 70-space line (typewriter) or 1-inch margins (computer) and double spacing. Correct all errors. Follow one of the procedures below.

WORDS

Keyboarding Procedure
On your typewriter or computer, key the following words at least two times, concentrating on the correct spelling and pronunciation.

Shorthand Procedure
On your typewriter or computer, key the following words once, concentrating on the correct spelling and pronunciation. Then write the shorthand outline for each word in your shorthand notebook or on your shorthand machine. Transcribe from the shorthand outlines one time on your typewriter or computer.

legatee	declarant	decedant
devise	testamentary instrument	testamentary trust
life estate	succession	distribute
exception	age of majority	statutory lien
secured claim	exempt property	lawful purpose
security deposit		

SENTENCES

Keyboarding Procedure
Key each of the following sentences one time on your typewriter or computer. Concentrate on the correct spelling and pronunciation of each underlined legal term.

Shorthand Procedure
Write the correct shorthand outlines for the following sentences in your shorthand notebook or on your shorthand machine. Transcribe from your shorthand outlines one time on your typewriter or computer.

These sentences will be used for practice dictation on the cassettes.

A legatee is a person to whom a legacy is given. In probate, a declarant is a person who signs a living will. In general, a declarant is a person who makes an unsworn statement of facts in a case. Decedant refers to a deceased person whether they died testate or intestate. The person to whom real property is given by will is a devise.

A written document that is in the nature of a will although it is not formally a will is a testamentary instrument. A testamentary trust is set up by the terms of a will and does not come into being until the death of the person who makes the will. Upon court approval, a testamentary instrument will have the same effect as a will. A life estate is one's right to the lifetime use and enjoyment of property that is owned by another. For example, a person may pass ownership of his or her home to children or other heirs but retain the right to live there until his or her death.

Succession is that which is established by law as to the rights of heirs to inherit property of a person who dies intestate. If a person dies without a will, the laws of succession determine how the property is to be divided and who is the heir at law. Distribute refers to a situation where a person dies intestate and the estate is divided equally among the legal heirs. Distribute is also referred to as per capita which is the opposite of per stirpes. <u>Exception</u> is the excluding or intentionally leaving someone out of a will. Exception also may refer to a document filed with the court which disputes the claim of a creditor against an estate.

The age established by law at which a person is entitled to manage his or her own affairs is the <u>age of majority</u>. Eighteen is the age of majority in most states.

A <u>statutory lien</u> is an encumbrance imposed on property by law. An indebtedness for which property was pledged as security is known as a <u>secured claim</u>. <u>Exempt property</u> is property as defined by federal or state statutes that is exempt from bankruptcy proceedings and that can, therefore, be retained by the person filing for bankruptcy.

<u>Lawful purpose</u> is an essential element of a legal contract and means that a contract cannot be enforced if it involves committing a crime, harming someone, or committing fraud. A <u>security deposit</u> is money paid by a tenant to a landlord as security for the tenant's performance in fulfilling the terms of the lease. State laws vary as to the amount of deposit that can be collected and under what conditions it can be retained by the landlord.

TRANSCRIBING FROM DICTATION

Directions: This dictation emphasizes and reinforces the legal terms and definitions you have studied. Listen carefully to the pronunciation of each of the legal terms. Unless otherwise directed, use a 70-space line (typewriter) or 1-inch margins (computer) and double spacing. Correct all errors. Follow one of the procedures below.

Keyboarding Procedure
Using the cassette from Lesson 32, Part B, transcribe the dictation directly at your typewriter or computer.

Shorthand Procedure
Using the cassette from Lesson 32, Part B, take the dictation using your shorthand system and then transcribe from your shorthand notes on your typewriter or computer.

When you have finished transcribing Part B of the practice dictation, check your transcript with the printed copy. If you made any mistakes in the transcription, you should practice those words several times before going on to Evaluation 16.

CHECKLIST
I have completed the following for Lesson 32:

	Part A, Date	Part B, Date	Submitted to Instructor Yes	No
Terminology and Definitions				
Self-Evaluation				
* Keying Legal Terms				
Words				
Sentences				
* Transcribing from Dictation				

When you have successfully completed all the exercises in this lesson and submitted to your instructor those requested, you are ready to proceed with Evaluation 16.

* If you are using a shorthand system, submit to your instructor your shorthand notes along with your transcript.

Evaluation No. 16   SECTION A

Directions: This dictation/transcription evaluation will test your spelling and transcription abilities on the legal terms that you studied in the two preceding lessons. Use a 5-space paragraph indention, a 70-space line (typewriter) or 1-inch margins (computer), and double spacing unless otherwise instructed. Correct all errors. Follow one of the procedures below.

Keyboarding Procedure

Using the cassette from Evaluation 16, transcribe the dictation directly at your typewriter or computer.

Shorthand Procedure

Using the cassette from Evaluation 16, take the dictation using your shorthand system and then transcribe from your shorthand notes on your typewriter or computer.

Sections B and C are available from your instructor.

Latin Words and Phrases

This section contains some additional Latin words and phrases that will expand your knowledge and understanding of Latin as it is used in the legal field. Even though the direction of the legal field has been to simplify the language and to use less Latin, many are still in common usage today. Therefore, it would be to your benefit if you are working in the legal field to be acquainted with as many of the Latin terms as possible.

Latin Term	Pronunciation	Definition
a fortiori	ə fōr-'shə-ə-rē	With greater force or with greater reason.
a priori	ə 'prī-ə-rē	From what has previously transpired; from the cause to the effect.
ab initio	əb in-'ish-ə-ō	From the beginning; entirely.
ad curiam	ad 'kyür-ē-əm	At a court; before the court; to the court.
ad infinitum	ad in-fə-'nī-tum	Without end; to any extent; indefinitely.
consortium	kən-'sòrt-ē-əm	The legal right each spouse has to the company, affection, and service of the other.
contra	'kän-trə	In opposition or contrast to; against; confronting; on the other hand.
duces tecum	'dü-cēz 'tek-kəm	Bring with you.
ex officio	eks ə-'fis-ē-ō	From office or by virtue of the office.
fiat	'fē-ət	Let it be done.
in camera	in 'kam-rə	In chambers; in private.
in loco	in 'lō-kō	In the natural place; in lieu; instead.
in personam	in pər-'sän-əm	Against the person.
in toto	in 'tō-tō	In the whole; completely; altogether.
indicia	in-'dish-ē-a	Signs; indications.
infra	'in-frə	Below, beneath, or under.
inter alia	in-'tər 'ā-lē-ə	Among other things.
inter vivos	in-'tər 'vi-vōs	Between living persons; from one living person to another.
intra	'in-trə	Within; in the space of.
locus delicti	'lō-kəs di-'lik-tī	The place of the crime or tort. The place where the crime was committed.
mala in se	'mal-ə in sā	Wrong in themselves. Acts that are morally wrong.
mala prohibita	'mal-ə prō-'hib-ə-tə	Acts that are prohibited by human laws but are not necessarily wrong in themselves.
non sequitur	nän si-'kwe-tər	It does not follow.
non sui juris	nän 'sü-ī 'jür-əs	Not his own master; not in its own right; not of full legal capacity.
nota bene	'nōt-ə 'bē-nē	Note well; take notice; used to call attention to something important.
onus probandi	'ō-nəs 'prō-band-ē	The burden of proof; burden of proving.
pro forma	prō 'fòr-mə	As a matter of form; tentatively.
pro tempore	prō 'tem-pə-rē	For the time being; temporarily. Abbreviated to pro tem.
supra	'sü-prə	Above; upon; in addition to.
vis a vis	'vis ə vē	Force against force; face to face; in relation to each other.

Proofreading Guidelines

Even though most word processing software programs have a feature to check spelling, you must still be able to proofread your work for errors that cannot be detected by the software program. A software spelling check program will only pick up misspelled words that do not make another word. For example, if you key "on" for "in," the program will not detect the error. Therefore, you cannot rely on your computer program to eliminate the need to proofread.

Following are some tips and guidelines to help you become a better proofreader.

1. Run your software program spelling check.
2. Read the document word for word for context. Say each word to yourself as you are reading so you can determine if there are any incorrect, omitted, or additional words.
3. If you keyed from rough draft copy, cross-check the keyed copy with the rough draft. This will help you find any omissions or additions.
4. Check for format, i.e., spacing, paragraph indentions, and punctuation.
5. Carefully double-check all numbers, land descriptions, citations, names, and addresses. When proofing land descriptions or other material with numbers, it is helpful to have someone read them to you as you proof the copy.
6. If you are proofreading hard copy, or if someone else will be making the corrections, use the proofreader's marks listed below. Additionally, it is helpful to put a mark in the margin beside any line that has a correction or use a contrasting ink color. This will help assure that you will see and make all the noted corrections.

Proofreader's Marks

∧	Insert	ss	Single space
⌒	Close up	ds	Double space
∼	Transpose	ts	Triple space
ℓ	Take out or delete	⌗	New paragraph
stet	Let it stand or leave as it was	no ⌗	No paragraph
⟳	Move as indicated	̂	Insert comma
[	Move to the left	⊙	Insert period
]	Move to the right	(:)	Insert colon
—	Underscore	(;)	Insert semicolon
#	Insert space	(?)	Insert question mark
≡ or cap	Capitalize	◯	Spell out or do not abbreviate
/ or lc	Lower case—no caps		

Enough emphasis cannot be placed on careful proofreading, and it is important that you take the necessary time to carefully proofread all your work. Remember: It is easier and less time-consuming to correct an error that could cause a problem than to correct a problem that was caused by an error.

Words Often Confused

There are many words that sound alike or are very close in spelling that are often confused. Following is a list of some of those words that often appear in legal documents or transcripts. Knowledge of these words and their definitions will help you make the correct choice when proofreading. If you are unsure about a word, check a dictionary for the definition to be sure that it fits the context of the sentence.

Word	*Definition*
accede	To become a party; give in.
exceed	To extend outside of; to be greater than; superior.
accept	To take; to receive.
except	To exclude; to object.
access	Right to use; approach.
excess	Extra; surplus.
adapt	Conform; change to suit.
adept	Highly skilled; proficient.
adopt	Take as one's own; choose.
adduce	To offer as example, proof, or reason.
educe	To elicit or bring out.
adjoin	To be next to or in contact with.
adjourn	To postpone or suspend.
advice	Recommendation. (noun)
advise	To give counsel. (verb)
affect	To influence or alter. (verb)
effect	Consequence or result. (noun)
affiance	To pledge; to solemnly promise.
affiants	Persons who swear to an affidavit.
err	To make a mistake or be wrong.
heir	One who inherits.
arraign	To call before a court; to accuse of a wrong.
arrange	To put in order or classify.
bail	Security to guarantee a court appearance.
bale	A bundle.
casual	Subject to, resulting from, or occurring by chance.
causal	Relating to or constituting the cause.
cede	To grant; give up.
seed	Source or origin.
collaborate	To assist; to cooperate.
corroborate	To support.
command	To order or lead.
commend	To entrust; praise.
complement	Something that fills up, completes, or makes perfect.
compliment	An expression of esteem; a flattering remark.

consul	A government official in a foreign country.
council	An assembly.
counsel	Advice; lawyer.
corpse	A dead body.
corpus	A collection or body of knowledge or evidence.
correspondence	Communication by letters.
correspondents	Persons who communicate by letter.
corespondents	Persons named as guilty of adultery with the defendant in a divorce action.
credible	Believable.
creditable	Deserving of praise.
decedent	A person who has died.
dissident	One who does not agree.
decent	Respectable.
descent	Lineage; a step downward.
dissent	Difference of opinion.
demur	To object or delay.
demure	Serious or modest.
elicit	To draw forth or bring out.
illicit	Illegal, unlawful, or prohibited.
farther	In space or distance.
further	To promote.
formally	According to established form.
formerly	Previously.
gilt	Something resembling gold.
guilt	Having committed a crime or offense.
grievance	Reason for complaint.
grievous	Severe pain, suffering, or sorrow.
hearsay	Rumor. Based on what someone else said.
heresy	An opinion, doctrine, or practice contrary to the truth.
incite	Stir up or arouse.
insight	Knowledge or understanding.
indict	To accuse one of a crime.
indite	To compose and write.
interstate	Between or among states.
intestate	Without a will.
intrastate	Within a state.
laches	Undue delay in asserting a legal right.
latches	Fasteners.
lean	To incline.
lien	An encumbrance.
liable	Responsible or answerable.
libel	Defamation of character.
mandatary	One to whom a mandate is given.
mandatory	Required.
marital	Of marriage.
martial	Of war or military.

meat	Flesh of animals; meaning; gist.
meet	To confront; to assemble.
mete	To give out; to allot.
militant	Aggressive; warlike.
militate	To influence.
mitigate	To lessen or make less severe.
ordinance	Law; a municipal regulation.
ordnance	Arms or ammunitions.
parol	Oral.
parole	Conditional freedom from incarceration.
peremptory	Putting an end to or precluding a right of action.
preemptory	Take precedence over.
perpetrate	To commit; to be guilty of.
perpetuate	To make lasting.
persecute	To torment.
prosecute	To sue.
plaintiff	The one who files a suit.
plaintive	Mournful.
precedence	Priority.
precedents	Things prior in time.
reality	That which is real.
realty	Real property or real estate.
residents	The ones who live there.
residence	The place where one lives.
statue	Figurine or sculpture.
stature	Natural height; achievement.
statute	A law.
steal	To unlawfully take another's possession.
steel	Metal; processed iron.
tort	A civil wrong.
torte	A rich cake.
tortious	Involving a tort or civil wrong.
tortuous	Crooked or winding.
torturous	Involving torture.
trustee	One who holds something in trust for another.
trusty	Dependable. A convicted person who is considered trustworthy.
undo	Untie or destroy.
undue	Unwarranted or improper.
waive	To forego or give up.
wave	Signal with hands.
waiver	The legal instrument by which one gives up a right.
waver	To fluctuate in opinion, allegiance, or direction.

Legal Transcription Basics

Since the format for legal instruments varies from state to state and there are so many variations in the computer software programs, the information presented in this section will serve only as a general guideline for the preparation of legal documents.

Margins:

(1) Left margin: Plain paper—1 1/2 inches
                      Legal cap—At least one space inside horizontal line.
(2) Right margin: Plain paper—1/2 inch
                      Legal cap—At least one space inside horizontal line.
(3) Top margin: Unbound—1 inch
                      Bound—2 inches
(4) Bottom margin: 1 inch

Spacing:

(1) Body—double spaced
(2) Land descriptions—single spaced

Paragraph indentations: 5 or 10 spaces

Capitalization:

Type the following in all caps:

(1) Title of document
(2) The first word or phrase of a paragraph (especially if it is the first or last paragraph of the document).
(3) Names of documents
(4) Names of individuals
(5) Names of firms

Numbers:

(1) Dates may be written in figures or spelled out.
(2) Amounts of money are first spelled out and then in figures in parentheses.
(3) Measurements are usually written the same as amounts of money.
(4) Numbers in land descriptions may be spelled out or written in figures.
(5) Symbols for feet, degrees, etc., may be used with numbers that are written in figures.

Signature Lines:

(1) Leave 3 to 4 blank lines between the last line of the document and the signature line.
(2) The witness signature lines start at the left margin and are approximately 3 inches long.
(3) The party signature lines start at the center and are approximately 3 inches long.
(4) Leave 2 to 3 blank lines between signature lines.

For more specific details for the preparation of legal instruments, you should check the guidelines for the state in which you will be working. Also, many legal offices have examples of their formats available for the use of new employees.

Key

Lesson 1
Self-Evaluation A

1. c
2. a
3. b
4. b
5. c
6. a
7. b
8. c
9. a
10. c
11. a
12. b
13. b
14. a
15. c

Lesson 1
Self-Evaluation B

1. j
2. i
3. g
4. e
5. k
6. h
7. l
8. b
9. f
10. n
11. m
12. d
13. a

Lesson 2
Self-Evaluation A

1. Corpus Juris Secundum
2. a. esquire
    b. Esq.
3. defense attorney
4. prosecuting attorney
5. lexicon
6. jurisprudence
7. lex
8. bar
9. judge
10. code books
11. bench
12. statute

13. a. in propria persona
    b. in pro per
14. jurist

Lesson 2
Self-Evaluation B

1. a
2. c
3. d
4. l
5. e
6. j
7. k
8. h
9. i
10. m
11. o
12. b
13. g
14. n

Lesson 3
Self-Evaluation A

1. petition
2. narratio
3. declaration or complaint
4. writ
5. plea
6. tribunal
7. contest
8. complaint or declaration
9. count
10. adjudicate
11. champerty
12. pleadings
13. gravamen
14. retainer

Lesson 3
Self-Evaluation B

1. a
2. c
3. b
4. a
5. a
6. b
7. c
8. a
9. a

10. c
11. b
12. c
13. b

Lesson 4
Self-Evaluation A

1. notary public
2. endorsement
3. ipso facto
4. acknowledgment
5. testimonium clause
6. seal
7. to wit
8. scilicet
9. sui generis
10. cause of action
11. interpolate
12. ancillary
13. locus sigilli
14. legal back

Lesson 4
Self-Evaluation B

1. a
2. e
3. f
4. h
5. d
6. l
7. j
8. c
9. n
10. b
11. k
12. m
13. g

Lesson 5
Self-Evaluation A

1. b
2. c
3. c
4. a
5. a
6. c
7. b
8. c

9. a
10. c
11. b
12. a
13. a
14. c

Lesson 5
Self-Evaluation B

1. i
2. k
3. h
4. o
5. l
6. j
7. a
8. c
9. m
10. g
11. b
12. e
13. f
14. n

Lesson 6
Self-Evaluation A

1. pretrial stipulations
2. contempt of court
3. fishing expedition
4. bench warrant
5. deposition
6. interrogatories
7. disclosure
8. subpoena
9. transcript
10. subpoena duces tecum
11. concealment
12. verbatim
13. court reporter

Lesson 6
Self-Evaluation B

1. a
2. b
3. a
4. c
5. b
6. a
7. c
8. b
9. c
10. b
11. a

12. c
13. c

Lesson 7
Self-Evaluation A

1. j
2. i
3. e
4. l
5. h
6. a
7. m
8. n
9. b
10. f
11. c
12. d
13. k

Lesson 7
Self-Evaluation B

1. direct examination
2. overruled
3. motion to strike
4. irrelevant
5. mistrial
6. cross-examination
7. physically expunge
8. opening statement
9. colloquy
10. testimony
11. admissible
12. objection
13. witness
14. sustained

Lesson 8
Self-Evaluation A

1. impeach
2. evidence
3. perjury
4. hostile witness
5. res gestae
6. averment
7. expert evidence
8. rebuttal
9. adduce
10. incompetent
11. exhibit
12. opinion evidence
13. hearsay
14. circumstantial evidence

Lesson 8
Self-Evaluation B

1. b
2. a
3. b
4. c
5. c
6. a
7. a
8. b
9. c
10. a
11. b
12. c
13. b

Lesson 9
Self-Evaluation A

1. d
2. b
3. c
4. m
5. k
6. g
7. n
8. e
9. a
10. h
11. j
12. f
13. l

Lesson 9
Self-Evaluation B

1. a
2. b
3. a
4. c
5. a
6. b
7. c
8. c
9. b
10. a
11. b
12. c
13. c
14. b

Lesson 10
Self-Evaluation A

1. a
2. c

3. b
4. c
5. a
6. a
7. b
8. c
9. b
10. a
11. c
12. b
13. c

Lesson 10
Self-Evaluation B

1. l
2. a
3. f
4. e
5. k
6. o
7. h
8. b
9. i
10. c
11. j
12. d
13. m
14. g

Lesson 11
Self-Evaluation A

1. c
2. b
3. a
4. b
5. c
6. c
7. a
8. b
9. a
10. a
11. c
12. b

Lesson 11
Self-Evaluation B

1. culpable negligence
2. duty
3. negligence
4. due care and diligence
5. in forma pauperis
6. liability

7. damnum absque injuria
8. contributory negligence
9. actio in rem
10. absolute liability
11. right
12. comparative negligence
13. imputation of negligence

Lesson 12
Self-Evaluation A

1. e
2. d
3. a
4. k
5. j
6. c
7. h
8. l
9. b
10. n
11. m
12. g
13. i

Lesson 12
Self-Evaluation B

1. knowledge of the peril
2. foreseeability of injury
3. act or omission
4. implied or imputed knowledge
5. sudden emergency doctrine
6. wanton, reckless, and intentional
7. res ipsa loquitur
8. Good Samaritan Statute
9. assumption of risk
10. constructive notice
11. sovereign immunity
12. probable consequences
13. ordinary, reasonable person

Lesson 13
Self-Evaluation A

1. c
2. a
3. a
4. b
5. b
6. b

7. c
8. c
9. b
10. a
11. c
12. c
13. b
14. a

Lesson 13
Self-Evaluation B

1. sine qua non
2. criminal intent
3. irresistible impulse
4. insanity
5. plea
6. Durham Rule
7. nolo contendere
8. non compos mentis
9. confession
10. defense
11. scienter
12. M'Naghten Rule
13. admission

Lesson 14
Self-Evaluation A

1. l
2. h
3. j
4. a
5. m
6. k
7. c
8. b
9. f
10. g
11. e
12. n
13. d

Lesson 14
Self-Evaluation B

1. homicide
2. manslaughter
3. murder
4. larceny
5. felonious homicide
6. animus furandi
7. utter and publish
8. forgery
9. assault and battery
10. malice aforethought

11. constructive breaking
12. break and enter
13. justifiable homicide
14. excusable homicide
15. robbery

Lesson 15
Self-Evaluation A

1. f
2. g
3. b
4. k
5. h
6. d
7. a
8. i
9. l
10. n
11. c
12. e
13. o
14. m

Lesson 15
Self-Evaluation B

1. c
2. c
3. b
4. c
5. b
6. a
7. a
8. a
9. c
10. b
11. c
12. b
13. a

Lesson 16
Self-Evaluation A

1. a
2. b
3. c
4. a
5. a
6. b
7. c
8. a
9. b
10. c
11. c

12. b
13. a

Lesson 16
Self-Evaluation B

1. conservatorship
2. guardian ad litem
3. indefeasible
4. guardian
5. ward
6. surrogate
7. trust
8. revocation
9. reversion
10. conservator
11. trust estate
12. animus revocandi
13. dower

Lesson 17
Self-Evaluation A

1. d
2. n
3. m
4. j
5. o
6. f
7. l
8. i
9. k
10. e
11. g
12. h
13. c
14. b

Lesson 17
Self-Evaluation B

1. plat
2. homestead
3. joint tenancy
4. partition
5. easement
6. conveyance
7. tenancy in common
8. land description
9. servitude
10. tenancy by the entirety
11. metes and bounds
12. abstract
13. convey

Lesson 18
Self-Evaluation A

1. a
2. g
3. b
4. i
5. m
6. f
7. e
8. k
9. h
10. j
11. c
12. l
13. d

Lesson 18
Self-Evaluation B

1. b
2. a
3. c
4. a
5. c
6. b
7. b
8. c
9. b
10. a
11. b
12. a
13. c

Lesson 19
Self-Evaluation A

1. b
2. a
3. a
4. b
5. a
6. c
7. c
8. a
9. c
10. b
11. c
12. b
13. a

Lesson 19
Self-Evaluation B

1. assignment
2. performance

3. accord and satisfaction
4. pro tanto
5. assumpsit
6. condition
7. subrogation
8. nudum pactum
9. assignable
10. mutual obligations
11. quid pro quo
12. competent parties
13. consideration
14. quantum meruit

Lesson 20
Self-Evaluation A

1. implied in fact
2. bilateral contract
3. privity of contract
4. escalator clause
5. default
6. rescind
7. vitiate
8. inchoate
9. implied in law
10. express contract
11. inchoate contract
12. unilateral contract
13. implied contract

Lesson 20
Self-Evaluation B

1. n
2. o
3. b
4. e
5. g
6. m
7. f
8. j
9. i
10. l
11. c
12. a
13. k
14. h
15. p

Lesson 21
Self-Evaluation A

1. i
2. j

3. m
4. b
5. h
6. k
7. f
8. l
9. e
10. a
11. c
12. n
13. g

Lesson 21
Self-Evaluation B

1. separation agreement
2. antenuptial agreement
3. privileged communications
4. consanguinity
5. affinity
6. cohabitation
7. a mensa et thoro
8. separate maintenance
9. counsel fee
10. premarital
11. separation
12. femme sole

Lesson 22
Self-Evaluation A

1. absolute divorce
2. corespondent
3. a vinculo matrimonii
4. limited divorce
5. no-fault divorce
6. contested divorce
7. uncontested divorce
8. divorce
9. dissolution of marriage
10. grounds for divorce
11. conciliation procedure
12. Enoch Arden Law
13. desertion

Lesson 22
Self-Evaluation B

1. a
2. b
3. b
4. b
5. a
6. c
7. c

8. b
9. a
10. a
11. c
12. c
13. a

Lesson 23
Self-Evaluation A

1. b
2. c
3. b
4. a
5. b
6. a
7. c
8. b
9. a
10. c
11. a
12. b
13. c

Lesson 23
Self-Evaluation B

1. payee
2. draft
3. bearer
4. draft-varying acceptance
5. comaker
6. trade acceptance
7. accommodation paper
8. holder in due course
9. maker
10. qualified acceptance
11. carte blanche
12. bill of exchange
13. payer

Lesson 24
Self-Evaluation A

1. a
2. i
3. b
4. h
5. e
6. c
7. l
8. f
9. m
10. d

11. j
12. k

Lesson 24
Self-Evaluation B

1. bogus
2. restrictive indorsement
3. indorsement
4. allonge
5. special or full indorsement
6. kite
7. successive indorsement
8. qualified indorsement
9. bona fide
10. blank indorsement
11. spoliation

Lesson 25
Self-Evaluation A

1. a
2. c
3. a
4. c
5. b
6. b
7. a
8. c
9. b
10. b
11. a
12. c
13. a
14. b

Lesson 25
Self-Evaluation B

1. balance of funds
2. account current
3. discharge
4. secured debts
5. composition
6. account stated
7. summary of debts and assets
8. insolvent debtor
9. deficiency decree
10. after-acquired property
11. assets
12. liquidate
13. liabilities

Lesson 26
Self-Evaluation A

1. del credere agent
2. agency
3. principal
4. undisclosed principal
5. universal agent
6. exclusive or irrevocable agency
7. implied agency
8. agent
9. power of attorney
10. special agent
11. primary agent
12. subagent
13. plenipotentiary
14. general agent

Lesson 26
Self-Evaluation B

1. i
2. f
3. h
4. o
5. n
6. d
7. j
8. e
9. g
10. m
11. b
12. k
13. c
14. a

Lesson 27
Self-Evaluation A

1. a
2. c
3. b
4. b
5. c
6. b
7. a
8. a
9. c
10. b
11. b
12. a
13. c
14. a

Lesson 27
Self-Evaluation B

1. rule of morality
2. right and duty
3. consent decree
4. estoppel in pais
5. sua sponte
6. de minimis non curat lex
7. doctrine of doing complete justice
8. clean hands doctrine
9. matter in pais
10. declaratory judgment
11. finding of fact
12. waiver
13. reformation
14. in pari delicto
15. remedial

Lesson 28
Self-Evaluation A

1. general partner
2. proprietor
3. severalty
4. Uniform Limited Partnership Act
5. junior partner
6. limited partner
7. partnership
8. Uniform Partnership Act
9. limited partnership
10. silent partner
11. sole proprietorship
12. senior partner
13. articles of partnership

Lesson 28
Self-Evaluation B

1. h
2. m
3. g
4. a
5. f
6. c
7. l
8. b
9. d
10. i
11. k
12. e

Lesson 29
Self-Evaluation A

1. c
2. a
3. b
4. a
5. a
6. c
7. a
8. c
9. b
10. b
11. c
12. b
13. b
14. c

Lesson 29
Self-Evaluation B

1. book value
2. watered stock
3. shareholder
4. preferred stock
5. transfer agent
6. stock certificate
7. par value
8. share
9. common stock
10. promoters
11. stock
12. treasury stock

Lesson 30
Self-Evaluation A

1. f
2. i
3. d
4. b
5. l
6. c
7. j
8. h
9. m
10. g
11. a
12. k

Lesson 30
Self-Evaluation B

1. dividend
2. sinking fund
3. working capital
4. auditor
5. debenture
6. income statement
7. financial reports
8. retained earnings
9. earnings per share
10. net worth
11. liability
12. balance sheet

Lesson 31
Self-Evaluation A

1. pluries summons
2. disclosure statement
3. sidebar
4. proffer
5. realtime
6. discovery
7. certificate of readiness
8. perfect
9. undue influence
10. chose in possession
11. cross-complaint
12. certificate of service
13. alias summons
14. clerk of the court
15. docket
16. joinder

Lesson 31
Self-Evaluation B

1. e
2. j
3. c
4. a
5. b
6. p
7. m
8. k
9. f

10. i
11. l
12. d
13. o
14. g
15. n

Lesson 32
Self-Evaluation A

1. c
2. b
3. a
4. a
5. c
6. a
7. c
8. c
9. a
10. b
11. a
12. c
13. b
14. a
15. b

Lesson 32
Self-Evaluation B

1. succession
2. testamentary instrument
3. statutory lien
4. age of majority
5. decedant
6. legatee
7. exempt property
8. security deposit
9. lawful purpose
10. declarant
11. secured claim
12. exception
13. devise
14. distribute
15. testamentary trust
16. life estate

Index